THE WORK OF MEMORY

THE WORK OF MEMORY

New Directions in the Study of German Society and Culture

EDITED BY ALON CONFINO
AND PETER FRITZSCHE

University of Illinois Press Urbana and Chicago

Manufactured in the United States of America
C 5 4 3 2 1

This book is printed on acid-free paper.

Library of Congress Cataloging-in-Publication Data
The work of memory : new directions in the study of
German society and culture / edited by Alon Confino
and Peter Fritzsche.
p. cm.
Includes bibliographical references and index.
ISBN 0-252-02717-5 (alk. paper)
1. Germany—Civilization.
2. Memory—Social aspects—Germany.
3. Memorials—Germany.
4. Germany—Histororiography.
5. National socialism—Psychological aspects.
6. Political culture—Germany.
I. Confino, Alon.
II. Fritzsche, Peter, 1959– .
DD61.W67 2002
943—dc21 2001004566

CONTENTS

PART 3: MATERIALITY

ACKNOWLEDGMENTS

We would like to acknowledge the generous support of the Department of History and particularly the funding from the College of Liberal Arts and Sciences at the University of Illinois at Urbana-Champaign that made possible the December 1998 conference on memory work in Germany out of which this volume has grown. And we want to thank our bus drivers, Glenn Penny and Joe Perry.

THE WORK OF MEMORY

Introduction: Noises of the Past

ALON CONFINO AND PETER FRITZSCHE

The current interest in memory, among both scholars and laypersons, has become almost an obsession. A term that ten years ago had little public resonance has entered household vocabularies and everyday speech, buttressing the claims of individuals, victims, and social groups for various forms of recognition, compensation, and entitlement. This valorization of memory has advanced the breakdown of common or conventional historical narratives to such a point that the ensuing fragmentation of what had been a shared (if distorted) past has become the focus of fundamental concern: professional historians lament the dispersion of collective traditions as much as family members contradict the testimony of trauma and abuse.[1] Memory studies are thus conducted in an atmosphere that is self-conscious and admonitory, one in which observers claim that memory is too short or too obsessive, that it proves to be evasive or operates hypercritically, that there is altogether too much of it or too little. Yet it is precisely the problem of the commemoration, trauma, and evasion of the past that justifies renewed emphasis on the topic of memory. The operations of memory in social settings and the subsequent study of memory in academic contexts are justified because, plainly, the past does not speak for itself.

The past does not speak for itself and it is therefore available for use and distortion and denial in strikingly diverse ways. Huge archives and databases of information, and sophisticated archeological and historiographical techniques, make the past accessible as never before. At the same time, the rapid movements of the capitalist economy have both destroyed connections to the past and commodified and commercialized them. Memory work reconfigures the nation into a set of past traditions, which themselves are contested by social groups and marginalized people, exiles and strangers, who tell quite different stories about the nation. Democratization and the elaboration of civic society has had the result of generating countless versions of the past and setting into motion alternative ethnic, gender, and personal subjectivities. The politics of historical and moral responsibility at the end of the bloody twentieth century, in particular the confrontation with fascism, National Socialism, and Communism, has further revised once-accepted renditions of the past. The historiographical recognition of the evasive nature of memory has energized more deconstructive ways of thinking about conventional and alternative historical narratives in general and about the disciplinary meaning of narrative itself.

Germany has been an exceptional site to explore the workings of modern memory. The Holocaust and World War II, and the subsequent forty-year division of Germany into two countries with very different versions of the twentieth-century past, confront scholars with fundamental problems of recollection, silence, and denial. Indeed the problem of explaining and historicizing the historical extremes of world war and mass death has more or less defined the topic of memory in Germany. The basic imperative of German memory is widely regarded to be the collective responsibility of coming to terms with the past, or *Vergangenheitsbewältigung.* A distinguished body of literature has made German history the place where common European values and rights can be clarified and justified, and has made the confrontation of German contemporaries with Germany's past a model of civic responsibility.[2] The extent to which this confrontation has been realized remains an issue, but its desirability is not. At the same time, the study of complicity, estrangement, and victimization in the social and political life of Germany in the 1930s and 1940s and the recognition of the different ability of victims and perpetrators to remember, to forget, and to evade, and to weave their stories into larger national narratives in the 1950s and 1960s have created an unusually supple and nuanced understanding of how the past can be reorganized and reshaped. This primarily German-oriented scholarship serves as a welcome example of an understanding of the conditions for remembering and forgetting.

However, the focus on *Vergangenheitsbewältigung* has kept a wide range of other troubling questions about the presence of the past in German life from being asked, while at the same time providing sophisticated methods for doing so. This collection of essays, which emerged from an interdisciplinary conference on memory work in Germany held at the University of Illinois at Urbana-Champaign in December of 1998, proposes to go beyond the identification of denial and the scandal of silence in the confrontation with Germany's National Socialist past. Our aim is to explore how memory operated in German culture and society before and after 1945: in part 1, to inquire into the historical development of the categories of the past and the present that enable historical subjects to think at all of memory and to use it in culturally significant ways; and in parts 2 and 3 to examine the power relations, social identities, and everyday situations that memory work served. Such an undertaking ends up posing the question of the place of Holocaust memory in modern memory: how is the memory of murder in the twentieth century connected to broader patterns of remembering and creating meaning?

There are no exact prescriptions in this book, for there is no one correct way to "do" memory; indeed, the power of memory as a historical concept lies in its openness to questioning and renewal. But taken together, the essays collected here point to contemporary problems and possible future directions in the study of memory in Germany. This book is an invitation to problematize memory as a concept that is worth thinking *about,* but also and especially worth thinking *with.* In what ways is the term "memory" useful to develop new insights about German history, to articulate new relationships, to shed new light on old topics?

* * *

The most common approach to the study of the work of memory in Germany has been to explore how the German past was represented in distinct cultural artifacts such as museums, monuments, former concentration camps, films, novels, poems, and memoirs. The majority of these studies centered on the memory of National Socialism, though the pre-1933 period as well as the attempts to legitimize West and East Germany have also been examined.[3] Most of this literature belongs to what Patrick Hutton has described as the first generation of studies in the history of memory. They are "self-consciously projects of commemoration" and politics of memory.[4] This scholarship has successfully illuminated how the past has been perceived and used in German society and culture, although by now it runs the danger of being predictable, as yet another (mostly Holocaust) memory is subjected to an analysis of its construction, representation, and contestation. The interest in Holocaust memory is also very presentist, not only focusing on post-1945 forms but adhering closely to contemporary political debates: it often admonishes rather than explains.

This volume seeks to take memory out of the museum and beyond the monument, into the wider field of social relations, beyond an indication of inadequate moral confrontation. Scholars of German history and culture need to broaden the range of topics beyond the Holocaust as well as beyond commemorative sites.[5] Innovative topics await their historian: the impact of the democratization of the past on German private and public memories, the commercialization and commodification of the past, and the construction of family memories.[6] For all its innovation, memory studies and, by extension, a certain rendition of cultural history have often picked topics within a field of representational artifacts from the world of art (broadly defined: museums, films, novels, monuments, and others). Matt Matsuda has shown in *The Memory of the Modern* the use and understanding of modern memory in rather unusual, but highly illuminating, contexts.[7] He examines the Paris stock exchange and its accelerated selling of futures as well as the state as a bureaucratic organization pursuing vagabond criminals. This kind of originality is still lacking in German memory studies, although the centrality of the economy to German identity, and of the state to German history, makes similar topics especially fruitful.[8] One suspects that cultural historians have ignored the topics of the state and economic relations because they view these subjects as traditional. But there are no traditional topics, only traditional historians. These topics should also be subjected to an analysis as cultural artifacts; arguably, they are more complex than a museum.[9] The result of overlooking such topics is a distorted and limited view of what memory is and how it operates in society.

Indeed, one problem with the first generation of memory studies has been a rather uncomplicated notion of how memories operate in society. Too often culture is regarded as an autonomous sphere disconnected from social experience.[10] As a genre, these studies suffer from a current weakness characteristic of a certain rendition of cultural history, namely, the emphasis on cultural representations at the expense of social relations, mediation, and reception. The result is an analysis of culture that is devoid of social conditions. Images of the past are presented as circulating in an autonomous sphere of representations, while analysis of these images ignores social differentiation, roles, and structures, as well as the class, gender, generational, and other relations that made these representations possible and gave them meaning.[11] We thus learn more about memory than about the effect of memory on the organization, hierarchy, and arrangements of social and cultural relationships; more about cultural representations than about their effect on social processes; more about single artifacts and discourses than about the relations among them. The picture that emerges is often of several narratives of the German past in symbolic and cultural isolation, without an elucidation of how these narratives built a German symbolic universe with opposing crosscurrents and conflicting imageries.[12]

Consequently, a weakness of memory studies is the tendency to conceive of memory as an entity of symbols without actions, of culture without society, of representations without material goods and interests. This is an internalist view of culture because, in explanatory terms, memory often functions as a reflection of the culture around it, rather than its shaper. This internalist view of culture has a limited notion of power because the question "who wants whom to remember what and why?" is ultimately answered by using the representation as the source as well as the outcome of power. It illuminates little about what is the explanatory value of memory. The emphasis is on how memory represents social relations, but not how memory shapes them. Indeed, in many studies the function of memory appears to be purely rhetorical. When scholars attempt to interpret memory from a representation of the past, but without intermediaries that connect the representation to the social world, the risk of a circular argumentation through "cultural" reading is high.[13]

Recently, a second generation of memory studies has emerged, aiming at rescuing memory from an exclusively representational approach and the often-limited conception of power it has encouraged. These studies attempt to analyze memory as embedded in social networks, and as a commingling of immaterial and material interests and motivations. The term "generation" is, in a sense, a poor choice to describe this body of work that has lacked a self-conscious theoretical statement and a comprehensive overview of that which defines it. This new scholarship is characterized by separated fields of relatively intense research highlighted against a broad backdrop still left untouched or dealt with only superficially. Research has centered on post-1945 East and West Germany, exploring topics such as the interplay between memory and urban space, public and social policy, and official, popular, and counter-gender memories.[14] Fewer studies concentrate on the pre-1945 period[15] or cover modern German history as a whole.[16] These studies share an attempt to go beyond the approach of first-generation memory studies and to explore what people actually "do" with their memories. The practice of memory has been explored as a vehicle to destabilize long-existing boundaries in German culture and historiography, such as the boundary between the local and the national in the German Empire or the boundary between repression and memory in post-1945 West Germany.[17]

While building on this impressive but uneven historiography, the essays in this volume seek to push the topic of memory further. We ask explicitly the essential question: how memory *forms* social relations—as opposed to the traditional way of asking how memory represents social relations. Instead of wondering what memory might be at any one point in time, we ask: how does memory operate? The present volume offers concrete examples of new directions in memory studies that investigate a whole range of topics such as everyday life, families, consumption, economics, death, nostalgia, and the state as a site of memory. Our aim is to propose new topics, but also to point to innovative directions by illuminating subjects that, while being a mainstay of German history and historiography, had hitherto been largely neglected in memory studies and cultural history, such as the state and the economy. We view memory as a symbolic representation of the past embedded in social action. To take memory out of the museum and away from the monument means to view it not as a location, or a group of people, or a thing, but as a set of practices and interventions. Differently put, in order to understand how memory forms social relations we have to understand the practical uses of the category "memory," the way it comes to structure perception, to inform thought, to construct identities, to determine policies, and to explain situations.

Part 2 of the book explores memory in the setting of everyday life. Andrew Bergerson explores the evolution of a notion of normalcy that made the Nazi national community (*Volksgemeinschaft*) possible, as well as its denial after the war. Elizabeth Snyder Hook focuses on the broken life of a post-1945 West German family in which the husband and wife, relieved to leave the war behind and resume "normal" life, discover the difficulties in fitting back into family life because their war memories, traumas, and feelings of guilt could not be so easily left on the outside. And Elizabeth Ten Dyke tells the story of the unsettling experience of East Germans after the 1989 *Wende*, which withdrew basic markers of identity and orientation, as a familiar mode of life represented in the coveted consumer goods disappeared.[18] Central to the essays is the relation between the everyday world of memory and specific historical conditions that calls previous perception of the normal into question. What happens when a pattern of life breaks down completely? How did people integrate—after 1945 and 1989—their new life experiences with old habits, memories, and crimes? How did they succeed or fail in connecting notions of personal experience with notions of collectivity? The essays put the agents of memory front and center, while at the same time placing personal experiences within larger historical conditions.

Part 3 views memory as a material as well as symbolic good in three cases. In Paul Lerner's study, based on post-1918 claims for military pensions on grounds of psychological distress, the focus is on the struggle over defining the "true" memory and meaning of the war: on one side, veterans pressed compensation claims based on narrated memories that stressed the power of traumatic wartime events to transform their identity; on the other side, psychiatrists responded to their patients' stories by asserting a kind of a counternarrative that undermined patients' pension claims and supported the collective identity of the nation. The materiality of memory is the topic of Jonathan Wiesen, who, by linking the process of memory with that of public relations, explores the attempt of West German industry to construct a meaningful and profitable narrative of its role in the Third Reich. And weaving together gender, political symbolism, state policy, and memory,[19] Elizabeth Heineman explores the hidden assumptions about the war and post-1945 society as they played out in public policy concerning war widows as well as the wives of prisoners and missing men in the two Germanys. These essays move from the attempts of subjects to create meaning to the confines set by institutions in their attempt to secure or discount entitlement claims based on memories that reworked the experience of the war. The "official transcripts" that result indicate the political requirements to represent the past and to organize memory in efforts to manage social order. For public institutions were locations where power was defined, knowledge constructed, and rules set and then legitimized as natural, presumed, and beyond question. The essays in part 3 thus explore memory in terms of dollars and cents and cost-benefit considerations that give it the materiality and tangibility that has so far been largely neglected by scholars.

The benefit of these essays' broader approach is great. We ask: how does the use and understanding of memory inform the policies of state, medical, and economic institutions, which determine the paycheck at the end of the month or the political rights at the end of the day? We approach institutions in an anthropological key. Some years ago Mary Douglas set out to describe "how institutions think." Of course, Douglas is well aware that "institutions cannot have minds of their own"; they cannot behave, still less think or feel. But by probing the relations between individuals and institutions, she illuminates the extent to which thinking, our processes of classifying and recognizing, remembering and forgetting, depends upon institutions, and that institutions have powerful stakes in the organization of the past.[20] One need not necessarily agree with her statement—that "public memory is the storage system for the social order," which is influenced by Maurice Halbwachs's Durkheimian notion of the social—in order to see the usefulness of her approach to the study of memory.[21] Institutions give memory a structure and an organization that is decisive for its reception. In public institutions, Germans carried, cultivated, and propagated memories, and their activity gave memory social continuity and regularity, and also made memory the ally of evasion. Study of the history of how institutions construct memories and narratives can be useful to illuminate how memory is linked to a social order and social relations, and how institutions use memory to attain power.

Exploring memory in the setting of everyday life and as constitutive of perceptions of normality, showing how it operated as a material as well as a symbolic good in the private sphere and in public institutions and the state, is a useful approach to capture the multiple links that existed between memory and power, and that enabled memory to shape social relations. When power is located so firmly in common representations (museums, monuments, films, etc.) then other kinds of power are made to seem falsely peripheral by comparison. As the essays under discussion here show, many kinds of links between memory and power operated in society, in different locations and practices. Memory played out in various kinds of power, often in competition with one another; not all forms of memory and power were interchangeable, but all of them were important.

We are aware, of course, that the emphasis on social practice can be in itself primarily rhetorical, since scholars often "emphasize practice in order to oppose what they see as an overly linguistic or discursive definition of culture."[22] But our emphasis on memory as practice has a different purpose. We are not interested in showing, by way of "practice," how the public received a given museum or film. Similarly, we do not claim that one needs to add social action to the study of representation, for this theoretical position assumes the existence of two separate spheres, while in fact these are intertwined. Rather, we wish to link perceptions of memory to decisions and actions by individuals, institutions, and the state. We need to ask: how influential was the category of memory in making social, political, economic, and everyday-life decisions? Our aim is to destabilize the boundaries between memory as representation and memory as social action: we wish to explore whether and in what way the presence of memory is not so much a manifestation of the culture around it but a shaper of culture, of beliefs and values as well as of everyday life, institutional settings, and the processes of decision making.

* * *

A further aim of this volume is to think critically about how to write the history of memory in Germany. If the impulse to organize the past is the basis for the construction of identity, then this impulse achieves intelligibility as a compelling story or narrative. These stories have authority precisely because they are organized in a way that effaces the contingent, discontinuous, and indeed dangerous (because multivocal) quality to the past. Without this management of the past, the coherence that connects individuals with collectivities and makes social action in a public setting possible would be unimaginable. Narratives establish authority by telling a plausible story, and by providing social meaning to otherwise scattered individual experiences.[23] These narratives may be tendentious, gendered, conflict-ridden, and violent, but one thing that emerges from this volume is that states, institutions, and individuals are dependent on them for legitimacy and coherence. But there is more to them. Narratives provide storied claims for entitlement and they thus generate historical subjectivity that has proven notoriously difficult to deconstruct by a critical scholarship. Collective memories are a weak form in that they are potentially integrated into any number of narratives, but once embedded in a narrative stream they turn out to be remarkably strong and they thus deflect counternarratives and counterarguments.[24]

The authority of narrative provides a way to think about the link between the organization of collective memory and the construction of identities, that is, about how identity is increasingly grounded in recognizable memories. But this commonsensical relationship is itself historical. The deliberate work of memory is energized by the way historical subjects locate themselves in the space opened by modernity between the past and the present. Cultural memory becomes increasingly important when the past is recognized as cut off and different from the present. This temporal perspective gains authority in the modern era. The urgency of constructing usable pasts is also associated with the project of the nation-state, with national attempts to resist imperial designs and to create distinctive, vernacular histories. In this respect, the history of memory is entangled with the history of being conscious of one's modernity—the sense of displacement from the endurance and legitimacy of tradition and the recognition of the contest among new, politically potent identities. The overall theme that unites the essays in part 1 is the modern context to the obsession with memory. It is not a question of whether memory is modern.[25] More useful is an interrogation of what is peculiarly modern about memory and an attempt to historicize the discourses of memory and of being modern.[26] The increasingly plausible notion that time is accelerating and the feeling that the past seems remote and in a state of ruin makes the issue of the past more and more present, and makes achieving relations to the past an endeavor that is difficult and important. What emerges from the essays is that being modern is experienced as the purported absence or disintegration or jeopardy of tradition, a term which itself is coined as part of a modern worldview. As a result, people in the modern age feel a more compelling need to tell historically situated stories in order to understand themselves and to motivate collective action. The past becomes present as a reconstructed set of relations of distance and intimacy.

Covering a period from the Reformation to the twentieth century, the essays in part 1 provide four signposts to writing the history of memory in Germany. They are not about how a given past was commemorated but rather about how notions of temporality, that is, perceptions of the past, present, and future and their relations, changed, and how these transformations created the conditions for people to use and think about memory in new, at times complex and at times simplistic, ways. Where, when, and why did there emerge categories for past and present that make it possible as well as useful for people to think of memory? Rather than taking modernity itself as the hard and set context within which memory operates, the attempt is to elucidate the genealogy of our own historical understanding and use of these categories.

Craig Koslofsky attempts to historicize the creation of "the modern memory order." He argues that the Reformation, by propagating the doctrine of salvation by faith alone, made death a barrier that demarcated the sovereignty of God as well as the historical formation of the individual. This laid the foundation for the modern memory order based on time as linear and directional, which in turn composed a past of dead individuals, with whom the living could have only the most disturbing, incomplete contact. "Compared with the medieval presence of the dead," Koslofsky concludes, "the modern past is always unmasterable: it can be interpreted, but never set right." The ironic trope is unmistakable: there is an unmasterable past, and it has a German connection, but it is unexpectedly linked to the Reformation.[27] Jonathan Hess goes against a cherished argument in memory studies, namely that the Jews as the people of memory were forced by modernity to forsake tradition for history. Hess is not interested in discounting this account. Rather, he explores the genealogy of this narrative of memory's suppression. Ultimately, Hess subjects the narrative of modernity itself to investigation, and explores the relation between historical understanding and the problematizing of modernity. Peter Fritzsche examines nostalgia after the French Revolution in terms of the emergence of modern categories for past and present. Far from being a reflexive reaction of antimodernism or a kind of a reactionary by-product of rapid change, nostalgia reflected the distinction between past and present that is a hallmark of modernity. At the same time, nostalgia facilitated historical consciousness by placing personal experiences into a general historical narrative. Changing genres of memory are also the focus of Marcus Funck and Stephan Malinowski's report on the commemorative culture of the German nobility, a group that cultivated the traditions of family and estate over hundreds of years. The authors cast some doubt on just how remorseless historical transformations have been, and discover that until the end of the twentieth century the mastery of noble memory worked surprisingly well. Their focus is especially useful because most studies in memory tend to take as their subjects either the representational artifact (the museum, film, and the like) or the event rather than the social group, and have mainly ignored the aristocracy.

What emerges from these essays is the proposition that to be modern is to be conscious of one's historicity: to be able to see oneself in historical terms.[28] Only this condition makes it sensible and useful to think of memory as a category with which to explain the world. Memory as a modern category has meaning when the past is perceived to have become irretrievable. The essays take as their subject the acknowledged difficulty of mastering the past and the cultural activity that has been generated as a result. They explore how and why the past came to be seen as troubled and indeterminate, and why it should require the strenuous effort of mastery. Modernity replaced the self-evident authority of tradition with a self-conscious historical sensibility that is premised on the knowledge of the demolition of tradition. This fundamental proposition of modernity made modern memory a vexed, compelling activity. In the modern age, the past—every past—is, potentially, a problem.[29] Differently put, the need to master the past is a modern phenomenon and preoccupation; mastering the past is not a specifically German concern.

For German historiography, the potential subversiveness of this argument—that the modern need to come to terms with the past and the subsequent endeavor to gain mastery over it are the preconditions for the work of memory—should be clear. It runs against one of the most cherished master narratives of modern German memory, namely, that of the sui generis "unmasterable past" qualities of the Holocaust. Certainly, the Nazi regime and the Holocaust pose enormous problems of owning up to the past and attempting to come to terms with it. Who, among those who seek truth, would deny it? But the question should be different: is the problem of understanding the Holocaust, on a fundamental level, so different from the troubled relations modern people have to the past? It is not without interest to note that parallel to the body of work on the difficulties, if not outright impossibility, of mastering the Holocaust past there is an important literature on the intransparent, protean, and, in short, problematic relations to the past in the modern age as a whole. The link between these two bodies of work is the proposition of this volume: coming to terms with the past is a modern endeavor. The essays in part 1 have profited immensely from the scholarship on the Holocaust and particularly on the capacities of perpetrators and victims to remember and represent the past, but the contributors shift focus to explore the difficulty of mastering the past as a constituent part of modern identity.

Writing a history of memory in Germany should therefore begin, in our view, with the recognition that on the spectrum of modern reactions to the past the Holocaust represents the most extreme case, but not, on a fundamental level, a qualitatively different case that stands alone. The ambiguities, traumas, repressions, and negotiations that made the relations of Germans to the past before and after 1945 so troubled need to be put in relation to the overall problem of the past in the modern world. The work of memory also needs to be analyzed in terms of the historical narratives it enables. Distinctive histories are tendentious and selective, and they privilege the particular over the general precisely in order to distinguish a cohesive social group. Collective memory thereby enables the fanciful continuities of national history—it authorizes a sense of historical subjectivity for separate nations, and it thereby provides the mechanisms for collective political action. This perspective highlights the paradox of memory: it leads and misleads and yet only remembering and forgetting provide the ability to act and to judge.

* * *

This approach does not fit neatly with current views on mastering the past in Germany. The literature on the subject is so vast now, and the literary, political, and artistic scandals in Germany and elsewhere so common, that the calls on Germany to master its past, while morally laudable, sound like a formulaic mantra with little thinking behind it. It repays to think more critically about this. This quest must begin with the recognition that memory in Germany is a subject whose raison d'être, in public and scholarly discourse, has been intimately connected to the topics of the Holocaust and World War II.[30] The importance of studies on coming to terms with the past has been fundamental. They have used a vocabulary, originating largely in psychoanalysis, whose interpretative value has been significant to the field of memory as a whole.[31] Key terms such as "silence," "amnesia," "repression," "denial," "guilt," "shame," "trauma," "mastering the past," and "the burden of the past" have provided studies on *Vergangenheitsbewältigung* with their themes and concepts. The essays in the present volume are indebted to the vocabulary, historical findings, and moral urgency of this rich body of literature.

But the accusation that Germans have not mastered the past has become a ritualistic statement that often ignores two fundamental questions: What does it really mean to master the past? And is it at all possible? It seems that for some people, scholars as well as laypersons, mastering the past is a thing: if only the past will be mastered more energetically, adding another museum, building another monument, then at the end a mastering will be reached. As if mastering the past is a journey with a final stop, where one reaches finality and reconciliation that bring closure. Others seem to think that nothing Germany has done or will do can suffice to show that it has mastered its past. Neither view is useful. Mastering the past is not a process that leads to reconciliation with Nazi crimes but rather a process of learning how to live with the realization that Nazi crimes are part of your history and identity, and nothing, in a sense, can reconcile you to them. At the same time, the idea of mastering the past is so open-ended that no matter how German society confronts it, there can always be people who can say this is not enough.

For how do you measure a mastering of a past? What does it mean? It means that the past in question is relevant to the identity and politics of a society, and that it can be confronted critically. In thinking about mastering the past we should not assume a production of an absolute coherent, univocal voice, but rather the presence of multiple voices, often contradictory and opposed to each other but in dialogue. These voices exercise self-criticism about the past that ultimately brings self-consciousness. In their classic book on the inability of Germans to mourn and to come to terms with the past, Margarete and Alexander Mitscherlich defined the process as "a sequence of steps in self-knowledge."[32] The Mitscherlichs, as it is well known, argued that such steps were not taken in postwar Germany.

On one level, applying this definition, the sequence of steps taken in West Germany and then in the united Germany in the last twenty years is in fact quite remarkable. They include, among others: the 1979 TV series "Holocaust," the 1985 Bitburg affair, the 1986 historians' debate (*Historikerstreit*), and, just in the last several years, the Goldhagen controversy, the introduction of a Holocaust commemoration day on 27 January, and the debate surrounding the Berlin Holocaust memorial.[33] The Holocaust is now a mainstay of German public life, political liturgy, and national identity. And this becomes clear precisely in cases where the significant role of the Holocaust, in historical inquiry and in public life, was questioned, such as the historians' debate. A common view in studies on mastering the past is to interpret these cases as symptoms of the continuing refusal of Germans to face up to the past. But this is a mistaken view based on the unspoken assumption that mastering the past must produce a univocal voice. There will always be in German society shades of opinions about the German pasts. And why should we assume differently? There are certainly contradictory and opposing voices in Germany about World War II and the Holocaust, some of which are outright repulsive (such as the refusal of German companies who gained from slave labor to contribute to the compensation fund). But these voices must operate within a dominant discourse in German public life that recognizes the crimes of the Nazis and the perils of apologetics. If we have heard so much in the last two decades about Holocaust controversies it is not because Germans fail to master the past; it is precisely because they are in the process of mastering it.

On a second level, and perhaps more importantly, the idea that we should expect a complete mastery of the past—namely, an absolute agreement over the memory of the Holocaust—is not only wishful thinking, it is a mistake. Mastery of the past is always incomplete; it can't be expected because the distortions, lies, and evasions that remain are the building blocks of social and individual identities. Coming to terms with the Nazi past is not a process in which Germans will, at some point, reach mastery over it. Instead it is a process in which

Germans internalize this past as an integral part of their national identity by renouncing all the internal resistance they feel against acknowledging the enormity of the atrocities and the fact that they were committed by Germans.[34]

Significantly, when and if the Holocaust becomes a topic about which everyone can agree, this will also be a sign of its insignificance. Disagreement is a sign of importance, not of irrelevancy. Viewed in this way, disagreements over the Holocaust are constitutive to the process of coming to terms with past, not its contradiction. Rather than being so preoccupied with every controversy, we should look at the overall picture: the controversies do not signify that the past is not mastered, but, on the contrary, they are the evidence that the Nazi past has been, in various degrees and speeds, internalized as inherent to German national identity. It is indeed a question of degree and proportion: which public discourse is prevalent, the one of Ernst Nolte, the scholar who diminished the Holocaust in the historians' debate, or the one of the German president Johannes Rau, who, in a historic speech to the Knesset delivered in German, the first time that language has been spoken from the rostrum of the Israeli parliament, declared in February 2000: "I bow my head in humility before those who were murdered, those who have no graves at which I could ask their forgiveness."[35] Scholars, journalists, politicians, and intellectuals who lament the state of coming to terms with past in German society invert, in fact, the relations of cause and effect. It is not that we talk about the Holocaust because the past has not been mastered, but that we talk about it because it is in the process of being internalized as a mainstay of German identity, a past that will not go away because it should not go away.

A comparison between Germans' attitudes toward the Holocaust in the present and in the two decades after 1945 is illuminating. What are the conditions under which memories are shared? Pierre Nora argued that memories can be usefully shared by a nation only when their original nature has been so transformed as to be emptied of any real significance, at which point they stop being divisive.[36] We don't think the Holocaust has been emptied of any real significance; this is clearly an error. But the perception of the Holocaust has transformed between the generation of 1933–45 and the following generations of the children and grandchildren. A society may be thought of as a system of symbols and practices that, however diverse, share a certain thin coherence.[37] German society presently manifests a thin coherence that places the Holocaust at the center of public life, though there are disagreements over how to translate this coherence economically (slave labor compensations), politically (relations to Israel), and morally (the historians' debate). This coherence is wholly different from the one that existed in the post-1945 period, when the Holocaust was not at the center of East and West German public culture and identity. In West Germany, in the first years after the war, as much as 70 percent of the population rejected the idea that Germany itself bore total responsibility for the war. Most believed that Hitler and the Nazi party were responsible for the war, but not the German nation as a whole. Today, most Germans reject these opinions. The arguments of Andreas Hilgruber and Ernst Nolte, who provoked the historians' debate of the mid-1980s with their analyses of the links between Communist and Nazi crimes, were common among West Germans after 1945, but today collapsing the Nazi crimes into a general universal or Western evil is rather unacceptable in German society.[38] The arguments of Hilgruber and Nolte were viewed as an attempt to whitewash the crimes of the Third Reich and were opposed by many, headed by the philosopher Jürgen Habermas. The notion that Nolte, Hilgruber, and others were a vanguard of a 1980s conservative *Wende* seems misplaced; theirs was rather a conservative rearguard battle. Could we even remotely think of a similar popular liberal reaction to Nazi apologetics in the 1950s?

The distinction between the two periods brings into sharp focus the argument that, when compared to the postwar period, the period from the 1970s seems to be a time in which the past is in the process of being internalized. Above the surface, in public life, there have been considerably more discussions on the Holocaust after the 1970s than before. But the earlier period may be the more interesting and challenging for scholars. Here existed genuine tensions about the Holocaust, for this was after all a society of, among others, many murderers and many more bystanders. In this society tensions flared between perpetrators and honest Germans (of the Nazi period: because perpetrators of the Third Reich turned into honest, law-abiding citizens in East and West Germany, which created for some another tension—in their inner selves), Auschwitz and moral taboos, guilt and belief in God, personal memories and public silences, shooting children and educating your own. The years after the war, which are so often uncomplicatedly labeled as years of denial and repression, may be much more important than previously thought for molding the memory of war and genocide.[39] An investigation of this period, where the Holocaust as well as anti-Semitism became a taboo in German society, calls for imagination and subtlety, for one must enter people's private lives, intimate desires, and worst nightmares. Where is the history of German dreams in this period? Our stories on mastering the past and German memories tend to be too predictable; we need to constitute a new space of memory possibilities.[40]

The distinguished historiography on memory in German history, overwhelmingly centered on the Holocaust and World War II, has been overdetermined by descriptive and explanatory terms such as "silence," "absence," and "repression." This is, no doubt, true: German society after 1945 has often refused to own up to its past. But it is only a partial truth. Before and after 1945, the noises of the past reverberated loudly in German society and culture. We may not like the articulation of some of these pasts, but "silence" is not the right term to describe the presence of the past in modern German history. The question is not how Germans repressed the past, but whether they repressed it at all so completely. It is not whether Germans articulated their memories, but how they articulated traces of the past, and where, and how scholars are to find these traces. This volume, by focusing on everyday life, materiality, and the history of memory, is written precisely to encourage more probing into these questions.

There is no closure to this introduction, just as there is no closure to the modern struggle with memory and with the past. We began this text by warning against identifying German memory studies with the Holocaust, and we ended up talking quite a lot about the Holocaust. But this is not a contradiction. It would be absurd to talk about memory in Germany while avoiding the Holocaust, just as it would be reductive to study memory only in relation to the Holocaust. The two are connected, part of the same history. We therefore choose to end with an open-ended intervention. Steven Ostovich's essay is a theological and philosophical meditation on the dangerous quality of modern memory, and the uses of memory work in promoting social recognition and political transformation. "Dangerous memories" illuminate the impermanence of dominant historical narratives, and they thereby facilitate the construction of alternative, subversive historical subjectivities.

Here again "the noise of the past" is a useful term because it takes the full measure of the evasions, silences, and tendentious emphases of memory work.[41] Images of the past often opposed and contradicted each other; Germans were ready to imprison and kill each other over disagreements regarding identity and ideology. And yet the noise was never a complete cacophony. Polyphony seems to be the sound that characterizes German memory. This, perhaps, is the most suitable metaphor for German memory: the polyphony of memories in German history meant that different readings of the past, violently different in some cases, coexisted within a certain cultural coherence, one that was contested and changing, but one that was also delimited by certain themes, rhetorics, symbols, and practices. And to subject German history to such an investigation means to place the Holocaust within history, the history of memory in the light of the trauma of the Holocaust, and German memory within modern memory.

NOTES

1. Robert Hughes, *The Culture of Complaint: The Fraying of America* (New York: Oxford University Press, 1993); Arthur M. Schlesinger, Jr., *The Disuniting of America: Reflections on a Multicultural Society* (New York: Norton, 1992); Allan Young, *The Harmony of Illusions: Inventing Post-traumatic Stress Disorder* (Princeton: Princeton University Press, 1995).

2. See, for example, Etienne François, "Von der wiederelangten Nation zur 'Nation wider Willen.' Kann man eine Geschichte der deutschen 'Erinnerungsorte' schreiben?" in *Nation und Emotion: Deutschland und Frankreich im Vergleich 19. und 20. Jahrhundert,* ed. François et al. (Göttingen: Vandenhoeck & Ruprecht, 1995).

3. The literature is enormous, and continues to grow. See, for example: James Young, *The Texture of Memory: Holocaust Memorials and Meaning* (New Haven: Yale University Press, 1993); James Young, ed., *The Art of Memory: Holocaust Memorials in History* (New York: Prestel-Verlag, 1994); and Edgar Wolfrum, "Geschichtspolitik und deutsche Frage: Der 17. Juni im nationalen Gedächtnis der Bundesrepublik (1953–89)," *Geschichte und Gesellschaft* 24 (1998): 382–411. And see n. 30 below.

4. Patrick Hutton, "Mnemonic Schemes in the New History of Memory," *History and Theory* 36 (Oct. 1997): 380.

5. For two important collections on commemorations see John R. Gillis, ed., *Commemorations: The Politics of National Identity* (Princeton: Princeton University Press, 1994); and Gerald Sider and Gavin Smith, eds., *Between History and Histories: The Making of Silence and Commemorations* (Toronto: University of Toronto Press, 1997).

6. Indeed, in spite of the common perception that memory as a topic of research is everywhere, in reality the range of topics covered by scholars is quite bounded. Thus, in the burgeoning field of German cultural history, memory as a field of research for the pre-1945 period is often neglected. Although "memory" is one of the leading terms in cultural studies, Geoff Eley does not discuss it in his introduction to *Society, Culture, and the State in Germany, 1870–1930,* an edited collection that meant to present the state of the field. Only one essay, by Rudy Koshar, takes the theme of memory. Eley also does not discuss the problems, methods, and potential of the term in his essay "Theory and the Kaiserreich: Problems with Culture: German History after the Linguistic Turn," *Central European History* 31 (1998): 197–227. Hans-Ulrich Wehler's critique of Eley's volume points to other possible and fruitful directions of research, but memory is not one of them. See Geoff Eley, ed., *Society, Culture, and the State in Germany, 1870–1930* (Ann Arbor: University of Michigan Press, 1997), and Hans-Ulrich Wehler, "A Guide to Future Research on the Kaiserreich?" *Central European History* 29 (1996): 541–72.

Some sixteen years after the publication of Pierre Nora's first volume in the masterful *Les lieux de mémoire,* a multivolume work on German *Erinnerungs-Orte* is to be published soon, edited by Etienne François and Hagen Schulze. It is too early to tell whether it will be an important contribution in terms of method, approach, and subject matter, or whether it will replicate Nora's project while introducing new information on German sites of memory.

7. Matt K. Matsuda, *The Memory of the Modern* (New York: Oxford University Press, 1996).

8. Raphael Samuel's *Theatres of Memory,* vol. 1: *Past and Present in Contemporary Culture* (London: Verso, 1994), is also an instructive example. Samuel's study attempts to document and explore the current obsession, in all modern industrial societies, with preservation and conservation, as industrial artifacts become images of heritage, whether it is a Victorian pier, an old mine shaft, or the Abbey Road's Beatles studio. He argues that heritage and conservation are profoundly democratic, carried by "Clio's underlabourers" (ordinary folks such as collectors, photographers, museum curators, book-fair hunters) who, more than official historians, have shaped our sense of the past. The book is encyclopedic more than analytical, but offers a wide range of topics, as well as an agenda, that goes beyond our existing knowledge of Heimatlers and preservationists in Germany. The true followers of Samuel's agenda in Germany are local historians who in the last twenty years have practiced history from below and history of everyday life as a counterculture response to official and professional renditions of the past.

On Samuel's book see Krishan Kumar, "History and Heritage," *Radical Philosophy* 77 (May/June 1996): 41–43; Bill Gale, "Staging the Practices of Heritage," *Labour/Le Travail* 37 (Spring 1996): 289–99; Matt Matsuda, "The State of Things: Honoring Memory," *Radical History Review* 67 (Winter 1997): 199–205. On Heimatlers and preservationists in Germany see Celia Applegate, *A Nation of Provincials: The German Idea of Heimat* (Berkeley: University of California Press, 1990); Rudy Koshar, *Germany's Transient Pasts: Preservation and National Memory in the Twentieth Century* (Chapel Hill: University of North Carolina Press, 1998); and Alon

Confino, *The Nation as a Local Metaphor: Württemberg, Imperial Germany and National Memory, 1871–1918* (Chapel Hill: University of North Carolina Press, 1997). On everyday life history as a professional and antiestablishment movement, see Alf Lüdtke, ed., *The History of Everyday Life: Reconstructing Historical Experiences and Ways of Life* (Princeton: Princeton University Press, 1995); and Geoff Eley, "Labor History, Social History, *Alltagsgeschichte:* Experience, Culture, and the Politics of the Everyday—A New Direction for German Social History?" *Journal of Modern History* 61 (1989): 297–343.

9. This is an ironic twist on the work of Michel Foucault, one of the greatest historians of institutions in the West. While his overall work and agenda have been very influential for cultural studies, the subject matter of institutions was left on the sideline for memory studies.

10. For a very different study of commemoration, which commingles representation and social experience and rejects artificial fixed meanings and coherent closure, see Alf Lüdtke, "Histories of Mourning: Flowers and Stones for the War Dead. Confusion for the Living—Vignettes from East and West Germany," in *Between History and Histories,* ed. Sider and Smith, pp. 149–79.

11. An exemplary case of this problem is Y. Michal Bodemann's essay "Eclipse of Memory: German Representations of Auschwitz in the Early Postwar Period," *New German Critique* 75 (Fall 1998): 57–89. Bodemann's aim is to explore how "Auschwitz and the final solution were represented in the public arenas of postwar Germany . . . [as a] nexus of silence and memory" (pp. 59, 63). His method is to analyze several cultural artifacts as representatives of larger discourses in German society. Thus, Eugen Kogon's *The NS State,* published in 1946, represented the Nazis as criminals and the Jews as victims. A second discourse, found in memoirs and novels, reversed or blurred the roles of victims and perpetrators. A third narrative, epitomized in Carl Schmitt's *Glossarium,* provided apologetics for the Third Reich, while a narrative of silence pervaded postwar German sociology. Bodemann presents a picture of varying attitudes toward the past, while avoiding the false dichotomy between silence and memory. But this is an analysis of culture that is devoid of social conditions.

12. See Alon Confino, "Collective Memory and Cultural History: Problems of Method," *American Historical Review* 102 (1997): 1386–1403.

13. In this sense, the term "memory" shares a similar problem as the term "culture." Ann Swindler's observation about culture applies to memory as well: "Too-easy embrace of the notion that culture is ubiquitous and constitutive can undermine any explanatory claim for culture. Then emphasis on culture becomes a species of intellectual hand waving, creating a warm and cozy atmosphere, while other factors continue to carry the real explanatory weight." Swindler is quoted by Victoria Bonnell and Lynn Hunt in their introduction to *Beyond the Cultural Turn: New Directions in the Study of Society and Culture,* ed. Bonnell and Hunt (Berkeley: University of California Press, 1999), p. 32, n. 32.

14. On West Germany, see Robert Moeller, *War Stories* (Berkeley: University of California Press, 2001) and "War Stories: The Search for a Usable Past in the Federal Republic of Germany," *American Historical Review* 101 (1996): 1008–48. See also Elizabeth Heineman, "The Hour of the Woman: Memories of Germany's 'Crisis Years' and West German National Identity," *American Historical Review* 101 (1996): 354–95. On memory and state policy in East Germany, see Jeffrey Herf, *Divided Memory: The Nazi Past in the Two Germanys* (Cambridge: Harvard University Press, 1997), and Catherine Epstein, "The Production of 'Official Memory' in East Germany: Old Communists and the Dilemmas of Memoir-Writing," *Central European History* 32 (1999): 181–202. On urban space, see Brian Ladd, *The Ghosts of Berlin:*

Confronting German History in Urban Landscape (Chicago: University of Chicago Press, 1997), and Gavriel Rosenfeld, *Munich and Memory: Architecture, Monuments, and the Legacy of the Third Reich* (Berkeley: University of California Press, 2000).

Some studies discuss the nexus between public policy, social legislation, and the legacy of the war in West German society, though they do not use memory explicitly as narrative or explanatory vehicle. See James Diehl, *The Thanks of the Fatherland: German Veterans after the Second World War* (Chapel Hill: University of North Carolina Press, 1993); Constantin Goschler, *Wiedergutmachung. Westdeutschland und die Verfolgten des Nationalsozialismus (1945–1954)* (Munich: Oldenbourg Verlag, 1992); and Michael Hughes, *Shouldering the Burdens of Defeat: West Germany and the Reconstruction of Social Justice* (Chapel Hill: University of North Carolina Press, 1999).

A case apart is the important research of Lutz Niethammer and his collaborators, who placed memory of the Third Reich in the post-1945 era in the minutiae of everyday life and social networks. Their work on oral history, originally linked to historiographical concerns of the social history of the 1960s and 1970s, connected to memory topics of cultural history of the 1980s and 1990s. See *"Die Jahre weiß man nicht, wo man die heute hinsetzen soll." Faschismuserfahrungen im Ruhrgebiet* (Berlin: Dietz, 1983); *"Hinterher merkt man, daß es richtig war, daß es schief gegangen ist." Nachkriegserfahrungen im Ruhrgebiet* (Berlin: Dietz, 1983); and "'Normalisierung' im Westen: Erinnerunsspuren in die 50er Jahre," in *Ist der Nationalsozialismus Geschichte? Zu Historisierung und Historikerstreit,* ed. Dan Diner (Frankfurt am Main: Fisher Taschenbucher Verlag, 1987).

15. Susan Crane, *Collecting and Historical Consciousness: New Forms for Collective Memory in Early Nineteenth-Century Germany* (Ithaca: Cornell University Press, 2000), and Christopher Clark, "The Wars of Liberation in Prussian Memory: Reflections on the Memorialization of War in Early Nineteenth-Century Germany," *Journal of Modern History* 68 (1996): 550–76.

16. The work of Rudy Koshar is fundamental here. See Koshar, *Germany's Transient Pasts* and *From Monuments to Traces: Artifacts of German Memory, 1870–1990* (Berkeley: University of California Press, 2000).

17. Confino, *Nation as a Local Metaphor;* Moeller, *War Stories.*

18. On consumer culture and memory see also Alon Confino and Rudy Koshar, "Regimes of Consumer Cultures: New Narratives in Twentieth-Century German History," *German History* 19 (Spring 2001): 135–61. See also in this special issue on German consumer culture, Elizabeth Ten Dyke, "Tulips in December: Space, Time and Consumption before and after the End of German Socialism" (pp. 253–76); and Paul Betts, "The Twilight of the Idols: East German Memory and Material Culture," *Journal of Modern History* 72 (2000): 731–65.

19. On gender and memory see Selma Leydesdorff, Luisa Passerini, and Paul Thompson, eds., *Gender and Memory* (Oxford: Oxford University Press, 1996). For a discussion of gender differences in recollection, see Elizabeth Loftus, Mahzarin Banaji, Jonathan Schooler, and Rachael Foster, "Who Remembers What? Gender Differences in Memory," *Michigan Quarterly Review* 26 (Winter 1987): 64–85; and Lucy Noakes, *War and the British: Gender, Memory and National Identity* (London: I. B. Tauris, 1998).

20. Mary Douglas, *How Institutions Think* (Syracuse, N.Y.: Syracuse University Press, 1986), pp. 3, 8.

21. Douglas, *How Institutions Think,* p. 70.

22. Bonnell and Hunt, "Introduction," in *Beyond the Cultural Turn,* ed. Bonnell and Hunt, p. 12.

23. Key texts include David Carr, *Time, Narrative, and History* (Bloomington: Indiana University Press, 1986); Saul Friedlander, ed., *Probing the Limits of Representation: Nazism and the "Final Solution"* (Cambridge: Harvard University Press, 1992); Hayden White, *Metahistory: The Historical Imagination in Nineteenth-Century Europe* (Baltimore: Johns Hopkins University Press, 1973); Hayden White, *Tropics of Discourse: Essays in Cultural Criticism* (Baltimore: Johns Hopkins University Press, 1978); Hayden White, *The Content of the Form: Narrative Discourse and Historical Representation* (Baltimore: Johns Hopkins University Press, 1987); and W. J. T. Mitchell, ed., *On Narrative* (Chicago: University of Chicago Press, 1980). See also *Beyond the Cultural Turn*, ed. Bonnell and Hunt, part 3.

24. See the argument in David Campbell, *National Deconstruction: Violence, Identity, and Justice in Bosnia* (Minneapolis: University of Minnesota Press, 1998).

25. The views of Maurice Halbwachs and Pierre Nora are well known. Halbwachs sharply distinguishes between memory as a premodern, malleable rendition of the past and the discipline of history, emerging in the nineteenth century, as a scientific, accurate rendition of it. Nora provides a nostalgic view of memory, and views modernity as the destroyer of it. He believes that there once existed a "real memory—social and unviolated, exemplified in but also retained as the secret of so-called primitive or archaic societies." But now, in the modern era, memory as a social practice, as "a milieu of memory," has been replaced by voluntary and deliberate memory. Speaking of creating a warm and cozy atmosphere . . . See Maurice Halbwachs, *The Collective Memory*, trans. Francis J. Ditter, Jr., and Vida Yazdy Ditter (New York: Harper and Row, 1980), pp. 78–87, 105–7. On Halbwachs's conceptions of history and memory, see Patrick Hutton, *History as an Art of Memory* (Hanover, N.H.: University Press of New England, 1993), chap. 4. See also Pierre Nora, "Entre mémoire et histoire," in *Les lieux de mémoire*, ed. Nora, vol. 1: *La République* (Paris: Gallimard, 1984), pp. xvii, xx–xxx.

26. See, for example, James Chandler, *England in 1819: The Politics of Literary Culture and the Case of Romantic Historicism* (Chicago: University of Chicago Press, 1998); Reinhart Koselleck, *Futures Past: On the Semantics of Historical Time* (Cambridge: MIT Press, 1985); and Richard Terdiman, *Present Past: Modernity and the Memory Crisis* (Ithaca: Cornell University Press, 1993).

27. For an illuminating discussion on the relations between memory and power in medieval society, see Gadi Algazi, "Lord Asks, Peasants Answer: Making Traditions in Late-Medieval Village Assemblies," in *Between History and Histories*, ed. Sider and Smith, pp. 199–229; and Algazi, "'Sich selbst vergessen' im späten Mittelalter: Denkfigur und soziale Figurationen," in *Memoria als Kultur*, ed. Otto Oexle (Göttingen: Vandenhoeck & Ruprecht, 1995), pp. 387–427.

28. Obviously, to view oneself in historical terms is not an invention of the moderns. The ancient Greeks, to name one example, viewed their existence against a past, though a mythic one. The difference introduced by the moderns is the idea that the past is irretrievable and the present is constantly changing and moving inexorably forward, whether one thinks this is good, a disaster, or a combination of both. Medieval historical perception, in contrast, was based on the familiarity and likeness between the past and present. This perception of the past was first broken in the Renaissance and Reformation and later demolished with the Enlightenment. On medieval historical mentality, see the excellent studies of Amos Funkenstein, *Heilsplan und naturliche Entwicklung. Formen des Gegenwartsbestimmung im Geschichtsdenken des Mittelalters* (Munich: Nymphenburger Verlanshandlung, 1965) and *Theology and the Scientific Imagination from the Middle-Ages to the Seventeenth Century* (Princeton: Princeton University Press, 1986).

29. "Potentially," is the key word here, for clearly many past events in personal and collective life do not pose any problem but still get totally forgotten.

30. The literature is huge. See, for example, Thomas Fox, *Stated Memory: East Germany and the Holocaust* (Rochester, N.Y.: Camden House, 1999); Herf, *Divided Memory;* Geoffrey Hartman, ed., *Holocaust Remembrance: The Shapes of Memory* (Oxford: Blackwell, 1994); Caroline Wiedmer, *The Claims of Memory: Representations of the Holocaust in Contemporary Germany and France* (Ithaca: Cornell University Press, 1999); Omer Bartov, *Murder in Our Midst: The Holocaust, Industrial Killing, and Representation* (New York: Oxford University Press, 1996); Saul Friedlander, *Memory, History and the Extermination of the Jews of Europe* (Bloomington: Indiana University Press, 1993); and James Young, *At Memory's Edge: After-Images of the Holocaust in Contemporary Art and Architecture* (New Haven: Yale University Press, 2000).

31. Dominick LaCapra, especially, has used concepts from psychoanalysis. See his *Representing the Holocaust: History, Theory, Trauma* (Ithaca: Cornell University Press, 1994) and *History and Memory after Auschwitz* (Ithaca: Cornell University Press, 1998).

32. Alexander Mitscherlich and Margarete Mitscherlich, *The Inability to Mourn: Principles of Collective Behavior* (New York: Grove Press, 1975), p. 14.

33. The screening of the American TV miniseries "Holocaust," starring Meryl Streep, caused a lively debate in Germany about the Nazi past. The Bitburg affair concerned a ceremony commemorating the fortieth anniversary of the war in which President Reagan laid wreaths on the graves of SS men. For an overview of the Bitburg debate, see Ilya Levkov, ed., *Bitburg and Beyond: Encounters in American, German, and Jewish History* (New York: Shapolsky Publishing, 1987).

The 1986 historians' debate centered on the uniqueness of the Nazi crimes and on the place of the Third Reich in modern history. The debate was not confined to academia but engulfed German cultural life as a whole for months. See Charles Maier, *The Unmasterable Past: History, Holocaust and German National Identity* (Cambridge: Harvard University Press, 1988); Richard Evans, *In Hitler's Shadow: West German Historians and the Attempt to Escape from the Nazi Past* (New York: Pantheon Books, 1989); and Peter Baldwin, ed., *Reworking the Past: Hitler, the Holocaust and the Historians' Debate* (Boston: Beacon Press, 1990).

The Goldhagen controversy followed a book that blamed all Germans for exterminatory tendencies against the Jews. See Daniel Goldhagen, *Hitler's Willing Executioners: Ordinary Germans and the Holocaust* (New York: Knopf, 1996); Marouf Hasian, Jr., and Robert Frank, "Rhetoric, History, and Collective Memory: Decoding the Goldhagen Debates," *Western Journal of Communication* 63 (Winter 1999): 95–114; and Lars Rensmann, "Holocaust Memory and Mass Media in Contemporary Germany: Reflections on the Goldhagen Debate," *Patterns of Prejudice* 3, no. 1 (1999): 59–76. On the reaction to the book in Germany, see Andrei Markovitz, "Störfall im Endlager der Geschichte: Daniel Jonah Goldhagen und seine deutschen Kritiker," *Blätter für deutsche und internationale Politik* 6 (1996): 667–74.

On the debate surrounding the Berlin Holocaust memorial, see Michael Cullen, ed., *Das Holocaust-Mahnmal: Dokumentation einer Debatte* (Zurich: Pendo, 1999); Michael Jeismann, ed., *Mahnmal Mitte: Eine Kontroverse* (Cologne: DuMont, 1999); Lea Rosh, ed., *"Die Juden, das sind doch die anderen": Der Streit um ein deutsches Denkmal* (Berlin: Philo, 1999); and Ute Heimrod, Günter Schlusche, and Horst Seferens, eds., *Der Denkmalstreit—das Denkmal? Die Debatte um das "Denkmal für die ermordeten Juden Europas": Eine Dokumentation* (Berlin: Philo, 1999).

34. See Christian Meier, *Vierzig Jahre nach Auschwitz: Deutsche Geschichtserinnerung heute,* 2d ed. (Munich: C. H. Beck, 1990), p. 10.

35. *Haaretz Daily Newspaper,* 17 Feb. 2000, 1 (in Hebrew).

36. See Francis Haskell, "Thanks for the Memories," *New York Review of Books* 35, no. 19 (1988): 48.

37. On thin cultural coherence, see William Sewell, Jr., "The Concept(s) of Culture," in *Beyond the Cultural Turn,* ed. Bonnell and Hunt, pp. 35–61.

38. See Anna Merritt and Richard Merritt, eds., *Public Opinion in Occupied Germany: The OMGUS Surveys, 1945–1949* (Urbana: University of Illinois Press, 1970), p. 36; and Josef Foschepoth, "German Reaction to Defeat and Occupation," in *West Germany under Construction: Politics, Society, and Culture in the Adenauer Era,* ed. Robert Moeller (Ann Arbor: University of Michigan Press, 1997), p. 77.

Among CDU Catholic circles and probably beyond, it was not uncommon to blame Nazism on Western civilization itself. Nazism, according to this view, was the "demonic mixture" of "the world views of the Enlightenment, [that is] free thinking, individualism, Marxism, communism, bolshevism, nationalism, chauvinism, [and] militarism." And in an argument that eerily reminds one of the historians' debate, Nazism and Marxism were frequently seen as twin brothers: "[Marxism and fascism] are nothing but powerful reactionary movements, grown out of the native soil of the same liberal capitalistic thinking" (Maria Sevenich, "Neue Wege in der Politik," *Schriftenreihe "Neue Politik" Stuttgart,* no. 1 [Oct. 1966], cited in Maria Mitchell, "Materialism and Secularism: CDU Politicians and National Socialism, 1945–1949," *Journal of Modern History* 67 [1995]: 285, 290 n. 45). Moreover, after the war, the notion that Jews and Germans experienced the same kind of persecution was prevalent among scholars and the public alike. Germans suffered, so the argument ran, as they were expelled, raped (in the case of women), and occupied. See, for example, Moeller, "War Stories."

39. See Tony Judt, "The Past Is Another Country: Myth and Memory in Postwar Europe," *Daedalus* 121 (1992): 83–118.

40. See Alon Confino, "Traveling as a Culture of Remembrance: Traces of National Socialism in West Germany, 1945–1960," *History and Memory* 12 (2000): 92–121.

41. Rudy Koshar uses the term "noise," in contrast to silence, to describe Germany's problem with the past in this century. See Koshar, *Germany's Transient Pasts,* p. 336. Jay Winter and Emmanuel Sivan describe the working of collective memory by using an analogy to choir singing. See Winter and Sivan, "Setting the Framework," in *War and Remembrance in the Twentieth Century,* ed. Winter and Sivan (Cambridge: Cambridge University Press, 1999), p. 28. Both metaphors are imaginatively fruitful.

PART I

HISTORICITY

CHAPTER 1

From Presence to Remembrance: The Transformation of Memory in the German Reformation

CRAIG KOSLOFSKY

Remembering the Dead

In the classical world, memory was an aspect of rhetoric, which treatises divided into its five fundamentals: *inventio, dispositio, elocutio, memoria,* and *pronuntiatio.* In his discussion of *The Orator* Cicero (106–43 B.C.E.) described the invention of the "science of mnemonics" by the poet Simonides of Ceos (c. 556–468 B.C.E.) in the aftermath of sudden disaster:[1]

> Simonides was dining at the house of a wealthy nobleman named Scopas at Crannon in Thessaly, and chanted a lyric poem which he had composed in honour of his host, in which he followed the custom of the poets by including for decorative purposes a long passage referring to Castor and Pollux; whereupon Scopas with excessive meanness told him he would pay him half the fee agreed for the poem, and if he liked he might apply for the balance to his sons of Tyndareus [i.e., Castor and Pollux], as they had gone halves in the panegyric. [In fact, the gods would quickly reward Simonides] . . . a little later a message was brought to Simonides to go outside, as two young men were standing at the door who earnestly requested him to come out; so he rose from his seat and went out, and could not see anybody; but in the interval of his absence the roof of the hall where Scopas was giving the banquet fell in, crushing Scopas himself and his relations underneath the ruins and killing them.

In this legend death brings separation and anonymity, cutting the victims off from their kin: "when their friends wanted to bury them . . . they were altogether unable to know them apart as they had been completely crushed." Memory, however, could recover their identities. Cicero continues: "Simonides was enabled by his recollection of the place in which each of them had been reclining at table to identify them for separate interment; and . . . this circumstance suggested to him the discovery of the truth that the best aid to clearness of memory consists in orderly arrangement." As Frances Yates has pointed out, this is a vivid story of the invention of the "art of memory."[2] But the death of the banqueters, crushed and mangled by the collapsed roof, conveys more than a memorable legend. It also calls our attention to a specific relationship between death, the dead, and memory in the Western intellectual tradition, in which the past is understood as the memory of dead individuals.

In the story of Simonides, memory overcomes the anonymity of death, allowing the dead to be given their rightful burial places. As Quintilian (c. 35–100 C.E.) relates the story: "Simonides, who remembered the order in which the guests had been sitting, succeeded in restoring to each man his own dead."[3] It is no accident that this legend of the invention of mnemonics concerns the memory of the dead, who were central to the social practices of memory in ancient and medieval society.

In premodern Europe, the work of memory that is the subject of this volume unfolded very differently from its modern counterparts. Indeed, several fundamental aspects of modern memory, such as the absence of the past and the finality of death, developed out of the failure of medieval practices of memory in the course of the Protestant Reformation. In this essay I will historicize the creation of the modern memory order by describing developments that led from the presence of the dead to the memory of the past in early modern Europe.

Memoria: The Presence of the Dead in Medieval Society

Medieval Christendom was suffused with the presence of the dead.[4] In everyday life and in marvelous, terrifying apparitions, in relics and in the Eucharist, the dead interacted with the living. This was *memoria,* the social presence of the dead in medieval society. A system of doctrines, beliefs, and memorial practices worked to erase the gulf between past and present so fundamental to modern memory.

The body lay at the center of this medieval system. The Christian emphasis on the body and the physical presence of the dead began to emerge in the second century, marking a sharp break with Roman practices of memory. The early Christians' promiscuous contact with the bodies of their dead disgusted educated pagans. The emperor Julian the Apostate (b. 331, r. 361–63) can speak for them all: "who could detest as they deserve all those doctrines that you have invented as a sequel, while you keep adding many corpses newly dead to the corpse of long ago? You have filled the whole world with tombs and sepulchres, and yet nowhere in your scriptures is it said that you must grovel among tombs and pay them honor."[5] Corpses and tombs were immensely important for Christians because the body symbolized, and indeed made possible, the presence of the dead among the living. This is especially (though not exclusively) apparent in medieval death ritual.

Medieval Christians dwelt in a community of the living and the dead: the traditional ritual of Christian burial summed up this close relationship by bringing the body of the deceased to rest in a consecrated churchyard at the center of a village or town while the clergy offered prayers and masses for the soul of the deceased. Medieval death ritual interwove themes of continuity and separation. Death marked a transition within the community of Christians: in late medieval ritual books (liturgical guides for parish clergy), the prayers and responses offered on the deathbed were repeated after death in the house, at the burial itself, and on the anniversaries of the death.[6] Despite the passage from life to death, the Christian remained within the Church, and continued to benefit from her intercession.

After death, the proper place for the body was the churchyard; the most likely abode for the soul was Purgatory. For Latin Christians before the Reformation, death marked a passage into another social group: the *ecclesia dolens* of suffering souls in Purgatory. These souls were the object of lay and clerical intercession: almsgiving, prayers, masses, and (after 1475) indulgences for the dead, all anchored in the sacrament of penance and the doctrine of Purgatory.

The funeral mass was the highest expression of the intercessory purpose of the entire ritual: to commend the soul to God. Indeed, many late medieval German ritual books refer to the entire funeral liturgy as the "Commendatio animae mortuorum."[7] "With four things can one help [free] the soul," relates the Franciscan Marquard of Lindau (d. 1392), "from the bonds of Purgatory." Following Gregory the Great, Marquard listed the four traditional means to aid the dead: holy masses, devout prayers, alms, and fasting.[8] The most effective of these intercessions, as Marquard of Lindau explained, was the Mass.[9] When in 1466 the Saxon noblewoman Barbara von Schönenberg obtained for herself, her daughter Elizabeth, and all their descendants the spiritual benefits of membership in the Franciscan order, the charter of membership (*Brüderschaftsbrief*) guaranteed to them all the "suffrages for the dead" ("suffragia defunctorum") received by the brothers and sisters of the order.[10] She had joined a spiritual community which transcended past, present, and future in order to intercede for the souls of its members.

The history of Christian burial shows that Emperor Julian's complaint was prophetic: by the fifteenth century Western Christians had indeed "filled the whole world with tombs and sepulchres." The bodies of the dead were laid to rest in churches or churchyards, woven into the fabric of daily life. The physical location of the body reflected the closeness of the soul to the intercession of the living. As the recusant Biberach patrician Joachim von Pflummern related: "After [the funeral mass] a Christian would be buried in consecrated ground, that is in the churchyard, and was laid in the grave facing the rising sun."[11] At the graveside service, more prayers might be offered for the deceased. The body's place of burial served as a visible reminder that solicited the prayers of the living. Heretics, criminals, suicides, and the excommunicated were denied Christian burial in a churchyard: the exclusion of their bodies reflected the separation of their souls from salvation and the Christian community.[12]

With the burial and service at the grave, the funeral itself was over. But the Church could intercede for the deceased at any time, and the prayers of the funeral liturgy echoed on in masses for the dead sung on the seventh and thirtieth days after the funeral, on All Souls' Day, and on the anniversary of the funeral.[13] The rituals of intercession could be repeated long after death: few practices had so powerful an influence on the development of the Church in the Middle Ages.

"The souls of the dead need help if they are in Purgatory." The influential German alphabetical compendium of canon law and church doctrine of the Dominican Berthold of Freiburg (translated from John of Freiburg's *Summa confessorum* in the fourteenth century and circulated widely in the fifteenth century) succinctly summarized for a lay readership the predominant relationship between the living and the dead in late medieval society.[14] A belief in interaction between the dead and the living is certainly far older and more widespread than Latin Christendom. But the goal of late-medieval eschatology was to channel the manifold hopes, fears, superstitions, and apparitions which connected the dead and the living into an acceptable understanding of Heaven, Hell, and the cult of Purgatory.[15]

Visitors from Purgatory and visions of the afterlife brought orthodox eschatology into popular preaching and piety. From Dante's sublime vision to the earthy humor of Johannes Pauli's *Schimpf und Ernst* (*Ridiculous and Serious*), the cult of Purgatory flourished in vernacular literature, exempla, and sermons. In a sermon Johannes Tauler (c. 1300–1361) described a suffering soul in Purgatory who appeared to a priest and asked for an intercessory mass. After it was said, Tauler reported that the soul was "freed from all his unendurable pain and went immediately into eternal life."[16] The living and the dead were united in the penitential cycle of the medieval Church.

Beyond the spoken word, medieval devotional images made visible the presence of the dead in daily life and in extraordinary circumstances, reminding Christians that the dead might erupt into the present and interact with the living.[17] This possibility reflects a sense of the past utterly different from that of modern memory. Death did not necessarily prevent individuals from righting wrongs, seeking justice, or aiding the living.

Marginalizing the Dead in the German Reformation

The ties that connected the dead to the world of the living were strained in the fifteenth century before they were consistently severed by the Reformation. The closeness of both the souls *and* the bodies of the dead to the world of the living was at issue: recent scholarship has argued that the Reformation helped separate the living from the dead both spiritually and physically, and that this parallel separation was fundamental to the development of the Reformation.[18]

The permanent physical separation of the dead from the world of the living began in the late fifteenth century. In Swiss and German cities, contemporaries began to complain of crowded and indeed overfilled urban churchyards (in some areas, the result of rapid urban population growth combined with high mortality). The urban churchyards could not be expanded, and the stench which arose from these crowded places of burial was increasingly considered a threat to public health. For reasons of hygiene, densely populated cities and towns closed their urban churchyards and established new cemeteries outside city walls, separated from the sacred locus of the parish church.[19] In the early 1520s leading Protestant cities like Nuremberg were especially vigorous in their support of extramural burial. Martin Luther published the first theological endorsement of the practice in 1527.[20]

Parallel to the physical separation of the dead from the living inherent in extramural burial, the theologians of the Protestant Reformation imposed a spiritual separation that eliminated the dead from Christian society. Intercession for the dead came under massive attack; its denial was one of the very few points on which all Protestant reformers agreed. Indeed, the elimination of intercession for the dead was overdetermined in Protestant theology. The doctrine of salvation by faith alone meant that even the holiest of the dead, Mary and the saints in Heaven, could no longer intercede for the living. Purgatory itself was denounced as an unscriptural, mercenary trick; and all Protestant reformers, from Luther and Calvin to the Anabaptists, denied the sacrificial power of the Mass. Luther proposed the doctrine of soul-sleeping, or psychopannichism, arguing that the souls of the dead slept until the Last Judgment and so could not appear to the living. All purgatorial spirits who did appear, pleading for intercessory masses or vicarious penance, Luther denounced as diabolical illusions.[21]

This separation of the dead from the living meant a new understanding of death itself. No longer did death mark a passage into another social group (for most, the "poor souls" in Purgatory), still closely connected to the living by mutual responsibilities. Instead, death became a barrier which demarcated both the sovereignty of God (since neither individuals nor the church could intercede for the dead) and the historical formation of the individual (who alone could have the faith essential for salvation).

In 1522 Luther preached on this theme, shocking his Wittenberg listeners with a relentless emphasis on the isolation of death: "The summons of death comes to us all, and no one can die for another. Every one must fight his own battle with death by himself, alone. We can shout into each other's ears, but every one must himself be prepared for the time of death: I will not be with you then, nor you with me."[22] Ultimately, the prayers of the faithful and the intercession of the clergy were useless. The radical separation of the dead from the living began on the deathbed, where each individual "must for himself be armed and prepared for battle with the devil and death."[23] The dead are absent from the Protestant funeral rituals based on this theology of separation, and there is no intercession for them.

The theology and piety of the Protestants was based upon the absence of the dead. The living would pray for one another, and families might imagine themselves united after death in Heaven, but no prayer or intercession could connect the living with the dead.[24] Instead, the dead person was socially concluded, and Protestant death ritual focused on his or her faith, life, and ancestry. The dead were becoming a part of history. The contrast between late-medieval *memoria* and the simple remembrance of the past is summed up by Calvin who, as in other aspects of Protestant theology and culture, developed and systematized the insights of the first-generation reformers. In his explication of divine foreknowledge as it relates to predestination, Calvin contrasts the eternal presence of all things before God with the absence of the thing remembered in human memory: "When we attribute foreknowledge to God, we mean that all things always were, and perpetually remain, under his eyes, so that to his knowledge there is nothing future or past, but all things are present. And they are present in such a manner that he . . . truly looks upon them and discerns them as things placed before him."[25] Human minds, in contrast, "merely conceive of" things remembered "from ideas formed in [the] mind." Calvin notes that "things remembered by us appear present to our minds."[26] In this understanding of memory, the past can only *appear* present—its essence is absence. In traditional Christianity, spiritual communities had joined the living and the dead in the hope of salvation: now only God could connect past, present, and future.

Supporters of the Reformation promoted the new practices of memory in everyday life. In Wittenberg, for example, the burial of the dead was moved outside the town to the extramural Hospitalfriedhof in 1527.[27] In Leipzig pro-Lutheran city councillors established an extramural cemetery (the Johannisfriedhof) as the city's main place of burial well before the city was able to adopt the Reformation.[28] The city council's support for extramural burial at the Johannisfriedhof rejected *memoria* while maintaining the hierarchy of prestige that had been marked by burial inside the city's churches and churchyards. Arched tombs were built into the wall surrounding the cemetery, and these vaults corresponded in prestige to burial within one of the city's churches. When the wall of the Johannisfriedhof was completed in 1538, twenty-seven family tombs were sold at ten *Gulden* each (a hefty price). Of the twenty-seven spaces, the names of twenty-one original purchasers are known, among them seven Leipzig councilmen and a city clerk. Heinrich Stromer von Auerbach, the mayor Wolf Wiedemann, and and other supporters of the Reformation purchased family tombs there.[29] Their mothers, fathers, and ancestors lay in prestigious tombs in the city inside its churches, but these men chose to break with the past and the social practices of memory that sustained *memoria.*

Absence and Remembrance: Toward the Modern Sense of the Past

In medieval Christian society, what we call "the past" was made of the memory of the dead, both as individuals and as members of groups. The dead were named in intercessory prayers and masses, and each passed through Purgatory during a period of human time, assisted by the intercession of the living. This was *memoria,* the presence of the dead among the living. If the living failed to honor their commitments, the dead could appear and make their demands clear. The presence of the dead expressed through *memoria* was an interactive presence in which the living and the dead could affect each other in fundamental ways.

The failure of *memoria* shook medieval culture at its foundations, calling our attention to the role of this failure in the development of modernity. (It also leads us to consider what a similar failure of modern social practices of memory would mean.) The rejection of *memoria* was essential to the modern order of memory based on linear, directional time and a past of dead individuals, absent, with whom the living could have only the most disturbing contact. The implications of this rejection of the presence of the dead are wide-ranging: here I will trace two specific developments in the social practices of remembering and understanding the past.

In the immediate context of death ritual, the clearest result of the collapse of *memoria* was the rise of a secular, historical memory of the dead person.[30] In Lutheran Germany the biographical funeral sermon flourished from 1550 to 1750 and became the focus of the entire funeral service. This was a distinctive Lutheran development, singular among the funeral services of the Protestant churches.[31] Today some three hundred thousand printed funeral sermons remain in German libraries and archives, evidence of the importance of the printed funeral sermon as the single most popular form of occasional literature in early modern Germany.[32] Of course, funeral sermons were preached before the Reformation, and also grew in importance in seventeenth-century Catholic France, but the biographical emphasis is distinctly Lutheran.

By the end of the sixteenth century the sermon was firmly established as part of the Lutheran funeral; this just precedes the first peak in the printing of funeral sermons in the decade before the Thirty Years' War.[33] As the use of the funeral sermon became more widespread, however, its content shifted. Originally intended to teach and to edify, by 1600 the funeral sermon had become an uneasy mixture of doctrine and moral instruction with lengthy praise of the deceased and his or her family.[34] In 1600 a Brandenburg church visitation commission ordered the pastors of the town of Gardelegen to stop "canonizing" the dead in their funeral sermons, and to stop filling the sermons with "stories of the deceased's ancestry and his great deeds, life, and ways."[35] Clerical criticism could not stop this development: funeral sermons developed a highly specialized form (and grew much longer) as the life and ancestry of the deceased occupied an increasingly larger portion of the sermon.

The sermon preached by the pastor Joachim Schwarzkopf at the funeral of Anna Litzmann, who died in childbirth on 8 December 1627 in Neuruppin (Brandenburg), is typical of the genre. After a brief discussion of the story of the death of Rachel (Gen. 35: 16–21), the sermon describes the death, life, and ancestry of the deceased townswoman. It presents Litzmann's "honorable, notable, and learned" husband Burchard Palzow, as well as the social position of her parents, sisters, children, and first husband.[36] Preached (at almost every adult funeral) and printed (if the family could afford it), this sort of biographical funeral sermon developed in the second half of the sixteenth century and reached its height a century later.

Within a generation of the introduction of the funeral sermon, Lutheran churchmen began to criticize the display of social status central to the Lutheran funeral. These critics argued that the emphasis on biography in the typical Lutheran funeral obscured the Christian meaning of the ritual and glossed over the actual character of the deceased. Their criticism had little effect, however. Death initiated the telling of a life story and a family history. By focusing on the biographical sermon, the Lutheran funeral apprehended the dead individual as part of the absent past, a completed story ready to be retold in the funeral sermon. Narrative and history/biography had replaced *memoria.*

At the same time, the presence of the dead became much more disturbing. The place of the ghost in the modern memory order suggests some connections between the absence of the dead and the modern self. As Keith Thomas and Natalie Zemon Davis have noted, the radical removal of the dead from the world of the living enacted through the Reformation transformed purgatorial spirits into dangerous ghosts.[37] Luther and Calvin stated that revenants of any kind were simply diabolical spirits sent to threaten the faith of the living. Medieval encounters with the dead could be also terrifying or unresolved, but with the Reformation the ghost became a transgressor whose presence denied the absence of the dead fundamental to modern memory.

What were ghosts in premodern society? Medieval ghosts came with specific needs and demands. Pay my debts, they asked; or intercede for my soul, or make peace with someone.[38] Often, we suspect that they were created by the displacement of emotion onto *memoria.* The hopes, fears, passions, or guilt of the living combined with a sense of the presence of the dead to call forth dead individuals. But the interaction between the living and the dead fundamental to *memoria* meant that the appearance of the dead also offered possibilities for resolution and redirection of the emotions that were externalized and embodied by the ghost.

Early modern Protestant culture, on the other hand, tended to direct faith and emotion into the self. No dialogue with the dead was possible: they were utterly gone, and anything left unresolved at an individual's death could only be worked out in an interior monologue.[39] When the Pietist barber-surgeon Johann Dietz (1665–1738) began writing his autobiography at the age of seventy, he began with the story of the ghost of his maternal grandfather, Martin Nitzsche.[40] The family of Dietz's mother was divided by some typical early modern tensions: his mother's father had been "cunningly tricked" into marrying his housemaid, who became his third wife. Fearful that this younger wife would take everything upon his death and deprive his other heirs, Martin Nitzsche allegedly buried all his wealth and refused to reveal its location. The sixty-nine-year-old man fell ill, lost his speech, and died in January 1680 without telling anyone the location of the buried treasure (if such really existed).[41] Dietz was fifteen when his grandfather died; fifty-five years later he described the tensions unleashed on the night of the old man's death. "That same night the monstrous noises and banging were indescribable."[42] To quiet the poltergeist and perhaps find the hidden hoard, Dietz's father hired a treasure hunter (*Schatzgräber*), who indicated with a divining rod that they should dig under a tree in the garden. As they all began to dig, "at night between eleven and twelve," immediately "a horrible Ghost, in the form of the one who had buried [the hoard]" appeared and drove the terrified family into the house. The next night the grandfather's ghost appeared again. The treasure hunter explained that the treasure was "possessed" and that he would have to go to the mountains to get a special root to be able to uncover it. He never returned and no hoard was ever found. Dietz speculated that the treasure hunter secretly stole the hoard, perhaps with the help of the greedy step-grandmother. As he commented, "*Summa:* it [the ghost] was gone, and all quiet."[43]

In contrast with medieval encounters between the living and the dead, here the appearance of the revenant resolves nothing. Did the grandfather really have a hoard of wealth? Did the treasure seeker steal it? Was the step-grandmother to blame? In the introspection of his memoirs, Dietz warned his readers to beware of any such "tricks and conjuring, in which the holy name of God is abused, and nothing remains but a bad conscience, as many cases show."[44] For Dietz, the lesson was clear: the ghost was a dangerous interloper who could not help the living. The past and its conflicts remained unresolved, and in this case could only be retold in a Pietist autobiography.

The elimination of *memoria* in the Protestant culture was the most fundamental development on the path to the modern memory order, but not the only stage along the way. The first major changes in daily practices regarding the dead and their memory in European Catholic culture came in the eighteenth century, when health officials began to eliminate parish burial and create large extramural cemeteries. The Cemetery of Innocents in the heart of Paris, for example, was closed in 1780.[45] Catholic clergy in France and Austria struggled against these Enlightenment plans, arguing cogently that the removal of the dead from local daily life would be a powerful blow against traditional piety and belief.[46]

For someone like Johann Dietz, the past was absent and concluded, but he could look back over more than a half-century with the assumption that daily life had not really changed. Recent work by Reinhart Koselleck, Stephen Bann, Aleida Assmann, and Peter Fritzsche suggests that the next major shifts in European memory cultures came with the French Revolution and the Napoleonic era, as the sense of an absent past promoted by the Reformation and the Enlightenment was intensified by rapid social change and political reorientation.[47] Now the past was not only absent, it was also foreign and unfamiliar. As Fritzsche has argued, after the broad social and cultural impact of Napoleon, territorial and legal reorganization, and the Wars of Liberation, Germans could no longer assume that the village of their grandparents was like the village of their own day.

Conclusion

As the legend of Simonides' invention of the art of memory suggests, death and oblivion have long evoked the need for individual and social practices of memory. In late medieval Christian culture, the social practice of memory had become *memoria,* the real presence of the dead in the world of the living. This presence meant interaction with the dead—in the name of corporate piety, justice, revenge, satisfaction, love, or loyalty. I have argued that the social practices of memory termed *memoria* became problematic in the fifteenth and early sixteenth centuries, especially in Swiss and German cities. A new theology and piety arose which articulated, justified, and systematized the rejection of *memoria.* This new understanding of the dead and the past was established by the Protestant state churches of early modern Europe.

The rejection of *memoria* was the single most important step to a past that is history: profane, finite, finished, and separate. From the perspective of *memoria,* the gap between loss and recovery is a permanent part of modernity. The past is truly dead, and death is what makes the past history. Compared with the medieval presence of the dead, the modern past is always unmasterable: it can be remembered and interpreted, but never set right. In this sense it is irretrievable. But the past can nevertheless be historicized: it is not the passage of time that creates the past, but specific attitudes toward death and the dead that establish the past in the modern order of memory.

NOTES

1. Cicero, *De oratore,* II, lxxxvi, 351–54. English translation from the Loeb Classical Library edition.

2. Frances Yates, *The Art of Memory* (Chicago: University of Chicago Press, 1966), pp. 1–4.

3. Quintilian, *Institutio oratoria,* XI, ii, 17–22. English translation from the Loeb Classical Library edition.

4. See Otto Gerhard Oexle, "Die Gegenwart der Toten," in *Death in the Middle Ages,* ed. Herman Braet and Werner Verbecke (Leuven: Leuven University Press, 1982), pp. 19–77, and the literature cited there.

5. Julian, *Against the Galileans* (363 C.E.), Loeb Classical Library edition, 415 (335B). See Peter Brown, *The Cult of the Saints: Its Rise and Function in Latin Christianity* (Chicago: University of Chicago Press, 1981).

6. Hugo Grün describes the variety of medieval death rituals in "Das kirchliche Begräbniswesen im ausgehenden Mittelalter," *Theologische Studien und Kritiken* 102 (1930): 341–81, here pp. 353–54. The discussion in E. Döring-Hirsch, *Tod und Jenseits im Spätmittelalter* ([Berlin: K. Curtius, 1927], pp. 16–62), is also very useful. See also the well-illustrated studies from Martin Illi, *Wohin die Toten gingen: Begräbnis und Kirchhof in der vorindustriellen Stadt* (Zurich: Chronos, 1992), and Paul Binski, *Medieval Death: Ritual and Representation* (Ithaca: Cornell University Press, 1996), and the literature cited there.

7. Grün, "Begräbniswesen," pp. 353–54.

8. Jacobus Willem van Maren, ed., *Marquard von Lindau. Die Zehe Gebot (Straßburg 1516 und 1520)* (Amsterdam: Rodopi, 1980), pp. 39–41. The catechism based on the Ten Commandments by Marquard of Lindau enjoyed wide popularity in the fifteenth century, with over 120 surviving German and Dutch manuscripts as well as several printings, including the 1516 Strasbourg edition cited here.

9. Van Maren, *Marquard von Lindau,* pp. 39–40. On the changing demand for masses for the dead, see Jacques Chiffoleau, "Sur l'usage obsessionnel de la messe pour les morts à la fin du Moyen Age," in *Faire croire. Modalités da la diffusion et de la réception des message religieux du 12e au 15e siècle,* Collection de L'école Française de Rome 51 (Rome: École française de Rome, 1981), pp. 235–56.

10. Hubert Ermisch, ed., *Urkundenbuch der Stadt Freiberg in Sachsen,* vol. 12 of *Codex Diplomaticus Saxoniae Regiae* (Leipzig: Giesecke & Devrient, 1883), vol. 1, p. 387.

11. "Darnach so hat man ein Christen Menschen in das geweycht Erdtreich vergraben, alls in den Khürchhoff, und hat ains in das grab gelegt, daß eins gegen der Sonnen aufgang gelegen ist" (A. Schilling, ed., "Die religiösen und kirchlichen Zustände der ehemaligen Reichsstadt Biberach unmittelbar vor Einführung der Reformation," *Freiburger Diözesanarchiv* 19 [1887]: 1–191, 166). On the 137-page manuscript, see Otto Borst, "Biberach. Geist und Kunst einer schwäbischen Stadt," in *Geschichte der Stadt Biberach,* ed. Dieter Stievermann (Stuttgart: Theiss, 1991), pp. 88–89.

12. See W. Thümmel, *Die Versagung der kirchlichen Bestattungsfeier* (Leipzig: J. C. Hinrichs, 1902).

13. The services held before and with the burial were usually termed *de presenti funere, Sepultura,* or *Begräbnis.* These are distinct from the postfuneral intercessory services, usually summarized under the term *Begängnis,* which could refer to vigils (sung or recited the evening before or during the Requiem or *Seelenmesse*) or to the Requiem Mass itself, also termed *Messe an den Begängnissen, Seelenmesse,* and *Seelenamt.* On the German and Latin terms for clerical intercession for the dead, see Nikolaus Müller, *Die Wittenberger Bewegung 1521 und 1522,* 2d ed. (Leipzig: Heinsius, 1911), pp. 155–58, and Karl Müller, "Die Esslinger Pfarrkirche im Mittelalter. Beitrag zur Geschichte der Organisation der Pfarrkirchen," *Württembergische Vierteljahrshefte für Landesgeschichte,* n.s. 16 (1907): 237–327.

14. Georg Steer et al., eds., *Die "Rechtssumme" Bruder Bertholds: eine deutsche abecedarische Bearbeitung der "Summa confessorum" des Johannes von Freiburg. Synoptische Edition der Fassungen B, A und C* (Tübingen: M. Niemeyer, 1987–), vol. 1, p. 1955: "Sele der toten leut pedürffen hilff, sein sie in dem fegefeür."

15. The cult of Purgatory rested on doctrines formulated at the Councils of Lyon (1274) and Florence (1439). See the detailed article by A. Michel in the *Dictionnaire de Théologie Catholique* (Paris: Letouzey et Ané, 1908–50), 13, 1: 1163–1326.

16. ". . . und was von dem einen empfengnisse alle siner inlidelichen pinen quit worden und fur alzuhant in daz ewige leben" (Ferdinand Vetter, ed., *Die Predigten Taulers* [Berlin: Weidmann, 1910], p. 131).

17. An excellent collection is reproduced in Peter Jezler, ed., *Himmel, Hölle, Fegefeuer: das Jenseits im Mittelalter: eine Ausstellung des Schweizerischen Landesmuseums in Zusammenarbeit mit dem Schnütgen-Museum und der Mittelalterabteilung des Wallraf-Richartz-Museums der Stadt Köln,* 2d ed. (Munich: W. Fink, 1994).

18. See Craig Koslofsky, *The Reformation of the Dead: Death and Ritual in Early Modern Germany, 1450–1700* (New York: St. Martin's Press, 2000).

19. I use a distinction often made in the sources: "churchyard" (*Kirchhof*) refers to an intramural place of burial while "cemetery" (*Friedhof, Gottesacker*) refers to nonparish, extramural burial.

20. See Koslofsky, *Reformation of the Dead,* chap. 3.

21. See Koslofsky, *Reformation of the Dead,* chap. 2.

22. From a sermon preached at Wittenberg on 9 Mar. 1522, the first of the eight "Invocavit sermons" (*D. Martin Luthers Werke. Kritische Gesamtausgabe* [Weimar: H. Böhlau, 1883–] 10, 3: 1–2): "Wir seindt allsampt zu dem tod gefodert und wirt keyner den andern sterben, Sonder ein yglicher in eygner person für sich mit dem todt kempffen. In die oren künden wir woll schreyen, Aber ein yglicher muß für sich selber geschickt sein in der zeyt des todts: ich würd denn nit bey dir sein noch du bey mir." Cf. J. Pelikan and H. T. Lehmann, eds., *Luther's Works* (St. Louis: Concordia Publishing House, 1955–86) 51: 70.

23. From a later printed edition of the sermon of 9 Mar. 1522: "ein iglicher in eigner Person mus geharnischt und gerüstet sein fur sich selbs mit dem Teufel und Tode zu kempffen" (*D. Martin Luthers Werke. Kritische Gesamtausgabe,* 10, 3: 1). See also Werner Theide, "Luthers individuelle Eschatologie," *Lutherjahrbuch* 49 (1982): 7–49.

24. Cf. Calvin's position on prayer for the dead: "Now, since the entire law and gospel do not furnish so much as a single syllable of leave to pray for the dead, it is to profane the invocation of God to attempt more than he has bidden us" (*Institutes of the Christian Religion,* ed. John T. McNeill [Philadelphia: Westminster Press, 1960], 3.5.10). The medieval doctrine of the real presence of Christ in the Eucharist, maintained by Luther but rejected or radically reinterpreted by Zwingli, Calvin, and the south German reformers, left Christ as the only one among the dead who could be present among the living in the interactive sense of medieval *memoria.* For all others, death enshrined a person in memory as a permanent absence.

25. Calvin, *Institutes,* 3.21.5.

26. Calvin, *Institutes,* 3.21.5.

27. See Wolfgang Böhmer, "Martin Luther und das Wittenberger Medizinalwesen zu seiner Zeit," *Zeichen der Zeit* 37 (1983): 107–16.

28. See Koslofsky, *Reformation of the Dead,* chap. 3.

29. Cf. Gustav Wustmann, *Der Wirt von Auerbach's Keller: Dr. Heinrich Stromer von Auerbach, 1482–1542* (Leipzig: H. Seeman, 1902), pp. 80–81, and Paul Benndorf, *Der alte Johannisfriedhof in Leipzig: Ein Beitrag zur Stadtgeschichte* (Leipzig: Haessel, 1922), pp. 21–31. On urban elites, memorials, and social/regional mobility, see Dietrich W. Poeck, "Rat und Memoria," in *Memoria in der Gesellschaft des Mittelalters,* ed. Dieter Geuenich and Otto Gerhard Oexle (Göttingen: Vandenhoeck & Ruprecht, 1994), 286–335; and Albert Cremer, "Religiosität und Repräsentation: Zum Tod der hohen Pariser Magistrate (2. Hälfte 16. und frühes 17. Jahrhundert)," *Francia* 19, no. 2 (1992): 1–22.

30. The Lutheran funeral sermon is a distinctive Protestant cultural expression of a nar-

rower intellectual change, a "secularization of time and memory." See Aleida Assmann, *Erinnerungsräume: Formen und Wandlungen des kulturellen Gedächtnisses* (Munich: Beck, 1999), pp. 45–46: "Die Renaissance unterscheidet sich vom Mittelalter durch die aus der Antike wiederaufgenommene Wertschätzung des Ruhms. . . . Diese Umwertung des Ruhms hängt mit der Säkularisierung von Zeit und Gedächtnis zusammen. In der Renaissance tritt die Totenmemoria, die Erinnerung an die Toten und an den eigenen Tod, zurück hinter die Hoffnung auf Unsterblichkeit durch kulturelle Leistungen: das Leben nach dem Tode ist aus der exklusiven Verfügungsgewalt Gottes genommen und findet sich irdische Variante im Nachleben, 'a life beyond a life', wie Milton es ausdrücken wird." Of course, "immortality through cultural achievement" was not a hope for most early modern people. A cultural history of memory must connect intellectual developments with practices of daily life, such as changing attitudes toward the dead, the local community, or the nation.

31. See Fredric Tromly, "'Accordinge to sounde religion': The Elizabethan Controversy over the Funeral Sermon," *Journal of Medieval and Renaissance Studies* 13, no. 2 (1983): 293–312.

32. See Koslofsky, *Reformation of the Dead,* chap. 4.

33. Hugo Grün, "Die Leichenrede im Rahmen der kirchlichen Beerdigung im 16. Jahrhundert," *Theologische Studien und Kritiken* 96 (1925): 287–312, 297.

34. See Rudolf Mohr, *Der unverhoffte Tod. Theologie- und kulturgeschichtliche Untersuchungen zu außergewöhnlichen Todesfällen in Leichenpredigten* (Marburg: Schwarz, 1982), pp. 148–52, and Jill Bepler, "Women in German Funeral Sermons: Models of Virtue or Slice of Life?" *German Life and Letters* 44, no. 5 (1991): 392–403.

35. "Dieweil aber die Visitatores berichtett werdt, das in den Leichpredigten ein großer Mißbrauch sey, in deme, das die prediger die Verstorbenen *canonisieren* und mitt allzu übermäßigen *encomiis extollieren* und dadurch von dem abgelesenen text abschreiten, und die gantze leichpredigt mit erzahlung der Verstorbens her= und ankunft, seiner herlich thaten, lebens und wandels zubringen" (Brandenburgisches Landeshauptarchiv Potsdam, Pr. Br. Rep. 40A, 372, fol. 6).

36. Joachim Schwartzkopf, *Rahels Kreis und Todes Bette. Das ist die trawrige Historie aus Gen. 35 von dem kläglichen Tod der heligien Ertzmutter Rahel / bey dem Christlichen Leichbegengnis / der weyland Ehrbaren und Vielehrentugendreichen Frawen Fr. Annä Litzmannin . . .* (Wittenberg: August Boreck, 1628). See Arno Böttcher, "Neuruppinische Leichenpredigten," *Brandenburgia Monatsblatt* 17 (1908–9): 535–66, 539.

37. Keith Thomas, *Religion and the Decline of Magic* (New York: Scribner, 1971), pp. 587–606, and Natalie Zemon Davis, "Ghosts, Kin and Progeny: Some Features of Family Life in Early Modern France," *Daedalus* 6 (1977): 87–114.

38. Davis, "Ghosts," 94.

39. Some of these tensions between the presence of the dead and the self are explored in *Hamlet,* for example. The protagonist attempts to internalize the contradictory values of his world and direct his actions through his own values. The ghost of Hamlet's father appears as an external force to demand revenge, and this unleashes a tragic series of events. From the start of the play, Shakespeare and his audience would have considered (as Hamlet did) the possibility that the ghost was, as Luther and Calvin insisted, a diabolical spirit sent to threaten the faith of the living. One lesson of the ensuing tragedy is that ghosts and specters destroy the finality of the past, violate the boundaries of the self, and deny the memory order of modernity.

40. Johann Dietz, *Meister Johann Dietz des Großen Kurfürsten Feldscher: Mein Lebenslauf,* ed. Friedhelm Kemp (Munich: Kösel-Verlag, 1966).

41. The burial register of the St. Lawrence Church in Halle-Neumarkt records the funeral of Martin Nitzsche on 18 Jan. 1680 (Dietz, *Lebenslauf,* p. 310).

42. "Was dieselbe Nacht für ein Ungeheuer und Poltern im Hause gewesen, ist nicht zu beschreiben. Es hat kein Mensch im Haus mehr bleiben wollen, bis der selige Vater einen Schatzgräber kommen lassen . . . unter einem Apfelbaum mit Gewalt niederschlagen. Da denn unter selbigen Baum in der Nacht zwischen elf und zwölf Uhr sie angefangen zu graben. Was geschicht? Ein greulich Gespenst, in des Vergrabers Gestalt, stellet sich Gleich da hin, siehet zu und lehnet auf das Gegatter" (Dietz, *Lebenslauf,* p. 11).

43. "Summa: es war weg, und alles stille" (Dietz, *Lebenslauf,* p. 11).

44. Dietz, *Lebenslauf,* p. 11.

45. See Christine Métayer, "Un Espace de vie: les charniers du cimetière des SS. Innocents à Paris, sous l'ancien Regime," *Journal of the Canadian Historical Association* 4 (1993): 183–206, and Madeleine Foisil, "Les Attitudes devant la mort au XVIIIe siècle: Sépultures et suppression des sépultures dans la cimetière Parisien des Saints-Innocents," *Revue Historique* 521, no. 2 (1974): 303–30.

46. These struggles are described in John McManners, *Death and the Enlightenment: Changing Attitudes to Death among Christians and Unbelievers in Eighteenth-Century France* (New York: Oxford University Press, 1981), pp. 303–67, and Johannes Wimmer, *Gesundheit, Krankheit und Tod im Zeitalter der Aufklärung: Fallstudien aus den Habsburgischen Erbländern* (Vienna: Böhlau, 1991), pp. 176–202.

47. See Reinhart Koselleck, *Futures Past: On the Semantics of Historical Time* (Cambridge: MIT Press, 1985); Stephen Bann, *Romanticism and the Rise of History* (New York: Twayne Publishers, 1995); Assmann, *Erinnerungsräume;* and Peter Fritzsche's contribution to this volume.

CHAPTER 2

Memory, History, and the Jewish Question: Universal Citizenship and the Colonization of Jewish Memory

JONATHAN M. HESS

> The great and noble business of government is to weaken the exclusive principles of all these various societies [in the state] so that they are not disadvantageous to the great union that comprises them all. Each of these divisions must awaken only competition and activity rather than aversion and distance. Government seeks to dissolve these societies in the great harmony of the state. Each of these particular associations is allowed its pride, and even its non-damaging prejudices. Government seeks, however, to give each member an even greater love for the state, and it realizes its great intention when the nobleman, the peasant, the scholar, the artisan, the Christian and the Jew are all, more than anything else, *citizens.*
>
> —Christian Wilhelm Dohm, *Ueber die bürgerliche Verbesserung der Juden* (1781)

In his introduction to *Les Lieux de mémoire,* Pierre Nora transforms Maurice Halbwachs's opposition between "collective memory" and "history" into a master narrative for modernity.[1] Bemoaning the displacement of the living forces of collective memory by history—which he, like Halbwachs, equates with nineteenth-century positivist historiography—Nora privileges Jewish memory as one of the last vestiges of the *milieux de mémoire* characteristic of the premodern world:

> This uprooting of memory, its eradication by the conquering force of history, has had the effect of a revelation, as if an ancient bond of identity had been broken, calling into question something once taken for granted: the close fit

> between history and memory. . . . If we still dwelled among our memories, there would be no need to consecrate sites embodying them. *Lieux de mémoire* would not exist, because memory would not have been swept away by history. Every one of our acts, down to the most quotidian, would be experienced, in an intimate identification of act and meaning, as a religious repetition of sempiternal practice. With the appearance of "the trace," of distance and mediation, however, we leave the realm of true memory and enter that of history. Think of the Jews faithfully observing their traditional ritual: as the "people of memory," history was no concern of theirs until exposure to the modern world obliged them to discover a need for historians.[2]

The master narrative Nora charts here—the annihilation of memory by history, the shift from holistic *milieux de mémoire* toward a fragmented world painfully aware of its rupture with the past and thus driven to consecrate *lieux de mémoire*—posits the Jews as some of modernity's exemplary victims. Cast as the people of memory par excellence, a people traditionally unconcerned with history, the Jews elucidate both the displacement of memory by history and the causality underlying this displacement. For Nora, the Jewish turn toward history generally identified with the *Wissenschaft des Judentums* in the nineteenth century is neither the product of internal Jewish forces nor the outgrowth of a creative encounter with modernity, but simply the result of modernity's memory-destroying forces. The Jews are "obliged" to forsake memory for history, and what obliges them to do so is their mere "exposure" to the modern world.

What Nora's hopelessly nostalgic master narrative obscures, of course, is the historicity of its own stance vis-à-vis the premodern past. In mourning the loss of the holistic, all-encompassing environments of memory, Nora engages in a form of nostalgia that is itself a product of a distinctly modern discourse, an elegiac view of the premodern world that marks Nora as the Romantic par excellence. In many ways, indeed, the introduction to *Les Lieux de mémoire* revives the pose of the "sentimental" poet as Friedrich Schiller delineated it in his influential 1795 treatise *Über naive und sentimentalische Dichtung.* There are, however, two critical differences between the sentimental relation to the past Schiller celebrates and the historiography underlying Nora's opposition between the premodern *milieux de mémoire* and the modern drive to rescue the memory he sees as conquered by history. Schiller's sentimental poet mourns the loss of an intact world he also concedes never actually existed as such, and he engages in this self-conscious exercise not as a historian but as a poet, longing for a past ideal he recognizes as his own projection.[3] Unlike the sentimental poet, then, Nora ignores the extent to which the nostalgic vision of the past that organizes his discourse has its origins in precisely that modern world he seeks to overcome. In this way, he presents a classic modernist master narrative that essentializes collective memory, one that equates memory with authenticity, continuity, and presence and history with discontinuity, mediation, and absence.

Much recent literature has questioned Nora's opposition between memory and history, contending that both memory and history are heavily mediated discourses. Suspicious of the type of nostalgia that underwrites Nora's project, recent scholarship has typically stressed the extent to which traditions, commemorative practices, and nostalgic fictions are "invented" in the modern world, the way in which even the holistic *milieux de mémoire* Nora celebrates are socially, politically, and ideologically constructed rather than mere givens that become the victims of modernization.[4] For many recent scholars, accordingly, Nora's model of chronological supersession does not sufficiently explain the relations between memory and history. In much contemporary discourse, collective memory and history figure as interrelated and at times interdependent modes of constructing a community's relation to its past, the difference between them being less a question of a rigid opposition than one of differing sets of formal and disciplinary conventions.

In this essay, I would like to approach Nora from a slightly different angle. Rather than discarding his account of memory being conquered by history, I would like to explore the *genealogy* of this narrative of memory's supersession, and I would like to do so by interrogating the paradigmatic status Nora and others claim for "Jewish memory" in their configurations of the relationship between memory, history, and modernity. For like his view of memory in general, Nora's vision of the Jews as the quintessential people of memory forced by their "exposure to the modern world" to forsake memory is also a fundamentally modern notion, one that emerged first in the course of the widespread debates on Jewish emancipation that began in Germany with Christian Wilhelm Dohm's 1781 book *Ueber die bürgerliche Verbesserung der Juden.*[5] Particularly in the initial stages of the debates over Jewish emancipation, I shall argue, Jewish memory was rarely seen as a given that needed to be eradicated. Jewish memory typically appears, rather, as a dynamic site of contest, with Enlightenment historiography emerging as the ultimate means of recrafting and reconstructing Jewish memory. Against Nora, then, I shall contend that Jewish memory is not in fact destroyed by the Jews' "exposure" to the modern world with its destruction of the "ancient bond of identity" between history and memory. Enlightenment historiography, rather, seeks to *reinvent* Jewish memory, and it does so as an integral part of a more general process of imagining new forms of collective memory germane to a political order grounded in concepts of universal citizenship. In this context, we will indeed encounter a vision of the displacement of Jewish memory. This conception of the supersession of Jewish memory, however, relates less to any particularly Jewish mode of memory destroyed by modern historiography than to competing blueprints for the nation-state, to Enlightenment intellectuals' struggles to envision new forms of collective memory that would, in Dohm's words, enable the state to realize its great "intention" of enabling "the nobleman, the peasant, the scholar, the artisan, the Christian and the Jew" to conceive of themselves, "more than anything else, [as] *citizens*." Anything but an adequate description of a specifically Jewish relation to memory that became the victim of political modernization, Nora's vision of "Jewish memory" will emerge here as a trope constructed in retrospect, one that proves absolutely crucial to the early nation-state's own attempt to imagine new forms of political community.

* * *

Before we move into the late eighteenth century, it will prove helpful first to situate Nora's celebration of the Jews as the ultimate "people of memory" within contemporary historical scholarship on Jewish memory. In this field, Nora is not without parallels. Indeed, in *Zakhor: Jewish History and Jewish Memory,* a seminal 1980 series of lectures in which Yosef Hayim Yerushalmi sought to reflect on the historical novelty of his own position as a Jewish historian, Yerushalmi maps out a similar relationship between modernity, history, and Jewish memory.[6] Coming from Halbwachs, Yerushalmi also charts a radical shift from the self-sufficient medieval world of Jewish memory toward a modern Jewish historiography that sought to destroy memory, a movement he identifies with the discipline of Jewish history that first emerged with the *Wissenschaft des Judentums* in the 1820s. Unlike modern Jewish history, Yerushalmi argues, the forms of Jewish collective memory that persisted from Rabbinic Judaism through the eighteenth and nineteenth centuries typically saw themselves as ritually commemorating an ancient historical world. The Bible represented in this context "not only a repository of past history but a revealed pattern of the whole of history," a remote historical past that contained archetypes that could be used for the interpretation of contemporary events as well.[7] In the self-sufficient, all-encompassing memory world of premodern Jewry, historical and liturgical time seemed to merge, the past representing "a series of situations into which one could somehow be existentially drawn" in the present rather than events to be contemplated at a distance.[8]

Like Nora, Yerushalmi also charts the rise of a modern Jewish historiography that sought to subject the inherited forms of Jewish memory to critical and historical scrutiny. Unlike its non-Jewish historiographical peers, he notes, the emergent discipline of Jewish history did not seek to construct a national history. Positioned antithetically toward collective memory, rather, the *Wissenschaft des Judentums* typically "reconstructed a Jewish past in which the national element was all but suppressed, and the hope for national restoration seemed an anachronism."[9] In this sense, Yerushalmi argues, Jewish history "began precipitously out of that assimilation from without and collapse from within which characterized the sudden emergence of Jews out of the ghetto. It originated, not as a scholarly curiosity, but as ideology, one of a gamut of responses to the crisis of Jewish emancipation and the struggle to attain it."[10] For Yerushalmi, then, Jewish history is ultimately apologetic, an assimilationist effort to obliterate

Jewish memory and reconceptualize Judaism so that modern Jews appear acceptable citizens for a non-Jewish state.

Yerushalmi's vision of the relationship between Jewish memory and Jewish history thus follows Gerschom Scholem's famous indictment of the *Wissenschaft des Judentums* for their "liquidation" of Jewish tradition, a view that has come to be challenged in recent scholarship.[11] In her 1998 book *Abraham Geiger and the Jewish Jesus,* Susannah Heschel positions nineteenth-century Jewish historiography alongside the Protestant theologians with whom it often entered into dialogue. Contextualizing modern Jewish history in this manner, Heschel exposes the *Wissenschaft des Judentums* as a dynamic form of counterhistory, a challenge to the power of Christian theological scholarship within the academy. Particularly in accounts of the Jewish origins of Christianity and of Jesus's own Judaism, writers like Geiger radically inverted liberal Protestant theologians' constructions of Judaism and Christianity. Geiger envisioned Judaism, namely, not as the superseded, degenerate "other" of Christianity but as a religion with a world-historical significance, a religion that gave rise to Christianity as the degenerate other of Jesus's own Judaism. With this appropriation of the historical Jesus, Geiger clearly subverted Protestant historical theology's accounts of the relations between Judaism and Christianity and sought to unsettle the hegemony of Christian theology—a strategy that is difficult to accommodate in Yerushalmi's visions of nineteenth-century Jewish historiography as an assimilationist apologetics that set out to destroy Jewish memory.

Yerushalmi's account of Jewish memory has also not been without its critics. In a 1989 essay, "Collective Memory and Historical Consciousness," Amos Funkenstein challenges Yerushalmi's strict opposition between Jewish history and Jewish memory, emphasizing instead a continuity of creative thinking about history, a Jewish "historical consciousness" that long predates the modern era.[12] This historical consciousness, Funkenstein contends, rarely contradicts collective memory; rather, it is a developed and organized form of it. For Funkenstein, Jewish history and Jewish memory are thus fundamentally interrelated, and the fact that Jewish historical consciousness is secularized in the nineteenth century should not lead us to conclude that the ritual-liturgical collective memory Yerushalmi and Nora celebrate was all-encompassing for the premodern period. Medieval Jews, Funkenstein insists, were in fact less typological than their Christian peers. What happens in the nineteenth century, he argues, is not a radical rejection of collective memory but a transformation of Jewish historical consciousness whereby the uniqueness of Israel began to signify not its difference from others but its universality. Theologians like Geiger, he comments, did not liquidate Jewish tradition and obliterate Jewish memory; rather, they actually continued the grounding of Jewish uniqueness in an understanding of history.

Clearly, then, the notion of an opposition between Jewish memory and Jewish history has limits as a methodological framework for studying Jewish memory, Jewish history, or the relation between them. Yet the significance of these narratives of the destruction of Jewish memory lies not simply in their potential explanatory power. The vision of the Jews as a people forced to forsake memory needs to be interrogated in its historical novelty for the modern period, in terms of the function it assumes and the discourses that make it possible within the debates over the question of Jewish emancipation. For by the time the *Wissenschaft des Judentums* emerged in the early nineteenth century, its Jewish writers were entering a discursive field that was already saturated with discussions on crafting and recrafting Jewish memory. The question that needs to be posed here is not solely whether the modern discipline of Jewish history destroyed, preserved, or transformed Jewish memory. We need to consider, rather, the functions ascribed to Jewish memory by the (non-Jewish) writers participating in the debates over Jewish emancipation, the ways in which, long before the emergence of the formal discipline of Jewish history, Enlightenment historiography had already constructed Jewish memory as a site of contest where the more general process of crafting a new political order might be acted out.

* * *

Let me start here in the realm of historical theology, considering the position of the Göttingen Orientalist Johann David Michaelis (1717–91), one of the late eighteenth century's premier authorities on the history of Judaism and a major player in the early debates over Dohm's *Ueber die bürgerliche Verbesserung der Juden.* Michaelis was one of the Enlightenment's foremost admirers of ancient Judaism. He produced popularly oriented Bible translations, edited the first major German journal dedicated to biblical criticism, the *Orientalische und exegetische Bibliothek,* and wrote a widely read, Montesquieu-inspired historical reconstruction of the spirit of Mosaic law, *Mosaisches Recht* (1770–75), that was quoted by Dohm and others arguing for Jewish emancipation. As an historian of ancient Israel, importantly, Michaelis had little interest in Jewish memory. For him, as for Dohm and nearly all Enlightenment intellectuals, there existed a sharp discontinuity between contemporary Jews and the ancient Israelites they claimed as their spiritual ancestors.[13] In *Mosaisches Recht* and other works, he set up his own historical methods in explicit opposition to the spirit of contemporary Judaism. For Michaelis, as for so many of his peers, Jewish postbiblical traditions such as the Talmud consisted of "oral traditions of somewhat ignorant Rabbis," useless for the proper historical study of the Hebrew Bible; lacking a true understanding of their own religion and its "Oriental" origins, Michaelis concluded, Jews often interpreted Mosaic law "as the direct opposite of that which Moses commanded," fulfilling the "letter of the laws of Moses" at the expense of their "soul."[14] Characterized by their continued adherence to an antiquated legal system they fail to comprehend, contemporary Jews represent the ultimate anachronism, out of sync with both their own historical origins and the modern historical methods that inspire Michaelis's admiration of their ancient religion. Judaism for Michaelis knows neither continuity nor development. The only continuity he grants the Jews, accordingly, is not that of memory but that of "race," a category he adapts from his Göttingen colleague Johann Friedrich Blumenbach's anthropological writings; Jews, as an "unmixed race of a more southern people," have a poor physical stature and a problematic "national temperament, which remains unchanged, because they never mix with others."[15]

In Michaelis's writings, however, the modern historical methods he adopts from Montesquieu and others are never deployed in order to supersede or annihilate ritual-liturgical memory. In his *Mosaisches Recht,* as elsewhere in his biblical scholarship, he generally uses historical-critical methods to uphold traditional understandings of scripture. But the memory Michaelis wishes to preserve is not the Jewish one, as his polemics against Dohm make clear. In the lead article of a 1782 issue of his *Orientalische und exegetische Bibliothek,* he argues against emancipation, insisting that "the Jews will always view the state as a temporary dwelling, which, if they are lucky, they will be able to leave so as to return to Palestine, almost in the way in which their forefathers were suspicious to the Egyptians (2nd book of Moses, 1:10). . . . A people that has such hopes will never become completely native."[16] In this context, the Bible continues to function as a collection of archetypes for the interpretation of present events. The memory preserved here, however, is not that of the Jews but that of the Egyptians—a nation, Michaelis wants us to recall, that was rightly "suspicious" of the Israelites' longings to be delivered from Egyptian bondage. The Hebrew Bible serves here not as a vessel for Jewish commemoration but as a record of Egyptian memory. Michaelis the historian appropriates the Hebrew Bible against contemporary Jews, finding in the second book of Moses—the account of the exodus from Egypt—a memory of Egypt that gives the modern German states a persuasive argument against Jewish emancipation.[17]

In his attempt to appropriate the Hebrew Bible against contemporary Jews, Michaelis nevertheless also opens up the question of Jewish memory. In the passage above, he envisions the anticipation of messianic redemption that Jews construct around their memory of Egypt as fundamentally unsettling to the modern state, as a *countermemory* that will prove disruptive to the efforts to create a new political order. In this context, it is crucial that Michaelis in his polemics against granting Jews civil rights openly supports Dohm's basic blueprint for political modernization. Like Dohm, he envisions a multiconfessional, multinational political order that would "naturalize" and "melt together" its subjects, an all-encompassing, all-assimilating state that he conceives of as incompatible with the forms of memory promoted by contemporary Jews' misunderstanding of their own historical origins: "Do the laws of Moses contain anything that would make it impossible or difficult for the Jews to be completely naturalized and melt together with other peoples? One should nearly think so! Their intention is to preserve the Jews as a people separated from all other peoples, . . . and as long as the Jews retain the laws of Moses, . . . they will never melt together with us—like the Catholic and Lutheran, the German, Wend and Frenchman, who all live in a single state."[18] Groups as disparate as Germans, Sorbs, and Frenchmen can apparently be easily melded into a new political state. With the countermemory of ancient Egypt fostered by their improper understanding of Mosaic law, however, contemporary Jews will prove resistant to projects of "bürgerliche Verbesserung." For Michaelis, Jewish countermemory constitutes a threat to the model of universal citizenship Dohm wishes to see instituted. The ideal solution the former proposes to the Jewish question, accordingly, is one of colonial deportation; it would be best to send this "unmixed people of a more southern race" off to imaginary German "sugar islands which, with the wealth they produce, nevertheless have an unhealthy climate."[19] In this context, Egyptian memory becomes an explicit model for European political modernization, issuing an imperative to view Jews as the modern equivalents of Israelite slaves, as African slaves on West Indian sugar plantations.[20]

The differences between Dohm and Michaelis are manifold, and too complex to be explored in their entirely within the context of this essay. What I would like to investigate here is one of their fundamental similarities, the extent to which Dohm, like Michaelis, also constructs his model of the state in relation to an understanding of Jewish countermemory. Clearly, Dohm's notion of "civic improvement" rejects the protoracial undertones of Michaelis's argument; indeed, Dohm explicitly claims, in reference to critics like Michaelis, that the notion of an "unimprovable race of humans"—an *unverbesserliche Menschen-Raçe*—is an unthinkable proposition.[21] Unlike Michaelis, accordingly, Dohm argues that granting Jews civil rights will enable these "unfortunate Asiatic refugees" to regenerate themselves and become useful citizens who might be able to be successfully integrated into the modern state.[22] He makes his arguments for the "civic improvement" of the Jews, however, by following a strategy analogous to that underlying Michaelis's construction of Jewish memory as a countermemory unsettling to the modern state. He deals with the issue of Jewish memory, however, not by seeking to contain it but by appropriating it for the modern state, transforming the Jewish concept of Diaspora into a symbolic model for a modern body politic grounded in concepts of universal citizenship.

* * *

From the beginning, Dohm grounds his argument for the civic improvement of the Jews in a very particular understanding of the Jewish experience of Diaspora, that space of exile which makes Jewish memory both possible and necessary. Rather than constructing Jewish memory as a danger to the modern state, he opens his treatise by reinterpreting the Jewish concept of Diaspora, offering up his own vision of what Funkenstein posits as the continuity of Jewish "historical consciousness":

> The author of this work had made a plan several years ago to study the *history of the Jewish nation since the destruction of its own state.* The cultural and political circumstances in which the Jews found themselves in different times and countries; the mutual influence of the nations among which they lived, the consequences of the various constitutions, the direction that the Jews' character was given by the occupation prescribed to them; and the influence which this nation has had in industry, trade and culture; the course of its knowledge; the alteration of its original spirit:—these might have been approximately the topics he would have paid attention to and attempted to develop by examining the sources, all of this with an eye toward perhaps communicating the results of such research to the public. The motivation to publish this work would have derived not merely from the thought of filling in a still left-over, but not unimportant lacuna of history, but also from the intention of drawing a conclusion from the unfortunate history of the Jews: namely, that the oppressive condition in which the Jews live even now in most states is only a remnant of the inhuman and unpolitical prejudices of the darkest centuries and as such, not worthy of persisting in our times.[23]

Constructing the "history of the Jewish nation" through the lens of modern concepts of national sovereignty, Dohm reads Jewish history as a simple regression from national autonomy to extranational heteronomy. Jewish history begins in this scenario with the loss of political autonomy, and it culminates, it seems, in the Jews' complete loss of any positive identity of their own. The true "original spirit" of the Jews, apparently present in the ancient Jewish state, has eroded with the loss of political autonomy, Dohm insists, yielding a series of subjections to external influences that would seem to leave little room for the continuity of Jewish memory. The Jews exist in the present only as a "remnant," and what they are a remnant of is not the Jewish nation of antiquity. The Jews as they exist under the "oppressive condition" of modernity are not a positive remainder of lost Jewish totality but lingering traces of modern Europe's own unfortunate prehistory, products of the "inhuman and unpolitical prejudices of the darkest centuries."

Dohm begins his argument, then, by emptying Jewish memory of its content. The contemporary Jewish condition is marked not by the continuity of Jewish memory but by the Jews' anachronistic subjection to "inhuman and unpolitical prejudices" inherited from an earlier, less civilized period. In this carefully crafted opening, the frames of Jewish memory—the experience of exile and anticipation of messianic return—already begin to cede to Dohm's project of social engineering, his vision of transforming Jews into productive citizens. Conceiving of contemporary Jews as a "remnant of the inhuman and unpolitical prejudices of the darkest centuries" enables Dohm to issue the "human" and "political" imperative to eradicate modernity of such anachronism:

> If he [the author] had demonstrated from history how the Jews were only corrupt as human beings and citizens because they were denied the rights of both, he would have believed himself to be able even more successfully to encourage state governments to increase their number of *good* citizens by no longer causing the Jews to be *bad* ones. A changed external position and several occupations forced the author, however, to interrupt these investigations and no longer allowed him to spend the time necessary for careful study of the various writers of all the centuries. Meanwhile, though, he has penetrated deeply enough into the material to convince himself of these truths and to feel at once the wish to contribute to the realization of his intention without having already executed the more extensive historical scaffolding. ("Vorerinnerung," n.p.)

Once the Jews have been properly recognized as relics of archaic prejudices, the pressing task at hand is not to reconstruct the unfortunate history of the Jews but to take action to put modernity temporally in sync with itself, to establish the present as present by seeking to rid it of these holdovers from its past. In this context, the true protagonist of *Ueber die bürgerliche Verbesserung der Juden* is the modern state, not the Jews whom it needs to improve. The politics of Jew-hatred is but a "remnant of the barbarism of past centuries, an effect of the fanatic religious hatred that is unworthy of the enlightenment of our times and that should have long since been eradicated by such enlightenment" (vol. 1, p. 39). The persistence of Jew-hatred marks for Dohm a symptom of modernity's dissatisfaction with itself, a disaggregation within the modern state that prevents it from realizing its true potential.

For Dohm, then, Jewish memory hardly constitutes a threat for the modern state. In this initial framework, it seems to play no role whatsoever. In Dohm's scenario, indeed, the Jews are not the people in Diaspora awaiting a return to the holy land. It is, rather, the modern state that is in the disaggregated condition of Diaspora; in its anachronistic Jew-hatred, the modern state is only perpetuating holdovers from its own past, keeping itself from firmly arriving in the present. The modern state can find its way out of Diaspora and form a cohesive, self-sustaining whole, accordingly, by purging itself of its prime anachronism, by subjecting its Jews to a program of civic improvement. Clearly, then, Dohm's historiography does much more than simply dispose with the Jewish concept of Diaspora and its furtherance of Jewish memory: Dohm also colonizes the concept of Diaspora as the master narrative for the modern, non-Jewish state. Insisting that Jewish history came to an end with the onset of Diaspora, Dohm casts the modern, secular state as the nation in Diaspora that can properly establish its national autonomy only by incorporating the Jews. Dohm's project to assimilate the Jews hinges thus on an historiography that both negates Jewish memory and transforms the Jewish concept of Diaspora into a negative model for the modernity of the non-Jewish body politic.

In colonizing the Jewish concept of Diaspora, Dohm structures his entire argument as a historical narrative culminating in modernity's anticipated return to itself. Quoting from both eighteenth-century historical literature—largely Michaelis's *Mosaisches Recht* and Anton Friedrich Büsching's *Geschichte der jüdischen Religion*—and a wide variety of classical sources, Dohm constructs an account of Jewish history from the Exodus to the late Middle Ages that serves as the crux for his vision of the modern state. Adopting the archetype of Jewish exile and return, Dohm's project for the modern state to overcome its temporal disaggregation coincides in this context with the resurrection of a very particular political precursor. Unlike Michaelis, Dohm does not seek to appropriate the Hebrew Bible against the Jews and resurrect the memory of Egypt. Dohm constructs the modern state's project of "civic improvement" also in reference to an ancient model, but its model is the Roman empire, that is, precisely that political order that destroyed the last traces of Jewish political state autonomy in 70 C.E.[24]

Dohm finds in the ancient Roman republic a presciently modern separation of church and state, a political order he regards as far superior to the Jewish state it conquers. He describes the ancient Jewish state as a relatively primitive, chauvinistic theocracy that perpetuated mistrust and enmity toward all non-Jews (vol. 1, pp. 18–21) and that thus fought against the Roman "destroyers of Jerusalem" with "raging national-hatred" to "stubbornly defend its freedom and capital city" (vol. 1, p. 40). Dohm's Rome, in contrast, wisely recognizes the proper distinction between religious and political societies. Arguing that in the centuries before Christianity became a state religion, the "wise and mild politics" (vol. 1, p. 40) of the Roman empire gave the Jews an unprecedented opportunity for participation in civic life, Dohm marks the ancient Roman republic as a model for both Jewish civic virtue and civic virtue per se. In colonizing the Jewish concept of Diaspora for the modern state, then, Dohm secularizes Jewish memory, marking a secular political order that represents the antithesis of the ancient Jewish theocracy as the state whose return he hopes to effect. This secularization of Diaspora completely inverts the anticipatory logic of Jewish homecoming. Dohm subordinates Jewish memory to the memory of that political order that conquered the Jewish state and sent the Jewish nation into its final exile. The memory work Dohm's treatise performs symbolically reenacts the victory of Rome over Jerusalem, marking the conquering power that initiates the final Jewish Diaspora as the political order to be resurrected in modernity. In its "emancipation" of the Jews, the project of civic improvement reenacts the fall of Jerusalem.[25]

Dohm maps out the cyclical history of the modern state almost entirely between these two poles of Rome and Jerusalem, locating the origins of this key problem of modernity—the persistence of premodern Jew-hatred—in the degeneration of the ancient Roman republic. In Dohm's treatise, not surprisingly, Rome is not destroyed from without but from within, by a violation of the boundaries between politics and religion reminiscent of the ancient Jewish theocracy. The politics of Jew-hatred that Dohm marks as a "remnant of the barbarism of past centuries" has a precise date of inception in this context. It ensues with the politicization of Christianity:

> Certainly one never would have doubted this truth [that Jews, just as well as all other humans, can be useful members of civil society] if the wise principle of Roman government had not been abandoned and if one had bound this nation even more firmly to society by allowing it to enjoy all of society's privileges. The Jews would certainly have remained more enlightened and less corrupt if in the ensuing period fanatical fathers of the church had not misled weak monarchs to suspend the wise ordinances of their precursors and to regard it as proof of their zeal for the religion of love to treat those who thought differently in a unloving manner. (vol. 1, p. 45)

Establishing Christianity as a state religion destroys the boundaries between the religious and the political realms, and does so with disastrous consequences for both. As the "religion of love" is transformed into its antithesis, it violates the "wisdom" governing the political realm. In this context, anti-Jewish persecution is a political phenomenon of enormous significance, an improper entry of religion into politics that marks the beginning of the end of the Roman republic.

Christian Rome represents thus a regression to a lower level of political culture, a return to the religiously motivated political antagonism toward others that characterized the ancient Jewish state. The modern state goes into exile, as it were, by returning to the ancient Jewish model of theocratic government, by allowing Jerusalem to gain its hold over Rome. Implicitly invoking a long tradition that sees the anti-Jewish elements in Christianity as part of its Jewish heritage,[26] Dohm marks the emergence of political Jew-hatred here as a revival of the antagonism toward others characteristic of the ancient Jewish state; political Jew-hatred figures as an outgrowth of the politics of Jerusalem. The final descent of Rome into "barbarism" in Dohm's narrative, accordingly, does not need to be cast as a moment in which Rome is conquered from without. Rather, the "Nordic peoples" only complete the process of civic degeneration initiated by the politicization of Christianity:

> This was the condition in which the Jewish nation found itself when the various Nordic peoples invaded the Roman empire and established their own new states in its provinces. Since the free-born Romans and the other original inhabitants of the empire were treated almost like slaves by their new conquerors, the Jews, already despised by these people, naturally had to receive an even harsher treatment from the barbarians, who knew no other virtue than that of war, a virtue which had long since been eradicated in the Jews. The religion of the conquered Romans soon became that of the victors, and the only way the victors knew how to express their zeal for this religion was to persecute the un-

> fortunate nation that steadfastly refused to take on a faith that Goths, Vandals and Franks so easily exchanged with that of their fathers. (vol. 1, pp. 50–51)

The politicization of Christianity that destroyed the Roman republic from within withstands the political collapse of Rome; indeed, the final fall of Rome marks the political victory of Christianity, the completion of the transformation of the "religion of love" into its antithesis. Like Dohm himself, who both commemorates the Roman victory over Jerusalem and colonizes the Jewish concept of Diaspora, the "barbarians" who conquer Rome also take on the religious self-consciousness of their victims—with the essential difference that the Vandals, Goths, and Franks do not have to transform the "religion of love" into anything else. The Romans themselves have already taken care of this task.

It is at this juncture that Dohm locates the origins of premodern Jew-hatred, marking it as a "remnant of the barbarism of past centuries" that can be properly eradicated only by means of resurrecting the Roman political order, by symbolically reenacting the victory of republican Rome over theocratic Jerusalem. How, though, does he actually stage this triumph? Elsewhere, I have analyzed the particular role that the revival of the "virtue of war" plays in Dohm's program of civic improvement, particularly in his program for disciplining the Jewish body.[27] What we need to consider at this juncture is the strategy Dohm's historiography uses to discipline the Jewish mind. The project to resurrect Roman republicanism and restore the Jews' lost civic virtue hinges, not surprisingly, on an act of direct intervention into the space of Jewish memory. Dohm introduces the modern project of civic improvement not as a deviation from the course of Jewish history but as the ultimate Jewish homecoming, as the ultimate realization of the spirit of Mosaic law. In incorporating the Jews into a non-Jewish body politic, civic improvement claims to be restoring Jewish memory:

> Certainly, the unnatural oppression in which the Jews have lived for so many centuries has contributed not just to their moral corruption, but to the degeneration of their religious laws from their original goodness and utility. Moses wanted to found a lasting, flourishing state, and his law contains nothing that would contradict this goal. In the observation of this law, this state too had its golden age, and until well into the fifth century the Jews were good citizens in the Roman empire. It is only afterward, when all civil societies of the earth excluded them, that they forgot how their religious doctrine related to civil societies. The singular occupation of trade gave them pleasure and also an inclination toward hair-splitting speculations. For the lack of anything better to do they then tampered with their religious prescripts, anxiously [*ängstliche*] observing certain customs and times in an effort to achieve exquisite holiness and greater rights to heaven—all this because civic virtue was forbidden to them, because their participation in the happiness of this earth was so limited. This anxious spirit of ceremonies and minutiae [*ängstliche Ceremonien- und Kleinigkeiten-Geist*] that has crept into the Jewish religion will cer-

> tainly disappear again as soon as the Jews receive a greater sphere of activity. Having become members of political society, the Jews will be permitted to make its interest into their own. They will then also rework [*umbilden*] their religious constitution and its laws accordingly; they will return to the freer and nobler ancient Mosaic constitution and will even find in their *Talmud* the authorization to apply this constitution according to the changed times and circumstances. (vol. 1, pp. 142–44)

Strangely conflating the ancient Jewish state founded by Mosaic law with the "golden age" of the Jewish nation under Roman rule, Dohm finds the process of Jewish civic degeneration reflected in a lack of Jewish memory, in the Jews' collective amnesia. Forgetting his own earlier characterization of the Jewish state as a chauvinistic theocracy that perpetuated enmity toward all non-Jews, Dohm insists that Jews have themselves simply forgotten the proper relationship between Judaism and political power, between Judaism and civic virtue. Excluded from political society and forced into the "singular occupation of trade," they simply "had nothing better to do" than to pay excessive attention to Jewish ceremonial law, ultimately creating in this way a perverted religious constitution that now stands in the way of civic reintegration. Rabbinic Judaism in this context does not serve to foster Jewish memory and hold together a nation in exile. Dohm casts Rabbinic Judaism essentially as a compensatory phenomenon, an *Angst*-ridden attempt to produce a canon of minute religious and ceremonial laws that would take the place of the properly political sphere of activity the Jews lose once Christianity becomes the official religion of the Roman empire. In Dohm's scenario, contemporary Jews are anything but a people of memory. Judaism as it is is merely a substitute for Roman politics, and a rather poor one at that.

The project of civic improvement, then, emerges here as a project to "restore" Jewish memory of civic virtue by wresting the Jews out from under the pseudo-authority of Rabbinic law and resuscitating their memory of the grandeur of Rome. As an essential negation of politics, Rabbinic Judaism's attention to the letter of Jewish law betrays what Dohm sees as the true spirit of Mosaic law. In the scenario mapped out above, moreover, the perverted religious constitution of Jewish ceremonial law standing in the way of civic integration also betrays itself, allowing Dohm to find in the Talmud an authority for the incorporation of Jews into a non-Jewish state. In symbolically reenacting the victory of Rome over Jerusalem, Dohm's program of civic improvement thus claims only to be restoring the true authority of Mosaic law, and to be doing so with the authority of Talmudic interpretation. Like the original conquest it seeks to reenact, this triumph of Rome over Jerusalem claims to liberate its victims, granting them possibilities for "participation in the happiness of this earth" that Dohm marks as the completion of Mosaic law. In resurrecting what he marks as the Roman distinction between church and state, Dohm's goal is not to secure freedom of conscience for the Jews. Rather, he intervenes directly into the realm of conscience here, "restoring" Jewish memory of civic virtue in such a way as to reinscribe the Roman victory over Jerusalem as the necessary completion of Mosaic law, the ultimate messianic homecoming. Unlike Mendelssohn's 1783 *Jerusalem, oder, über religiöse Macht und Judentum,* Dohm's *Ueber die bürgerliche Verbesserung der Juden* does not argue for the compatibility of traditional Jewish ceremonial law with the modern, secular state.[28] Civic improvement anticipates an explicit reformulation of Jewish law, a modernizing *Umbildung* that Dohm insists also represents a "return to the freer and nobler ancient Mosaic constitution." Dohm ultimately does much more in this way than simply colonize the Jewish concept of Diaspora and transform it into a master narrative for the modern state. Civic improvement also subjects the Jews to this non-Jewish homecoming, doing so in such a way as to mark it as a particularly Jewish homecoming as well. For the Jews who emerge from this project of civic improvement, the memory of Rome permanently replaces the memory of Jerusalem.

Before moving on to my third and last selection—Johann Gottfried Herder's 1802 essay "Bekehrung der Juden"—it will prove helpful at this point to step back and formulate some provisional conclusions about the way in which the discourse on Jewish emancipation figures Jewish memory as a site of contest. Written nearly forty years before the point at which Yerushalmi locates the emergence of modern Jewish historiography, Dohm's 1781 treatise on civic improvement works through precisely that negation of Jewish collective memory that Yerushalmi sees as a response to emancipation. By means of a historiographical strategy that colonizes the Jewish concept of Diaspora, civic improvement seeks to replace Jewish memory with the memory of Rome, staging in this way a homecoming for the modern state that claims to be a political homecoming for the Jewish nation as well. In Dohm's scenario, traditional forms of Jewish commemoration of the past do not simply fall apart in the face of modernization. In colonizing the concept of Diaspora, the program of civic improvement explicitly negates the forms of Jewish memory fostered by post-biblical Judaism, reducing Rabbinic Judaism itself to a perverse symptom of the exclusion of the Jews from political society that Dohm links to the politicization of Christianity. The negation of the forms of Jewish collective memory that Yerushalmi sees as a Jewish response to emancipation thus has to be seen instead as a constitutive moment of emancipation itself, as part and parcel of the political project to transform the Jews into productive citizens. Dohm's objective here, however, is not to replace Jewish collective memory with a modern historical consciousness that would subject inherited forms of Jewish collective memory to critical scrutiny; his historiography does more here than negate collective memory. The project of civic improvement also seeks to produce a new form of collective memory for the Jews. In his attempt to put an end to premodern Jew-hatred, Dohm reenacts the victory of Rome over Jerusalem within the space of Jewish collective memory, doing so in such a way as to produce a collective memory of this conquest as the primal moment of Jewish emancipation—and as a more general model for a modern political order grounded in concepts of universal citizenship.

* * *

In this context, Jewish memory does not mark a mode of commemorating the past that is destroyed or superseded by modern historiography. Like Michaelis, Dohm also constructs Jewish memory as incompatible with the modern state, but he solves this problem by appropriating it for the modern state, by using Jewish historical consciousness as a means to deliver the modern state from its own disaggregated Diaspora. Jewish memory for Dohm hardly marks something to be eradicated. It is, rather, of immense value for his vision of modernity, important because of its durable form and its malleable content, its ability to be adopted and colonized as a model for the modern state. Unlike so many nineteenth-century visions of the nation, the political order Dohm wishes to produce is very emphatically not constructed as "natural." The discourse on civic improvement does not conceive of the nation as a "natural" reflection of some perceived cultural homogeneity. For Dohm, indeed, the nation figures as a collective identity that is thoroughly mediated by historiography. This nation has to be produced, and it has to be produced by a political enactment, a staged remembering of Roman civic virtue for which the transformation of Jewish memory becomes both the paradigmatic test case and the symbolic example.

In this context, it should not come as a surprise that among Enlightenment intellectuals, it is Johann Gottfried Herder, the theorist of national cultures and the *Kulturnation,* who arguably expresses the most admiration for the continuity of Jewish memory. In his 1792 essay "Ueber Denkmale der Vorwelt," Herder concedes that for the Jews, "the ruins of Jerusalem" are "founded in the heart of time."[29] In his 1802 "Bekehrung der Juden," an essay which begins by marking attempts at religious conversion as alien to the spirit of the modern era, Herder states emphatically that "the religion of the Jews is, as they say themselves, an inheritance of their lineage, their inalienable heritage."[30] Unlike Michaelis, Dohm, and so many of his contemporaries, then, Herder claims to see the Jews as they see themselves, explicitly identifying modern Jews with the ancient Israelites they commemorate as their spiritual ancestors. Especially in "Bekehrung der Juden," however, this seeming respect for Jewish memory and Jewish uniqueness goes hand in hand with a concept of Jewish memory as being inextricably bound to the Jews' Near Eastern origin and thus inherently out of place in northern Europe. Like Michaelis and Dohm, Herder also sees Jewish memory as a problem for the modern state, as the primary impediment to emancipation:

> The religion of the Jews is, as they say themselves, an inheritance of their lineage, their inalienable heritage. Only the God of their fathers, who imposed

> these commandments on them, can (they believe) rescind these laws, and this could happen only through a ceremonial act as triumphant as the legislation on Mount Sinai. This people thus is and remains even in Europe an Asiatic people foreign to our part of the world, a people that is, as they confess, bound to an ancient, irrevocable law given to them in a distant clime. The question to what extent this law and the ways of thought and life it has brought about belong in our states is no longer a matter for religious dispute; the point is not to discuss opinions and beliefs. This is, rather, a simple question of state [*Staats-Frage*]. The problem is: how many of this *foreign* people that thinks, lives and conducts its business under this foreign national law [*Nationalgesetz*] can be dispensable, useful or harmful to any particular state. How should one regard them and make use of them? If we were talking about Chinese, Indians, Persians, Gypsies or Mamelukes who had immigrated from elsewhere, the question would remain the same. Every state has to decide this question for itself; no one can prescribe laws on this matter; least of all should the philosopher decide this question in an a priori manner. For the Mosaic-Sinaitic law and the people that observes it belongs, according to its own pronouncements, not in Europe but in Palestine. In its prayers Israel esteems itself as its own people distinct from all others; how could it be viewed by other nations differently?[31]

For Herder, then, "the ruins of Jerusalem" are not just "founded in the heart of time." Drawing on one of Michaelis's most prominent contributions to Enlightenment biblical scholarship—the vision of Mosaic law as the product of the climate and culture of the ancient Near East—Herder insists that Jewish memory is fundamentally place-oriented as well. Modern Jews do not just live in a self-contained memory world that is *symbolically* linked to Palestine. They are, quite literally, an "Asiatic people foreign to our part of the world."

What is important about Herder's argument here is not simply his conception of Jews as Asiatic foreigners—a notion shared by many Enlightenment intellectuals, Dohm included—but the functions he ascribes to place in his proposals for the reconstruction of Jewish memory. In the first section of his essay, he suggests mass repatriation to Palestine, invoking a proposal put forth by David Hartley but giving it a fundamentally new twist: "Good luck, thus, if a Messiah-Bonaparte leads them victoriously there, good luck to them in Palestine!"[32] Alluding to the French debates surrounding Napoleon's 1799 expedition to Palestine, Herder envisions a scenario here in which the French imperialist displaces the Jewish messiah, orchestrating a homecoming by setting up a European Jewish colony in Palestine.[33] Such an end to Jewish exile, however, is hardly a realistic possibility for Herder, not least of all because the industrious, trade-loving Jewish nation, he insists, would hardly be satisfied with the "cramped Palestine."[34] Jews constitute and are slated to remain an Asiatic people of memory with a fixed geographical origin but with no fixed roots in the Diaspora; in this context, relocation to Palestine would only create problems for what Herder posits as the continuity of Jewish memory. A "Messiah-Bonaparte," clearly, would fundamentally pervert the structure of Jewish memory.

The solution Herder proposes toward the end of his essay, accordingly, pairs a reconstruction of Jewish memory with a relocation not *to* but *of* Palestine. Palestine here loses its literal, historical, and geographical reference to become a purely figurative object of Jewish memory. The memory at stake here, accordingly, is no longer solely that of the Jews:

> What a prospect it would be to see the Jews, such a sharp-witted people, devote themselves to the culture of the intellect, to the good of the state that protects them, and to other objectives generally useful to humanity, to see them purely humanized [*rein-humanisirt*] in their occupations and way of thinking! If they were to lay down their ancient, proud national prejudices and dispose of the customs that are not appropriate for our time and constitution, and even for our climate, if they were to work not as slaves on a coliseum [*Colisäum*] but as fellow residents of educated peoples [*Mitwohner gebildeter Völker*] on the greatest and most beautiful coliseum [*Colloseum*], the building of the intellect, the collective culture of humanity. Not on the naked mountains of Palestine, that cramped, devastated land, but everywhere their Temple would spiritually rise up from its ruins. All nations would honor with them, and they with all nations, the creator of the world by developing and raising forth his image, reason and wisdom, generosity and charity, in the human race. The concession of new mercantilist advantages will not lead them to honor and culture [*Sittlichkeit*]. They will raise themselves by means of purely human, intellectual, and civic merits. Their Palestine, then, can become wherever they live and have noble effects.[35]

Like Dohm, Herder supports a program of civic improvement, a program of "humanizing" that seeks to transform the Jews into productive citizens. He sets forth his vision of Jewish regeneration here, moreover, by adopting the model of restructuring Jewish memory at the core of Dohm's treatise, the symbolic opposition between Rome and Jerusalem. Humanization here means de-orientalization, and the symbolic figure Herder uses to prescribe the integration of the Jews into the collective culture of humanity is that of the Roman "coliseum." In encouraging the Jews to leave behind their "oriental" prejudices to become "fellow residents of educated peoples," the modern state will apparently not be subjecting the Jews to its particular value system—it will not be enslaving them to work, literally, on the Roman coliseum [*Colisäum*]. Rome here gains symbolic value; it signifies the universal-human coliseum [*Colloseum*], the collective culture of humanity, that Herder envisions as the antithesis of the Jews' place of national origin. In this scenario, moreover, the symbolic "coliseum" of humanity does not just supplant the literal Temple at Jerusalem as the object of Jewish memory, the temple that was destroyed by the Romans. It also effectively replaces "the ruins of Jerusalem" that are "founded in the heart of time," enabling the Jews symbolically to find Palestine—to resurrect a symbolic Temple and stage their homecoming—wherever they are able to contribute to the "coliseum" of human culture.

Like Dohm, then, Herder does not annihilate Jewish memory; he reformulates it as the key mode of integrating Jews into a non-Jewish political order. The "conversion" he refers to in his title is not a religious conversion but a political one, and one that targets not so much the Jews as society as a whole: "Political conversion begins at the improper end if it concerns the Jews and not the Christian."[36] Society as a whole needs to be "humanized," and the symbolic conversion of the Temple at Jerusalem into the figure of the coliseum of the "collective culture" of humanity serves as a paradigmatic test case for this more general process of regeneration. The spiritual resurrection of the ancient Jewish Temple destroyed by the Romans is crucial for already "educated peoples" as well, as the ideals of universal humanity Herder articulates will blatantly fall short in practice as long as Jewish memory continues to link the Jews to their oriental origins. Like Dohm, Herder also reenacts the victory of Rome over Jerusalem in the space of Jewish memory, doing so in such a way as to stage a homecoming for the modern state as well, *its* entry into the symbolic Temple-Colosseum of human culture. Once emptied of its Jewish particularity and transformed into a figure for a universal-human collective memory, the "Temple" at Jerusalem rises spiritually up from its ruins to be a secular temple for all nations: "All nations would honor with them, and they with all nations, the creator of the world by developing and raising forth his image, reason and wisdom, generosity and charity, in the human race." Once converted into a symbolic Roman structure, the Temple at Jerusalem becomes the ideal object of both Jewish and non-Jewish collective memory, the perfect figure for a political order grounded in an ideology of universal citizenship.

* * *

When Dohm first introduced the question of Jewish emancipation in the 1780s, he did so within a more general discussion of internal colonization. Prussia under Frederick the Great pursued an aggressive policy of managed population growth and internal colonization, subsidizing foreign "colonists," primarily farmers and artisans, to settle in the country, particularly its eastern regions, and contribute to economic growth. By 1786, one-sixth of the Prussian population consisted of such colonists, a figure that surpassed that of all other European states.[37] Jews, of course, were never invited in as colonists, and the domestic Jewish population was closely controlled so as to be kept to a minimum. In the areas of West Prussia gained in the 1772 partition of Poland, in fact, four thousand Jews were removed from their homes in order to make room for foreign colonists.[38] Dohm, writing as a Prussian civil servant, opens his treatise by noting this apparent contradiction in Prussian colonial policy. Casting population growth as the "final purpose" and "most reliable barometer" of a state's general prosperity,[39] he insists that it hardly makes sense to continue the policy of limiting Jewish population and economic productivity while one expends large funds to attract foreign colonists. In this way, Dohm introduces his project as a challenge to Prussian colonial policy, offering up his proposals for the "civic improvement" of the Jews as a substitute for the current practice of subsidizing foreign colonists.[40]

Using the term "Jewish emancipation" in this context, of course, is a bit of misnomer, not to mention an anachronism.[41] For Dohm's goal is not to emancipate the Jews as Jews but to regenerate their character, to transform them into colonists who would be useful to the state. Given this dynamic, it makes sense that scholarship on the Jewish question has typically stressed its relation to the rise of the nation-state, a political order that, in Hannah Arendt's words, "perverts equality from a political into a social concept" and thus fails to constitute a "political organization in which otherwise unequal people have equal rights."[42] It is, indeed, by precisely such a perversion of equality from a political into a social concept that Dohm constructs his ideal of universal citizenship, issuing a call for civic improvement that inscribes Jewish otherness as an impediment to political modernization. When it comes to the question of Jewish memory, however, Jewish otherness very emphatically does not appear as something to be contained. Indeed, both Herder's and Dohm's blueprints for emancipation systematically appropriate Jewish memory for the modern state. Jews here are not just potential economic resources that are colonized by the state. They are also perceived to have a symbolic resource, a form of collective memory, that can be colonized by the state as well.

In this context, Nora's and Yerushalmi's narratives of the supersession of Jewish memory clearly only tell part of the story of modernity's dealings with Jewish memory. Their nostalgic visions of Jewish memory being destroyed by modernity obscure the dynamic role that Jewish memory plays in the very blueprints for political modernization. Viewing the Jews as the quintessential people of memory whose memory is eradicated by modernity engages in a form of nostalgia that obscures the crucial role that precisely this memory plays in the crafting of a new political order. Anything but an adequate description of premodern Jewry, the view of the Jews as the quintessential people of memory needs to be seen as a modern fiction produced by the discourse on Jewish emancipation, one of the most prominent means by which the modern nation-state begins to commemorate itself into existence.

NOTES

1. Pierre Nora, "General Introduction: Between Memory and History," in Nora, ed., *Realms of Memory: Rethinking the French Past,* 3 vols., trans. Arthur Goldhammer (New York: Columbia University Press, 1996–98); compare Maurice Halbwachs, *The Collective Memory,* trans. Francis J. Ditter, Jr., and Vida Yazdy Ditter (New York: Harper and Row, 1980).

2. Nora, *Realms of Memory,* vol. 1, p. 2.

3. Friedrich Schiller, "Über naive und sentimentalische Dichtung," in Schiller, *Sämtliche Werke,* ed. Gerhard Fricke and Herbert G. Göpfert (Munich: Hanser, 1989), 5: 730.

4. See here, for instance, Natalie Zemon Davis and Randolph Starn, introduction to a special issue on collective memory and countermemory, *Representations* 26 (1989): 1–6; John R.

Gillis, ed., *Commemorations: The Politics of National Identity* (Princeton: Princeton University Press, 1994); Eric Hobsbawm and Terence Ranger, eds., *The Invention of Tradition* (Cambridge: Cambridge University Press, 1983); Patrick H. Hutton, *History as an Art of Memory* (Hanover, N.H.: University Press of New England, 1993); Jan Assmann and Tonio Hölscher, eds., *Kultur und Gedächtnis* (Frankfurt: Suhrkamp, 1988); Alon Confino, *The Nation as a Local Metaphor* (Chapel Hill: University of North Carolina Press, 1997); and Liliane Weissberg and Dan Ben-Amos, eds., *Cultural Memory and the Construction of Identity* (Detroit: Wayne State University Press, 1999).

5. For background on Dohm and the debates on the question of Jewish emancipation, see David Sorkin, *The Transformation of German Jewry, 1780–1840* (New York: Oxford University Press, 1987), pp. 11–40, as well as my essays, "Sugar Island Jews? Jewish Colonialism and the Rhetoric of 'Civic Improvement' in Eighteenth-Century Germany," *Eighteenth-Century Studies* 32 (1998): 92–100, and "Rome, Jerusalem and the Imperial Imagination: Christian Wilhelm Dohm and the Regeneration of the Jews," in *Monstrous Dreams of Reason: Writing the Body, Self, and Other in the Enlightenment,* ed. Laura Rosenthal and Mita Choudhury (Lewisburg: Bucknell University Press, 2001).

6. Yosef Hayim Yerushalmi, *Zakhor: Jewish History and Jewish Memory* (New York: Schocken, 1989). See also the essays collected in *Jewish History and Jewish Memory: Essays in Honor of Yosef Hayim Yerushalmi,* ed. Elisheva Carlebach, John M. Efron, and David N. Myers (Hanover: Brandeis University Press, 1998), most of which support Yerushalmi's theoretical project.

7. Yerushalmi, *Zakhor,* p. 21.

8. Yerushalmi, *Zakhor,* pp. 34, 44.

9. Yerushalmi, *Zakhor,* p. 88.

10. Yerushalmi, *Zakhor,* p. 85.

11. On Scholem's views on the *Wissenschaft des Judentums* and their importance in the genesis of his own vision of "counterhistory," see David Biale, *Gerschom Scholem: Kabbalah and Counter-History* (Cambridge: Harvard University Press, 1979). Yerushalmi himself quotes Scholem (*Zakhor,* p. 142). For a recent challenge to this vision of the *Wissenschaft des Judentums,* see Susannah Heschel, *Abraham Geiger and the Jewish Jesus* (Chicago: University of Chicago Press, 1998).

12. Amos Funkenstein, "Collective Memory and Historical Consciousness," *History and Memory* 1 (1989): 5–26, reprinted in Funkenstein, *Perceptions of Jewish History* (Berkeley: University of California Press, 1993), pp. 3–21.

13. See Edward Breuer, "Politics, Tradition, History: Rabbinic Judaism and the Eighteenth-Century Struggle for Civil Equality," *Harvard Theological Review* 85 (1992): 357–83.

14. Johann David Michaelis, *Mosaisches Recht,* 3d ed. (Frankfurt am Main, 1793), vol. 1, pp. 56–58, 238.

15. Michaelis, *Orientalische und exegetische Bibliothek* 19 (1782): 1–40, reprinted in vol. 2 of Christian Wilhelm Dohm, *Ueber die bürgerliche Verbesserung der Juden,* 2 vols. (Berlin, 1781–83), here pp. 2, 51, 36. See my essay, "Johann David Michaelis and the Colonial Imaginary: Orientalism and the Emergence of Racial Antisemitism in Eighteenth-Century Germany," *Jewish Social Studies* 6, no. 2 (2000): 56–101.

16. Michaelis, in Dohm, *Ueber die bürgerliche Verbesserung der Juden,* vol. 2, p. 42.

17. In his conceptualization of the role of Egypt in the genesis of Judaism—which I discuss in greater detail in "Johann David Michaelis and the Colonial Imaginary"—Michaelis differs from some of his more radical Enlightenment peers, those for whom the resurrec-

tion of Egyptian memory and the figure of Moses the Egyptian strategically unsettled the opposition between monotheism and its polytheistic other; see here Jan Assmann, *Moses the Egyptian: The Memory of Egypt in Western Monotheism* (Cambridge: Harvard University Press, 1997).

18. Michaelis, in Dohm, *Ueber die bürgerliche Verbesserung,* vol. 2, pp. 40–41.

19. Michaelis, in Dohm, *Ueber die bürgerliche Verbesserung,* vol. 2, pp. 40–41.

20. See Hess, "Johann David Michaelis and the Colonial Imaginary."

21. Dohm, *Ueber die bürgerliche Verbesserung,* vol. 2, p. 23.

22. Dohm speaks of "unglückliche Asiatische Flüchtlinge" in *Ueber die bürgerliche Verbesserung,* vol. 1, p. 8.

23. Dohm, *Ueber die bürgerliche Verbesserung,* vol. 1, "Vorerinnerung," not paginated. All further references to Dohm will be given in the body of the text.

24. I should note that I am using the term "autonomy" here to refer to strictly political forms of state autonomy, and not to the relative autonomy of the Jews that Dohm himself sees thriving under Roman rule or the relative autonomy that scholars like David Biale argue was characteristic of nearly all ancient forms of Jewish political sovereignty; see Biale, *Power and Powerlessness in Jewish History* (New York: Schocken, 1986).

25. One cannot help but note the formal similarity here between Dohm's historiographical maneuvers and the commemorative narratives that have been so central to the implementation of Zionist ideology. Indeed, if Dohm's attempt to incorporate the Jews into a non-Jewish body politic hinges on a historiography that reenacts the victory of Rome over Jerusalem, Zionist historiography has typically done the exact opposite. Eager to stress its continuity with the ancient Jewish state, much Zionist historiography has traditionally viewed the entire period of exile as empty time, as a period of suppressed Jewish nationhood. The only historical moments in Jewish exile that gain prominence in this schema are typically events like the fall of Masada or the Bar Kokhba rebellion, events conceived of—in the case of Masada often with great difficulty—as expressions of Jewish political resistance to the Romans. See on this issue Yael Zerubavel, *Recovered Roots: Collective Memory and the Making of Israeli National Tradition* (Chicago: University of Chicago Press, 1995).

26. On this question see Marc Shell, "Marranos (Pigs), or From Coexistence to Toleration," *Critical Inquiry* 17 (1991): 306–35; also Daniel Boyarin, *A Radical Jew: Paul and the Politics of Identity* (Berkeley: University of California Press, 1994), p. 246ff.

27. See Hess, "Rome, Jerusalem and the Imperial Imagination."

28. The implicit differences between Mendelssohn and Dohm I illuminate in this particular passage should be understood as relative differences, not as a clear-cut opposition. Dohm wrote his treatise at Mendelssohn's request and closely cooperated with Mendelssohn during its composition; Mendelssohn also helped supervise Johann Bernouilli's French translation of *Ueber die bürgerliche Verbesserung der Juden.* On the relationship of Dohm to Mendelssohn, see Alexander Altmann, "Letters from Dohm to Mendelssohn," in *Salo Wittmayer Baron: Jubilee Volume on the Occasion of His 80th Birthday,* ed. Saul Lieberman, Arthur Hyman, and Jeanette Meisel Baron (Jerusalem: American Academy for Jewish Research, 1974), vol. 1, pp. 39–64, but also Breuer, "Politics, Tradition, History."

29. Herder, "Ueber Denkmale der Vorwelt," *Herders Sämmtliche Werke,* ed. Bernhard Suphan (Berlin: Weidmannsche Buchhandlung, 1879), vol. 26, p. 64.

30. Herder, "Bekehrung der Juden," *Adrastea* 4 (1802): 142–66, here p. 145. "Bekehrung der Juden" is also reprinted in *Herders Sämmtliche Werke,* vol. 24, pp. 61–75. As the Suphan edition contains errors—rendering *Vorurtheile* as *Vortheile* in a key passage on page 165, for in-

stance—I quote the original edition here. Herder's views on Jews and Judaism and the various function of these views in his thought as a whole are too complicated to be discussed in full in the context of this essay. See, however, Maurice Olender, *The Languages of Paradise: Race, Religion, and Philology in the Nineteenth Century,* trans. Arthur Goldhammer (Cambridge: Harvard University Press, 1992), pp. 31–50; Liliane Weissberg, "Juden oder Hebräer? Religiöse und politische Bekehrung bei Herder," in *Johann Gottfried Herder: Geschichte und Kultur,* ed. Martin Bollacher (Würzburg: Königshausen und Neumann, 1994), pp. 191–212; and Karl Menges, "Integration oder Assimilation: Herders Äußerungen über die Juden im Kontext der klassischen Emanzipationsdebatte," *Euphorion* 90 (1996): 394–416. Paul Lawrence Rose also discusses Herder in his delineation of a genealogy of the German antisemitic psyche; see Rose, *Revolutionary Antisemitism in Germany from Kant to Wagner* (Princeton: Princeton University Press, 1990), pp. 97–109.

31. Herder, "Bekehrung der Juden," pp. 145–46.

32. Herder, "Bekehrung der Juden," p. 152.

33. See Jeremy Popkin, "Zionism and the Enlightenment: The 'Letter of a Jew to His Brethren,'" *Jewish Social Studies* 43 (1981): 113–20.

34. Herder, "Bekehrung der Juden," p. 152.

35. Herder, "Bekehrung der Juden," pp. 165–66.

36. Herder, "Bekehrung der Juden," p. 158.

37. See here, for instance, W. O. Henderson, *Studies in the Economic Policy of Frederick the Great* (London: Frank Cass, 1963), here p. 126, but also the chapter on "Die preußische Einwanderung und ländliche Kolonisation des 17. und 18. Jahrhunderts" in Gustav von Schmoller, *Umrisse und Untersuchungen zur Verfassungs-, Verwaltungs- und Wirtschaftsgeschichte besonders des Preußischen Staates im 17. und 18. Jahrhundert* (Hildesheim: Olms, 1974).

38. Von Schmoller, *Umrisse,* p. 593.

39. Dohm, *Ueber die bürgerliche Verbesserung,* vol. 1, pp. 1–6, here p. 6.

40. See Dohm, *Ueber die bürgerliche Verbesserung,* vol. 1, pp. 89–94.

41. On the term "Jewish Emancipation," see Jacob Katz, "The Term 'Jewish Emancipation': Its Origin and Historical Impact," in his *Emancipation and Assimilation: Studies in Modern Jewish History* (Westmead: Gregg, 1972), pp. 21–45.

42. Hannah Arendt, *The Origins of Totalitarianism* (New York: Harcourt Brace Jovanovich, 1973), p. 54, but also pp. 290–302.

CHAPTER 3

How Nostalgia Narrates Modernity

PETER FRITZSCHE

Nostalgia stalks modernity as an unwelcome double, a familiar symptom of unease in the face of political and economic transformation, plain evidence also for the persistent inability to acknowledge the destruction of tradition or to work with the materials of the present. Nostalgia typically illustrates the incapacity of contemporaries; it takes the measure of the distance people have fallen short in their efforts to make themselves "at home in a constantly changing world."[1] From the very beginning, nostalgia has expressed incompleteness or impoverishment. Johannes Hofer, a young medical student who in 1688 combined the Greek words *nostos* (return home) and *algos* (pain) to describe the strange melancholy of Swiss soldiers serving abroad, held nostalgia to be nothing less than a "disorder of the imagination." Fixated on a single idea, "the desire to return," Hofer's stricken Swiss men had become indifferent and infirm, refused food and water, and even collapsed and died. In effect, they screened out the world around them. So well known and terrifying was this condition of lethargy that eighteenth-century travelers deliberately avoided extended trips away from home for fear of risking an incapacitating nostalgia.[2] One hundred years later, in the middle of the nineteenth century, nostalgia had found a secure place in household vocabularies, its general usage made tenable by the massive displacing operations of industrialization and urbanization which also standardized its meaning as a vague, collective longing for a bygone but half-remembered time rather than an individual desire to return to a particular place. Nonetheless, nostalgia continued to be recognized by medical professionals and cultural critics as a disability which kept its sufferers from responding fully to new sensations and varying experiences.[3] In their search for security, nostalgics supposedly failed to cultivate abstract relations among strangers in formal settings. Familiar intimacies compensated for lack of social adeptness, so that nostalgia appeared sweet, but dumb. It was a diminished outlook based on repetition rather than novelty, order rather than juxtaposition. Moreover, nostalgics not only protested modernity's hazards but misconstrued what had become imperiled. They blundered by reclaiming the distance between then and now with great simplifications about implausibly splendid aspects of the past. The reconstructed past stood as a norm against which the present had grossly transgressed. The one was imaginatively reworked as simple, ordered, and harmonious, bearing little relation to the contaminated, impure, and conflict-ridden other. Throughout the modern period, critics have described nostalgia as a pervasive failure of imagination that rewrote immediacy in the past tense and miscarried judgments in the present.

The social and political consequences of this failure have been generally held to be deleterious. The insecurities of economic and political revolution in the modern era ensured the political constant of dissatisfaction with the prevailing social order. This deep-seated illegitimacy generated quixotic mobilizations which have mistaken complex problems for moral blights and eschewed practical politics for crusading zealotry. A contemporary example of this mischievous operation is the ubiquitous reference to the traditional American family, which through the 1950s allegedly bolstered social stability and built personal character by keeping couples together, childhoods intimate, and wives at home. Of course, insists Stephanie Coontz, this is "the way we never were." Such wishful thinking represents a "nostalgia trap" with the unhappy result of misdiagnosing serious problems and creating guilt-fringed expectations.[4] For Coontz, nostalgia serves as an example of muddled thinking which evades the complexities of the present and forgets the differences of the past. Thus, in the epigrammatic formulation of Adrienne Rich, "nostalgia is only amnesia turned around."[5]

Identified by detractors as retrospection that is "anti-modern" or "pre-industrial," nostalgic strains can be found in all those movements which sought to regain collective stability in the politics of unquestioning moral authority and unblemished ethnic purity. For the German sociologist Helmuth Plessner, writing in the 1920s, what had become a pervasive, flightful return to community endangered society because it refused to recognize difference and individuality or to exercise tolerance. The rise of National Socialism was, of course, the most obvious and most perilous culmination of the widespread effort to restore an archaic community, but Plessner's warnings applied more generally as well: as long as men and women insisted on the familiarity of home they could not grow up. For Plessner, the widespread hankering for safety amidst admittedly uncertain conditions expressed an elemental nostalgia which grievously impaired civic culture because it kept people from cultivating the "anonymity, itinerancy, [and] dispersion" of modern life which alone offered a new "horizon of possibility."[6] Nostalgia denied the fullness of civic society in the name of one-dimensional community.

There is a striking consistency in scholarly appraisals of nostalgia. In the first place, an unabashed structural-functionalism explains nostalgia as a symptom of erratic cultural stress to social complexity. The sociologist Fred Davis, for example, concludes that "the nostalgia wave," of the 1970s has to be understood in terms of "the massive identity dislocations" of the 1960s.[7] The same logic applied three hundred years earlier to Hofer's soldiers, whose anxiety increased not only according to how far they were from home but also how remote their homes had been: which is exactly why the mountainous Swiss appeared to suffer so acutely from nostalgia. In other words, nostalgia is widely regarded as the by-product of rapid change. Secondly, the violence of displacement corresponds to the malapropos aspect of nostalgic melancholia. Thus almost all discussions of the subject make a great deal of the unsuitable and sentimental nature of the objects of nostalgic longing. A stern utilitarianism features the simplifying operations of nostalgia, which is nothing less than an evasion of the transformed nature of the present. Even the most casual references treat nostalgia as a kind of blindness.

Yet the pervasiveness of nostalgia in the modern world and the equally pervasive disdain for its temptations raise perplexing questions. The emphasis on systemic stress to explain the sudden proclivity of individuals to look backwards with longing is not satisfactory because it does not account for the improbable form that longing takes or the remarkable discernment of difference in the categories "past" and "present." In other words, how is it that nostalgia sees difference? And is there really such a clear relationship between the manifestation of material stress in society and the cultural appearance of nostalgia? Or are other, intervening historical understandings necessary before the past can be imagined as relief from the present? If nostalgia is taken not as blindness to the directionality of history and the necessity of the present but as a kind of sightfulness, then some rather interesting structures of temporality come into focus. These structures rest on a categorical distinction between past and present, on the ineffable and continuous movement toward the new and unknown, and on the partial visibility of the once-present past in bits and pieces of debris. I propose to argue that nostalgia is predicated on a "deep shift in optic identity," one that is singular and particular to the modern era.[8] To make my argument, I will to focus on the narration of the revolutionary years 1789–1815 in Germany, a place from which contemporaries first watched the revolution in France and then experienced the invasion of the French and thus were well placed to think about both national or patriotic dramas and deeper metapolitical shifts in society.

To introduce a regime of seeing which facilitates nostalgia rather than to posit a system in stress which produces it corresponds to a cultural turn in historiographical commentary that puts emphasis on categories of apprehension rather than on mechanics of function. Historians, anthropologists, and literary critics have come to regard the fabricated ways in which the world is organized by the cultural activity of social groups as being equally important as the material pressures that act on that cultural activity. Indeed, historical analysis of the categories in which modern men and women have come to understand the world—key words such as self and other, natural and artificial, or feminine and masculine—is central to the humanistic practice of our times, an effort committed to disassembling the naturalness and thus the silent authority of all social practices and the social subordinations they enforce. Unfortunately the temporal structures in which we operate, and particularly Western assumptions about directionality, continuity, and progress in history, have only slowly been critically examined in this manner. In the late 1950s, Claude Levi-Strauss made incisive distinctions between "hot" and "cold" societies on the basis of their assimilation of change, but the Marxist paradigm against which he argued remained in place for another generation. Narrative and temporal structures have gradually become more central in the ethnographic understanding of identity.[9] Literary criticism's "new historicism" has recently tackled the subject of historicism itself.[10] However, nostalgia itself has continued to be seen as a function of strain and tension, a product or by-product of the system, and not as a way of seeing and interpreting and making sacred the world. And yet a history of nostalgia promises a great deal because it not only is deeply implicated in the development of modern notions of historical change but is exemplary of a critique of those same notions. In turn, the possible historical demise of nostalgia, or its fundamental transformation by the mass media, may well withdraw possibilities for social and cultural criticism.

Mobilization and Narration

What makes nostalgia such a compelling correspondent for the modern phenomenon is that it is predicated on a deep rupture in remembered experience. Nostalgia takes the past as its mournful subject, but holds it at arm's length. Although the virtues of the past are cherished and their passage is lamented, there is no doubt that they are no longer retrievable. There is no nostalgia without the sense of irreversibility, which denies the wholeness of the past to the present.[11] If this were not so, nostalgia would not mourn the exhaustion of tradition or lovingly attend the bits and pieces that are scattered about, but rather protest widespread ignorance of tradition's validity, which is the duty of the reactionary. In other words, nostalgia constitutes what it cannot possess, and defines itself by the inability to approach its subject, a paradox that is the essence of nostalgia's melancholy. This displacement is lost on those critics who simply deride yesterday's questionable merits. Nostalgia is therefore premised on a fundamental break with the past. It maintains a necessarily troubled relationship to the past which is regarded as *past* and it is quite foreign to the ordinary reactionary, who inhabits wholly, without the nostalgic's dread, a verifiable universe in which today corresponds with yesterday.

The irreversible quality that nostalgia invests in time's movement conjures up the constant mobilization in the present which continually pushes away the past. Simply the consciousness that there is fundamental change in history is conspicuous. There can be no more than sporadic nostalgia without the shared sense of being taken from one place in time and deposited in another, from which one is unable to return. If yesterday is different from today merely because natural disaster has occurred and misfortune has come to pass, the authoritative status of yesterday is not really challenged and yesterday's fortune might well persist someplace else not afflicted by catastrophe. In the next valley, the world would still be whole. Nostalgia as a widespread social phenomenon depends on a collective understanding of historical change that is relentless and violent in character and general in scope. As such it makes socially poignant otherwise parochial misfortunes.

The French Revolution was perhaps the first great modern upheaval to fundamentally reorganize long-standing Western structures of temporality. It did so not only by cutting the present off from the past and visualizing the future as new but also by making these structures widely recognizable so that parochial misfortunes could be legible as poignant tragedies. Only with this sense of discontinuity, in which past, present, and future were imagined as ontologically distinct places, could nostalgia articulate itself. It is difficult to overemphasize the cumulative impact of the French Revolution on Western conceptions of historical continuity. Again and again, commentators laid aside well-worn rhetorical templates in which they compared modern with ancient revolutions and instead picked up a new vocabulary that articulated the unprecedented force of events between 1789 and 1815. "Everything seems out of nature," ascertained Edmund Burke at the outset of his *Reflections on the Revolution in France.*[12] "The pen quivers in the hand of the historian who takes hold of it in order to try to portray the scenes of a year which seem to have surpassed human powers of description and feeling and which future generations will hardly believe actually took place," wrote Wilhelm von Schirach, editor of Hamburg's *Politisches Journal,* who found no other formula than to constantly, though inelegantly, reiterate: "Never before . . . [has] such a monstrosity been so wicked"; "never before . . . [were so many] murderous battles fought"; "never before . . . have we seen such broad attacks and retreats."[13]

The acknowledgement of the ill fit between past and present became an ever more compelling description of the particular case of modern times. Johannes von Müller, after Gibbon perhaps the most noted historian at the turn of the nineteenth century, was haunted by the fear that the universal history of civilization he had just completed had been made obsolescent by the revolution in France. In a series of heartfelt letters to his brother, he wrote repeatedly of his bewilderment at the eighteenth century's unpredictable, furious end: "alles wird so ganz anders"—everything is becoming so different.[14]

"Everything is becoming so different" is the signature phrase of the modern. To be sure, fundamental transformations had roiled earlier centuries. Nonetheless, modern testimony insists on seeing it like this: "everything is becoming so different." However tendentious, this testimony enables both modern history and modern memory in critical ways.[15] For all the disconnections to the lives of the dead and for all the disorder of the individual soul which worried Renaissance and Reformation philosophers, anticipation of the future was still basically rooted in the experience of the past. In his explorations of historical discourse, Reinhart Koselleck explains that well into the eighteenth century "the future was a known quantity insofar as the number of politically active forces remained restricted to the number of rulers."[16] Each player had an army, a sustaining population, and a more or less robust economy, making politics a variation of statistics and history a relatively static analysis in which outcomes were uncertain but calculable, circumscribed, and thus susceptible to scientific prognosis. "Within the apprehendable space of the European republic of rulers, with its state organs and estates," continues Koselleck, "the pedagogic role of history was simultaneously surety and symptom of a continuity that connected the past to the future."[17] Potential experience was bounded by history, which is to say that the future was delimited by the past.[18] Whereas Enlightenment notions of progress still accepted classical models of behavior as exemplars, post-Enlightenment thinkers were more apt to dwell on the incommensurability of experiences between one epoch and another, and whereas the Enlightenment conceived of the present as the most forward point of a great continuum of progress that pushed itself on and on, after the French Revolution contemporaries began to regard the present as cut off from the past.[19] The future was no longer conceived as the place where the trends from the past culminated, but as a space in which new and unexpected things would be encountered. "We are not headed toward the future," which one approaches and foresees, wrote Rahel Varnhagen in the eventful year 1815; rather "the future comes from behind," an idea that "is breaking my head apart."[20]

Koselleck draws the useful distinction between the space of experience and the horizon of expectation, defining experience as what can be usefully recalled and applied from the past in ways that make the past present, while expectation is alert to the possibility of the not yet and the not now.[21] Over the course of the nineteenth century, he argues, the space of experience grew smaller, while the horizon of expectation became more sensible. This sudden disjuncture, Rudy Koshar agrees, became "the fundamental condition of societal relationships" in modern times; "anticipation of the future worked without deferring primarily to the authority of remembrance."[22] David Lowenthal emphasizes as well the basic reorganization of time. "Up to the nineteenth century," he writes, "the past seemed not a foreign country but part of our own. And chroniclers portrayed bygone times with an immediacy and intimacy that reflected the supposed likeness."[23] Thereafter, temporal structures became a crucial dimension of difference, distinguishing historical cases bounded by time and place and thereby denying to an unprecedented degree the commensurability of comparisons between periods and societies. If the mechanisms of historical change were not clear, its nature had come to be regarded as relentless and violent.[24]

The French Revolution gave a broadly accessible narrative form to these claims of discontinuity. It was so closely associated with a sense of difference because it dramatized in ideological terms the wars and pestilence it scattered so widely across the European continent, thereby making out of what was unfortunately rather common something quite singular. The ideological contest among self-conscious subjects whose social and programmatic variety was unknown to the political science of the eighteenth century had the effect of disassembling abstract or naturalistic renditions of social reality and thereby challenged the authority of custom and remembrance. Two intertwined forces were at work in this period: the massive dislocation that came with the French Revolution and the Napoleonic Wars and the narration of that dislocation in terms of historical change or progress which is seen to extinguish tradition. Without the machinery of narration—histories, prefaces, memoirs—material changes could not have been interpreted as of one piece or identified in terms of an encompassing historical passage that elevated parochial misfortunes into more meaningful, more readable common fates. And without the restless mobilization of men and women into new economic arrangements, new geographic places, and new political services, the narration would have lost its pertinence, its authority, and its urgency. As a result, in the first quarter of the nineteenth century, material unsettlement combined with new sorts of narrational devices. Extravagant conceptions of time filled the historical imagination of this period: irretrievable loss; disconnection from remembered lifeworlds; exhaustion of tradition; a fugitive, fleeting experience of the present; and an often ominous anticipation of the future.

The extensive mobilization of the revolutionary epoch is easily described: the levée-en-masse of French citizens, the soldiering across all of Europe, the mustering of home guards, the ebb and flow of refugees and exiles, the quartering of troops in what seems to have been every young writer's home, the tax and capital levies in occupied territories, the dissolution of religious orders, the introduction of the Napoleonic Code, the anguished anticipation and joyous celebration of peace, the commemorative calendar that followed the victories at Leipzig and Waterloo—all this maneuvered ordinary men and women into the flow of history. Follow Sulpiz Boisserée, the Cologne art collector, aboard a market boat to Mainz in summer 1815:

> Carpenter, Tailor, or Cobbler; one in a reserveman's uniform with a meerschaum pipe in his mouth speaks with a traveler, a noncommissioned officer, an Italian or a Pole, about Napoleon. . . . In the big cabin someone is reading aloud a newspaper, a Jew is listening and so is a farmer. . . . The black-bearded Jew believes that Napoleon will still escape. . . . After dinner, a small cabin in the back . . . a Catholic priest has gathered a crowd . . . he's from Nassau and

> complains about the Russians, about the Germans, and particularly about the Prussians and their pride. They demand everything double, wheel and deal at the expense of innkeepers—"are those liberators," as he snorts tobacco. . . . Soon the discussion turns to world affairs. Jacobins are in the courts, in Berlin, in Vienna.

The description is marvelous. Boisserée meanders from cabin to cabin, catching snippets of publicly informed conversation, pointing out the newspapers, the uniforms, the unordinary mix of travelers, and revealing just how the revolutionary wars had created a new historical awareness.[25] The market boat crowded with travelers and soldiers is indicative of the raucous movements of the revolutionary epoch. Thousands of exiles and refugees remained in motion throughout these years. And when peripatetic Europeans were finally at rest in their lodgings, diaries and letters repeatedly describe the view from the window as columns of soldiers and prisoners and wounded passed through town.[26] Even if people did not leave, conditions of life changed anyway. Housing foreign soldiers was such a commonplace during this period that aunts and uncles greeted visiting relatives with the half-alarmed cry "Die Inquartierung kommt!"[27] And "almost 60 per cent of the German population changed rulers during the revolutionary period," calculates James Sheehan. "Among them were the inhabitants of Hausen, a village that had once been part of the Habsburg's western lands and then was given by Napoleon to Frederick of Württemberg in return for his support during the campaign of 1805. . . . Perhaps they believed the political world of 1806 was just another version of the old," he writes. "Like Germans everywhere, however, they would discover that they were now part of a larger world, subject to forces at work far beyond the horizon of their village. Twenty-nine Hausener marched with the Grande Armée into Russia, sixteen—almost two complete age cohorts of the village's young men—did not return. 'Grimmige Kälte und Mangel an Brot übergab uns in Russland dem Todt,' reads the sentence above their names in the cemetery chapel."[28] "Whether their memories were bitter or sweet," notes Lynn Hunt, "thousands of men had tested the political waters in revolutionary France." The collective memory of revolution would be "so sharp, because so many had participated in shaping it."[29]

At the same time, private lives were increasingly read against the flow of public events and thus became historicized in ways foreign to the eighteenth century. William Wordsworth spent the summer of 1794 by the sea at Rampside. When crossing Morecombe Bay after a visit to relatives one day in early August, he "carelessly inquired if any news were stirring." A ferryman transporting travelers from Ulverston cried out: "Robespierre is dead!"[30] Given Wordsworth's detailed and shocked response to this event, his biographer Kenneth R. Johnston regrets not knowing "where William Wordsworth was standing when he heard the news of the fall of the Bastille," which was "one of those world-shaking events that tend to isolate spots of time for everyone."[31] But surely the reason for the absence of a detailed account in 1789 and the presence of such an account five years later is not simply archival accident but rather the fact that the French Revolution had not in 1789 come to be recognized as a universal drama. By the time of the terror, five years later, however, it had pressed a claim on even an ordinary band of travelers and the ferryman and on the most careless inquiries in ways that were not imaginable at the time of the fall of the Bastille. The measure of the profound impact of the French Revolution on the ways in which Europeans considered their private lives in terms of public eventfulness and both inquired about and answered inquiries concerning "any news stirring" can be found in the very availability of a report on 1794. And Robespierre's death was not the only event that Europeans instantly recognized because of the parts they came to play as ideological conscripts in the revolutionary drama. News of Napoleon's return from Elba constituted one of the "spots of time" of the nineteenth century. "No, never shall I forget," recalled Germaine de Staël, "the moment when I learned from one of my friends, on the morning of the 6th March, 1815, that Bonaparte had disembarked on the coast of France." "I thought that the earth was about to open under my feet. For several days . . . the aid of prayer failed me entirely."[32] An exhausted Rahel Varnhagen wrote her brother Markus in Berlin: "He is back . . . all the old misarrangements, vexations, bad customs, and mistakes which will now be stirred around. Basta! Everything is going to be different." Rahel felt sympathy for Napoleon, but also felt dizzied—"Basta!"—by the perpetual motion of contemporary history.[33] History during the French Revolution came increasingly to resemble a long-running drama. Contemporaries did not know the turns of the plot, but recognized the decidedly political context in which these occurred and the remarkable, often malevolent ways it affected them.

What the French Revolution was clearly not was a natural occurrence, on a par with catastrophes such as the earthquake that devastated Lisbon in 1755. The French Revolution and the Napoleonic Wars not only featured acting human subjects but produced broad and lasting consequences which anything but the most cataclysmic disasters lacked. This element of human ambition made the revolution so sublime to such horrified, astonished observers as Edmund Burke. Precisely this consciousness of being able to act violently on society is what Georg Lukacs found so distinctive about the events of the French Revolution: "the masses no longer have the impression of a 'natural occurrence.'"[34] That bright comets lit up the autumn skies in 1803, when Napoleon prepared to invade England, in 1807, and again in 1811, but barely left a trace in the written commentary on the revolution serves as a remarkable illustration of Lukacs's argument.[35] It was rather the case that motives were ascribed to ideology, or to what Friedrich Schlegel termed "unselfish crimes," which were committed out of virtue, however misguided, not out of evil or want.[36] What the French Revolution validated was a view of history as a swift, comprehensive process of change in which men and women are complicit by virtue of being self-conscious subjects. "All human beings were subject to general disaster or exploitation as they were to disease," explains George Steiner. "But these swept over them with tidal mystery," and did not fundamentally alter the way people thought about change. "It is the events of 1789 to 1815 that interpenetrate common, private existence with the perception of historical processes." Steiner gets to the essence of the changes in these years with his wonderful remark that "wherever ordinary men and women looked across the garden hedge, they saw bayonets passing."[37] Steiner is not simply referring to the presence of large mobilized armies, which would not be qualitatively different from the grand armies of the seventeenth century, or even to the levee-en-masse, which involved millions of citizens in the affairs of the nation, but rather to the ongoing dramatization of events in terms of a recognizable and comprehensive transformation which shaped private lives and gave the ensuing disruption of individual fates a meaningful social context by providing experience with the narrative form that is history.

At the end of the revolutionary epoch an awareness of the speeded-up movement of time persisted. The revolution ended, but the production of difference did not, a realization which summarized the disillusion among adherents of the restoration. The consciousness of the intrusion of "new time" made contemporaries increasingly sensitive to the unknown and obscure quality of the future and the superannuated aspects of the past. "How are old customs supposed to maintain themselves?" asked Rahel Varnhagen in 1816—"now that the entire world is traveled and known; now that compass, telescope, printing press, human rights, and who knows what have been discovered; now that whatever happened is known in fourteen days."[38] Technology was a sure marker of the colonization of the present by the future, but, as Varnhagen's itemization makes clear, political and industrial revolution were two parts of the same perceptible process. "By the time of the failed Restoration of 1815, at the latest," concludes Koselleck, "the consciousness of a transitional period had become the common property of the peoples of Europe, increasingly induced from the social changes resulting from the Industrial Revolution."[39]

The narrative force and material disruption of the French Revolution had the effect of elevating merely parochial tragedies into poignant political fates which bound social groups together over time and space. For this reason, the memoir literature of the revolutionary era found such a broad audience; it portrayed events that became meaningful and recognizable to readers. That Talleyrand's famous postwar aphorism about the sweetness of life before the revolution quickly became a standard nineteenth-century cliché is evidence for the common discursive understanding of the revolution in terms of temporal disruption. Vigorous literary genres such as diaries, letters, and memoirs, and especially the recollections of ordinary men and women and the regular soldiers who fought in the Napoleonic Wars, testified to the public's comprehension of historical change and general fascination with the reverberation readers recognized in the experiences of strangers.[40] "In all the novels which deal with the French

Revolution," observed Agnes von Gerlach, "it is always the case that unhappiness separates families and divides lovers, and now I"—she was writing from French-occupied Berlin—"find this to be the case."[41] The novels, memoirs, and letters that circulated more and more easily around the European republic of letters demarcated the common ground of historical experience. The drama of this revolutionary epoch was maintained by a burgeoning memory industry which distinguished book publishing in the early nineteenth century from its eighteenth-century counterpart.[42] The point is not that people came to a consensus regarding the historical place of the French Revolution but rather that a general discourse regarding anarchronism, the break with tradition, and long-term continuity preoccupied statesmen, journalists, and ordinary readers. What Koselleck has termed the "singularization" of history in which "the Revolution" became a widely recognizable entity that could be shorthanded as "1789" or even "'89" gave Europeans of all classes a remarkably uniform historical and political vocabulary.

Strangers to Themselves

The French Revolution became a constituent part of the collective memory of nineteenth-century Europeans. Out of ongoing and completely ordinary conversations the revolution and the consequences it was said to have had were narrativized, cited, and recalled. This common frame did not determine individual responses to the revolution. Rather, it made it possible for the most personal and deeply subjective memories to make themselves heard. This was so because the apprehension of the radical and cumulative nature of revolutionary change had the effect of uniting in a single generation dramatically different experiences. "The monstrous contrasts of the years 1750, 1789, and 1815," wrote the bookseller Friedrich Perthes, "appear in men now living not as a sequence but as coexistence, according to whether they are grandfather, father, or grandson." What had once been a shared experience of time and expectation, in which changes were only slowly perceptible, if at all, had fragmented into a "coexisting plurality of times" that carefully distinguished generations. At the same time, the insistently ideological terms in which the French Revolution manifested itself ensured that responses would vary according to class and nationality. "Generations did live in the same experiential space," argues Koselleck, "but their perspective was interrupted according to political generation and social standpoint."[43] Each of these perspectives corresponded to a particular or personal story of the revolution. Therefore, the availability of a general narrative about the movement of history made socially sensible the most individual experiences and invited counternarratives based on those particulars. Indeed, historical narratives gave poignancy and depth to personal experiences that would otherwise have seemed unremarkable. This is consistent with Maurice Halbwachs's insights into the workings of collective memory. "It is in society that people normally acquire their memories," insists Halbwachs: "It is also in society that they recall, recognize, and localize their memories."[44] Once a social frame was in place, diverse evidence was easily summoned by all sorts of witnesses, and vernacular renditions multiplied in countless variations. These were usually unauthoritative, often nostalgic, but always telling. Personal experience traced the scars of the dominant revolutionary narrative, indicating tears and gaps in its credibility. Two correspondents, Friedrich Gentz and Rahel Varnhagen, illustrate how historical narratives emptied and refilled individual lives.

Being in a time when subjects felt dispossessed from the past could be terrifying. For example, at the beginning of the nineteenth century, what Gentz, an advisor to Metternich, saw stretched before him was an "Illiad of storms and battles and adversities." He spoke repeatedly of fiends and leviathans overtaking him. Napoleon was dead; nonetheless, "the revolution had incorporated itself into every monster; the revolutionary spirit has traveled around the world in a thousand forms."[45] By 1831, after the July Revolution, this monstrousness had become a general condition. "The world is becoming more savage and more gloomy," he commented.[46] The course of events had pushed him "further and further into a corner"; "my role is played out and the work of forty years has been lost."[47] For Gentz, the space of experience has narrowed considerably. The symmetry between the text of his life and the text of history—"the work of forty years"—had been wrecked—"my role is played out." He was plainly lost and he reached out to Rahel Varnhagen, a friend whom he had abandoned many times for her Jewishness and her inopportunism: "what are you doing? how do you feel? what is going on? what is going on *in* you?"[48]

Varnhagen too felt the panic of homeless, but for her it was not only an end—Gentz's corner—but an insistently personal beginning. For a time, the cosmopolitan literary world at the turn of the nineteenth century had given her, a Jewish woman, place and identity. Napoleon's war against Prussia in 1806, however, destroyed this precarious security. Prejudice against French ideas, Jewish persons, and cosmopolitan sensibilities mounted, and Varnhagen was left alone. "Where is our time, when we were all together," she recalled ten years later: "Went down in '06, went down like a ship with the most beautiful of life's treasures, with the finest of life's pleasures. . . . Adieu, adieu."[49] Forced to flee embattled Berlin in 1813, Varnhagen took on—she says so explicitly—"the title and the status: Stranger," *Fremde*.[50] Even after her marriage to a German diplomat, after Napoleon's defeat, and after returning to Berlin, the place of her birth, she still found herself in exile. "I don't have a real home, not a material one," she confessed to her friend, the actress Auguste Beste. "What I see are lots of out-of-date characters; what I meet are last year's opinions, worn out judgments, stuffy knowledge, and, on top of all this, unbearable pride!"[51]

Like Gentz, Varnhagen was no longer in synchrony with time—her time, 1806, was smashed up; back in Berlin, she recognized "lots of out-of-date characters"—and she wrote as an exile, who felt wreckage swirling around her body ("adieu, adieu"). Given her self-conscious status as "Stranger," Varnhagen drew some remarkable conclusions. She was not to be cornered and she did not seek shelter. On the contrary, "her whole effort," Hannah Arendt wrote one hundred years later, "was to expose herself to life so that it could strike her 'like a storm without an umbrella.' ('What am I doing? Nothing. I am letting life rain upon me.')"[52] In a letter to her future husband, she wholeheartedly embraced this asynchronic identity. To Karl August Varnhagen she presented herself as a paradox. "Compare me to a tree," she explained, "a tree that a storm has uprooted so violently" that it has "buried its top" deep into the ground.[53] These wonderful images are strikingly dissonant—Rahel in "a storm without an umbrella," Rahel upside down, her roots in the air. She was not sure exactly what was going to happen next, and not sure what belonged properly to the past and what would occur in the future. But she was very clear about the tentative—in her words, paradoxical—composition of the world: truths are not yet manifest; fashions are already obsolete. She was distinctly out of step and that was her distinctive vantage.

In a wonderful sidenote written just as the drama of Napoleon's "One Hundred Days" got underway, she indicates the degree to which she had reconsidered her private self in the light of public events. "It will not come out the way I say it will or the way I think it will," she reflected: "If one thinks things will turn up suddenly and violently, they come gradually; if one thinks they will come gradually and smoothly, they turn up unwanted, like the one from Elba, and disturb the world, instead of coming as I had imagined, at the first sign of trouble. Peace and quiet and whatever I had imagined—you shouldn't rely on that at all!"[54] Again and again, Varnhagen looked at herself from the position of exile, which provided her a rich, evocative, and melancholy reading of her own life. She expressed what one literary scholar has labeled "sideshadowing," the felt presence of counter-lives and the nagging absence of foregone conclusions.[55]

The sense of exile pervades the work of the German poet Joseph von Eichendorff as well. The French Revolution figured as the central organizing principle by which Eichendorff narrativized himself: "I was born (1788) with the revolution," he noted, by which he meant the political revolution and the subsequent literary engagement in which he figured so prominently.[56] He felt an irresistible affinity to the revolution because he understood his life and his difficulties in its tumultuous terms. The legibility he achieved for himself in autobiography and for his readers in poetry and prose he accomplished through his confrontation with the French Revolution. In his autobiographical sketches, Eichendorff worked and reworked the storm-brewed scene set at his family's provincial Silesian estate as the news of the execution of Louis XVI was announced. The composition is constructed in the form of recollection, but it is clear from its careful fabrication that Eichendorff only gave importance to the scene after the consequence of the revolutionary lurch forward had become clear many years later. This storm continued to blow throughout Eichendorff's work, cutting off the remembered *"gute alte Zeit"* ("good old days") from the present day of recollection, upsetting secure and ordered social relations and carting off the young men he wrote about as itinerant soldiers, apprentices, and musicians. Eichendorff's poetry provided sweet lyrics to Robert Schumann's songs and served as sentimental adornments to the provincial culture of nineteenth-century Germans, but there was an unsettling aspect to his words. Theodor Adorno, who set out to rescue Eichendorff from his admirers, described him not as "a poet of the homeland," as his place in Biedermeier company might suggest, but rather as "a poet of homesickness." "When one first hears many of Eichendorff's lines," admitted Adorno, who knew them from his school days, "they sound like quotations learned by heart from God's primer."[57] Indeed well-worn images of ruined castles, dark forests, and rushing brooks give his verse a treacly, rounded-off quality. However, a second look reveals a sentimental rather than naive Eichendorff who had assumed the status of stranger. He narrated from a position once removed, as passerby or conscript. Native regions and cozy parlors are viewed from the open road. While Eichendorff's nouns described a familiar, even static romantic landscape, his verbs and tenses indicated the scars of history and the "unrest of longing."[58] Although Eichendorff allowed people to look back at what has been lost—"die gute alte Zeit"—he denied them any return and thereby took the measure of the unsettlement of the postrevolutionary era. The ruptures and hauntings of historical time had created all sorts of distancing effects. They had mustered up the "incomprehensible" and the "strange" which were not only characteristic themes for romantic poetry as Eichendorff defined it but also unmistakable elements of his own self as he apprised it.[59]

Eichendorff's imagery of the storm, like Varnhagen's shipwreck "in '06," is auspicious because it counterpoints so well personal experience to general narrative, or rather determines the investment of the one in the other, and indicates also the plain facts of wreckage, the debris that the revolution has left behind in private lives. "The prospect of shipwreck looms ever on the horizon," Steven Rendall writes about this powerful metaphor, "and pursuing the project of human self-assertion in our present situation means being prepared to abandon whatever patched-up craft is currently bearing us across the turbulent seas of existence, in order to leap into the waves and begin, again and again, the task of constructing a new vessel from the materials at hand—including, perhaps, the debris from earlier shipwrecks."[60]

Just how authoritative or resonant the postrevolutionary testimony of exile was is not clear, and Eichendorff's own imperiled status as an aristocrat certainly gives his melancholy a class-conscious feel. Yet it would be a mistake, I think, to dismiss nostalgia simply as an aristocratic malady, or to recall the huge numbers of people who remained oblivious to the import of the French Revolution. Not only did the émigré literature remain surprisingly popular throughout the nineteenth century but the personal cast of émigré stories corresponded to the individual's newly enfranchised status in the nineteenth century and to readers' fascination with domestic or anecdotal versions of history. Contemporaries increasingly saw themselves in historical terms, considered their own lives through a developmental schema, and therefore were more sensitive to the losses of historical transformation. What distinguished postrevolutionary society, notes Suzanne Nash about France in ways that are applicable to nineteenth-century Germany, was that it was represented as much in terms of "what it had lost—as debris or ruins, quagmire or sewer"—as it was in terms of "the solidity of its foundations."[61]

Postrevolutionary witnesses such as Varnhagen and Eichendorff made the world look completely different by scattering across its face the ruins of its people. The ruins they see are the ruins of the present, visible in their own lives and in the political turmoil around them. Indeed, the French memoirist and exile François René de Chateaubriand noted once that the best way to "depict society in 1789 and 1790" was to liken it to "the collection of ruins and tombs of all ages heaped pell-mell . . . in the cloisters of the Petits-Augustins: only, the ruins of which I speak where alive and constantly changing."[62] The shift in perspective from the unchanging ruins of Greece and Rome to the accumulating ruins of present-day revolution itself traced a fundamental transformation in the structures of temporality. Even the recent past had been broken off from the present to assume the antique status of ancient civilizations. Whereas seventeenth- and eighteenth-century "moderns" had lived with a sense of being different from and even disconnected to the "ancients," they did not visualize the reproduction of that difference and disconnection in the present day or in their own lives. Both the recent past and the anticipated future remained on a single plain of experience. What Tocqueville referred to as the "forty years" that had "tried everything, and settled nothing" destroyed the reliability of experience.[63] It is this rift between experience and expectation, between the memory of the past and hope for the future, that generated widespread feelings of exile and displacement. A tormenting sense of estrangement prevailed even among people who had never left their homes, since historical and political forces had moved through particular places and robbed them of familiarity. Without authoritative and permanent markers, tossed about by storms or cast away by shipwreck, contemporaries felt more and more like exiles who no longer knew their way and would not know it in the future. Exile served as a reliable summation of modern fate, in which the longing for home was not just a passing malaise but a conspicuous condition of longing and of living at a remove from remembered experience. This articulated sense of displacement increasingly shaped how more and more nineteenth-century contemporaries made sense of their lives even after the revolution.

The stress I am putting on the presence of absence is a nod to the diasporic turn in historical studies generally. Exile, displacement, and diaspora are central categories in the work of anthropologists, literary critics, and historians. Given the conditions of globalization, the impact of the mass media, the mobility of capital, and the extent of migrations there has been much more close attention to cultural hybridities worldwide. Exemplary of the nomadic turn is James Clifford's recent argument that travel and movement is as constitutive of identity as home and that unsettlement is as much a part of the historical process as settlement.[64] This provocative reading, however, needs to be historicized. With the narratives of historical change introduced by the French Revolution, conditions of unsettlement in Europe acquired a much more culturally specific quality and could be experienced as radical estrangement even by those who never left the place of their birth. Nineteenth-century strangers were not simply the product of widespread conditions of unsettlement but of a compelling historical understanding that appeared to deny the possibility of resettlement. Narratives of the revolution configured the notion of homelessness in powerful ways.

Treasures of the Past

More homeless Germans: in an 1809 letter to the young Cologne art collector Sulpiz Boisserée, Dorothea Schlegel confessed that she felt completely cut off from the past. "Time now moves so rapidly," she wrote: "It is not possible to keep up; between one mail day and the other lies an entire historical epoch. I feel like I am watching the most diabolical card tricks." Like Eichendorff's storm or Varnhagen's shipwreck, the gambling play of revolutionary politics had upended the inheritance of the past. At the same time, Schlegel took comfort in the antique landscape of the Rhine Valley. "Towers, spires, capitals, and columns"—all these provided evidence of "past greatness" which "evoked memories." And "soon we forgot the present." By contrast, ruins on the the Danube which she had surveyed earlier were "confusing" and "raw" and kept Schlegel from forming a picture of the past. She concluded her letter by thanking Boisserée for reminding her that "monuments and art objects" still existed amidst the destruction of war and revolution.[65] What is remarkable about this communication is Schlegel's consciousness of the rupture of continuity and her insistence on the articulation of the past. She felt at once disconnected from previous mail days and connected to Rhenish ruins, and she was uneasy both about the prospect of a present that she cannot forget (one without "monuments and art objects") and that of a past she cannot read (Danubian ruins, which are "confusing" and "raw"). What Schlegel sees and fails to see is available thanks to a newly honed historical optics which bring to light all sorts of ruins and thereby dramatize the destructive work of even contemporary history but, at the same time, which enable quite particular emotional relationships to those ruins.

What is left unspoken are the national values attached to present and past. Dorothea Schlegel does not explicitly describe the ruins she sees as German and destruction as French, but such a correspondence would not be surprising. Indeed her husband Friedrich, upon arriving in France from Germany in 1802, purported to be immediately aware of dullness of the landscape west of the Rhine. It was without remarkable features, pretty but superficial, and without the wild residue of Germany's history.[66] Even in Paris, he reported, "luxury is the all-absorbing deity that governs the hasty revolutions of the fleeting day, amid an universal irregularity of existence, buildings, garments, and the ornamental refinements of life, interrupted only by the fantastic caprice of ever-varying fashion."[67] Living without memory, the French lacked the possibilities of retrieving alternative historical itineraries. Their "ever-varying fashion" was as unworkable as the Danube landscape was confusing. What is interesting is not whether Schlegel was right, but how forcefully he, Dorothea, and their contemporaries made judgments about places without memory, the value of ruins, and the stories imputed to them. The obsession with ruins and the alleged indifference with which they were treated indicates that for nineteenth-century observers such as the Schlegels ruins were no longer part of a natural landscape of decay and regeneration but evidence of abrupt endings and new beginnings, of calamity, destruction, and possible rebirth. They were the signs of a distinct historical case which had been overwhelmed; they indexed a particular national history.

The campaign to complete the cathedral in Cologne indicates just how the ruins that evinced a conditional past (that which might have been) also suggested a conditional future (that which might yet be). Difficult as it was to overlook the huge, unfinished structure, throughout the eighteenth century the cathedral did not seem particularly interesting because it was broken down and had been left behind by the political developments that had taken place since the Thirty Years' War. After the French Revolution, however, it was seen afresh. Suddenly the cathedral stood for alternative (German) subjectivities that had been defeated but might be rearticulated. French occupation authorities prohibited religious services in 1796, and used the cathedral to house Austrian prisoners of war, to store grains, and, finally, in 1802, to stable horses, which only heightened the sense of what the cathedral had been and was no longer. An impressive array of literary figures came to cherish it as a monument to a specifically German "prehistory." In their view, the completion of the cathedral made it possible to imagine following up the lost itinerary of German prehistory and thus introducing a new greatness and cohesion to German actions once the French had been defeated. For the journalist Heinrich Steffens, Cologne's cathedral beckoned an "indeterminate future," a space in which various possibilities of history remained alive. The subjunctive future corresponded to the conditional past, in which defeat and demolition were no longer regarded as foreordained. To complete the cathedral in Cologne, or to discover a worthy medieval heritage amidst the dilapidated streets of Nuremberg or to identify ruins along the Rhine River, which revealed itself as a "huge national museum"—all these were critical elements in the dramatization of difference that allowed nineteenth-century Germans to fashion for themselves a new national subject and a new national history.[68]

The endeavors of the Brothers Grimm also can be understood in the light of the French Revolution. They too collected bits and pieces of a past they insisted was irretrievably ruined and only partially comprehensible. In the introduction to the first edition of their fairy tales published in 1812, they compared the stories they transcribed to small shafts of grass that had been protected by hedges and bushes after storms had flattened a field of crops.[69] Tucked away in hidden places, the bits of grass urged the collector to bend down close to the ground. Jacob recalled the method: "quietly pick up the leaves and carefully bend back the twigs, so as not to disturb the *Volk* and to furtively glimpse this small, rare part of nature, smelling like fallen leaves, meadow grass, and fresh rain." This work of collecting had to proceed quickly, the Grimms urged, before "total decomposition ensues,"[70] making clear that the summer storm was not merely a recurring seasonal danger but a very particular historical catastrophe. The revolutionary armies whom the brothers had seen move back and forth across their native Hessen, and the surveyors and road builders who arrived in the decades that followed, flattened fields as surely as any summer's storm, wiping away older lifeways in the name of progress. Folksongs, a few books, and "these innocent fairy tales" were all that remained. And even these bits and pieces survived only along the edges of ordinary life: "around the fireplace, the kitchen stove, the cellar stairs."

Given how violently and thoroughly the storm of modern development had acted—"flattening a whole field of crops"—how fragile individual customs had become—collectors had to "carefully bend back the twigs"—and how hard the traditional villages were to find—places "where few paths led"—the Grimms insisted on preserving old folkways as they found them. They conceded that the stories and legends were no longer integral elements in the larger society that collected them, and that as a result efforts to translate them into a more accessible vernacular would ruin them. On the one hand, the folktales formed a link to a distant past, which justified their collection, preservation, and dissemination. On the other, they had to be accepted as artifacts of a broken whole that could no longer be repaired. "The past" (*das Alte*) could not be "transplanted into our time, where it no longer belongs," insisted Jacob Grimm to his brother Wilhelm. The wording suggests that today had once been commensurate with yesterday, but was "no longer." Following Stephen Bann's distinction between exemplary specimens and recovered relics, a "shift in terms" around 1800 that "alerts us to a radical change in conceiving the relationship of the historical object to the past," I would argue that the tales entered nineteenth-century culture as relics.[71] That modern scholarship has disproven the Grimms' claim for the rustic, Germanic origins of the folktales in no way challenges that the brothers and their readers encountered the stories as recovered treasures. The "strange, noble creatures" that Jacob imagined his tales to be appeared both as eloquent expressions of the grandeur of the past and of estrangement with it. They were the pieces of an organic whole that had been shattered. Giving depth to national history, they also withheld an immediate link to it.[72]

The antiquitarians who carefully picked over these postrevolutionary places were self-conscious of the destruction that had been wrought and, at the same time, they undertook the work of cultural commemoration to take account of the losses that had been incurred. The momentous break in the continuity of history that Eichendorff, Schlegel, or the Grimms posited is only the first stroke of a two-stage process by which nineteenth-century nostalgia constituted itself. The second stroke was to attempt to reestablish some sort of connection to the past that has been lost. To be sure, "there is no return to natality—the past has not been stored in a warehouse until such time as it may be taken out, dusted and restored to its former beauty, it needs to be sewn anew," comments Zygmunt Bauman. "In this respect there is no status difference between back and forward, past and future, 'glorious heritage' and daring project. Whether the sought-after home is imagined in the past or knowingly located in the future—it is always a *postulated* home."[73] A home can only be postulated in the subjunctive tense, by summoning up what might have been or what might yet be. In this way, debris offered new cultural opportunities and opened up new imaginary byways.

Ruins were no longer regarded as decrepit, but suddenly reseen as treasure. Indeed the modern age was perceived as dangerous precisely because it threatened to efface the debris itself and thus the possibility of even a mediated connection to the past and the alternative identities it contained. Without monuments, a people would live in "empty space," warned Dorothea Schlegel; if you take away "the bones of their fathers," Chateaubriand wrote in another context, "you take away their history," you rob people "of the proofs of their existence and of their annihilation."[74] Thinking about the possibility of a land without monuments and cemeteries, where the bones of kings had been thrown into ditches, Chateaubriand and Schlegel came to regard ruins as half-hidden treasure. The experience of loss paradoxically endowed an acquisition of wealth because markers of rupture and contingency indicated possibility and variability. Physical refutations of immutability, ruins reidentified the variety of subjects available in the vicissitudes of history. These formal insights into the action and the mutability of the historical process encouraged their own efforts to "make" history in the present. The alternation of abrupt endings and new beginnings that was so evident in the past applied as well to the present, which suddenly appeared more fragile and less necessary. This archeological imagination anticipated Walter Benjamin's insistence on excavating and retrieving the aspirations of yesterday in order to set them against the certainties of today and thereby to resuscitate critical thinking.[75] Thus, the acknowledgment of loss, the recognition of historical transformation, and the sense of ill-ease in the present made it possible to imagine different pasts and to apprehend multiple possibilities of history in the future. It made possible the reenactment of national belief which Eichendorff described as the "superstitious belief in superstition" (*Aberglaube an Aberglaube*).[76] "Yes, the world is still full of wonder," he insisted, "we just don't see it anymore!" Here Eichendorff was echoing Novalis: "It is the weakness of our organs that keeps us from seeing fairies."[77] However, newly emergent structures of temporarity at the turn of the nineteenth century, premised on the recognition of the breakup of time, did in fact open up all sorts of new imaginary spaces in which both nations and individuals reconstituted themselves. The past, as much as the future, was the distinctive territory of modernity.

A final question might be posed: Is this modernity still with us? Today the fragments of the past are energetically manufactured and avidly consumed but do not correspond to the felt and lived evidence of experience. The interiorized voice and vernacular location of nostalgia has been made nearly obsolescent by the mass media's ability to package and repackage the past in a way that facilitates its omnipresence but diminishes its pertinence to particular lives. Bits and pieces of the past are scattered about all around us, but they lack provenience and therefore have lost some of the power to tell their own version of history or to undermine the versions of others. This is nostalgia without melancholy. Commodified in this way, the past is no longer a different place and the troubled, tenuous connections that made historical self-awareness possible are lost in easygoing consumption.[78] The possibility of envisioning in the present day the end of nostalgia or a nostalgia without melancholy calls attention to the historicity of the phenomenon. Nostalgia corresponds to the historical age that was not only saturated with narratives of transformation and movement but keenly aware of the estrangement that those motions called forth. At the very moment that the calamities that befall individuals are no longer comprehended in terms of a recognizable and comprehensible historical process, nostalgia simply shrivels into bad luck without wider social meaning. This was the case before the onset of the historical age more than two hundred years ago and may well be the case today, in the face of the disintegration of grand narrative. A study of nostalgia suggests how fragile has been historical consciousness and how apposite is the nightmare of an eternal present, a place which is undisturbed by the difference of the past because it cannot generate narratives to assimilate the signs of yesterday's lives.

NOTES

1. Marshall Berman, *All That Is Solid Melts into Air: The Experience of Modernity* (New York: Simon and Schuster, 1982), p. 6.

2. Jean Starobinski, "The Idea of Nostalgia," *Diogenes* 54 (1966): 86–87.

3. See, for example, Michael Roth, "Remembering Forgetting: *Maladies de la Mémoire* in 19th-Century France," *Representations* 26 (1989): 49–68; Roth, "Dying of the Past: Medical Studies of Nostalgia in Nineteenth-Century France," *History and Memory* 3 (1991): 5–29; and Roth, "The Time of Nostaliga: Medicine, History and Normality in 19th-Century France," *Time and Society* 1 (1992): 271–86; as well as Susan Stewart, *On Longing: Narratives of the Miniature, the Gigantic, the Souvenir, the Collection* (Baltimore: Johns Hopkins University Press, 1984).

4. Stephanie Coontz, *The Way We Never Were: American Families and the Nostalgia Trap* (New York: Basic Books, 1992).

5. Edward S. Casey uses the Adrienne Rich epigram and profitably discusses Emmanuel Levinas ("The World of Nostalgia," *Man & World* 20 [1987]: 361–84).

6. See Helmuth Plessner, *Grenzen der Gemeinschaft: Eine Kritik des sozialen Radikalismus* (Bonn: F. Cohen, 1924); and Helmuth Lethen, *Verhaltenslehren der Kälte: Lebensversuche zwischen den Kriegen* (Frankfurt: Suhrkamp, 1994), pp. 8–9.

7. Fred Davis, *Yearning for Yesterday: A Sociology of Nostalgia* (New York: Free Press, 1979), pp. 26, 105.

8. On "optic identity," see Rudy Koshar, *Germany's Transient Pasts: Preservation and National Memory in the Twentieth Century* (Chapel Hill: University of North Carolina Press, 1998), p. 3.

9. Aleida Assmann, *Erinnerungsräume: Formen und Wandlungen des kulturellen Gedächtnisses* (Munich: Beck, 1999); Jan Assmann, *Das kulturelle Gedächtnis: Schrift, Erinnerung und politische Identität in frühen Hochkulturen* (Munich: Beck, 1999); Johannes Fabian, *Time and the Other: How Anthropology Makes Its Object* (New York: Columbia University Press, 1983).

10. The best example is now James Chandler, *England in 1819: The Politics of Literary Culture and the Case of Romantic Historicism* (Chicago: University of Chicago Press, 1998).

11. Vladimir Jankélévitch, *L'Irréversible et la nostalgie* (Paris: Flammarion, 1974).

12. Edmund Burke, *Reflections on the Revolution in France,* ed. Conor Cruise O'Brien (London: Penguin Books, 1968), p. 92.

13. "Schilderung des Robespierre," *Politisches Journal,* Aug. 1794, p. 856; "Historisch-politische Uebersicht des Jahrs 1796," *Politisches Journal,* Jan. 1797, p. 3.

14. Johannes von Müller to his brother, 20 May 1797, in Johannes von Müller, *Briefe in Auswahl,* ed. Edgar Bonjour (Basel: B. Schwabe, 1954), p. 212. See also letter of 2 July 1796, p. 208.

15. See, for example, Hegel discussed in Perry Anderson, *A Zone of Engagement* (New York: Verso, 1992), p. 293; Marx, in David Harvey, *The Condition of Postmodernity* (Oxford: Blackwell, 1990), p. 261; Walter Benjamin, "The Storyteller," in *Illuminations,* ed. Hannah Arendt, trans. Harry Zohn (New York: Schocken Books, 1969), p. 159; Herbert Fischer in Modris Eksteins, *The Rites of Spring: The Great War and the Birth of the Modern Age* (Boston: Houghton Mifflin, 1989), p. 291; and Eric Hobsbawm, *The Age of Extremes* (New York: Pantheon, 1995), particularly his chapter on the "great landslide."

16. Reinhard Koselleck, *Futures Past: On the Semantics of Historical Time* (Cambridge: MIT Press, 1985), p. 15.

17. Koselleck, *Futures Past,* p. 26.

18. Koselleck writes: "The temporal structure of past history bounded a continuous space of potential experience" (*Futures Past,* p. 23).

19. Ingrid Oesterle, "Der Führungswechsel der Zeithorizonte in der deutschen Literatur. Korrespondenzen aus Paris, der Hauptstadt der Menschheitsgeschichte," in *Studien zur Ästhetik und Literaturgeschichte der Kunstperiode,* ed. Dirk Grathoff (Frankfurt: Peter Lang, 1985), p. 20.

20. Rahel Varnhagen to Karl August Varnhagen, 11 Oct. 1815, in Rahel Varnhagen von Ense, *Rahel Varnhagens Briefwechsel,* ed. F. Kemp, 4 vols. (Munich: Matthes & Seitz, 1979), p. 2: 355.

21. Koselleck, *Futures Past,* p. 271.

22. Koselleck, *Futures Past,* pp. 275–76; Koshar, *Germany's Transient Pasts,* p. 18.

23. David Lowenthal, *The Past Is a Foreign Country* (Cambridge: Cambridge University

Press, 1985), p. xvi. In addition to Koselleck, see also Karl Kroeber, "Romantic Historicism: The Temporal Sublime," in *Images of Romanticism: Verbal and Visual Affinities,* ed. Kroeber and William Walling (New Haven: Yale University Press, 1978), p. 150.

24. See A. Assmann, *Erinnerungsräume;* and Chandler, *England in 1819.*

25. Entry for 17 August 1815 in Sulpiz Boisserée, *Tagebücher,* vol. 1: *1808–1823,* ed. Hans-J. Weitz (Darmstadt: Roether, 1978), pp. 249–50.

26. In his *Erinnerungen aus meinem Leben,* Ludwig Emil Grimm writes: "In den französischen Revolutionszeiten wurde es auch bei uns unruhig. Es kamen immerwährende Durchzüge, bald die Franzosen, bald Österreicher, Holländer, Preussen, Mainzer und Hessen; da gab es denn immer etwas für uns zu sehen, und wir waren immer am Fenster; die gute Mutter war in grosser Angst und liess uns nicht in die Schule und auf die Strasse." See Gabriele Seitz, *Die Brüder Grimm: Leben—Werk—Zeit* (Munich: Winkler, 1984), p. 27.

27. Wilhelm Grimm to Jacob Grimm, 18 Jan. 1814, in Hermann Grimm, Gustav Hinrichs, and Wilhelm Schoof, eds., *Briefwechsel zwischen Jacob und Wilhelm Grimm aus der Jugendzeit* (Weimar, 1881; rpt. Weimar: H. Bölhaus, 1963), p. 238.

28. James J. Sheehan, *German History, 1770–1866* (New York: Oxford University Press, 1989), p. 251.

29. Lynn Hunt, *Politics, Culture, and Class in the French Revolution* (Berkeley: University of California Press, 1984), pp. 172–73, 181.

30. Kenneth R. Johnston, *The Hidden Wordsworth: Poet, Lover, Rebel, Spy* (New York: W. W. Norton, 1998), pp. 72, 419.

31. Johnston, *Hidden Wordsworth,* p. 162.

32. Germaine de Staël, *Considerations on the Principal Events of the French Revolution,* 3 vols. (London: Baldwin, Cradock, & Joy, 1818), vol. 3, p. 136.

33. Rahel Varnhagen to Markus Roberts, 29 Mar. 1815, in Varnhagen, *Briefwechsel,* vol. 4, p. 80.

34. Bruce James Smith, *Politics and Remembrance: Republican Themes in Machiavelli, Burke, and Tocqueville* (Princeton: Princeton University Press, 1985), pp. 139–42; and Georg Lukacs, *The Historical Novel* (Lincoln: University of Nebraska Press, 1983), p. 23. See also Ernst Behler, *Unendliche Perfektibilität: Europäische Romantik und Französische Revolution* (Paderborn: F. Schöningh, 1989), pp. 38–41.

35. On the comet in 1803, see Raphael Samuel, *Theatres of Memory* (London: Verso, 1994), p. 32; on 1807, Gentz to Müller, 18 Oct. 1807, in Friedrich Gentz, *Briefwechsel zwischen Friedrich Gentz und Adam Heinrich Müller, 1800–1829* (Stuttgart: J. G. Cotta, 1857), p. 112; and on 1811, François Hué, *Le Journal d'un paysan, 1799–1823,* ed. E. V. Veuclin (Paris: E. Veuclin, 1886), p. 24, and Hans Brandenburg, *Joseph von Eichendorff: Sein Leben und sein Werk* (Munich: Beck'sche Verlagsbuchhandlung, 1922), p. 217.

36. Quoted in Arthur Herman, *The Idea of Decline in Western History* (New York: Free Press, 1997), p. 39.

37. George Steiner, *In Bluebeard's Castle: Some Notes towards the Redefinition of Culture* (New Haven: Yale University Press, 1971), pp. 12–13.

38. Rahel Varnhagen to Ludwig Robert, 5 Feb. 1816, in Varnhagen, *Briefwechsel,* vol. 4, p. 101.

39. F. Ancillon, "Über die Perfectibilität der bürgerlichen Gesellschaft, ihre Bedingungen und Triebfedern," in *Zur Vermittlung der Extreme in den Meinungen* (Berlin: Dunker und Humblot, 1828), vol. 1, p. 192, cited and discussed in Koselleck, *Futures Past,* p. 251.

40. Gustav René Hocke, *Das europäische Tagebuch* (Wiesbaden: Limes, 1963), pp. 67, 201–

2; Peter Gay, *The Naked Heart* (New York: Norton, 1995), p. 109; Clive Emsley, *British Society and the French Wars, 1793–1815* (London: Macmillan, 1979), pp. 172–73. See also Celia Betsky, "Inside the Past: The Interior and the Colonial Revival in American Art and Literature," in *The Colonial Revival in America,* ed. Alan Axelrod (New York: Norton, 1985).

41. Agnes von Gerlach to Marie von Raumer, 23 Dec. 1808, in Hans Joachim Schoeps, ed., *Aus den Jahren Preussicher Not und Erneuerung. Tagebücher und Briefe der Gebrüder Gerlach und ihres Kreises, 1805–1820* (Berlin: Haude & Spenersche Verlagsbuchhandlung, 1963), pp. 368–69.

42. Stanley Mellon, *The Political Uses of History: A Study of Historians in the French Revolution* (Stanford: Stanford University Press, 1958), pp. 1–2.

43. Koselleck, *Futures Past,* p. 282.

44. Maurice Halbwachs, *On Collective Memory,* ed. and trans. Lewis A. Coser (Chicago: University of Chicago Press, 1992), p. 39. See also Halbwachs, *The Collective Memory,* trans. Francis J. Ditter, Jr., and Vida Yazdy Ditter (New York: Harper & Row, 1980), p. 19.

45. Gentz to Brinkmann, 8 Nov. 1824, in Friedrich von Gentz, *Briefe von und an Friedrich von Gentz,* ed. F. C. Wittichen and Ernst Salzer, 3 vols. (Munich: R. Oldenbourg, 1909–13), vol. 2, p. 341.

46. Gentz to Rahel Varnhagen, 8 July 1831, in Varnhagen, *Briefwechsel,* vol. 3, p. 194.

47. Gentz to Rahel Varnhagen, 21 Jan. 1831, in Varnhagen, *Briefwechsel,* vol. 3, p. 187.

48. Gentz to Rahel Varnhagen, 8 July 1831, in Varnhagen, *Briefwechsel,* vol. 3, p. 194.

49. Rahel Varnhagen to Pauline Wiesel, 26 June 1816, in Barbara Hahn, *"Antworten Sie Mir" Rahel Levin Varnhagens Briefwechsel* (Basel: Stroemfeld/Roter Stern, 1990), p. 60.

50. Letter of 23 May 1813, cited in Hahn, *"Antworten Sie Mir,"* p. 141, n. 27.

51. Rahel Varnhagen to Brede, 11 Nov. 1819, in Hahn, *"Antworten Sie Mir,"* p. 181.

52. Hannah Arendt, *Rahel Varnhagen: The Life of a Jewish Woman,* trans. Richard Winston and Clara Winston (New York: Harcourt Brace Jovanovich, 1974), p. xvi.

53. Rahel Varnhagen to Karl August Varnhagen, 19 Feb. 1809, quoted in Barbara Breysach, *Die Persönlichkeit ist uns nur geliegen: Zu Briefwechseln Rahel Levin Varnhagens* (Göttingen: Königshausen & Neumann, 1989), pp. 189–90.

54. Rahel Varnhagen to Markus Roberts, 2 Apr. 1815, in Varnhagen, *Briefwechsel,* vol. 4, p. 83.

55. Michael André Bernstein, *Foregone Conclusions: Against Apocalyptic History* (Berkeley: University of California Press, 1994).

56. Cited in Wolfgang Fruehwald, "Der Entdeckung der Erinnerung. Zu Eichendorffs historischen, politischen und autobiographischen Schriften," in Joseph von Eichendorff, *Werke* (Frankfurt: Deutscher Klassiker Verlag, 1993), vol. 5, p. 845.

57. Theodor Adorno, "In Memory of Eichendorff," in Adorno, *Notes to Literature,* vol. 1, ed. Rolf Tiedemann and trans. Sherry Weber Nicholsen (New York: Columbia University Press, 1991), pp. 55–79, here p. 57.

58. Adorno, "In Memory of Eichendorff," *Notes to Literature,* p. 61.

59. Helmut Koopman, "Eichendorff, das Schloss Dürande, und die Revolution," in *Ansichten zu Eichendorff,* ed. Alfred Riemen (Sigmaringen: Jan Thorbecke, 1988), p. 120. See also Eichendorff to Jegor von Sivers, 14 Nov. 1853, in *Sämtliche Werke des Freiherrn Joseph von Eichendorff,* vol. 12 (Stuttgart: Kohlhammer, 1992), pp. 313–14.

60. Steven Rendall, "Translator's Introduction" to Hans Blumenberg, *Shipwreck with Spectator: Paradigm of a Metaphor for Existence,* trans. Rendall (Cambridge: MIT Press, 1997), p. 3.

61. Suzanne Nash, "Introduction," to Steven Rendall, ed., *Home and Its Discontents in Nineteenth-Century France* (Albany: State University of New York Press, 1993), p. 5.

62. François René de Chateaubriand, *The Memoirs of François René Vicomte de Chateaubriand,* trans. Alexander Teixeira de Mattos, 6 vols. (London: G. P. Putnam, 1902), vol. 1, p. 172.

63. Smith, *Politics and Remembrance,* p. 168.

64. James Clifford, *Routes: Travel and Translation in the Late Twentieth Century* (Cambridge: Harvard University Press, 1997).

65. Letter dated end of December, 1809, Dorothea von Schlegel, *Dorothea von Schlegel und deren Söhne Johannes und Philipp Veit. Briefwechsel,* 2 vols. (Mainz: Kirchheim, 1881), vol. 1, pp. 396–99.

66. Schlegel, "Reise nach Frankreich," *Europa* (1803): 17–18.

67. Friedrich von Schlegel, "Principles of Gothic Architecture: Notes of a Journey through the Netherlands, the Rhine Country, Switzerland, and a part of France in the Years 1804, 1805," in *The Aesthetic and Miscellaneous Works of Friedrich von Schlegel,* trans. E. J. Millington (London: G. Bell, 1875), pp. 198–99.

68. On the Cologne cathedral, see Gertrud Klevinghaus, "Die Vollendung des Kölner Doms im Spiegel deutscher Publikationen der Zeit von 1800–1842" (Ph.D diss., Saarbrücken, 1971), pp. 12, 27. Nuremberg is discussed in W. D. Robson-Scott, *The Literary Background of the Gothic Revival in Germany* (Oxford: Clarendon Press, 1965), pp. 120–21, and the Rhine in Gerhard Schulz, *Die deutsche Literatur zwischen Französischer Revolution und Restauration* (Munich: Beck, 1989), pp. 143–44.

69. Jacob Grimm and Wilhelm Grimm, "Vorrede," 3 July 1819, *Kinder- und Hausmärchen,* ed. Heinz Rölleke (Stuttgart: P. Reclam, 1980), p. 15.

70. "Aufforderung an die gesammte Freunde deutscher Poesie und Geschichte erlassen" (1811), in Heinz Rölleke, *Die Märchen der Brüder Grimm* (Munich: Artemis, 1985), pp. 63–69, here p. 65.

71. Stephen Bann, *The Clothing of Clio* (Cambridge: Cambridge University Press, 1984), p. 86.

72. Jacob Grimm to Wilhelm Grimm, 17 May 1809, in Grimm et al., eds., *Briefwechsel zwischen Jacob und Wilhelm Grimm,* p. 101. On Grimm scholarship see Rölleke, *Märchen.*

73. Zygmunt Bauman, *Life in Fragments* (London: Blackwell, 1995), p. 137.

74. Dorothea Schlegel to Sulpiz Boisserée, 4 Mar. 1814, in Schlegel, *Dorothea von Schlegel und deren Söhne Johannes und Philipp Veit,* vol. 2, p. 254; and Chateaubriand, *Memoirs,* vol. 1, p. 231.

75. Graeme Gilloch, *Myth and Metropolis: Walter Benjamin and the City* (London: Blackwell, 1996).

76. Joseph von Eichendorff, "Troest-Einsamkeit," in *Sämtliche Werke,* vol. 5, p. 387.

77. Eichendorff and Novalis quoted in Lothar Pikulik, *Romantik als Ungenügend an der Normalität. Am Beispiel Tiecks, Hoffmanns, Eichendorffs* (Frankfurt: Suhrkamp, 1979), pp. 295–96.

78. See the very different reflections of David Gross, *The Past in Ruins: Tradition and the Critique of Modernity* (Amherst: University of Massachusetts Press, 1992); and A. Assmann, *Erinnerungsräume.*

CHAPTER 4

Masters of Memory: The Strategic Use of Autobiographical Memory by the German Nobility

MARCUS FUNCK AND STEPHAN MALINOWSKI

The Nobility's Culture of Memory

No social group relied more on the strategic deployment of memory in shaping its identity than the nobility, and no social group developed techniques as finely honed in order to recall and guide memories. The quality and significance of the nobility's culture of memory are among those achievements of the nobility that have been preserved into the present,[1] something which even the fiercest critics of the nobility cannot overlook. In view of the colorful show of splendor in which they appeared in order to display their own superior qualities, nobles can appropriately be called "experts of visuality."[2] Closely connected with this capability is a second quality: nobles are masters of memory. The intention of this essay is to analyze the masterful creation, selection, and deployment of memory, which must be seen as an indispensable component of the cultural model of the German nobility. And it was in the twentieth century, in particular, that German aristocrats rediscovered and refined techniques of memory in order to reinvent their gravely imperiled cultural and political identities.

The mastery of noble memory can be described on three different levels. The noble culture of memory is unique, first, for its historical depth; second, for the variety of remembrance techniques specific to the nobility; and, third, for the consciously controlled selectivity of what is remembered. It is worth commenting on these three different levels.

1. Nobles possess the unique ability to trace their forefathers back not only two or three generations, which more or less encompasses the personal time horizon of most non-nobles, but two or three and even as many as ten centuries. And regardless of how far back in time nobles can trace their ancestors, they

look upon these previous generations as members of a single "family." Thus in 1931 it was possible for a member of an ancient noble family whose National Socialist party comrades insinuated the presence of Jewish forefathers to defend himself with reference to his family tree, on which all of his forefathers were "known" to him back to 1000 A.D. and, with a seventy-year gap, back even to the year of Charlemagne's imperial coronation.[3] The most complete possible recall of the nobility's forefathers is connected with its concept of family. For the nobility, family means a close community of the dead, living, and still unborn generations into which the individual must fit in order to preserve noble lineage and name. As a unidirectional continuum that seemingly eludes historical change, this concept of the supratemporal noble family corresponds to that traditional *milieux de mémoire* which has not yet broken with the past. Pierre Nora's assessment of the peasantry as a "*collectivité-mémoire* par excellence"[4] can also be applied to the nobility. Indeed Nora's distinction between "*mémoire*" and "*histoire*" as two distinctive forms of remembrance can be well illustrated by the nobility. Nobles maintain a superb mastery of both forms. The aristocratic cast to the forms of memory that attach themselves to objects, symbols, places, and everyday gestures ("*mémoire*") is still apparent throughout Europe. Villages which for centuries have borne the name of a local lord; coats of arms embedded in ancient, moss-encrusted ruins; and regiments and barracks named after famous forefathers are the material evidence of forms of memory which do not depend on writing or textualization. Castles that rest on foundations that date from the Middle Ages or nineteenth-century palaces rebuilt in the most pompous architectural styles are instantly recognized and understood even at a great physical distance. Nora also identifies a second of memory ("*histoire*"), one that is more intellectual and reflective and relies on written communication, but it too was cultivated by nobles over long centuries when a bourgeois historiography was not yet imaginable: aristocratic families preserved written texts and genealogical documents and paid scribes to compose heroic family histories. No other social group provided such historical depth for itself.

In the autobiography of the Prussian *Landrat* Joachim von Winterfeld there is a remarkable instance of the direct, material form of memory. Trees are transformed into powerful memorial symbols that express the double nature of the rootedness of the family. The forest to which the author feels such a strong link represents the connection both to nature and to the past. In Winterfeld's description, he walks through the family woods accompanied by family members who have long since passed away. "As I walk through woods of birch and oak, past tall elders and across cuttings, my ancestors accompany me every step of the way. I live immersed in the past, and not simply my own. I feel myself to be a link in a long chain."[5] The basic principle of noblesse oblige is based to no small extent on this extension of remembrance which even the best bourgeois families cannot approach. The newspaper of one noble family boasted proudly (in 1926): "The year '1229' appears at the top our family paper. It wants to impress on every member of our house this admonishment: Soon seven hundred years of documented Bülow history will be looking down upon you! Be worthy of it!"[6] The unique depth of noble memory served as a mark of distinction and a constant call for achievement. It was also an important source of the noble self-confidence and sureness of style which bourgeois critics so jealously and ubiquitously noted.

The memory of the family's ability to stay "on top" and its mastery of past crises in turn gave it the self-confidence to overcome the crises of the present. In 1921 in the palace of Prince Christian Ernst zu Stolberg-Wernigerode, a play written by the hereditary prince was performed, in which this form of strength-giving memory was allegorically dressed up. The prologue and epilogue of the piece entitled "From Christian Ernst to Christian Ernst: Five Scenes through Two Centuries" feature a dialogue between two princes of the Stolberg house separated by two centuries. In a conversation mediated by an allegorical character called Time, a form of communication occurs which should be seen as a variation of the image on the chain described above, one in which the links are supernaturally joined. Each cousin reassures the other of the timeless greatness of the Stolberg family down the centuries. In a kind of trance, each family member, separated from the other by many generations, is granted the opportunity to observe the worries and struggles of his descendant or ancestor and to summon up strength for his own present. While gently stroking the head of the sleeping prince, Time reminds him of the continuing splendor of the family's coat of arms and the eternal values that both cousins have defended and fostered to the family's glory.[7] In this sense, memory in depth proved to be a fortification against time.

2. Next to their diversity, the noble media of memory show a series of special features, which do not completely lose their distinctive noble stamp even where they are copied by the bourgeoisie. Castles, palaces, galleries of ancestors, proofs of descent, coats of arms, family archives, orders of knights, family and noble associations, family trees, collections of weapons, court ceremonies, hunting conventions, family crypts, special burial rituals, genealogical works (especially the famous "*Gothaer*"), family histories, memorial albums for sons who fell in war (the so-called *Heldengedenkmappen*),[8] privileged seats in the local church or in the cadet school mess hall—where the young noble officer candidate sat in the same place his forefathers had and used the very same cutlery with which they had dined[9]—all point to a complex system of noble techniques of remembrance elaborated over the course of centuries. Centuries-old family properties, and the manors, castles, and natural surroundings that have been shaped by ancestors, serve the nobility as *lieux de mémoire,*[10] which are essential for the creation and maintenance of noble identity. The strength of this identity comes from the physical and visible nature of these *lieux de mémoire.* Many localities of noble memory testify to the "rootedness in the concrete" which Pierre Nora describes as the nature of *mémoire* in contradistinction to *histoire.*[11] Since the

end of the nineteenth century, with the advent of the age of individualization and democratization, and the accelerated loss of political privileges and social advantages, these localities of memory have become more rather than less important. They offer the nobility a unique opportunity to maintain an aura of distinction. Recalling his family's old medieval castle, for example, Count Oswald von Finckenstein describes the mystical connectedness of all the generations who have seen the castle "lying in the quiet moonlight . . . who once drew in the deep breath of six centuries." In a description of his family's imposing palace in Mark Brandenburg, Count Dankwart von Arnim speaks of the "sheer power of the family's history emanating from all the walls, pictures, and people."[12] Objects less grand than moss-covered castle walls also have important commemorative functions. Augmenting the coats of armour that still bear the traces of medieval battles, the corridors of family portraits, and even the five-hundred-year-old bones of forefathers, on display after being rediscovered, are more recent memorial objects: the silver spoon Immanuel Kant had given to great-grandfather, which was "saved from the Russians" in 1945; the tobacco tin that Tsar Alexander I presented to yet another great-grandfather; and the oil portraits bequeathed to Count Dönhoff by Frederick the Great. These are not curiosities, but the insignia of noble rule and greatness. The memory of this greatness uses a variety of physical aids to convey that central message, which even in the twentieth century has been formulated again and again in countless variations: that is, the assertion that the nobility "is something by birth and therefore does not need to become something."[13]

3. The nobility achieves a consciously controlled selectivity of memory by concentrating its remembrance on outstanding individuals. The value of the entire group is assessed according to the achievements of particular individuals, who are immortalized through a variety of remembrance techniques. Mediocre nobles, failures, and "duds" are systematically excluded from the process of remembrance, or they are concealed or "sent to America."[14] America, in fact, becomes the symbolic and physical place where nobles who have transgressed against aristocratic codes are banished. In transatlantic exile, they no longer disrupt the ideal picture of the family. However, after several years, transgressors can be reintegrated, provided that the down-and-out nobles have married a "wealthy widow" and are thus able to return to Germany and entertain their well-born friends in provincial outposts. In that case they have once again become "*hoffähig*" and worthy of remembrance.[15] The more successfully the glory of individuals can be emphasized, the higher the credit for which the great "family" of nobles as a whole can hope. Bourgeois sociologists and theorists of elites, including Maurice Halbwachs, Georg Simmel, Robert Michels, and Werner Sombart, have repeatedly pointed to the ability of the nobility to convince others that judgment of the estate should rest on its best representatives, not its average members. Noble memory always amounted to an attempt to keep alive in other classes the impression that titles of nobility were "bequeathed from generation to generation

with the personal qualities that they represent, so that their contemporary holders can claim as their own the great deeds of those who first attained them."[16] If noble memory often emphasizes impressive achievements, this is due to, first, the abundant wealth of experience it collected during its thousand years "on top" and, second, to the splendor of carefully selected individuals in whose shadow the bulk of the ancestors disappear.[17] "Twenty-five generals in the ancestral line of a single family, along with eighty officers killed upon the field of honor,"[18] are indeed impressive, especially when respect for such achievement keeps questions about the rest of the family from coming up.

Only if noble-born mediocrity is filtered out of public perceptions and the impression is thereby gained that aristocratic families consist exclusively of remarkable individuals can the nobility have confidence that the core of its self-identity, which has remained stable for centuries, is accepted by the outside world. The nobility understands itself as a chosen minority with high-quality qualifications for rule and leadership, based on experience and tradition and bequeathed from one generation to the next. The task of noble memory is to strengthen this view within the nobility and to communicate and represent it without. The most important functions of noble memory have remained the same in the course of the centuries: cohesion, delimitation, and, above all else, symbolic allusion to the nobility's singularity and superiority. To describe this self-understanding, Georg Simmel used the metaphor of the precious metal that changes its form during constant recastings but that does not lose its everlasting essence and value.[19]

Noble memory has played a crucial role in both the preservation of noble traditions and their adaptation to the changing needs of the present. The most important forms and techniques of noble memory are subject to innovation and revision. An ancient, relatively stable core stock of techniques, which has survived into the present, has been expanded during the recent past. The *lieux de mémoire* already mentioned above, the castles, palaces, galleries of ancestors, coats of arms, family trees, collections of weapons, court ceremonies, hunting conventions, family crypts, hereditary funerals, and stylized techniques for the symbolic representation of rule, all indicate that the noble culture of memory was not primarily written. Many of these *lieux* appeal less to the cognitive side of memory than to its affective, sensory side. Noble memory traditionally relied on a metaphorical language of images, especially when it was trying to have a public effect. The reason for this is clear: these images of memory were supposed to be "read" and understood, not least by subjects who could neither read nor write. Written products of noble memory (travel accounts, family histories) were mainly intended for consumption within the nobility.

The need to expand and modify traditional forms of noble memory arose from the growing pressure to which the nobility was exposed during the "long" nineteenth century. Defeat in war, the flight of the kaiser, and the November Revolution all marked 1918 as a radical break in the history of the German nobility. The real experiences of loss in this period were described by countless noble families as an incomparably long "fall" from a great "height."[20] Technically, the nobility in the German republic was no more than a tiny minority of 60,000 to 100,000 individuals, who made up little more than 0.15 percent of the total population.[21] In a world in which the nobility had been constitutionally abolished, stripped of its last privileges, and cut off from portions of its traditional bastions of power, the significance of noble remembrance grew dramatically. In the first place, it became ever more difficult to distinguish a nobility no longer protected by formal barriers or recognized by special privileges. The drastically accelerated slide of countless nobles into "ignoble" occupations and petit bourgeois livelihoods further aggravated the nobility's existential need for distinction. Second, in the fierce postwar ideological debates among right-wing intellectuals, who began to legitimize concepts such as "nation" and "*Volk*," the nobility was forced to go on the counteroffensive in order to justify its distinctive leadership qualities. Nobles claimed a new political role by presenting themselves as "*Führer*" to overcome the "rule of the inferior."[22] In postwar years, then, the importance of the nobility's culture of memory grew significantly not only to bolster the self-image of the nobility but to enhance its public image. The noble culture of memory and the symbols it created had always helped to increase the symbolic capital of the group and to improve its power prospects. Reverent groups of visitors in the portrait galleries of old castles, through which the bored son of the castle owner occasionally passed, testified to a culture of memory that continued to impress the outsider more than it did the insider—for the latter knew better the faulty structure behind the impressive facade. Under the conditions of a shaken social order, in which considerable portions of the disoriented (bourgeois) élites were looking for new forms of leadership—which were summarized by the term "*Führertum*"—the nobility's dual mastery of representation and memory offered the estate new political opportunities. Bourgeois opponents of bourgeois culture, already influential before 1918, despised the universe of middle-class values, which they dismissed as one of "the most boring dreams ever."[23] Sooner or later, these critics were bound to (re)discover and use the "cornucopia of symbolism and visual memory"[24] that the nobility had prepared for centuries, and thereby lend the nobility new credibility and unforeseen popularity.

In a "de-nobled" society, nobility is determined by the specific "*Lebenswelten*,"[25] the value systems and exceptional cultural features its members can preserve and outwardly convey. It is therefore hardly surprising that the postwar nobility, whose existence was more dependent than ever on its ability to define itself through its way of life and culture, discovered a genre for remembering that had been used hitherto by the bourgeoisie: the autobiography. Historians have traditionally "either ignored [this genre] completely or treated [it] as a minefield to be avoided by all but the most experienced veterans."[26] The aim of this essay is to show what the social and cultural history of the nobility can hope to gain by venturing into this minefield.[27] What the autobiographies describe is not "how it actually was," but the specific ways in which noble authors perceived and took account of their surroundings. The reconstruction of the strains of aristocratic remembrance, which is made possible thanks to the autobiographies, provides new insights into what at first were the extremely aggressive reactions of nobles to the threats to and the destruction of their *Lebenswelten.* Only in the last two decades of the twentieth century did this reactionary stance give way to a more nostalgic farewell, in which remembrance is no longer deployed to discredit what is taken to be an unbearable present.

From Memory Offensive to Nostalgic Farewell

When modern bourgeois authors remembered their lives through autobiography, they fashioned each published life as an account of a personality and emphasized above all else the special value of the self, to which the written journey to the individual's interior had gained access.[28] This form of written remembrance also offered the individual the opportunity to give meaning to the life already lived and therefore to join in the collective process of identity formation.[29] In the stable hierarchical society of orders, the nobility, by contrast, did not need individual reassurance of its social and cultural position. Written remembrance of individuals was left either to paid clerks or to descendants, who celebrated the life and deeds of their master or ancestor in the style of hagiography, presenting him as an unshakable, self-evident monument. Even in the autobiographical nineteenth century, few nobles published memoirs, and those that did were exceptional individuals who had held leading positions in the court, in the state administration, or in the military and had "something to say" about national politics. In these memoirs, often posthumously published apologia, the authors reconstructed public events of significance to the state from carefully chosen official and private documents and emphasized their own important roles, without intending to fathom private and everyday life or to analyze their own actions. The often glossy presentation of these voluminous books and the partly anecdotal, light conversational tone of the authors reflected the reality of a noble world that for the most part still functioned.[30]

A clear break was marked by the collapse of the *Kaiserreich,* when noble authors began to present their messages to the public with much greater frequency. From a sample of some four hundred noble autobiographies published in the nineteenth and twentieth centuries, well more than half of them appeared in the period between 1918 and 1945. The second, though less voluminous, wave of publication began directly after Germany's unconditional surrender and the collapse of the National Socialist regime, which for the nobility east of the Elbe was synonymous with the loss of sometimes centuries-old property. Beginning in the 1960s, this wave was followed by a third phase, which brought forth a new, more introspective type of noble autobiography. The dramatic breaks of war and revolution point to the reasons and circumstances why people wrote publicly about their lives. "The night-lamp of self-examination burns only rarely," writes Peter Sloterdijk, in a general statement that applies particularly to the nobility: "There are very specific crises in which the individual is forced to look in the mirror and observe his injured consciousness under a reflective light."[31] When the old world of nobility was threatened, its collapse was perceptible, and the decline of the nobility accelerated, the need for clarification of one's own standpoint grew accordingly, as did the need for making sure of one's own values, leitmotifs, relationships, and delimitations.

This impression is confirmed by a survey of those nobles who used public autobiographical memory after 1918 and those noble groups that continued to avoid it. Besides the highly educated, cultivated representatives of the high and diplomatic nobility, who enjoyed writing and who comprised a very small group, the newly emerging authors included the fallen, exiled kaiser, and former royal officers who now earned their livings as businessmen on Wall Street. Nobles in economically stable circumstances who were able to preserve their traditional lifestyles after 1918 were far less apt to write autobiographies. It was mainly people who had lost their sense of certainty along with their former ways of life who tried to come to terms with their experiences of material and cultural loss through autobiography. This is probably why many of the most famous Prussian names in the group of authors that published between 1918 and 1945 were represented only by later-born sons, younger brothers, or the daughters of still established big landowners. The heads of high noble and mediatized princely houses and the politically dominant members of the rich low nobility in southern Germany were barely represented among the autobiographers of this period.

Like the middle class before them, the nobility used the written conveyance of its canon of values to establish the estate's interior and exterior boundaries over a period of generations, as well as to reflect on the noble cultural model, justify it anew, and sometimes even reinvent it.[32] Yet noble autobiographies differed from their bourgeois counterparts to such a remarkable extent in terms of structure, form, arrangement, and choice of subject that one should see the texts as a special form within the genre. In general, noble autobiographies lacked the introspective relationship to the self and the concept of personal development that distinguished middle-class autobiographies. Noble autobiographies always remained more self-portrayal than self-analysis. Even in periods of individual and collective crisis for the nobility, one senses the hold of deeply rooted noble conventions, which Countess Marion Dönhoff accurately has called "banisters of certainty."[33] The stunning unity of formal structure and the set of anecdotes and leitmotifs that has remained the same for generations indicate the long-term, far-reaching, and formative strength of this cultural model.

The fall of the monarchy released the first wave of noble autobiography. A large part of the recollections that noble authors brought before the public after 1918 by no means went *à la recherche du temps perdu,* as one might have expected. The natural supposition that one should find a nostalgic transfiguration of the past, the fashioning of a lost golden age in noble memoirs published after 1918 is confirmed only by exceptions. Unlike the French nobility after 1789, and as distinct from the most important (noble) authors of the Counter-Revolution, who joined hatred for the Revolution with celebration of the old regime,[34] the majority of German noble authors did not look backward, but rather forward. In step with bourgeois intellectuals of the "conservative revolution," the memory of the *Kaiserreich* for remarkably many of the (male) authors served less as a bridge back to the past than as a reservoir of experience that offered support for an uncertain future. The sharp critique in many memoirs of conditions in the immediate past fitted smoothly into the atmosphere of the New Right, which perceived—or at least fashioned—the end of the *Kaiserreich* not only as a collapse but as a breakthrough.[35]

Noble autobiographies were written precisely to present authors as vigorous and forceful opponents of the "prattle of the parliamentary system."[36] While the exiled kaiser sought in his two volumes of memoirs—which were edited several times by "advisors"—to present himself as an elder statesman, a paternal figure who would focus the alleged monarchical yearnings of his people, his son followed a markedly different strategy of self-representation.[37] Crown Prince Wilhelm had the ghostwriters of his memoirs cast him as a battle-hardened leader, who stood ready as heir apparent in new political and social conditions.[38] Leading officials of the old empire who did not want to retire from the political stage shaped their autobiographies mainly into antiparliamentary blueprints, whether in the wooden military language of the former head of the Supreme Command, Paul von Hindenburg, or the aggressive and surly landowners' idiom of the eccentric Reichstag member Elard von Oldenburg-Januschau, or in appreciation of the coming "Third Reich" that Moeller van den Bruck conjured up.[39]

To develop a sense of the aggressive style that dominated many of the works in the first phase of written noble memory after 1918, it is worth looking at descriptions and interpretations of the November Revolution. In terms of language and content, it is possible to distill a remarkably homogeneous narrative pattern from a wide range of depictions and anecdotes: "The human beast"—a people gone wild, who had mutated into a "disgusting mass"[40]—had managed to destroy the institutions of the old state, but over the long term had failed miserably in its attempt to break the timeless superiority of noble leadership. The superiority of the nobility had shown itself to be unshakable, in marked contrast to the sansculotte "riffraff" behind the lines and in the navy, who seemed to have risen from the "port bordellos" of the big cities.[41] In the typical version, the determination of a single noble sufficed to bring a group of heavily armed, insurgent workers in Berlin to their senses; the nobleman on horseback rode toward the insurgents and spoke "down" to them in an appropriate tone.[42] Likewise, the revolt on the rural manor was crushed by pulling "the laborer" by his ear to the ground, threatening him with the cudgel, and thereby making clear who was "the master" of the estate.[43] In another version, the speech of a noble lieutenant barely of age was enough to intimidate the chairman of the Social Democratic Party and future president of the Reich. The empress imperiously put to flight a revolutionary soldier who had forced his way into the Potsdam palace. Far from the capital, the son of a Saxon king restored the discipline of his insurgent frontline troops with a single speech. A determined republican who had dared to question the prince's leadership wore the look of "an ox when lightning is flashing" after this rebuke and gave "a salute to the others."[44]

There were also brutal variations to this representation of the nobleman's presumption to rule. In his memoirs, the free corps leader and National Socialist Manfred von Killinger recounted the struggle against the revolution in Munich and how he had smashed the faces of prisoners and had a woman whipped by his men "until no white spot was left on her backside." In his account, he degraded the woman with dirty language, calling her a lecherous "female" and a "*Schwabinger Malweibchen.*" Killinger, who, like many from his social background, interpreted the revolution in 1918 and the failure of the Kapp Putsch in 1920 as the results of insufficient "severity" and "leadership," defended his methods with words that were as simple as his conception of the world: "Some will say 'brutal.' True, but [I acted] correctly. Anything else would have been understood by the riff-raff as weakness."[45] These examples, which could be multiplied many more times[46] contained a central message that was endlessly repeated: In the struggle against the revolution and the republic, nobles were standing ready as reliable rulers, whose ancient experience in leadership would not fail, even under the changed circumstances.

The publication stream of noble recollections did not abate with the Nationalist Socialist seizure of power in 1933. To be sure, prefaces were added to some new editions of older works and some passages were adapted to the tone of the new age; however, the content and function of noble autobiography stayed the same. The nobility's memory remained oriented toward political purposes and concentrated on the reaffirmation of aristocratic pretensions to rule.

Nineteen forty-five brought the second and final defeat of the German nobility, but it did not bring any change in its image of the world as presented here. Though disavowed as an independent social and political force and—with the loss of the big family estates in the east—irrevocably robbed of the economic and cultural basis of its position of power, the nobility from east of the Elbe River continued to dominate the authorship of noble recollections in the early post–World War II period. Prominent noble functionaries in the society, state, and political parties of the *Kaiserreich,* the Weimar Republic, and the Third Reich took up their pens to clarify—or transfigure—their own political past. Former career officers made up the bulk of this group of authors for obvious reasons.[47] In the process, authors like the *Herrenreiter*[48] and former Reich chancellor Franz von Papen or retired general field marshal Erich von Manstein used the technique of contrasting refined origins and the aristocratic milieu with the brown morass of National Socialist parvenus, against whose dilettantism even the superior political and military leadership of (noble) generals, their *Führerkunst,* could achieve only "lost victories."[49] Despite an apologetic tone, the account of noble superiority remained completely unbroken. The masses gone wild in the recollections of the 1920s and 1930s gave way to philistines in brown uniforms, who were seduced and led by a poorly dressed character without style, culture, or manners. In the stunningly corresponding concentration of the criticism of Adolf Hitler on the outer details of his stylistic failings, this man was described as a soup-slurping, bloated plebeian with a ridiculous haircut, who became a nervous wretch whenever he was faced with true (that is, noble) *Herrentum.* As in 1918, nobles appeared once again as *rocher de bronze,* embodiments of a superior culture and way of life, which had not been able to halt the Nationalist Socialist masses but which had maintained an insurmountable distance from them.

Well-born memoirists of the resistance movement of 20 July 1944, whose leadership was one-third noble, followed a basically similar apologetic strategy in which they linked the activities of the "other Germany" to firm aristocratic values and thereby carefully elevated their origin from the so-called petit bourgeois masses of National Socialism.[50] In sum, the public autobiographical memory of the nobility in early postwar Germany was shaped mainly by contemporary political debates, while individual memory remained in the background.

Only in the late 1960s did the beginnings of a calm and in part also a critical treatment of the nobility's own past emerge, sustained by a generation that had still spent its early childhood in manors, but that had not filled any significant social or political functions before 1945 and that had experienced the loss of their *Heimat*—their homes, their homelands, their entire social, cultural, and physical universes—as an irreversible break.[51] In these accounts memory is the medium for a painful personal farewell—taken without any aggression—from the shattered *Lebenswelten* of the nobility. The excessive self-elevation and contempt for the masses of earlier autobiographers made way for a nostalgic tone, in which even modestly self-critical echoes have a place. Only now can we view the fascinating details of the nobility's rich culture and way of life, its *Lebenswelten,* which were attached so closely to nature and seemed so foreign to modernity's rules and conventions. Behind this shift in tone and approach lies a change in the dominant group of authors. The producers of nostalgic remembrance at the end of the twentieth century did not belong in the front row of power in either the *Kaiserreich* or the Third Reich. They usually are not in the middle but at the end of their lives, in which they have accomplished those tasks that the majority of German nobles after 1918 had refused to do, which was social and ideological integration into a democratic republic. Thus emerged instructive noble self-portraits, in which the nobility's world and everyday lives were given much more attention than the great affairs of state, which tried to explain the "misdevelopment" of recent German noble history through the description of their milieu from the inside.[52] With increasing temporal and mental distance grew the acceptance of the loss of land and of the pretensions to political leadership. Instead of reporting on heroic battles and revolutionary encounters, memory tended to concentrate on preserving its masters' lost childhood world from oblivion through descriptions of nature and landscapes.

Even the titles pointed to the displacements in the aims of noble remembrance. They no longer indicated military events and heroic figures, the search for truth, or evocations of decline; instead they registered private recollections of everyday human interaction and impressions of nature. The childless epigone Joachim von Winterfeld-Menkin's *Life's Seasons,* published already in 1942, flowed into the metaphorical "world-melancholy" of autumn, because of the author's knowledge of the foreseeable end to a family's history. The more characteristic autobiographies that appeared forty years later under programmatic titles such as *Marsh Marigolds and Lilacs, Leaves Scattered in the Wind* or *Only the Storks Remained* documented not only the collective experience of loss and irretrievability but a nostalgic attachment to what had been, although one that came without material claims of ownership.[53] Only now did the destructive and aggressive "memory-offensive" after 1918 give way, slowly but surely, to nostalgic memory as farewell.

The definitions of the memory of a lost world, the passing of which has been painful but complete, are clearly visible in the recollections that Maria von Maltzan, a countess from a family of the ancient Silesian nobility, published in 1986: "With every thread of my being, I hung on to [my family's property in] Militsch. I loved the land, the palace, and everything that went with it. Although in later years I often was offered the chance to see Militsch again, I abstained from doing so. I would rather carry my home in Silesia as an untouched memory deep in my heart."[54] The East Prussian Count Oswald von Finckenstein ends his memoirs in a similar manner. After reporting in detail on the disappearance of his noble social-emotional *Heimat,* he ends by demanding a final departure from the territorial homeland: "Release our children from this wistful hope for our homeland. It is lost, like our children, like the *rocher de bronze,* like the house, upon which we worked for nothing. We will not rest in the earth of our homeland. We will disappear in some dust."[55] Klaus von Bismarck, until 1945 a front officer in the *Wehrmacht* and later president of the Goethe Institut, ends his recollections with a description of a single pine, which "I planted in Pomerania by myself and which has withstood several tests in Poland." The "strong shoots" the tree has developed in a changed world symbolize for him the beginnings of a world to which he will no longer belong and from which he parted with the words: "I look back on a rich life, for which I have not only myself to thank."[56]

Count Hans von Lehndorff strikes a similar tone. At the end of his memoirs, this doctor from one of the most famous East Prussian noble families depicts a mystical connectedness with the lost worlds of his ancestors. But he does not make any claims or demands:

> When I walk with my sons through the park, which has become completely overgrown, but in which the oak-lined avenues planted almost four hundred years ago still exist, then I experience in myself a concentration of all those things which give the concepts of Prussia, *Heimat,* [and] family their content. The panels with the poems are no longer there, and several of the massive oaks look as though they would not survive the next storm. But memory still reconstructs what has been with ease. . . . In this place the centuries melt into one piece of eternity, that eternity in which they are secure and in good keeping, from which they have come and to which they shall return.[57]

Finally, Countess Marion Dönhoff calls the urban-industrialized surroundings of her Hamburg present "a paltry world." Yet here the memory of the splendid impressions of nature from her East Prussian youth also assumes nostalgic tones, which, however, explicitly reject "hatred against those who took possession of [our homeland]." The change from militant-aggressive memory to nostalgic-loving memory—a central theme in this essay—becomes explicit in Dönhoff's recollections. "When I think about the forests and lakes of East Prussia, of the broad meadows and old tree-lined avenues, then I am sure that they are still just as unforgettably beautiful as they were, when they were *Heimat* to me. Perhaps this is the highest degree of love: to love without possessing."[58] Despite an often arrogant undertone, in which the nobility's thousand-year-old conviction of its superiority continues to be perceptible, no trace remains of the offensive of memory on the present, which once had so clearly dominated nobles' autobiographical reports after World War I. Not until a half-century after the "great fall" has noble memory achieved that which noble mentalities and noble habitus had allowed only as exceptions in the aftermath of 1918 and 1945: nostalgic remembrance and loving farewell from a lost world.[59]

Since advanced industrial society has "overcome" this former world, together with its rules and ideals, once and for all, a refined form of retrospective memory should become possible not only for noble autobiographers but also for historians—a look backward that can calmly place the analysis of the anti-democratic aggression and destruction, which flowed from influential subgroups of the nobility after 1918, next to those elements of noble *Lebenswelten* that appear to us to be worth preserving, or at least worth remembering. From the perspective of our increasingly homogenized lifestyles in the present, such a look back definitely appears desirable. It appears to be worth using the nobility and its uniquely maintained treasure of memory as a valuable optical instrument with which to enlarge our image of the twentieth century to include important new facets, which are not always disagreeable. Next to arrogance, elitism, hatred of humankind, and hindrances to "progress," the sharpened and refined view of the products of memory introduced here should reveal something else: "a world we have lost," to use Peter Laslett's fine phrase.[60]

NOTES

1. Cf. Eric Mension-Rigau, *Aristocrates et grands bourgeois: éducation, traditions, valeurs* (Paris: Plon, 1994); and Monique de Saint-Martin, *L'espace de la noblesse* (Paris: Métailié, 1993).

2. The term was introduced by Heinz Reif, "Adeligkeit." See "Historische und elitentheoretische Überlegungen zum Adelshabitus in Deutschland um 1800," unpublished manuscript (Berlin, 1996), p. 5.

3. Letter by Werner von Alvensleben, 1931, in Landeshauptarchiv Magdeburg, Außenstelle Wernigerode (LHAM), Rep. H Neugattersleben, no. 225, fol. 441.

4. Pierre Nora, "Entre Mémoire et Histoire. La problématique des lieux," in Nora, ed., *Les lieux de mémoire,* vol. 1: *La République* (Paris: Gallimard, 1984), pp. xvii–xlii, here p. xvii.

5. Joachim von Winterfeld, *Jahreszeiten des Lebens. Das Buch meiner Erinnerungen* (Berlin: Propyläen, 1942), p. 325.

6. LHAM, Rep. H von Bülow, no. 52, fol. 1.

7. LHAM, Rep. H Stolberg-Wernigerode, O, L, no. 8, fols. 18–21. The play was written and performed by members of the princely family on the occasion of the silver jubilee of the prince's "reign." The prince and his sons organized a series of political conferences in the 1920s, for which nobles from all parts of Germany assembled at their majestic castle in the Harz mountains.

8. Alexis von Schönermarck, *Helden-Gedenkmappe des deutschen Adels* (Stuttgart: Petri, 1921); *Ehrentafel der Kriegsopfer des reichsdeutschen Adels 1914–1919* (Gotha: Perthes, 1921); and *Gedenkbuch des deutschen Adels (1939–1945),* ed. Matthias Graf Schmettow (Limburg: Starke, 1967). Cf. the internal lists of the families von Arnim and von der Marwitz in Brandenburgisches Landeshauptarchiv Potsdam (BLHA), Rep. 37 Boitzenburg, no. 3356, and Rep. 37 Friedersdorf, no. 259, fols. 105–20.

9. Rudolf von Gersdorff, *Soldat im Untergang* (Frankfurt: Ullstein, 1977), p. 38; and Ludwig Renn, *Adel im Untergang* ([East] Berlin: Aufbau Verlag, 1946), p. 27.

10. On bonding to past generations through specific noble *lieux de mémoire,* see for many others Helene von Nostitz, *Aus dem alten Europa. Menschen und Städte* (Berlin: K. Wolff, 1933), pp. 13f., 38f.; Wolfgang Edler Gans zu Putlitz, *Unterwegs in Deutschland* ([East] Berlin: Verlag der Nation, 1956), p. 17; Tilo Freiherr von Wilmowsky, *Rückblickend möchte ich sagen. . . . —An der Schwelle des 150jährigen Krupp-Jubiläums* (Oldenburg: Stalling, 1961), pp. 15, 23; Tisa von der Schulenburg, *Ich hab's gewagt. Bildhauerin und Ordensfrau—ein unkonventionelles Leben* (Freiburg: Herder, 1983), p. 26; Marion Gräfin Dönhoff, *Namen, die keiner mehr nennt* (Düsseldorf: Diederichs, 1963), pp. 17f.; Christian Graf von Krockow, *Die Reise nach Pommern. Bericht aus einem verschwiegenem Land* (Stuttgart: Deutsche Verlagsanstalt, 1985), p. 225; Ernst Heinrich Prinz von Sachsen, *Mein Lebensweg vom Königsschloß zum Bauernhof* (Munich: List, 1968), p. 225; Hedwig von Bismarck, *Erinnerungen einer 95jährigen* (Halle: Muehlmann, 1910), p. 209; Alexander Prinz von Hohenlohe, *Aus meinem Leben* (Frankfurt: Societäts-Druckerei, 1925), p. 241; Katrine von Hutten, *Im Luftschloß meines Vaters. Erzählung* (Zurich: Arche, 1983), p. 152; Maria Gräfin von Maltzan, *Schlage die Trommel und fürchte Dich nicht* (Berlin: Ullstein, 1986), pp. 10f., 176–78; and the very influential Udo von Alvensleben, *Adelssitze zwischen Altmark und Masuren. Besuche vor dem Untergang. Aus dem Tagebuch von Udo von Alvensleben,* ed. Harald von Königswald (Berlin: Ullstein, 1968), pp. 37f., 42–46, 87f.

11. Nora, "Entre mémoire et histoire," p. xix.

12. Ottfried Graf von Finckenstein, *Nur die Störche sind geblieben. Erinnerungen eines Ost-*

preußen (Munich: Langen Müller, 1994), p. 10; Dankwart von Arnim, *Als Brandenburg noch die Mark Hieß* (Berlin: Siedler, 1991).

13. Alois Fürst Löwenstein, Aufgaben des Adels in der Gegenwart, in "Adel," *Staatslexikon der Görres-Gesellschaft* (Freiburg: Herder, 1926), vol. 1, col. 44. During the Weimar period, this Bavarian prince was president of the most important catholic noble associations.

14. Marion Gräfin Dönhoff, *Kindheit in Ostpreußen* (Berlin: Siedler, 1988), p. 57.

15. Hellmut von Gerlach, *Von rechts nach links* (Zurich: Europa-Verlag, 1937), p. 33; Joachim von Dissow, *Adel im Übergang. Ein kritischer Standesgenosse berichtet aus Residenzen und Gutshäusern* (Stuttgart: Kohlhammer, 1961), pp. 109f.

16. Georg Simmel, "Exkurs über den Adel," in *Soziologie. Untersuchungen über die Formen der Vergesellschaftung* (Frankfurt: Suhrkamp, 1992), p. 824.

17. Maurice Halbwachs, *Das Gedächtnis und seine sozialen Bedingungen* (Frankfurt: Suhrkamp, 1985), p. 315.

18. Wilhelm Freiherr von Reitzensteins, 25 Oct. in Deutsches Adelsarchiv Marburg, DAG, Landesabteilung Bayern, vol. 2, "Protokolle." Cf. Paul von Hindenburg, *Aus meinem Leben* (Leipzig: Hirzel, 1934), pp. 4f.; Elard von Oldenburg-Januschau, *Erinnerungen* (Berlin: Koehler & Amelang, 1936), p. 14; Karl von Einem, *Erinnerungen eines Soldaten 1853–1933* (Leipzig: Koehler, 1933), p. 7; Paul Freiherr von Schoenaich, *Mein Damaskus. Erlebnisse und Bekenntnisse* (Berlin: Neue Gesellschaft, 1926), p. 13; Dietrich von Oppen, ed., *Lebensskizzen aus der Familie von Oppen vornehmlich im 20. Jahrhundert. Ein zeitgeschichtliches Lesebuch* (Freiburg: Herder, 1985), p. 151; Dissow, *Adel,* p. 20.

19. Simmel, "Exkurs über den Adel," p. 825.

20. Erinnerungen von Antonie Gräfin zu Eulenburg born Gräfin zu Stolberg-Wernigerode in Bundesarchiv Koblenz (BAK), Kl. Erw. no. 708, written in 1950/51, cit. fol. 118. On the noble understanding of the 1918 revolution see Erwein von Aretin, *Krone und Ketten. Erinnerungen eines bayerischen Edelmannes,* ed. Karl Buchheim and Karl Otmar von Aretin (Munich: Süddeutscher Verlag, 1955), p. 22; Hugo Freiherr von Freytag-Loringhoven, *Menschen und Dinge wie ich sie in meinem Leben sah* (Berlin: Mittler, 1923), pp. 193, 331; Charlotte Freifrau von Hadeln, *In Sonne und Sturm* (Rudolstadt: Verlag der Fürstlich privaten Hofdruckerei, 1935), pp. 182, 201; Wilhelm Kronprinz von Preußen, *Erinnerungen,* ed. Karl Rosner (Stuttgart: Cotta, 1922), p. 329f.; Werner Freiherr von Rheinbaben, *Kaiser, Kanzler, Präsidenten "wie ich sie erlebte"* (Mainz: Hase & Koehler, 1968), p. 164; Fedor von Zobeltitz, *Ich habe so gern gelebt. Die Lebenserinnerungen* (Berlin: Ullstein, 1934), p. 202; Karl Alexander von Müller, *Im Wandel einer Zeit. Erinnerungen,* vol. 3 (Munich: Süddeutscher Verlag, 1966), pp. 273, 286; Fritz-Günther von Tschirschky, *Erinnerungen eines Hochverräters* (Stuttgart: Deutsche Verlags-Anstalt, 1972), pp. 32, 37; Manfred Freiherr von Killinger, *Ernstes und Heiteres aus dem Putschleben* (Munich: Franz Eher Nachfahren, 1942), p. 13; Werner Otto von Hentig, *Mein Leben. Eine Dienstreise* (Göttingen: Vandenhoeck & Ruprecht, 1962), p. 208; Karl Anton Prinz Rohan, *Heimat Europa. Erinnerungen und Erfahrungen* (Düsseldorf: Diederichs, 1954), p. 46; Maria von Oertzen, *Mein Leben. Eine Selbstbiographie von M. von Oertzen* (Lahr-Dinglingen: St.-Johannis-Druckerei, 1935), p. 104. For many more see Marcus Funck and Stephan Malinowski, "Geschichte von oben: Autobiographien als Quelle einer Sozial- und Kulturgeschichte des deutschen Adels in Kaiserreich und Weimarer Republik," *Historische Anthropologie* 7 (1999): 263–70.

21. Iris Freifrau von Hoyningen-Huene, *Adel in der Weimarer Republik* (Limburg: Starke, 1992), pp. 17–20.

22. This was the title of one of the most important publications of the right-wing intelli-

gentsia in the 1920s: Edgar Julius Jung, *Die Herrschaft der Minderwertigen* (Berlin: Struckum: Verlag für ganzheitliche Forschung und Kultur, 1930).

23. Ernst Jünger, *Das abenteuerliche Herz* (1929; Stuttgart: Klett-Cotta, 1987), p. 131. Cf. Manfred Hettling and Stefan-Ludwig Hoffmann, "Der bürgerliche Wertehimmel. Zum Problem individueller Lebensführung im 19. Jahrhundert," *Geschichte und Gesellschaft* 23 (1997): 333–59, here pp. 352–59.

24. Reif, "Adeligkeit," p. 7. For the conception of "Adeligkeit," see Funck and Malinowski, "Geschichte von oben," pp. 245–47.

25. The term *Lebenswelt* (literally "lifeworld") denotes the more or less clearly perceived reality in which social groups and individuals act, which they reproduce in turn through their thoughts and actions. Cf. Rudolf Vierhaus, "Die Rekonstruktion historischer Lebenswelten. Probleme moderner Kulturgeschichtsschreibung," in *Göttinger Gespräche zur Geschichtswissenschaft,* vol. 1: *Wege zu einer neuen Kulturgeschichte,* ed. Hartmut Lehmann (Göttingen: Wallstein, 1995), pp. 7–28.

26. Kenneth D. Barkin, "Autobiography and History," *Societas: A Review of Social History* 6 (1976): 83–108, here p. 83.

27. Cf. our suggestions in Funck and Malinowski, "Geschichte von oben," pp. 236–47.

28. Georges Gusdorf, "Voraussetzungen und Grenzen der Autobiographie," in *Die Autobiographie. Zu Form und Geschichte einer literarischen Gattung,* ed. Günther Niggl (Darmstadt: Wissenschaftliche Buchgesellschaft, 1989), pp. 124–47, here p. 133.

29. Cf. John M. Fitzgerald, "Autobiographical Memory and Conceptualizations of the Self," in *Theoretical Perspectives on Autobiographical Memory,* ed. Martin Conway (Dordrecht: Kluwer Academic, 1992), pp. 99–114. The best historical treatment of this mechanism for the formation of bourgeois identity is Michael Maurer, *Die Biographie des Bürgers. Lebensformen und Denkformen in der formativen Phase des deutschen Bürgertums (1680–1815)* (Göttingen: Vandenhoeck & Ruprecht, 1996).

30. See, for example, Hedwig von Bismarck's memoirs of a 95-year-old, which do not make any claims although they reflect the author's increasing alienation from modern society. Short selections of typical memorabilia: *Unter den Hohenzollern. Denkwürdigkeiten aus dem Leben des Generals Oldwig von Natzmer,* ed. Genomar Ernst von Natzmer, 4 vols. (Gotha: Perthes, 1887–89); and S. M. Gräfin Voß, *Neunundsechzig Jahre am preußischen Hofe. Aus den Erinnerungen der Oberhofmeisterin* (Leipzig: Duncker & Humblot, 1876). A late climax of this form of immortalization of the self was reached with the vain memoirs by the former chancellor Bernhard von Bülow, *Denkwürdigkeiten,* 4 vols. (Berlin: Ullstein, 1929–31), and the memoirs commissioned by the Eulenburg family, *Aus 50 Jahren: Erinnerungen, Tagebücher und Briefe aus dem Nachlaß des Fürsten Philipp zu Eulenburg-Hertefeld,* ed. Johannes Haller (Berlin: Paetel, 1923).

31. Peter Sloterdijk, *Literatur und Organisation von Lebenserfahrung. Autobiographien der Zwanziger Jahre* (Munich: Hanser, 1978), p. 11. See also Barkin, "Autobiography and History," pp. 95f.

32. The term "reinvention" is borrowed from David Cannadine, "The Making of the British Upper Classes," in *Aspects of Aristocracy* (New Haven: Yale University Press 1994), pp. 9–36. This concept is also used in the impressive study about the French nobility in the nineteenth century by Claude-Isabelle Brelot, *La noblesse réinvintée. Nobles de Franche-Comté de 1814 à 1870,* 2 vols. (Paris: Diffusion Les Belles Lettres, 1992).

33. Dönhoff, *Namen,* p. 42.

34. We are referring to those two noble authors who decisively formed French conserva-

tism: Louis de Bonald, *Théorie du pouvoir politique et religieux* (1796; Paris: Blond & Barral, 1880); Joseph de Maistre, *Considérations sur la France* (1797; Paris: Vrin, 1936) and *Les soirées de Saint-Pétersbourg* (1821; Lyon: Vitte et Perrussel, 1886).

35. Peter Fritzsche, "Breakdown or Breakthrough? Conservatives and the November Revolution," in *Between Reform, Reaction and Resistance: Studies in the History of German Conservatism from 1789 to 1945,* ed. Larry Eugene Jones and James Retallack (Providence: Berg 1993), pp. 299–328.

36. Oldenburg-Januschau, *Erinnerungen,* p. 75.

37. Wilhelm II, *Ereignisse und Gestalten aus den Jahren 1878–1918* (Leipzig: K. F. Koehler, 1922); Wilhelm II, *Aus meinem Leben 1859–1888* (Leipzig: K. F. Koehler, 1927).

38. Wilhelm Kronprinz von Preußen, *Erinnerungen.* This "book of memories" was written by ghostwriters from the crown prince's inner circle and repeatedly revised in order to increase its political effect.

39. Hindenburg, *Leben;* Oldenburg-Januschau, *Erinnerungen;* Einem, *Erinnerungen.*

40. Bogislaw von Selchow, *Hundert Tage aus meinem Leben* (Leipzig: Koehler & Amelang, 1936), pp. 291–99.

41. Wilmowsky, *Rückblickend,* p. 89 ("riffraff in the navy"); Hadeln, *Sonne und Sturm,* p. 182 ("riffraff behind the lines"); Müller, *Wandel,* p. 286 ("port bordellos").

42. Fabian von Schlabrendorff, *Begegnungen in fünf Jahrzehnten* (Tübingen: Wunderlich, 1979), p. 23.

43. Oldenburg-Januschau, *Erinnerungen,* pp. 208f.

44. Sachsen, *Lebensweg,* pp. 116f.

45. Killinger, *Ernstes,* pp. 13f., 52f.

46. Aretin, *Krone,* p. 22; Rohan, *Heimat,* pp. 46, 49; Dissow, *Adel,* p. 108; Freytag-Loringhoven, *Menschen,* p. 193; Hadeln, *Sonne und Sturm,* pp. 21, 182f., 220f.; Hentig, *Mein Leben,* p. 208; Killinger, *Ernstes,* pp. 13–15; Wilhelm Kronprinz von Preußen, *Erinnerungen,* pp. 329f.; Müller, *Wandel,* pp. 273, 286; Nostitz, *Europa,* pp. 135f.; Oldenburg-Januschau, *Erinnerungen,* pp. 208f.; Oppen, *Lebensskizzen,* pp. 169–71; Putlitz, *Unterwegs,* p. 15; Rheinbaben, *Kaiser,* p. 164; Sachsen, *Lebensweg,* pp. 116–30; Edith Gräfin Salburg, *Erinnerungen einer Respektlosen* (Leipzig: Hammer, 1927), p. 22; Tschirschky, *Erinnerungen,* pp. 32, 36f.; Wilmowsky, *Rückblickend,* pp. 89f.; Winterfeld, *Jahreszeiten,* pp. 249f.; and the anecdotes throughout Walter Görlitz, *Die Junker. Adel und Bauer im deutschen Osten* (Lüneburg: Starke, 1981), e.g., p. 340.

47. Cf. Friedrich Gerstenberger, "Strategische Erinnerungen. Die Memoiren deutscher Offiziere," in *Vernichtungskrieg. Verbrechen der Wehrmacht 1941–1944,* ed. Hannes Heer and Klaus Naumann (Hamburg: Hamburger Edition, 1995), pp. 620–29.

48. Papen was frequently referred to as a Herrenreiter, because he was visibly a noble (Herr) who conspicuously owned and rode horses (Reiter).

49. Franz von Papen, *Der Wahrheit eine Gasse* (Munich: Paul List, 1952). See also Erich von Manstein, *Verlorene Siege* (Bonn: Athenäum, 1955); Erich von Manstein, *Aus einem Soldatenleben 1887–1939* (Bonn: Athenäum, 1958).

50. Cf. Gersdorff, *Soldat;* and Schlabrendorff, *Begegnungen.*

51. Albrecht Lehmann sees the acceptance of loss as the prerequisite for the new style of noble memoirs in recent times; see "'Grafenerzählungen': Gehobene Heimat- und Erinnerungsprosa für Bürger von heute," in *Medien popularer Kultur. Erzählung, Bild und Objekt in der volkskundlichen Forschung,* ed. Carola Lipp (Frankfurt a. M.: Campus, 1995), pp. 60–70, here p. 61.

52. The first and probably best work of this kind is Dissow, *Adel.*

53. Editha von Münchhausen, *Dotterblumen und blaue Lilien. Eine Kindheit im Spreewald* (Heilbronn: Salzer, 1987); Finckenstein, *Störche;* Krockow, *Bericht;* Klaus von Bismarck, *Aufbruch aus Pommern* (Munich: Piper, 1992); Hutten, *Luftschloß;* Mary Gräfin von Seckendorff-Aberdar, . . . *gelebt und gewebt im blauen Schloß* (Neustadt an der Aisch: Ph. C. W. Schmidt, 1979); Hans Graf von Lehndorff, *Menschen, Pferde, weites Land* (Munich: DTV, 1983); Camilla von Stackelberg, *Verwehte Blätter* (Berlin: Siedler, 1992); Heinrich Prinz von Hessen, *Der kristallene Lüster* (Munich: Piper, 1994); Clara von Arnim, *Der grüne Baum des Lebens* (Bern: Scherz, 1989).

54. Maltzan, *Schlage die Trommel* p. 223.

55. From the concluding passage in Finckenstein, *Störche,* p. 266.

56. Concluding passage and final sentence in K. Bismarck, *Aufbruch,* p. 334.

57. From the concluding passage in Lehndorff, *Menschen, Pferde, weites Land,* pp. 286f.

58. Last sentence in Dönhoff, *Kindheit,* pp. 221 ("love") and 210f. ("paltry"). Cf. for similar nostalgic farewells Krockow, *Bericht,* p. 255; Maltzan, *Schlage die Trommel,* pp. 176–82; and Hessen, *Lüster,* p. 313.

59. Besides the very rare democratic and Communist renegades these exceptions can only be found in authors who were closely associated with academic and artistic circles dominated by the bourgeoisie. See, e.g., Harry Graf von Kessler, *Gesichter und Zeiten. Erinnerungen* (Berlin: Fischer, 1962).

60. Peter Laslett, *The World We Have Lost: England before the Industrial Age* (London: Scribners, 1965).

PART 2

EVERYDAY LIFE

CHAPTER 5

Hildesheim in an Age of Pestilence: On the Birth, Death, and Resurrection of Normalcy

ANDREW STUART BERGERSON

> The *unusual* events described in this chronicle occurred in 19– at Oran. Everyone agreed that, considering their somewhat *extraordinary* character, they were out of place there. For its *ordinariness* is what strikes one first about the town of Oran.
>
> —Albert Camus, *The Plague,* 1947 (opening paragraph; my emphases)

> Neighborhood was something completely *normal.* You lived on a street where many people lived. You knew each of them, greeted them, chatted with them. As a child, I hardly thought seriously about it at all.
>
> —Lotte Schohl, a Hildesheimer, 1992 (my emphasis)

The Problem with Being "Ordinary"

In recent scholarship, it has become commonplace to refer to the perpetrators of the Holocaust as "ordinary Germans."[1] In his best-seller, *Hitler's Willing Executioners,* Daniel Jonah Goldhagen reduced the problem of personal responsibility for Nazi crimes against humanity to a population universally committed to "eliminationist anti-Semitism." Goldhagen's almost demonic intentionality resurrected an earlier rhetorical strategy that made normalcy an a priori condition of life in a modern civil society: in the postwar era, a comforting boundary had kept Germany's abnormal Third Reich categorically distinct from our allegedly normal societies. In this sense, Goldhagen relegated the Nazi's brown revolution back to its status as a temporary aberration of modernization.[2] Meanwhile oral interviews with ordinary Germans have convinced some historians that we need to take seriously the claim that life during the Third Reich remained quite normal, at least for some.[3] In a comparable move, other scholars have begun to consider seriously how the behavior patterns of ordinary Germans fit into the larger patterns of modernity.[4] The *Historikerstreit* of the 1980s concerned these issues in part—the normality or abnormality of the Third Reich and its place in German and European history.[5] Yet the dramatic success of Goldhagen's book in the 1990s suggests that many would still prefer not to reflect seriously on how a sense of normalcy is generated in modern societies and how that category of experience could draw self-styled ordinary men and women into systems of mass destruction.

Certainly the uniqueness of the Holocaust demands that historians closely scrutinize the behavior of ordinary Germans for evidence of collusion. Yet after considerable research over the past three decades into the question of participation and resistance, most historians have come to realize that we cannot draw simple distinctions between collaborators and resisters. Both elite and ordinary Germans demonstrated conformist and nonconformist behaviors vis-à-vis specific Nazi policies.[6] Rather than label individuals, it would be more productive to investigate everyday behaviors and their historical consequences. We can certainly sympathize with the desire to deny the normalcy of the Third Reich out of hand, fearing that any such normalization could in turn relativize Nazi crimes. Yet it would be more productive and more accurate to integrate a critical assessment of normalcy into our models for explaining the Nazi revolution. Instead of trying to resolve the paradox of whether the Third Reich was a normal or an abnormal society, we need to historicize normalcy as a category of experience produced in and through specific customs of everyday life.[7]

This essay will sketch a history of normalcy in the first half of the twentieth century. It treats normalcy as the by-product of struggles for power and identity in everyday life between and among elite and ordinary Germans. These subtle contests were expressed primarily in cultural terms, though culture here refers less to ideas (such as anti-Semitism) or aesthetic objects (such as paintings) and more to the daily habits that shape experience, interpret meaning, and communicate identities in the public sphere.[8] The cultural responses of ordinary men and women to existing systems of domination (*Herrschaft*) are fascinating from a human perspective: the recent shift toward cultural history and historical ethnography rides this wave of interest in forms of everyday resistance. Yet historians and anthropologists treat these acts of self-expressive revolt against conformity (of *Eigensinn*) as if they cannot fundamentally alter historical events and their underlying structures.[9]

This essay will show that eigensinn can and did result in revolution—a Nazi revolution. It will focus on that society that most challenges the normalcy of Western civilization, the Third Reich. It will show that one cause for the brown revolution lay in the way that self-styled ordinary Germans altered their behavior among friends and neighbors. In the early 1930s, National-Socialist enthusiasts altered the customs associated with conviviality (*Geselligkeit*) so that they corresponded to the policies and principles of the Third Reich. These fascist rebels worked proactively and in anticipation of Nazi policy in order to challenge the civil society on which the Weimar Republic was based, to transform it into a *Volksgemeinschaft* (a Nazi racist community) and to lay claims for personal status and power in that new order. Yet they simultaneously disguised this transformation of local custom behind a cultural facade of normalcy that insulated ordinary men and women from world history and politics.

In the 1990s, many ordinary Germans, even those who did not participate directly in genocide, could nonetheless remember how they or their neighbors had renegotiated the boundaries and qualities of their informal social relations, how they had adjusted their customs to fit Nazi principles. Self-styled ordinary Germans are plagued by these memories; they disrupt the postfascist sense of normalcy that characterized the 1950s. These memories remind them of their personal complicity in laying the everyday foundations for the Holocaust in their communities. As late as the 1990s, these memories still awaken in them that disturbing sense of cultural disjuncture that they first experienced when they or their neighbors nazified neighborly relations in the 1930s. This model for thinking critically about the everyday qualities of life during the Third Reich will thus provide new insight into two questions of long-standing concern to historians: the highly politicized debates about the origins and nature of the Nazi revolution as well as what made the Holocaust uniquely memorable in the postwar era.

I will spend much of this essay discussing conviviality in Hildesheim, a socially diverse, mid-sized, provincial town in north-central Germany. I selected Hildesheim as the site of my case study because it is representative of the German Reich in this era. My dissertation described in detail the many insights I gained about informal social relations from oral interviews with elderly Hildesheimers as well as textual and visual sources. This essay will place these historical facts about conviviality in Hildesheim into a different context: that of Albert Camus's *The Plague*, an existentialist novel of mass death in Oran.[10] By reading Hildesheim against Oran, I will show the conceptual error of reducing the problem of National Socialism to a presumed German national character. Camus's novel suggests that the disease of fascism lies dormant in all modern societies. The question then becomes how that pestilence is activated and propagated. Typically modern, the fascist plague spread to all kinds of communities throughout Europe as more and more individuals chose to adjust their convivial relations to fit its principles: to participate in it while imagining their distance from it. Still, historians should neither ignore the fact that this particular plague was first engineered in the German *Heimat*, for example, in provincial hometowns like Hildesheim, nor that the society engendered by this plague represents a particularly inhumane version of modernity, as per Peter Fritzsche: a *Nazi* modern.[11] So I will also read Camus's story of

Oran against my history of Hildesheim in order to highlight the realities of life in Hildesheim in an age of pestilence.

The Birth of Normalcy

The Plague is a fictitious firsthand account of everyday life in an era of mass death. It is set in the 1940s in Oran, a large port on the Algerian coast (then a part of France). Its inhabitants include Spanish, Italian, and French colonists as well as an indigenous population of Berbers, Arabs, and Jews.[12] They are all "at once so dull and happy," Camus writes. What keeps them in this state of casual and thoughtless tranquility is neither an authoritarian government nor a mass consumer regime; the Oranais created a sense of banality through their everyday customs. The most telling example of this dynamic is the "dapper little old man" with a military bearing who used to stand on his balcony everyday after lunch. While most Oranais stayed indoors enjoying the siesta, he would call sweetly to the street cats, enticing them to come closer by dropping scraps of white paper. Then, "taking careful aim, the old man would spit vigorously at the cats and, whenever a liquid missile hit the quarry, would beam with delight." Camus explained: "you can get through the days [in Oran] without trouble once you have formed habits. And since habits are precisely what our town encourages, all is for the best."[13] Then the plague came to Oran: first all the rats died, later the cats disappeared from the streets as well. "Hence the old boy's plight. His hair isn't as well brushed as usual, and he looks less alert, less military. You can see he is worried." The plague interfered with their accustomed ways. "Our townsfolk . . . had never dreamed it possible that our little town should be chosen out for the scene of such grotesque happenings . . . in broad daylight." Had it been a matter of a few deaths, "force of habit would doubtless have gained the day, as usual." But it was a matter of mass death.[14]

Plague disrupted the sense of normalcy in Oran. In response, the Oranais refigured mass death to fit into their myth of normalcy. In Camus's rendition, the plague came to Oran, as plagues always do: "disasters always come out of the blue." The plague was a strange, exogenous phenomenon: the Oranais never concerned themselves with the historical questions of where it came from and how it spread to Oran. This oversight derived partially from the fact that "the townsfolk were like everybody else, wrapped up in themselves." Still Camus believed that the root cause was ontological: "a pestilence isn't a thing made to man's measure; therefore we tell ourselves that pestilence is a mere bogey of the mind, a bad dream that will pass away." The plot never brings the reader outside of Oran, and once the plague arrived, the town is quarantined. An inhuman abstraction determines life and death rather than personal antagonists. By definition, this plague lies beyond the scope of the control, agency, and responsibility of ordinary Oranais. All they can do is respond to it, perhaps "rise above themselves" in the process, but more likely they simply try to survive it physically and ethically.[15]

Camus may not have intended *The Plague* as an allegory for life during World War II and pestilence as a direct metaphor for National Socialism. More likely, his book was intended as a measure of the modern human condition writ large, as he wrote in the first pages: "It will be said, no doubt, that these habits are not peculiar to our town; really all our contemporaries are the same."[16] Still, Camus wrote *The Plague* while living in territories either occupied by the Nazi regime or controlled by Nazi collaborators (in biographical order: Vichy-controlled Algeria, Vichy France, occupied France). Clearly, Camus's measure of the modern human condition was influenced heavily by the kind of world that the Nazis had created. As a result, Camus was not simply addressing the problem of a mass society, as is often the case for existentialist writers. He was focusing on particular elements within the Nazi style of modernity: heartrending individual struggles of innocents (like the Othon boy) against an abstract yet gruesome process of murder, that "same thing [death] over and over and over again," with "the selfsame suffering going on and on," a "social order" based on "the death sentence." Camus even placed mass graves, concentration camps, and crematoria into plague-ridden Oran.[17] Consciously or not, *The Plague* represents Camus's confrontation with the mass death that conditioned life in Nazi-occupied Europe.

Interwar Hildesheim was much like Oran: what Camus depicted as banality Hildesheimers experienced as conviviality. In the 1920s, Hildesheimers of different classes, confessions, genders, generations, ethnicities, political opinions, even sexual proclivities and mental faculties lived next to one another in its neighborhoods. In spite of these social differences, they regarded each other perhaps as friends, colleagues, or comrades but always at the very least as neighbors and locals. A wide variety of customs laid a foundation of civility for these relationships: defining how one greeted and whom one knew, how one narrated the locality, its character and its boundaries, how one perceived its art and architecture, how resources and knowledge were exchanged and distributed, and even how one treated foreign guests, from tourists to national statesmen, seasonal laborers to vagabonds. These habits of conviviality enabled interwar Hildesheimers to preserve familial and communal respectability and status while they also figuratively excluded certain neighbors from their neighborhood. Consider salutations as one example.[18] Hildesheimers were able to greet neighbors in different ways (some with more intimacy, others with less) in order to lay claim to status and express their identity in the local public sphere. Yet proper Hildesheimers were obliged to greet all neighbors at least in some minimal way. Whether or not neighbors had anything further to do with each other was a matter left open for individual negotiation, but at the very least, interwar Hildesheimers recognized their neighbors as legitimate members of their local community.

To be sure, there was considerable hostility in interwar Hildesheim between the classes, confessions, ethnicities, and so on. Originating in imperial Germany, these social cleavages widened by the 1920s and were reinforced by an elaborate structure of competing institutions (including clubs, newspapers, schools, and political parties). In a provincial town like Hildesheim, however, the members of these divergent milieux tended to live in the same neighborhoods, shop in the same stores, stroll in the same parks. The fact was that people who sought little formal contact with one another faced the reality of extensive informal contact. Herein lies the tactical significance of conviviality. Interwar Hildesheimers used informal habits of neighborliness to reinforce formal distinctions that might not otherwise have been so obvious in the neighborhood. Customs of conviviality enabled them to differentiate themselves from those neighbors with whom they did not want to be associated. These same customs also ensured a fair distribution of material and symbolic resources in the neighborhood (in cultural if not in actual terms) and a minimum of mutual respect. The customs of conviviality should not be romanticized as purely benign influences in daily life; nonetheless they did ensure the civility of this civil society.

The challenge then became how to disguise the contradictions inherent in this everyday process of identity formation. In the case of greeting, one was supposed to greet everyone, yet it was perfectly obvious that one greeted some neighbors differently than others in order to distinguish oneself from people beneath one's station (real or imagined). Herein lies the tactical significance of normalcy. Hildesheimers promoted the fantasy that their neighborhoods were insulated from the conflicts that plagued the formal institutions of German political culture, as if that community stood apart from the barbaric, threatening, alienating, modernizing society beyond its walls. Evoked through conviviality, *Alt-Hildesheim* was a social imaginary characterized by historical and cultural monumentality. It was surreal in that it did not correspond to Hildesheim's social realities but to their dreamlike fantasies. Interwar Hildesheimers invented a sense of tradition, insularity, security, and respectability in an era of turbulent change. Alt-Hildesheim constituted a provincial heimat, happily isolated from the grand yet disruptive flow of history, its modern conflicts, its incessant modernization. Said in another way: through rituals of conviviality, interwar Hildesheimers imagined themselves and their town to be quite ordinary.[19]

I understand normalcy to refer to the naturalized notion that there are two distinct realms of human activity: a *system* and a *lifeworld.* When ordinary Germans complained with eigensinn about "them up there" (*die da oben*), they distinguished between, on the one hand, a set of abstract historical events and processes dominated by an elite over which they had no influence and, on the other, a pragmatic yet strictly bounded reality which they could influence directly.[20] In modern Central Europe, formal political institutions had become stalemated by unworkable majorities and antidemocratic forces, and in spite of democratic constitutions, they seemed impregnable to effective influence by individual constituents. Germans turned increasingly to the informal realm of everyday life as an alternate sphere for the conduct of politics. The elite could dominate there without risking political capital by naturalizing their principles in the lifeworld, and rebels could tweak the nose of the elite without fear of retribution by enacting their revolts in the lifeworld. Though vastly different in technique and unequal in power, both conspired to conduct these contests as if they were insignificant.

The by-product of this struggle to colonize everyday life was therefore a culture of normalcy,[21] characterized by a paradoxical duality: the reality that everyday life had become a primary realm in which one laid claim to and contested power, status, and meaning, combined with the fantasy that everyday life was a realm immune from politics, conflict, and historicity. As such, normalcy represents one of the "great divides" of modernity.[22] National Socialism became revolutionary in effect when the Nazis focused the dynamic, typically modern tension between system and lifeworld on radical change. Yet rather than in the Nazi elite, my interest here lies more in the part played by self-styled ordinary Germans in the construction of normalcy because I wish to show that the brown revolution *also* emerged from below, disguised behind the normalcy of everyday life. In the case of the Nazi modern, the overriding significance of this imagined distinction lies in the comfort gained from it: that agents acting in their lifeworld were not personally responsible for events or dynamics of the system.

In Hildesheim, among other places, this sense of normalcy was born when the imposing and hierarchical amalgam of bourgeois and feudal forms that supported the empires of Central Europe dissolved into chaos. While the processes of industrialization, rationalization, and civilization had increasingly alienated individual agency from outcomes, nineteenth-century Europeans of almost all political allegiances sported an historical imaginary that allowed them to link the events of their personal biographies, affirmatively or negatively, to the new historicity of their nations, classes, races, genders, and so on.[23] Rather than giving meaning to the everyday activities of individuals, this core element of the nineteenth-century sense of self threatened their survival in the early decades of the twentieth. It was precisely one's enthusiasm for and involvement in world-historical events like the Great War of 1914 to 1918 that seemed to endanger one's future. These "hard times" included not only momentous political, economic, and social crises but also a cosmological uncertainty that continued well after these formal systems stabilized themselves somewhat in 1924. As Peter Fritzsche has argued, the sequence of rapid-fire crises that began in 1914 invalidated "the grand narrative of 'History' as it had been developed over the course of the nineteenth century." In its place, Central Europeans not only experienced a continual "state of emergency" but also exploited the opportunity to manage that chaos and contingency through innovation, a contradiction typical of modernity. To survive this extended crisis of meaning, many Hildesheimers simply severed the conceptual connection between their lifeworld and those larger systems: one imagined a "return" to normalcy.[24]

To re-create a sense of stability in their lives in the absence of stable formal institutions, interwar Hildesheimers turned to one aspect of prewar experience that they could still control directly: the rituals of informal social relationships.

Conviviality now supported what the system formerly secured. Through neighborly exchange relations, Hildesheimers ensured a fair distribution of resources. Through greetings, they created a sense of community; through selective familiarity, hierarchies of social status. Storytelling and selective modes of perception restored a sense of civility, culture, and history to their hometown in contrast to "barbarian" hinterlands beyond its imaginary walls. They reestablished a sense of continuity for their political system through the local adoration of great men; yet through selective reading patterns and carefully orchestrated parades, they constituted a locality distinct from the outside world. Hildesheimers of all social positions reinvigorated a tradition of conviviality that reasserted their sense of self-reliance, self-respect, insularity, and control over their lived reality by exiling (culturally) all evidence of conflict and change that threatened civil harmony and disturbed their social imaginary. Though some of these customs could trace medieval ancestry, interwar Hildesheimers altered them in subtle ways, giving conviviality a new centrality in everyday life. These invented traditions filled the cultural void left by the suicide of the old regime: conviviality created a sense of normalcy in Alt-Hildesheim.

The Uses of Normalcy

Normalcy in turn engendered that which would ultimately undermine it. Customs of conviviality stood outside the rigid control mechanisms to which formal institutions were typically restricted. Even ordinary Hildesheimers could renegotiate power relations and status hierarchies by altering the style of their interaction with friends and neighbors. Consider the example of how Hildesheimers interacted with their architectural monuments.

It was customary in interwar Hildesheim for parents to take their children on walks around town to instruct them on the cultural and historical significance of their local art and architecture. Children learned to see within modernizing Hildesheim that surreal, premodern cityscape of historical and cultural value called Alt-Hildesheim. One monument that "belonged" to Alt-Hildesheim was the Kaiserhaus, so named because of its Renaissance facade adorned with medallion reliefs of the Roman emperors. Toward the end of the Great War, the younger generation of Hildesheimers began to spit on the medallion of Nero—so often that it has been captured in photos, with Nero's face covered in a damp darkness.[25] It is not exactly clear why they did so: was this a Catholic criticism of Nero since he was known to be a torturer of Christians? a way to mock the cultivated pretensions of their parents? an anti-Semitic slur against Nero who, some Hildesheimers incorrectly believed, had been Jewish? Or was this simply target practice in a militarized society, akin to the behavior of the "small-game hunter" of Oran? Most likely, young Hildesheimers spat on Nero for a variety or combination of different reasons. In all cases, however, spitting on Nero was an act of eigensinn: they were expressing themselves and laying claim to power and status in their lifeworld by altering their habits of conviviality.

These meanings were not lost on older Hildesheimers, who felt that the younger generation was desecrating the Kaiserhaus. They complained about the immoral habits of youth, a trope of intergenerational tension particularly characteristic of the modern era. Yet my informants dismissed these acts as the normal pranks of youth (*Jugendstreiche*). After all, spitting on Nero still proved that these young boys and girls had learned to see the monuments of Alt-Hildesheim for their cultural and historical significance. Taken together, the damp darkness on the facade of the Kaiserhaus illustrates that Hildesheimers were good modernists: they had learned to manage the chaos of the 1920s through cultural innovation, allowing for power struggles in everyday life while preserving their sense of normalcy. By using informal cultural mechanisms to express a variety of opinions from the mundane to the violent, Hildesheimers shifted the boundaries of the political. As seen in the possible hint of anti-Semitism in this prank, conviviality offered a normatively apolitical and ahistorical medium through which self-styled ordinary Hildesheimers could introduce revolutionary claims for the reorganization of their lifeworld without bearing personal responsibility for them.

The political implications of eigensinn can be seen more clearly in a second example. Günther Seidner (n.b., I have used pseudonyms for the names of my interview partners) explained that when *Gymnasium* students became upperclassmen, they went to a *Kneipe* and had a beer with their teachers to celebrate. Günther experienced this initiation into adulthood in 1930, the year in which the Nazi party's popularity grew dramatically in Hildesheim and throughout Germany. In the photo taken to commemorate the occasion, Günther showed me that two of his classmates, both convinced National Socialists, had taken the opportunity to raise their arms in the Hitler greeting. "This was quite typical. They wanted to make an example, so you could see. They were only individuals in 1930, still just a few individuals. He [one of the boys] just felt he had to express his political convictions at this visit to the pub by showing the fascist greeting."[26] The overriding purpose of a greeting had been to erase social differences between neighbors, especially those, that could lead to conflict, such as politics. This integrative function was reinforced by the norm that proper Hildesheimers must greet all neighbors at least in some minimal way. Yet salutations were dynamic and flexible in practice: one could hide the self-expressive implications of greeting behind the normalcy of its ritual repetition. With a gesture, these boys from Günther's class challenged the legitimacy of the Weimar Republic and laid claim to status and power in a proposed new order. Still, Günther recounted this memory dismissively, as if it were simply the normal pranks of youth. Thanks to the sense of normalcy associated with conviviality, these boys could promote the brown revolution and still remain "ordinary" Hildesheimers.

These seemingly insignificant acts of eigensinn held even more radical implications after the Nazi seizure of power in 1933. In prior decades, it had been customary in Hildesheim to announce life-cycle events in the local pages of the daily paper. Such announcements were one way for Hildesheimers to imagine a locality distinct from the trials and tribulations of the outside world: the latter events appeared on the front page of their daily papers in a very different narrative style. Beginning in the Great War, Hildesheimers used these life-cycle announcements as an indirect means to announce their political persuasions in the local public sphere. Bereaved families competed to show their persistent patriotic support for the war and sacrifice for the Fatherland by printing increasingly large announcements of the loss of a husband and son.[27] A similar dynamic took place during the Third Reich. In 1933, Dora Pröbst (a Protestant woman) and Erich (a Jewish man) wanted to get married. Since "interracial" marriage was taboo according to Nazi principles, they eloped to England and tried to disguise their union after they returned by living in separate homes. Several months later, Dora began to "show" that she was pregnant. So, she did what women had "always" done in Hildesheim: she announced her new status in the daily paper. Yet, her announcement was published not as it would have appeared for an Aryan couple, as one small entry among many others. The publisher drew particular attention to Dora's so-called *Rassenschande* (betrayal of her race) with a half-page announcement. "The publisher had a lot of fun," Dora concluded with self-mockery.[28] By simply changing its size, the publisher infused a local news item with political principles from the front page. He used this seemingly ordinary circumstance to express his support for Nazi ideology, to pressure his neighbors to adjust informal social relations to fit Nazi ideological premises, and to lay claim to status and power in that new world order. Clearly this act of cultural innovation was much more than just a mean prank: it helped transform Hildesheim from a civil society based on the equality of human dignity into a volksgemeinschaft based on essential racial hierarchies.

In Camus's Oran, there was no person to blame for the plague, only an abstraction. Similarly, historians traditionally credited Hitler's terror state with creating the volksgemeinschaft, though they now recognize that this process comprised both the seizure and the consolidation of power by the Nazi regime over the course of the 1930s. Yet the process of coordination (*Gleichschaltung*) was never just a matter of seizing control of the formal institutions of politics, economics, and society; the Nazis aspired to penetrate far deeper. The Nazi volksgemeinschaft required a revolution in the informal customs of everyday life. Over the course of the 1930s, ordinary Germans introduced Nazi principles in their local public sphere through a symbolic discourse conducted in greetings, flags, and uniforms. This semiotic dialogue among friends and neighbors challenged all "Aryans" to participate and all "degenerates" to exile themselves, or face retribution.[29] In Hildesheim, high-school boys openly challenged Günther to collaborate before the formal seizure of power in 1933; the publisher of this daily newspaper publicly branded Dora before the Nuremberg Laws made miscegenation illegal in 1935. The fact that both pranks were then dismissed as normal, even by their "victims," only reinforces the conclusion that these pranks succeeded in recalibrating conviviality according to new standards of barbarity behind a veil of normalcy. We should not reduce this informal process of coordination solely to the pressures, legal or extralegal, exerted on so-called ordinary Germans by the Nazi regime. As the chronology above suggests, Hildesheimers were conscious of changes in the system but acted in the lifeworld relatively independent of them. It was sufficient for these Hildesheimers to know the Führer's will to adjust their behavior to it. In keeping with the polycratic structure of the Nazi state, the realization of Nazi racial politics in Hildesheim could be left to relatively free agents staking claims and competing for power and status in the new world order.

The Propagation of the Plague

Still, these events were unsettling. In Oran, the moment when the cats disappeared so disturbed the "ancient small-game hunter" that his long years of military composure collapsed. Each day he went out onto his balcony at the usual hour and waited; he tapped his right hand on the balustrade and waited; he tore up some sheets of paper and waited. No cats appeared. Finally he retreated back into his room, slamming the French windows behind him. Each day for the rest of the week he did the same thing, growing all the more sad and bewildered. "On the eighth day," Camus writes, "the windows stayed resolutely closed."[30] The absence of cats was hardly remarkable in an objective sense: the small-game hunter noticed it only because it forced him to deviate from the banally violent habit that gave him a sense of eigensinn and normalcy. Still it was the absence of cats that forced him to recognize the propagation of the plague. National Socialism spread in Hildesheim in much the same way. The first signs of disease (e.g., a new greeting) could be dismissed as a prank or nuisance. Yet such acts of informal coordination changed the experience of social life from integration to alienation.

In Oran, "the first thing that plague brought to our town was exile. . . . In this extremity of solitude none could count on any help from his neighbor; each had to bear the load of his troubles alone. . . . The attempt to communicate had to be given up." Like the plague itself, this growing sense of alienation seemed to come from beyond the town walls, imposed on Oran with the quarantine. Yet closer inspection suggests that conviviality also collapsed from within because the Oranais changed their habits of neighborliness. "Ordinary people living in these districts used to spend the best part of the day on their doorsteps, but now every door was shut, nobody was to be seen, even the venetian blinds stayed down, and there was no knowing if it was the heat or the plague that they were trying to shut out." Eventually plague even destroyed friendships and romances. "By the end of their long sundering they had also lost the power of imagining the intimacy that once was theirs or understanding what it can be to live with someone whose life is wrapped up in yours."[31] In a time of plague, conviviality dissolved into anomie.

Historians have long debated the nature of social relations during the Third Reich. Over the years, they have interpreted the presumed sense of alienation in various ways: as the direct result of Hitler's totalitarianism, as the indirect result of pervasive denunciations by friends and neighbors, or as part of a transhistorical modernization process from a traditional community to a modern society. I view the problem differently: in both a civil and a *völkisch* society, the experiences of alienation and integration existed when the inhabitants of a particular neighborhood chose to create them. Both were mediated by customs of conviviality that stood within the scope of the control of ordinary Germans. Yet alienation and integration must be communicated interpersonally through symbolic acts that held meaning for both parties: that is, through their shared culture. Therefore, Hildesheimers experienced a sense of integration in moments of cultural conjuncture: when convivial behavior in the present corresponded to expectations based on prior experiences and transmitted through habit memories. Alienation emerged in moments of cultural disjuncture: when there was dissonance between past memory and present experience, either due to a shift in custom or a change in circumstance.[32] This dissonance usually surprised Hildesheimers not only because of the complacency of habit but also because of the myths of normalcy. Moreover, the chronology of alienation varied from person to person depending on circumstances as well as on their sociological, political, and moral nature. Still, this sense of exile grew rampant in Hildesheim in the 1930s as increasingly more Hildesheimers adjusted their conviviality to fit Nazi principles.

Consider three stories.[33] Radios were "very, very rare" in Franz Meissner's lifeworld: his family and friends did not own or use such luxury items. Still, when he walked down the street he listened to the radio from loudspeakers in front of store windows. This practice had been common in Hildesheim in the 1920s: broadcasting one's radio so that neighbors could hear was one way to take part in the lives of neighbors (*Anteil nehmen*), reinforce existing bonds of reciprocity, and ensure what Hildesheimers believed was a fair distribution of limited resources. Starting in the mid-1930s, however, store owners in the center of town made a point of broadcasting Hitler's speeches from their radios: "You could hear it from the restaurants, coffee houses." This decision was certainly in keeping with the principles and methods of Nazi propaganda, organized and propagated by Goebbels through the Reichskulturkammer, but there was no law requiring the public broadcasting of Hitler's speeches at this time. These store and restaurant owners chose proactively to alter the atmosphere of the local public sphere at the center of town, and they hid their Nazi politics behind the normalcy of sharing expensive resources with neighbors. Being Jewish, Franz responded in turn. He walked past these stores and "heard dogs barking." This adjustment in the nature of his reception from attentive listening to background noise was not simply the product of totalitarianism. These store owners were also doing their part to change *neighbors* into *Aryans* and *Jews.* It is perfectly understandable that Franz then revolted (with eigensinn) against the aryanization of conviviality by adopting the alienated listening habits of a mass society. This subtle act of inner migration in turn prepared Franz for his road to actual exile: he left for Palestine in the summer of 1936 at the age of fifteen, never to return.

At the core of Dora's story was a similar experience of disjuncture and exile. At first, she and Erich both stubbornly refused to recognize the anti-Semitism of their community. As the Nazis gained influence in town, they spent more time together with their good friends Gerdl and Ulrich Ossenkopp. These friendships helped to insulate Dora and Erich, keeping them from recognizing how many of their fellow Hildesheimers were joining the Nazi party. Then Ulrich joined the Nazi party. Dora knew that he was a Nazi by convenience not conviction, that he joined the party to keep his government job. Every time she ran into him on the street and greeted him, he tried to hide his new swastika insignia by slipping it under his lapel before she could see. The more she caught him doing this, however, the more distressed she felt. She said nothing to him: she did not want to place him in the awkward situation of having to choose between his job and his friends. More to the point, she did not want to admit to herself that Hildesheim was becoming a volksgemeinschaft. Dora then made a significant decision: she walked on the other side of the street. She pretended not to see Ulrich, so that he did not have to hide his insignia, and so that she did not have to greet him at all. And once she had alienated herself from her friends in this way, it was easy for Dora to choose her husband over her heimat: she convinced him to emigrate with her to the United States.

The third example follows a series of events that began in 1937 when Gerhard Mock met a stately tourist couple, the Diltheys, on the street. In true Hildesheim form, he offered to take them on a tour of town so that they could learn to see Alt-Hildesheim as he had: as a welcoming heimat of historical and cultural monumentality. They tested each other in order to determine their relation to the Nazi regime, a conversation spoken in codes. They all disclosed their antifascist postures, but Gerhard did not reveal that he was (half) Jewish, and when the tour was over he felt that something had been left unresolved. What he felt was not so much his Jewishness per se as his alienation from his heimat on that account, a strange new dissonance in conviviality. Instead of producing the sense of integration that Gerhard expected, giving a tour of his town to strangers forced him to realize that he was becoming estranged from his neighbors. His new identity (as of yet unnamed) threatened to break out of the "closet" again when he visited his new friends at their home in a Berlin suburb. The exchange of visits pressured him to reveal what he did not want to admit, but once again he left their company without making any disclosures. Only when he returned to his heimat was he then able to compose a letter to the Diltheys in which he "came out" to them and to himself.[34] He labeled himself "a German in the other sense," by which he meant a Jew in Nazi Germany who must flee the home he loved.

In each of these three accounts, my interview partner described initiating a ritual of conviviality on the basis of habit memory in which they anticipated feeling integrated and insulated into their heimat. Yet a change had taken place either in behavior (for Franz), circumstances (for Gerhard), or both (for Dora). The resulting dissonance between expectation and experience forced them to recognize their alienation. The choice to remove physically the offending element (themselves) could follow quite reasonably. Here it is important to recognize that even after they recalibrated their informal social relations to fit the Nazi principles, these Hildesheimers acted as if these matters were still just as ordinary as spitting on Nero. Only with great reluctance were they willing to recognize the full implications of this disjuncture. They redefined themselves as émigrés and exiled themselves from Hildesheim in part as a way to preserve their fantasy of Alt-Hildesheim and the integrity of their local customs of conviviality. No wonder, then, that the Third Reich could seem so normal to some and so abnormal to others. Gerhard, Dora, and Franz felt like they had been swept up into the tides of history, but most of their neighbors continued to act as if they were still just ordinary Hildesheimers. The myths of normalcy were that addictive.

The transformation of Hildesheim from a civil society to a volksgemeinschaft hinged on these early Nazi enthusiasts who transposed the formal principles of the Nazi movement into the informal realm of friendship and neighborliness. When they acted, they knew that the power of the movement stood behind them; and after 1933, what had been acts of nonconformity to the Weimar Republic now became conformity to a radically violent regime. Nonetheless, these Hildesheimers acted with relative independence from the Nazi regime. The result was a Nazi seizure of power in both the system and the lifeworld, effectively aryanizing not only of the institutions of German government, economy, society, and culture but also the semiautonomous world of friendship and neighborliness. Ordinary Hildesheimers thus played a critical role in the propagation of the Nazi plague.

The Death of Normalcy

In Oran, "the word 'plague' had been uttered; true, at this very moment one or two victims were being seized and laid low by the disease. Still, that could stop, or be stopped. It was only a matter of lucidly recognizing what had to be recognized; of dispelling extraneous shadows and doing what needed to be done." Camus defined that strategy pragmatically: "when abstraction sets to kill you, you've got to get busy with it." Unfortunately, most Oranais preferred living with shadows. They did not "call this disease by its name." They avoided "taking an alarmist view." They adopted a "wait-and-see attitude." They insisted on Oran's normalcy. "Plague was for them an unwelcomed visitant, bound to take its leave one day as unexpectedly as it had come." Self-interest reinforced normalcy's resilience. In Oran, the criminal Cottard benefited from the plague because it distracted attention from his arrest. The typical collaborator, he was content to live in the midst of mass death because his social circumstances improved and he was integrated into society through the common experience of pestilence.[35]

In Hildesheim, a wide variety of nonconformist responses emerged to challenge the new volksgemeinschaft. For instance, in response to broadcasting Hitler's speeches from storefront windows, some Hildesheimers chose to listen to foreign stations in the privacy of their home, if necessary with the receiver to their ear and under several pillows in bed in order to avoid detection. When greeted with "Heil Hitler," some courageous Hildesheimers replied with a resolute "Guten Tag," or sneezed, or only raised their hands "so high": that is, not very high at all. Like the profascist declarations analyzed above, these antifascist demonstrations may have expressed deeply held political beliefs or simply a querulous personality. Yet in all cases, such acts of revolt entailed significant risk on the part of the performer because the officers of the Nazi state punished such public expressions of defiance with violence and because Nazi neighbors responded to deviance with denunciation. In effect, early Nazi enthusiasts had initiated an informal debate in the local public sphere that was expressed in terms of competing styles of conviviality. Hildesheimers of all political persuasions redefined their identities, measuring themselves and each other according to the degree to which each act demonstrated that one participated, or refused to participate, in the new volksgemeinschaft. Because conviviality became a matter of public contention, acts of both conformity and nonconformity helped tear down the imaginary walls that protected Hildesheimers from history, politics, and barbarism. From a purely analytic perspective, then, the recalibration of conviviality to fit both fascist and antifascist purposes contributed to the death of normalcy.

Hildesheimers struggled to find a "third way" in a cultural field polarized into pro- and antifascist styles of conviviality. Threatened by the plague, some quarantined themselves: they simply waited until Hitler was "gone from the table" (*weg vom Tisch*), preserving their sense of normalcy by exiling themselves into an even more intimate lifeworld into which the Nazi system had not yet penetrated. This choice was self-delusional and harmful to others: it exaggerated the already surreal quality of informal social relations in Alt-Hildesheim and created an atmosphere in which the Nazi regime could implement its violent policies against local Jews without public outcry. Others "got busy" dealing with the plague: Franz, Dora, and Gerhard emigrated physically. This choice was eminently rational: it attempted to preserve the health of older customs in the face of corruption through self-sacrifice. Unfortunately this choice also helped facilitate the exclusion of Jews from German society. As Zygmunt Bauman argued, the Nazi regime "solicited the aid of its victims" by intentionally creating circumstances in which rational choices would lead ordinary Jews, as well as ordinary Germans, to help the regime achieve its solutions to the "Jewish Question." The evidence from Hildesheim suggests that ordinary Hildesheimers created an analogous circumstance in everyday life: individuals were faced with seemingly rational choices that ensured temporary survival but nonetheless helped the Nazis reorganize informal social life in racist-fascist terms. Arguably, it was this quality of everyday life to which Camus's character Tarrou was alluding when he said: "Each of us has the plague within him; no one, no one on earth is free from it."[36]

Because they came to terms with the Nazi plague in the context of their own customs, these Hildesheimers could take reasonable steps to cope with and even fight against it. Before he met the Diltheys, Gerhard had volunteered for the German army to prove that Jews were also loyal German citizens; thanks to his encounters with the Diltheys, Gerhard was able to adjust his identity enough that soon after he arrived in the United States he could become an officer in the U.S. army with no conflict of conscience. Yet most Hildesheimers (even many Jews) piously defended normalcy in spite of fascist realities. For instance, Jürgen Lüdewig recounted the filming of a movie in Alt-Hildesheim in 1938. To stage the historical fiction *An Immortal Heart* with Hildesheim as its backdrop, Veit Harlan had to erase all evidence of modern Hildesheim. Avidly watching this process, Jürgen could see his town being transformed into what he had always imagined it to be: a premodern community of historical and cultural monumentality. This surreal way of seeing had been typical of the interwar years for both the tourist and the local: the process of moviemaking merely reinforced existing traditions. Yet cinematic magic also served a new purpose in the months before the so-called Night of Broken Glass: Jürgen could hide the reality of fascist violence behind the surreal fantasy of Alt-Hildesheim, now mechanically reproduced.

Widow Ohlendorf, who lived in the twin house to Gerhard's, was far more direct. Her daughter had been such close friends with Gerhard's younger sister that they used to crawl through a hole in the fence between the two gardens to play. "And then the Nazis came and much changed." The older Ohlendorf daughter had married a man who became the mayor of a nearby spa town after 1933. Because of her status in the new volksgemeinschaft, "Mrs. Ohlendorf did not seem to know us anymore." She no longer greeted or spoke to the Mock family. Like Dora and Ulrich, the Mocks and the Ohlendorfs tried not to catch each other's attention on the street. "You just walked past each other." Such habits are violent, even if only in a social and cultural sense: the Ohlendorfs made their Jewish neighbors "irrelevant" in their lifeworld.[37] Yet precisely because these aryanized customs of conviviality made living in the Third Reich more agreeable, it became easier to repeat than to revise them, and like an addiction, the reiteration of symbolic violence could be exaggerated as physical violence, particularly if one wished to reinforce the righteousness of the original decision.[38]

The schema of anti-Semitism existed for millennia throughout Europe, yet the crucial turning point in the biography of ordinary Germans (Jewish and

Gentile) took place when some of them began to enact that schema for violence symbolically in terms of friends and neighbors. Just as the Jews of Hildesheim could escape their fate only by recognizing their new identities within the context of a disjuncture in their own culture, the Gentiles of Hildesheimers transformed themselves into potential murderers of Jews by enacting anti-Semitism within their own heimat in terms of their own culture. Of course, one cannot argue that these first small steps of symbolic violence directly caused the Holocaust: the death camps, the mobile killing squads. There were many moments when individuals could have opted to break their addiction to Nazi barbarism and many independent factors (propaganda, charisma, polycracy, war, and so on) which contributed to translate this process of radicalization into world history. Moreover, the Nazi state itself actively promoted both normalcy and violence in everyday life in order to further its racist goals. All the same, a cultural dynamic, parallel to the regime's efforts, originated in the hometowns of Germany prior to and independent of the Hitler state. Here, I am thinking neither of the burning of the synagogue during the Night of Broken Glass nor of the hundreds of forced laborers who died in Hildesheim and were buried in its cemeteries, some in mass graves. I am thinking of these small, seemingly insignificant modifications of existing customs that expressed a fascist-racist identity in the neighborhood, of the initial public acts of rebellion against the civility of the preexisting civil society.

This process of "sealing off" the Jews from German society and the "psychic numbing" of survivors and perpetrators did not result solely from a series of incremental, formal policies, both legal and extralegal, on the part of a political and technocratic elite, both national and local.[39] An independent, informal process was simultaneously at work in which neighbors made themselves into Aryans by making Jews irrelevant as neighbors. With these small, often purely symbolic acts of coordination, Hildesheimers took the first steps down a road that led to Auschwitz: not inevitably or legally but biographically and historically. In response to communicative ghettoization, some Jewish Hildesheimers made the reasonable choice to cooperate with their Nazi neighbors and make themselves irrelevant by exiling themselves from their heimat. Precisely because this Nazi revolution also took place in informal social relations, however, it became increasingly difficult to imagine that Alt-Hildesheim was isolated and insulated from history and politics, particularly the inhumane and barbaric policies of the Nazi regime. Like Oran, Hildesheim became "a huge necropolis."[40] Ordinary Hildesheimers undermined their own sense of normalcy, then, when they linked the ordinary customs of the heimat with the Nazi system of racist murder.

The absurdity of the notion that modern life was conditioned by mass death meant that one must struggle against it, even if in vain. Refusing "to give in tamely to the plague," Dr. Rieux (the protagonist and, as we learn at the end, the narrator of the novel) strives to heal or at least to diminish human suffering.

"The essential thing was to save the greatest possible number of persons from dying and being doomed to unending separation. . . . There was nothing admirable about this attitude: it was merely logical." To find this "path of sympathy," Rieux thinks critically about his habits and his surroundings rather than letting his habits and surroundings numb his consciousness.[41] Camus realized that the plague of fascism could not be eliminated entirely, but one could still combat the condition of modernity that enabled it to propagate: the normalcy of everyday life. In Hildesheim, there were some notable exceptions of courage and ideological conviction, but most Hildesheimers adjusted their conviviality to fit Nazi principles and trusted their fates to normalcy.

The Nazi state then translated this local process of making people irrelevant into global-bureaucratic policies of segregation, deportation, selection, and ultimately systematic execution. This formalization of informal customs is evident for instance in the Nazi system of labels for clothing, identification cards, and bodies: the Nazi regime increasingly administered what Hildesheimers had already rearranged for themselves. By the time the Nazi regime began to demand increased sacrifices from Aryans for the war effort and initiate the "Final Solution" for the Jews, most Hildesheimers had grown accustomed to life in an age of mass murder. Racist violence was hard to avoid with some ten thousand forced workers (one-seventh of the total population) living and working in and around town. Going shopping on the streets of Hildesheim, Lotte Schohl saw Russian forced laborers fighting for heads of cabbage and then eating them raw, because they were starving. She could hardly ignore the fact that racism was no longer just an abstract affair of the system; this disruption occurred, as Lotte explained, "when shopping. . . . It arose right out of daily life, precisely as one goes into town today to get provisions and take care of whatever errands." Some Hildesheimers perpetrated acts of symbolic death and desecration, others just witnessed them, but witness, perpetrator, and victim responded similarly to this public discourse in violence: they compartmentalized their human sympathy, scaled down the scope of relevance in their lifeworld, and became numb to the pervasiveness of this plague as well as to its human carriers. "By this time," Rieux explained about Oran, "the plague had swallowed up everything and everyone. No longer were there individual destinies; only a collective destiny, made of plague and the emotions shared by all."[42] As the Nazi war machine conquered increasingly more territory, more ordinary people helped propagate this plague in small, everyday increments, just as the Hildesheimers had done, until it did indeed typify the human condition in Nazi-occupied Europe.

Only at the end of the war did normalcy itself fall victim to the plague. After 1943 especially, ordinary Hildesheimers came to realize that they too would pay the price for Nazi crimes because they were implicated in the initial propagation and achievements of Nazi totalitarianism. Listening to their radios, Hildesheimers heard how the war was turning against the German army and how death was approaching them on the wings of Allied bombers. Hildesheim was bombed almost to complete destruction in March of 1945, and Hildesheimers anticipated that forced laborers, concentration-camp victims, and Allied soldiers would seek justice or even vengeance. With neither their fantasies of normalcy nor the Nazi regime to protect them, Hildesheimers hid in bomb shelters or in basements, desperately trying to escape the plague, but they could no longer ignore it. For they had engineered it in the first place through small acts of social violence and cultural desecration. Hildesheimers did not make these choices as entirely free agents, but they did make them themselves. "One could always refuse to face this disagreeable fact, shut one's eyes to it, or thrust it out of mind," Camus wrote, "but there is a terrible cogency in the self-evident; ultimately it breaks down all defenses."[43]

Resurrecting Normalcy

The self-evident is even more terribly cogent in memory. Reading Tarrou's diary of life in post-plague Oran, Rieux noted: "The cats were back at their usual places, but at the ritual hour the shutters stayed closed. And never once did Tarrou see them open on the following days." The small-game hunter could not return to his old habits as if the plague had never come to Oran. In Tarrou, we see what happens to people years after they have contracted the plague: they remain obsessed with it even though they survived it. Tarrou confided to Rieux that he had had the plague long before he came to Oran, even though he believed that he had been fighting it. "I learned that I had had an indirect hand in the deaths of thousands of people; that I'd even brought about their deaths by approving of acts and principles which could only end that way." Having scrutinized everyday life during the plague, Tarrou drew the conclusion that it lay dormant in every human society, "and I have lost my peace."[44] My interview partners could also remember participating in acts and implementing principles in their neighborhoods which could have and unfortunately did end in mass death; they too struggled to find peace in the postfascist world. Normalcy came to their rescue, but its 1950s reincarnation differed in a crucial way from the 1920s "return" to normalcy. In the 1950s, personal memories of complicity disrupted the narrative of resurrected normalcy, a destabilization that in turn made its ritual reenactment all the more compulsive.

The stability of the Federal Republic was constructed on many pillars, some of which had foundations in the Third Reich: consumption, productivity (*Leistung*), the cold war, political moderation. The postwar consensus also rested heavily on a culture of normalcy. There was a widespread consensus in postwar Germany for resurrecting cultural categories that promised to preserve the ethical integrity and historical insularity of their heimat. While this consensus tolerated the responsibility of "important" Germans for the Holocaust on a systemic level (Hitler, his lieutenants, his bureaucrats, even key industrialists), it still implied the innocence of "ordinary" Germans in their lifeworld.[45] In

Hildesheim, local residents tried to restore a facade of normalcy in the late 1940s and 1950s, just as they sought to rebuild the actual facades of Alt-Hildesheim. Reconstructing their public identities, they ignored "ex-Nazi" neighbors and sent greetings to "former Hildesheimers of the Jewish faith." They greeted their neighbors from their prewar neighborhoods while complaining that young people in their postwar neighborhoods no longer greeted their elders properly. They acted as if Alt-Hildesheim still existed, as if no rupture had taken place. They romanticized, even marketed the buildings and people of Alt-Hildesheim that they had lost in "the Destruction" (*Zerstörung*) while ignoring the neighbors they lost in the Holocaust. They found noble acts of antifascist resistance in their lifeworld while blaming Hitler for the sins of his dictatorship. They castigated the Allies for carpet bombing their town only a few weeks before the war was almost over and honored the victims of Russian aggression with monuments facing the "German East." By using the term *Alt-Hildesheim* after 1945 with melancholic overtones, Hildesheimers made the Allies into the perpetrators of a barbaric attack on *Kultur* and ordinary Hildesheimers into the tragic victims of mass destruction. The climax of this story, as they tell it, came shortly after 1 P.M. on 22 March 1945, when Hildesheim was invaded by history just as the plague had come to Oran.[46]

Though some of these tropes have Nazi ancestry, in the postwar context they constitute a rebellious response to the Allied discourse of German responsibility (just as the metanarrative of the German *Sonderweg* salvaged normalcy for the rest of Western civilization). Hildesheimers resurrected their normalcy by containing the ethical challenge of everyday life during the Third Reich. At stake was what Camus called "the terrible cogency of the self-evident": my interview partners could not forget the fact that, in the first place and up until the very end, the Nazi revolution was facilitated by ordinary Hildesheimers like them, who by and large had coordinated their customs of conviviality to fit the Nazi system of mass destruction. By directing attention away from that fact, normalcy accomplished its goal. It redefined National Socialism as something that came *to* Hildesheim and remade Hildesheimers into powerless victims of abstract forces.

I experienced remnants of this postwar cult of normalcy firsthand when I was given guided tours by several of my interview partners in 1992–93. These tours focused not on Hildesheim but on Alt-Hildesheim. My tour guides tried to relive, in memory, how these convivial spaces and cultural monuments had helped them to feel integrated in a surreal, insulated community. Yet these artifacts were either fragmented or obviously missing, to such an extent that I was introduced to a ghost town that existed only in their memory. Any postwar tour of Alt-Hildesheim necessarily focused on its destruction, and such strolls into the past necessarily raised disturbing questions of the historical responsibility for that collapse. Of course, my tour guides tried to avoid all mention of the persecution and destruction of Hildesheim's Jewish community as well as any implication that ordinary Hildesheimers had collaborated in this deed. They gave me these tours in part to prove to me, as an American, that Hildesheimers are friendly to foreigners: "Friendly Hildesheim" is the town motto. Nonetheless the act of disinterring these dead monuments of Alt-Hildesheim for me to see necessarily drew my tour guides toward their personal memories of the missing Jewish community. Those memories erupted within, and disrupted, the authoritative narrative that depicted Hildesheim as if it had been invaded by the Nazi plague. Indeed, the best surviving monuments of Alt-Hildesheim were closely associated with Hildesheim's Jewish past: the stone Tempelhaus on the old market square and the streets of half-timbered houses in Neustadt and on Lappenberg. Topographically, these postwar remnants of Alt-Hildesheim stand next to medieval Jewish ghettos and destroyed Jewish synagogues. More importantly, this correlation made sense to the interwar generation in terms of their personal memories. When they traced the disease that killed Alt-Hildesheim in their memory, they find that the first symptoms of illness were those moments when certain neighbors were treated like Jews. It is in this sense that their private memories endanger their official histories and the postfascist stabilization was constantly at risk of being undermined by them.[47]

When surviving Hildesheimers resurrected the myths of normalcy in the postwar era, they did so to protect themselves from accusation. When I explained that I was researching everyday life in the Nazi era, local historians in Hildesheim insisted that their town was not a center (*Hochburg*) of the Nazi faith, that it had always remained moderate (*gemäßigt*), as if "normal" Hildesheim had nothing to do with the "abnormal" Third Reich. Yet Hildesheimers could not deny the evidence of their own experience. After the war, it was these memories that nagged: of symbolic acts of collaboration, of the instrumentalization of normalcy, of the historicity of everyday life. Käthe Stolte grew uncommonly animated and angry when she recalled how certain of her neighbors used to "toss around" (*rumgeprallt*) Nazi greetings and then suddenly "changed their opinions like a shirt" in 1945. She did not feel comfortable in the Third Reich because of the Gestapo; but she felt a broader sense of alienation after the war, "because you did not know: so, is he a complete Nazi now or not?"[48] We can now see why reenacting interwar customs of conviviality is both a public obsession and a private danger for the members of interwar generation. Every time they walked around the early modern walls of their town, drew reproductions of buildings that no longer exist, greeted those neighbors who could also remember Alt-Hildesheim, or even gave a tour of town to foreign academics, they were attempting to resurrect a collective veil of normalcy over and against the disruptive evidence of their own memories: that Hildesheimers had made Hildesheim fascist. They recounted those incidents for me in the interview process because they were the memories that remained inexplicable, because they continue to haunt them whenever they raised the dead facade of Alt-Hildesheim. Yet they reenact these interwar customs all the same, continually both buttressing and undermining the facade that protects Hildesheim from its own memories.

What makes the Holocaust so disturbing for most ordinary men and women is neither the scale of death per se nor even the technological developments that facilitated mass murder. The Holocaust shakes the foundations of Western civilization because the Nazi regime employed the full arsenal of modernity (scientific reason, industrial efficiency, and bureaucratic rationality) to accomplish its dystopian goals. The Holocaust stands out among genocidal programs because the primary goal of this modern, bureaucratic-polycratic state was to murder and enslave entire social groups, because the raison d'être of the Third Reich was mass destruction. An analogous argument can be made in terms of everyday life. What disturbed Hildesheimers after 1945 was the fact that they and their neighbors had incrementally coordinated their individual lifeworld to fit the bureaucratic rationality and the racist policies of the regime. By initiating a contentious, public, symbolic debate about membership in the new volksgemeinschaft, by shifting the rules and boundaries of civility and relevance to fit the Nazi modern, ordinary Hildesheimers helped implement that new social order in fact. Given the unique hubris of Nazi racial policy and the vast potential of modernity to realize these goals, it is all the more disturbing to suggest that the mass death of the 1940s was "homemade."[49]

It is important to note that the Nazi past is not "unmasterable" for those interwar Hildesheimers who came to terms with it already in the 1930s, like Franz, Dora, and Gerhard. In the case of Dora and Erich, their friendship with Gerdl and Ulrich cooled off in the 1930s, but only temporarily: after the war, they were able to reestablish this relationship because Hitler had never been able, as Dora said, "to teach us to hate." By exiling herself from her heimat, Dora was able to preserve her respect for its civil customs. In the case of Gerhard, the first thing he showed me when I visited him in his Chicago suburb was his collection of images of Alt-Hildesheim, taking up an entire wall in his home. In the 1990s, he was still giving tours of his heimat to strangers, just in Illinois instead of in Niedersachsen. Clearly the Nazi past is only unmasterable for those interwar Hildesheimers who still refuse to think critically and ethically about their everyday life in the 1930s.

Local historians of the interwar generation denied out of hand that I, as both a foreigner and a young man, could access and understand everyday life in Alt-Hildesheim. During my tours of Alt-Hildesheim, my tour guides often decried the fact that young Hildesheimers did not, and could never, share in this surreal community of conviviality, for they had never experienced it—or more accurately, its destruction. To me, these comments revealed the tacit claim of the interwar generation to exclusive ownership of the interwar and Nazi past. Like the reminiscences of Rieux, these claims were staked through photo albums and reconstructions of public spaces, picture books and museum exhibitions, patterns of greeting and alienation. Their comments implied that they feared the younger generation and jealously guarded the local past. Yet by relishing the past but not sharing access to it, by reiterating it without resolving its contradictions, the interwar generation set an unfortunate precedent for a distracted society, which Camus described as one that seeks "reunion with something they couldn't have defined but which seemed to them the only desirable thing on earth. For want of a better name, they sometimes called it peace." In our postmodern era of mutual recrimination, it bears noting that the habits of historical entitlement through "political melancholy" (in which individuals lay claim to social resources through group-specific memories of past suffering) was first introduced not by the victims of Nazi aggression but by ordinary Germans in an attempt to distract themselves and their children from the memory of their personal acts of collaboration.[50] It makes perfect sense, then, that the murders of the Nazi modern could not be contained in their mass graves and that they among all examples of modern genocide would hold such power over postwar memory. Only in the case of the Holocaust was normalcy used to introduce and then disguise the collaboration of ordinary men and women in systems of mass murder.

At first glance, Camus seems to have shared this desire to use the cultural balm of resurrected normalcy to heal the scars of the receding plague. Camus finished writing *The Plague* only in 1946: in the final chapters of Rieux's account, the plague seemed to regain its abstract qualities (Rieux says, "The disease seemed to be leaving as unaccountably as it had come") while ordinary people seem to have become ordinary once again (Tarrou says, "I leave it to others to make history"). The novel even reinforced the fable that the sole collaborators had been arrested, removed, and punished, and that those remaining can consider themselves vindicated as either victims or resisters. Read in this way, *The Plague* (here viewed as both Rieux's post-plague autobiography and Camus's postwar novel) should also be understood as an act of remembrance that offers authors and readers a way to isolate ordinary people once again from their memories of collaboration in systems of mass death. In an era when books were luxuries, *The Plague* sold 360,000 copies by 1955: it was the seventh-best seller in postwar France.[51]

Yet this interpretation of *The Plague* does not correspond to Camus's behavior. The self-appointed postwar spokesperson for "the rebel" (the title of a subsequent book), Camus thought and wrote despair but he never lost faith in the moral deed. "Just because you have pessimistic thoughts, you don't have to *act* pessimistically," Camus told a reporter for the *New Yorker* on 27 March 1946. "One has to pass the time somehow." Closer scrutiny reveals that Camus did appreciate the problem of a postfascist return to normalcy. As Tarrou realized, "naturally our fellow citizens' strongest desire was, and would be, to behave as if nothing had changed and for that reason nothing would be changed, in a sense. But—to look at it from another angle—one can't forget everything, however great one's wish to do so; the plague was bound to leave traces, anyhow, in people's hearts." Tarrou is Camus's proof that even a plague could be spiritually liberating if approached correctly. He balanced a scientific preoccupation with scrutinizing everyday life with an acute awareness of the ethical need to humanize it. If Tarrou is pessimistic, it is only because he lost his innocence in the plague; but that past is hardly unmasterable. On the contrary, the plague clarified his duty to his fellow human beings in a destructive society and enabled him to see clearly in spite of its distractions: "On this earth there are pestilences and there are victims, and it's up to us, so far as possible, not to join forces with the pestilences."[52]

The Choice to Be a Rebel

If we are to believe Camus, then we must learn to see through this distracting and dehumanizing culture of normalcy and struggle against it as a rebel. From an ethical perspective, this philosophy seems absurd: Camus's posture of rebellion is not so very different from that of the early Nazis of Hildesheim. Both attempt to restore the kind of consciousness that was typical of the nineteenth century but had fallen into disfavor in the first half of the twentieth in which individuals saw an ethical and historical relationship between their everyday agency and world history. And yet Camus's existential stance differs from the early Nazi rebels of Hildesheim in one critical aspect: Nazi rebels promoted terror and violence, while Camus's rebels seek only to heal. Camus recognized that it is absurd to strive to heal when there is little hope for ultimate victory, yet he also allotted the highest moral significance to the striving.[53]

My historical conclusion follows from the same existential framework, one that I believe belongs at the core of the history of everyday life (*Alltagsgeschichte*). To prevent the plague of fascism from becoming epidemic, Camus suggests, we must call it directly by name.[54] So historians should not hide behind the comforting terminology of "ordinary men." This myth of normalcy is itself a collective, if misguided, cultural response to the ethical challenges presented by a thirty-one-year civil war in which European governments committed unprecedented violence with the unprecedented collusion of European peoples. The trope of "the ordinary German" misleads us because it reproduces the same habits, myths, and power relations that played a crucial role in creating the Nazi volksgemeinschaft in the first place. It suggests that we have not yet come to terms with the ethical and historical problems at work in that everyday process. By treating normalcy instead as a category of experience, historians can focus their attention on the everyday dynamics that both facilitated Nazi crimes and removed them from public scrutiny as history and in memory. By exploring the cultural process that redefined the everyday as normal, historians restore a sense of the human agency behind the production of specific, lived, collective realities. This shift in focus should not disregard the broader context in which everyday agents act: of institutions, ideologies, resources, policies, and so on. It should focus on determining how lifeworld and system, rebellion (*Eigensinn*) and domination (*Herrschaft*), interact in everyday life to produce specific historical outcomes.

The contingent agency of ordinary Hildesheimers did help transform European society, just not in the way that Camus would have desired. Rather than effectively opposing fascism in everyday life, ordinary Hildesheimers helped the Nazi regime realize its volksgemeinschaft and then repressed their personal memories of collusion. In this way, Camus's awareness of both the absurdity and the necessity of everyday rebels acting humanely in the face of a fascist plague can help us better understand modernity in general and the origins, crimes, and legacies of the Third Reich in particular. This awareness may also help us to learn how to act ethically in our postmodern, distracted, and destructive society: that is, in our unmasterable present. Camus believed that only if we are armed with this kind of knowledge of everyday life will we be ready for action when pestilence, lying "dormant for years and years in furniture and linen-chests . . . rouse[s] up its rats again and send[s] them forth to die in a happy city." Maybe then we too will be prepared to say, like the character Grand: "Plague is here and we've got to make a stand, that's obvious. Ah, I only wish everything were as simple!"[55]

NOTES

An earlier version of this essay appeared in the *Tel Aviver Jahrbuch für deutsche Geschichte* (1999): 303–40. For their constructive criticism, I would like to thank James A. Bell, Michael Geyer, Jennifer L. Jenkins, Maria Mitchell, H. Glenn Penny, Stefan Senders, Bernd-Jürgen Warneken, Eric Zolov, the editors of this volume, the participants of the workshop, and the members of the Washington Area German History Seminar. For their collaboration in my research, I am indebted to my many interview partners, colleagues, and friends in Hildesheim. My research in Hildesheim was made possible by a generous grant from the Friedrich-Weinhagen Stiftung. This essay is dedicated to Jenny, my wife, who recommended that I read Camus.

1. E.g., Christopher R. Browning, *Ordinary Men: Reserve Police Battalion 101 and the Final Solution in Poland* (New York: Harper, 1992); Daniel Jonah Goldhagen, *Hitler's Willing Executioners: Ordinary Germans and the Holocaust* (New York: Alfred A. Knopf, 1996); Jan T. Gross, *Neighbors: The Destruction of the Jewish Community in Jedwabne, Poland* (Princeton: Princeton University Press, 2001); and Ian Kershaw, *Popular Opinion and Political Dissent in the Third Reich: Bavaria 1933–45* (Oxford: Clarendon Press, 1983).

2. Hannah Arendt, *The Origins of Totalitarianism* (New York: Harcourt Brace Jovanovich, 1951); Ralf Dahrendorf, *Society and Democracy in Germany* (New York: W. W. Norton, 1965); and David Schoenbaum, *Hitler's Social Revolution: Class and Status in Nazi Germany, 1933–1939* (New York: W. W. Norton, 1966).

3. Dan Diner, "Historical Experience and Cognition: Perspectives on National Socialism," *History and Memory* 2 (1990): 84–110; Ulrich Herbert, "Die guten und die schlechten Zeiten: Überlegungen zur diachronischen Analyse lebensgeschichtlicher Interviews," in *"Die Jahre weiß man nicht, wo man die heute hinsetzten soll": Faschismuserfahrungen im Ruhrgebiet,* ed. Lutz Niethammer et al. (Berlin: J. H. W. Dietz Nachf., 1983), pp. 67–96; and Frank Trommler, "Between Normality and Resistance: Catastrophic Gradualism in Nazi Germany," *Journal of Modern History* 64, suppl. (Dec. 1992): 82–101.

4. Hannah Arendt, *Eichmann in Jerusalem: A Report on the Banality of Evil* (New York:

Viking Press, 1963); Zygmunt Bauman, *Modernity and the Holocaust* (Ithaca: Cornell University Press, 1992); Peter Fritzsche, "Nazi Modern," *Modernism/Modernity* 3, no. 1 (1996): 1–22, here at pp. 10–15; and Detlev Peukert, *Inside Nazi Germany: Conformity, Opposition, and Racism in Everyday Life* (New Haven: Yale University Press, 1982).

5. David Blackbourn and Geoff Eley, *The Peculiarities of German History: Bourgeois Society and Politics in Nineteenth-Century Germany* (Oxford: Oxford University Press, 1984); Martin Broszat, "Plädoyer für eine Historisierung des Nationalsozialismus," *Merkur* (May 1985): 373–84; Diner, "Historical Experience"; Heide Gerstenberger and Dorothea Schmidt, eds., *Normalität oder Normalisierung? Geschichtswerkstätten und Faschismusanalyse* (Münster: Westfälisches Dampfboot, 1987); George M. Kren and Leon Rappaport, *The Holocaust and the Crisis of Human Behavior* (New York: Holmes & Meier, 1980); Saul Friedlander, "Some Reflections on the Historicization of National Socialism," *Tel Aviver Jahrbuch für deutsche Geschichte* 16 (1987): 310–24; and Martin Broszat and Saul Friedlander, "A Controversy about the Historicization of National Socialism," *Yad Vashem Studies* 19 (1988): 1–47.

6. See David Crew, ed., *Nazism and German Society, 1933–1945* (London: Routledge, 1994); Heide Gerstenberger, "Alltagsforschung und Faschismustheorie," in *Normalität,* ed. Gerstenberger and Schmidt, pp. 35–49; Peter Fritzsche, "Where Did All the Nazis Go? Reflections on Collaboration and Resistance," *Tel Aviver Jahrbuch für deutsche Geschichte* 23 (1994): 191–214; Robert Gellateley, *The Gestapo and German Society: Enforcing Racial Policy, 1933–1945* (Oxford: Clarendon Press, 1990); Kershaw, *Popular Opinion and Political Dissent;* and Peukert, *Inside Nazi Germany.*

7. Broszat, "Plädoyer für eine Historisierung"; and Joan W. Scott, "The Evidence of Experience," *Critical Inquiry* 17 (Summer 1991): 773–97.

8. Gerstenberger, "Alltagsforschung"; and William H. Sewell, Jr., "A Theory of Structure: Duality, Agency, and Transformation," *American Journal of Sociology* 98 (July 1992): 1–29.

9. Pierre Bourdieu, *Outline of a Theory of Practice* (Cambridge: Cambridge University Press, 1989); Michel de Certeau, *The Practice of Everyday Life,* trans. Steven Rendall (Berkeley: University of California Press, 1984); and Alf Lüdtke, ed., *The History of Everyday Life: Reconstructing Historical Experiences and Ways of Life* (Princeton: Princeton University Press, 1995). Cf. Marshall Sahlins's *Islands of History* (Chicago: University of Chicago Press, 1985); and John Comaroff and Jean Comaroff, *Ethnography and the Historical Imagination* (Boulder, Colo.: Westview Press, 1992).

10. Andrew Stuart Bergerson, "A History of Neighborliness in Alt-Hildesheim: Custom, Transformation, Memory" (Ph.D. diss., University of Chicago, 1998), pp. 32–37, being revised for publication under the title *Ordinary Germans in Extraordinary Times;* and Albert Camus, *The Plague,* trans. Stuart Gilbert (New York: Modern Library, 1948).

11. Celia Applegate, *A Nation of Provincials: The German Idea of Heimat* (Berkeley: University of California Press, 1990); Fritzsche, "Nazi Modern"; Rudy Koshar, *Social Life, Local Politics and Nazism: Marburg, 1880–1935* (Chapel Hill: University of North Carolina Press, 1986); Bauman, *Modernity;* Henry Friedlander, *The Origins of the Nazi Genocide: From Euthanasia to the Final Solution* (Chapel Hill: University of North Carolina Press, 1995); Charles Maier, *The Unmasterable Past: History, Holocaust and German National Identity* (Cambridge: Harvard University Press, 1988); and Mack Walker, *German Home Towns* (Ithaca: Cornell University Press, 1971).

12. Herbert Lottman, *Albert Camus: A Biography* (Corte Madera, Calif.: Gingko Press, 1997).

13. Camus, *Plague,* pp. 37, 24, 5 respectively.

14. Camus, *Plague,* pp. 25, 21–22 respectively; see also p. 92.

15. Camus, *Plague,* pp. 25, 35, 35, 115 respectively.

16. Camus, *Plague,* p. 4.

17. Camus, *Plague,* pp. 189–97, 148, 263, 226, 219, 159–61 respectively.

18. Bergerson, "History of Neighborliness," pp. 576–620.

19. Benedict Anderson, *Imagined Communities: Reflections on the Origins and Spread of Nationalism* (New York: Verso, 1983); Cornelius Castoriadis, *The Imaginary Institution of Society* (Cambridge: MIT Press, 1987); Eric Hobsbawm and Terence Ranger, eds., *The Invention of Tradition* (Cambridge: Cambridge University Press, 1983); and Eve K. Sedgwick, *Epistemology of the Closet* (Berkeley: University of California Press, 1990), pp. 1–11.

20. The terms derive from Alfred Schutz and Thomas Luckmann, *The Structures of the Life-World* (Evanston, Ill.: Northwestern University Press, 1973); cf. Jürgen Habermas, *Theorie des kommunikativen Handelns* (Frankfurt: Suhrkamp, 1981). They neither correlate perfectly with the categories of state and society (for there is a realm of everyday life in which agents stake competing claims for herrschaft and eigensinn in both) nor do they correspond directly to the geographic distinctions of locality, region, nation, world (e.g., James Sheehan in "What Is German History?" *Journal of Modern History* 53 [Mar. 1981]: 1–23). Rather they refer to different modes of historical experience and scholarly apprehension: individual subjectivity and agency as opposed to that which transcends it (e.g., Diner, "Historical Experience," and Kren and Rappaport, *Holocaust*). As for the expression "die da oben," see David Warren Sabean, *Power in the Blood: Popular Culture and Village Discourse in Early Modern Germany* (Cambridge: Cambridge University Press, 1984), p. 25.

21. Kristin Ross, *Fast Cars, Clean Bodies: Decolonization and the Reordering of French Culture* (Cambridge: MIT Press, 1995); and Sedgwick, *Epistemology,* pp. 4, 8, 67, 70–73. Of course, normalcy has other meanings that come into play at times: the repetitive, plebeian, and traditional qualities of everyday life as well as values shared by "everyone" in the form of "common sense." Yet events that introduce something extraordinary, elite, or new into everyday life will not undermine one's sense of normalcy in the long term. Actual experiences and their memories must always sustain and reconfirm the self-induced ethical-historical naivete or else normalcy collapses as a cultural system that functions efficiently and naturally in the service of power relations.

22. Andreas Huyssen, *After the Great Divide: Modernism, Mass Culture, Postmodernism* (Bloomington: Indiana University Press, 1986). Modern scholarship tended to reproduce this great divide. Historians have outlined the macrohistory of Nazi herrschaft in far greater detail than the microhistory of Nazi eigensinn. Yet it is the question of the contributions and experiences of ordinary Germans that remains theoretically unresolved. A model for revision in this direction is Peter Blickle, *Obedient Germans? A Rebuttal: A New View of German History* (Charlottesville: University Press of Virginia, 1997).

23. Anderson, *Imagined Communities;* Bauman, *Modernity;* Castoriadis, *Imaginary Institution;* Norbert Elias, *Power and Civility: The Civilizing Process* (New York: Pantheon, 1982); Peter Fritzsche, "Chateaubriand's Ruins: Loss and Memory after the French Revolution," *History and Memory* 10 (1998): 102–7; George L. Mosse, *The Nationalism of the Masses* (Ithaca: Cornell University Press, 1975); and Max Weber, *Economy and Society* (Berkeley: University of California Press, 1978).

24. Diner, "Historical Experience"; Fritzsche, "Nazi Modern," pp. 10–15; Peter Fritzsche, *Germans into Nazis* (Cambridge: Harvard University Press, 1998); Kren and Rappaport, *Holocaust;* and Herbert, "Die guten und die schlechten Zeiten." The culture of normalcy that

emerged in the 1920s did not entirely obviate ideological consciousness or awareness of world events, yet it was sufficient to insulate the individual from the instability of the system. The various milieux of Central Europe did not abandon their respective dreams of utopia; they simply reconstituted living environments and biographies that were distinctly apolitical, insulated, and isolated, whether in Red Vienna or in a provincial heimat: e.g., Applegate, *Nation of Provincials;* Koshar, *Social Life;* and Anson Rabinbach, *The Crisis of Austrian Socialism: From Red Vienna to Civil War, 1927–1934* (Chicago: University of Chicago Press, 1983). The phrase "return to normalcy" was first politicized in Chicago in 1920, when Ohio senator Warren G. Harding used it as his slogan as Republican candidate for the presidency of the United States; see George B. Tindall and David E. Shi, *America: A Narrative History,* vol. 2 (New York: W. W. Norton, 1984), pp. 1120–28.

25. Bergerson, "History of Neighborliness," pp. 258–68.

26. Bergerson, "History of Neighborliness," pp. 643–44.

27. Bergerson, "History of Neighborliness," pp. 489–500.

28. Bergerson, "History of Neighborliness," pp. 525–26.

29. Gerstenberger, "Alltagsforschung"; and Caroline Wagner, *Die NSDAP auf dem Dorf: Eine Sozialgeschichte der NS-Machtergreifung in Lippe* (Münster: Aschendorff, 1998).

30. Camus, *Plague,* p. 105.

31. Camus, *Plague,* pp. 65, 69, 102, 164; see also p. 154.

32. Paul Connerton, *How Societies Remember* (Cambridge: Cambridge University Press, 1989); Sahlins, *Islands;* and Schutz and Luckmann, *Structures.*

33. Bergerson, "History of Neighborliness," pp. 552–58, 658–62, 268–83.

34. See Sedgwick, *Epistemology,* p. 75.

35. Camus, *Plague,* pp. 38, 81, 39, 45, 85, 174–80; see also pp. 34–35.

36. Bauman, *Modernity,* pp. 117–68; and Camus, *Plague,* p. 229.

37. Bergerson, "History of Neighborliness," pp. 247–58, 672–74 respectively. Here, irrelevance refers specifically to the subjective realm of the lifeworld in which an ordinary person has historical influence and ethical responsibility. Obviously, Jews never became irrelevant in terms of the Nazi cosmology, even after they were removed physically from the public sphere in Germany.

38. See also Bauman, *Modernity,* p. 157; Andrew Stuart Bergerson, "Aufklärung durch Erzählung: Mündliche Geschichte und bürgerliche Gesellschaft nach Hitler," in *Inspecting Germany,* ed. Thomas Hauschild and Bernd-Jürgen Warnecken (Constance: Universitätsverlag Konstanz, 2002); and Camus, *Plague,* pp. 34–35.

39. Bauman, *Modernity;* and Robert Jay Lifton, *The Future of Immortality and Other Essays for a Nuclear Age* (New York: Basic Books, 1987), chaps. 17 and 18.

40. Camus, *Plague,* p. 155.

41. Camus, *Plague,* pp. 277, 115, 122, 150, 230; see also pp. 118–27, 194, 278; and Lifton, *Future of Immortality,* chaps. 17 and 18.

42. Bergerson, "History of Neighborliness," pp. 407–31, quote at p. 418; and Camus, *Plague,* p. 151.

43. Camus, *Plague,* p. 156; see also Lutz Niethammer et al. eds., *Die Menschen machen ihre Geschichte nicht aus freien Stücken, aber sie machen sie selbst: Einladung zu einer Geschichte des Volkes in NRW* (Berlin: J. H. W. Dietz Nachf., 1988), p. 11.

44. Camus, *Plague,* pp. 247, 227, 228.

45. Elizabeth Heineman, "The Hour of the Woman: Memories of Germany's 'Crisis Years' and West German National Identity," *American Historical Review* 101 (1996): 354–95; cf. Lif-

ton, *Future of Immortality,* chaps. 7, 17, and 18; Charles Maier, *In Search of Stability: Explorations in Historical Political Economy* (Cambridge: Cambridge University Press, 1987); and Alexander Mitscherlich and Margarete Mitscherlich, *The Inability to Mourn: Principles of Collective Behavior* (New York: Grove Press, 1975).

46. Bergerson, "History of Neighborliness," pp. 284–328, 444–54; Andrew Stuart Bergerson, "Zwischen Pflaumenbaum und Gartenzaun," *Hildesheimer Heimatkalender* (1995): 63–67; and Dennis Hollier, *Against Architecture: The Writings of Georges Bataille* (Cambridge: MIT Press, 1988).

47. Bergerson, "History of Neighborliness," pp. 295–321; Sahlins, *Islands;* and Trommler, "Normality and Resistance."

48. Bergerson, "History of Neighborliness," p. 676.

49. Bauman, *Modernity;* Maier, *Unmasterable Past,* pp. 75–77, following Eberhard Jäckel, "Die elende Praxis der Untersteller," *Die Zeit,* 12 Sept. 1986; and Comaroff and Comaroff, *Ethnography,* pp. 292–94.

50. Camus, *Plague,* p. 269; Bergerson, "Aufklärung durch Erzählung," and "History of Neighborliness," pp. 302–12; following Charles Maier, "A Surfeit of Memory? Reflections on History, Melancholy and Denial," *History and Memory* 5 (1993): 136–51.

51. Camus, *Plague,* pp. 243, 229, 272, 251; see also pp. 26, 266. Lottman, *Camus,* pp. 344, 450.

52. Lottman, *Camus,* pp. 402, 217; and Camus, *Plague,* pp. 251, 34; see also p. 118. Camus helped the Popular Front in Algiers in spite of serious ideological misgivings about Communism. He was active in the antifascist resistance in occupied France. From 1944 to 1945, Camus helped edit the underground newspaper *Combat,* which represented, to many, France's best hope for a new political morality, one that would prevent the nightmare of the past war from ever being repeated. After liberation, he was publicly critical of both Uncle Sam's materialism and Stalin's totalitarianism, an ethical posture that cost him his friendship with Jean-Paul Sartre.

53. Camus, *Plague,* pp. 118, 255; see also Lifton, *Future of Immortality,* chaps. 17 and 18.

54. Camus, *Plague,* p. 39; see also Lifton, *Future of Immortality,* pp. 255–56.

55. Camus, *Plague,* pp. 278, 123; see also pp. 34, 121–22.

CHAPTER 6

Awakening from War: History, Trauma, and Testimony in Heinrich Böll

ELIZABETH SNYDER HOOK

> We wrote about war, about coming home, about what we saw on the battlefield and what we found when we came back. We wrote about the ruins.
>
> —Heinrich Böll, *Erzählungen, Hörspiele, Aufsätze* (Cologne: Kiepenheuer & Witsch, 1961), p. 339

In his landmark work *Beyond the Pleasure Principle,* Freud presents trauma as a "wound inflicted not upon the body but upon the mind."[1] Perplexed by the record number of war veterans who returned home only to suffer mental breakdowns, the famed psychoanalyst would eventually conclude that the visible symptoms of shell shock did not emerge from a physical or bodily trauma but from a psychological one. Moving away from his earlier notion of trauma as "an effraction or breach of external origin" (specifically, sexual seduction and abuse), Freud's analysis of combat veterans marks an important theoretical shift from corporeal experience to psychical experience, "from the external to the internal."[2] Freud's investigation in *Beyond the Pleasure Principle* highlights the emotional and behavioral scars manifested by battlefield survivors—uncontrollable screaming and weeping, catatonic or "frozen" postures, the loss of memory and affect—and seeks to explain how the horrors of trench warfare could cause soldiers "to act like hysterical women."[3] Of primary importance was not the soldiers' encounter with death but their ongoing experience of having survived it.[4]

What is missing from Freud's explication of trauma, and what subsequent scholars have increasingly prioritized, is the link between catastrophic events (whether of natural origin or human design) and the survivor's struggle to bear witness. Analysts and scholars now contend that the devastating impact of traumatic phenomena exceeds the eruption of painful memories or the reenactment of events through compulsive, repetitive behaviors. Research of the last several decades reveals that the negative repercussions of trauma are compounded by the fact that, often, the survivor is rendered incapable of communicating his or her experience to others. The atrocities suffered are so painful, so overwhelming, that the victim's only means of psychic survival is to banish all memories of the event from the realm of discourse; in effect, to equate silence with an absence of suffering. This denial of trauma, both psychological and linguistic, can be viewed as a lifesaving defense, without which the victim would be too paralyzed to go on living.[5] Yet it is this very dismissal of trauma, and the resulting absence of any testimony to one's experience, that blocks the victim's path to recovery. Judith Herman emphasizes this "unspeakable" aspect of traumatic events and underscores the paradoxical necessity of truth-telling for the healing process:

> The conflict between the will to deny horrible events and the will to proclaim them aloud is the central dialectic of psychological trauma. People who have survived atrocities often tell their stories in a highly emotional, contradictory, and fragmented manner which undermines their credibility and thereby serves the twin imperatives of truth-telling and secrecy. When the truth is finally recognized, survivors can begin their recovery. But far too often secrecy prevails, and the story of the traumatic event surfaces not as a verbal narrative but as a symptom.[6]

In seeking to understand this tension between silence and testimony, or the juxtaposition of the "unknowing, injurious repetition and the witness of the crying voice,"[7] scholars have expanded the parameters of trauma research to include not only case studies of survivors but literary texts as well. Cathy Caruth, in her insightful exploration of trauma, narrative, and history, argues, for example, that literature has much to teach us about the complexities of trauma and language. Citing Freud's discussion of Torquato Tasso's *Jerusalem Liberated,* Caruth proposes that the power of this romantic epic lies not so much in the hero's unwitting repetition of a murderous act but in the words of his slain beloved, whose voice cries out for truth. It is the insistent presence of this sorrowful voice, Caruth writes, a voice "paradoxically released *through the wound,*" that best represents traumatic experience.[8]

Caruth's claim that literature, like psychoanalysis, exposes the "complex relation between knowing and not knowing,"[9] truth-telling and secrecy, is powerfully substantiated in Heinrich Böll's early postwar novel *Und sagte kein einziges Wort* (*And Never Said a Mumbalin' Word*).[10] Written in the aftermath of World War II, Böll's portrait of postwar German life exemplifies in literary form Freud's conceptualization of trauma as an unhealed psychic wound, a "breach in the mind's experience of time, self, and the world"[11] that lives on in the form of nightmares and compulsions. What is equally striking about Böll's novel, however, is its vivid and compelling depiction of the protagonists' struggle to bear witness. Set in Germany in the early 1950s, *Und sagte kein einziges Wort* establishes a fictional narrative through which the traumatizing effects of the war are communicated. The characters' voices provide, to quote Shoshana Felman, "the liberation of the testimony from the bondage of the secret."[12] Böll's central couple, Fred and Käte, succeed at various points in the novel in converting their buried traumas into language, bringing what was previously denied into the realm of discourse. At the same time, Böll's story concerns itself with the more elusive or secretive aspects of trauma, with that which remains unspoken. Just as Freud attributes survivors' posttraumatic behavior to a disavowal of overwhelming experiences, the unverbalized secrets of postwar Germany erupt in *Und sagte kein einziges Wort* as symptoms into the public and private sphere: familial estrangement, manic consumerism, anxiety, depression, and abuse. While the novel seeks to tell the truth of trauma, it simultaneously exposes the difficulties inherent to the articulation of these experiences and reveals the emotional and linguistic obstacles faced by those characters who seek to bear witness.

Und sagte kein einziges Wort reveals a country scarred by war. The physical landscape of the novel is punctuated by the haunting remnants of this national —indeed international—catastrophe: crumbling buildings, destroyed homes, half-preserved churches. Dust covers the streets and fills the lungs of the city's inhabitants. Cheap food is served in makeshift stands. At one point in the novel, Böll compares the war-torn German city to a remote nomadic village. The men of the village have gone and taken their flocks with them; all that remains is a handful of infirm old women, who in their solitude testify to an earlier time. Böll makes no pretense, however, of presenting the damages sustained during the war in purely physical terms. He considers Germany's inner destruction, brought about by over twelve years of fascist rule and six years of war, to be of even greater importance.[13] The composition of *Und sagte kein einziges Wort* is predicated upon the simultaneity of physical and emotional upheaval. Even as the city's buildings remain in ruins, children grow up without fathers, spouses carry on in the absence of husbands or wives, and poverty is a fact of life. Similarly, the rain that continues for much of the novel leaves a chalky residue on the somber parade of passersby, whose expressions betray a kind of spiritual collapse.[14] In an essay dating from 1952, one year prior to the release of *Und sagte kein einziges Wort,* Böll calls upon his fellow writers to see and bear witness to the long-term psychological repercussions of this human tragedy. "He who hath eyes to see, let him see. . . . The eye of the writer should be human and unerring. . . . It is our duty to remind the world that man exists not simply to be governed—and that the destruction in our world is not limited to that which is external; nor is it so trivial that we can presume to heal it within a few years."[15]

Und sagte kein einziges Wort is Böll's literary response to the ongoing trauma of the war and reinforces the importance of testimony for the healing of Germany's wounds. Despite the dismissive voice of critics, who dubbed his fiction a "literature of the rubble," Böll adamantly rejected the notion that postwar writers should renounce the topic of the war in favor of more uplifting, idyllic subjects.[16] Drafted into the German army in 1939, wounded four times in combat, and taken prisoner by the Allies in 1945, Böll remained haunted by the war long after his country's defeat. He writes to a fellow veteran of the sadness caused by his "long years as a soldier" and of the "terrifying memories" that overtake him when he lies down to sleep.[17] Böll considered it the task of the postwar writer to remind his fellow Germans that the destruction facing Germany in 1945 went well beyond the visible and concrete evidence of bombed-out buildings. And he made no secret of the fact that, in penning the lives of his fictional protagonists, he sought to give voice to "the central theme of my life—the war and all that has come after."[18]

Dori Laub suggests that it is only through speaking of trauma, in bearing witness to it, that traumatic experiences are truly known. But testimony also carries certain costs. To speak of trauma involves the virtual living out of these events and therefore poses the threat of additional trauma. Laub writes that the act of telling can itself become severely traumatizing. The price of speaking is often reliving—"not relief, but further retraumatization."[19] Böll's problematization of this tension between truth-telling and secrecy, communication and fear, finds fullest expression in his novel's central protagonists. Böll focuses his story on the lives of Käte and Fred, a couple who in the postwar years are unable to resume their prewar existence. The traumatic events of the war (the loss of two children, the destruction of their home, their exposure to widespread violence and death) have called into question their relationship as husband and wife. As the novel opens, the two spouses no longer share the same home. Fred Bogner, currently employed as a telephone operator by the Catholic church, has left his wife of fifteen years, claiming he can no longer live in their tiny, dilapidated apartment. The only contact Fred feels capable of maintaining is an occasional phone call and infrequently scheduled rendezvous at various cheap hotels. Käte, unable to escape so easily, is left to take care of the children and each day faces the same dull struggle against poverty and dirt. A first-person narrative told alternately by husband and wife, Böll's novel poignantly reveals the isolation and frustration that not only consume his protagonists' lives but spill over into the next generation. Mistreated by their father and kept silent by their mother, the two surviving Bogner children inherit the couple's unresolved conflicts in the form of extreme timidity and withdrawal. At one point in the novel, Käte confides in the reader a sense of gratitude that her now-dead infants were spared such a painful life.

Käte and Fred interpret their wartime experiences as a series of betrayals, a reaction that intensifies their psychological pain. Fred feels betrayed by his country because he was sent to fight in a brutal and senseless war. At various points in the novel, Fred supplies the reader with graphic descriptions of his wartime experiences: from being forced to crawl among the dead and dying, to being placed next to the bloody body of a soldier infested with lice. Böll makes clear, however, that those fighting Germany's war were not the only ones affected. In chapter 4 of the novel, we learn that Käte gave birth to twins during a military attack and sat clutching her children as grenades exploded over her home. These two children, Regina and Robert, did not survive the war. Käte informs us that the minister of health, reacting to the financial interests of his nephew, prohibited the very medicine which could have saved her children's lives. Unable to provide her newborns with proper medical treatment, Käte is forced to watch them die a slow and gruesome death. The losses sustained by Fred and Käte are not limited to the years of National Socialism; they continue on for years. It can be argued that Böll's protagonists are victims on two fronts: once as the survivors of a devastating war, twice as the casualties of Germany's postwar economy. They live in abject poverty but are surrounded by those like their neighbors the Frankes, whose lives persist virtually unchanged.

Due to the tenacity of Fred and Käte's desire to forget the past, specific references to their traumas are rare and intervene in the narrative primarily in the form of flashbacks. Through the use of flashbacks, Böll presents his readers with a history that refuses to be forgotten or contained, a history that continually erupts into the couple's postwar lives. Just as the dust and dirt in the Bogners' home can never be fully removed, so too do residues of the Nazi past intrude upon the couple's awareness, forcing them to confront what they desperately seek to forget: the death of their young twins, the destruction of their home, the onset of extreme poverty, and the strain of their marital conflict. These flashbacks dramatize, in effect, what Cathy Caruth terms a strange connection between "the *elision* of memory and the *precision* of recall." Those who are traumatized, she writes, are forced to relive an unbidden past, even as the memory of this past occurs paradoxically "through the very denial of active recollection."[20]

In order for survivors of trauma to make sense of their experiences, they must accommodate the traumatic incident into their current concept of self and into the ever-emerging text of their personal life histories. The path to such integration, Pierre Janet concludes, is language: the conversion of traumatic memory into narrative memory.[21] The enormity of Fred and Käte's linguistic imprisonment, their inability to transform their unarticulated suffering into the cooperative narration of story, is borne out in the structure of the novel itself. Mirroring the verbal dysfunction of the novel's central protagonists, *Und sagte kein einziges Wort* is arranged as a "doppelter Ich-Roman." The narrative is organized not as a dialogue between husband and wife but as a series of separate monologues. It is the reader alone who is privy to the couple's guilt, fears, and hopes. It is the reader who serves as witness to their hidden pain. It is not until the final three chapters of the novel that Fred and Käte summon the courage to openly discuss their separation. As one critic perceptively observes, "there is no community of narrative, just as there is no community in their marriage."[22]

Wilhelm Schwarz has noted that the language of *Und sagte kein einziges Wort* corresponds closely to the loneliness and monotony of Fred and Käte's postwar existence and describes it as "sober and unembellished, almost brittle."[23] It is true that Fred and Käte assess their experiences (both past and present) in a manner strangely devoid of affect and throughout the novel express no trace of sentimentalism or verbosity. What Schwarz omits in his analysis, however, is the fact that this seemingly apathetic discourse goes well beyond the harsh realities of the protagonists' present environment and exposes a desperate attempt at self-protection. The pronounced lack of emotion in Fred and Käte's speech bears a striking resemblance to what Robert Jay Lifton observes among trauma survivors as a "psychic closing-off." Unable to remain open to their psychic pain, Fred and Käte erect both in their language and in their lives a "protective symbolic screen" which enables them to resist the impact of their trauma. In effect, it allows them to endure psychologically by "simply ceas[ing] to feel."[24]

Such psychically imposed defenses are emphasized through many of the novel's key words, especially *Langeweile* (boredom) and *Gleichgültigkeit* (indifference). These nouns circulate throughout Böll's story as virtual leitmotifs and create an atmosphere of almost suffocating lethargy. Fred is not only uncertain about the meaning of life but seems wholly indifferent to success. He repeatedly describes both his present existence and his experiences during the war as "boring." Käte, too, is weary of the drudgery of everyday demands. She compulsively cleans the dirt from her home but is totally lacking in enthusiasm and self-confidence. Rather than aggressively combating the undesirable aspects of their lives, Käte and Fred betray in their words a weariness bordering on passivity. Whether it is Käte's description of her endless "battle against dirt" or Fred's humble appeals for money, one senses an inability (both physical and linguistic) to effect positive change. Fred is conscious of the apathy felt by him and his wife. Interestingly, however, he attributes it not to their recent psychological trauma but to their present lack of money and energy: "One needs money for a larger apartment; one needs what they like to call energy. But we have neither money nor energy. And that includes my wife" (p. 71).[25]

Böll's use of corporeal metaphors further underscores the intensity of his protagonists' traumas and illustrates the longevity of the war's psychological consequences. Fred and Käte respond to the tangible impurities of their environment as elements that produce both mental and physical ill health. Fred's departure from his family is attributed to a "sickness," a vague condition said to have arisen from inadequate living space. Fred later depicts the material privations of his life as dust. He can feel this dust on his tongue and senses that it penetrates his lungs, his heart, and his mind. Käte, too, presents the reader with an image of a sullied and poisonous milieu. She states that the dust and dirt of her apartment, which she attributes to the war, settles upon the helpless body of her sleeping infant. Käte's attempts to clean the visible impurities from her home coincide with a desperate desire to rid her psyche of the traumatic residue of war.

Yet in spite of these shared observations and behaviors, Fred and Käte are not identical in the strategies they adopt to cope with their traumas. Käte remains with her children and, despite her fear of poverty and personal failure, attempts to hold the family together. Fred, on the other hand, decides to leave his wife and children, finding it easier to face his forsaken commitment than the strain of everyday family life. Still, this is merely the most tangible and obvious difference between Käte's and Fred's responses to past and present conditions. The key to understanding the more intricate motivations behind their contrasting reactions lies in language itself: in what Käte and Fred tell us about themselves and their choices, in how and when they choose to say it, and, just as importantly, in what is left to silence.

It is Fred's voice that begins the novel. He introduces himself to the reader by way of a descriptive account of his hours after work. He picks up his paycheck, decides how much to send Käte and the children, and then visits various employers and acquaintances in hopes of procuring more. The remainder of the novel follows much the same pattern. Fred repeatedly counts whatever money he has left and mulls over how much he can afford to spend on *Schnaps* and *Würste.*[26] In an effort to avoid the psychic turmoil resulting from his trauma, Fred focuses on the external details of his past and present experiences, not on his emotional reaction to them. Fred claims to remember vividly his two dead children but, unlike Käte, provides no specific information about their deaths. And although he notices the physical devastation of his environment, Fred describes his surroundings in a detached, almost objective fashion. He does not (perhaps cannot) allow his emotions to surface or to interfere.

Fred's denial of the war's devastating impact and his concomitant disconnection from others is manifested through his choice of careers. Fred works both during and after the war as a telephone operator. He is responsible for facilitating linguistic exchanges, for keeping the lines of communication open. Fred is, in fact, well suited to his job and fulfills his duties with considerable skill and ease. He connects other people's voices but is absolved of any pressure to participate in their conversations. He listens to what others have to say but at the same time remains safely outside the content of their discourse. This freedom to be a passive listener fills Fred with a sense of calm rarely experienced elsewhere. It is tempting to view Fred's job as a sign of healthy social integration. He has a task to do and he does it well. Yet, when one compares Fred's daytime duties to his private life, it becomes apparent that Fred's job is but another form of denial, a substitute for his own linguistic lack. By conveying the appearance of communication, Fred's employment not only protects him against his personal inability to speak but compensates for the fact that language itself has been significantly devalued.

Ironically, despite his professed resentment toward empty, bureaucratic discourse, Fred has incorporated the same linguistic notions into his own speech. Whenever he does choose to speak, Fred's language is often clipped and impassive. As stated earlier, Fred has learned to rid his voice of emotion and even in moments of severe desperation he disguises his speech so as to sound sufficiently nonchalant. Fred's statements reveal that his crisis of language is not limited to his own, internal compulsion to simultaneously conceal and expose the trauma he has suffered. Fred also lives in a society that sends him conflicting messages. On the one hand, Fred feels those around him are extremely tolerant and understanding. Because he is a war veteran, he is excused for behavior that would otherwise be considered unacceptable: erratic moods, disorientation, and apathy. On the other hand, Fred has observed that such goodwill ends whenever his fellow citizens are asked to provide more thoroughgoing support. Not only are the city's inhabitants unaccustomed to expressing genuine sympathy, they are, in the final analysis, worried primarily about its effects on their pockets. Fred states, for example, that in a city of three hundred thousand residents, it is difficult to find a single person who will lend him the money to meet with his wife. Fred's irritability and, in some instances, violent anger is exacerbated by Germany's inability to acknowledge the magnitude of the war's psychological impact, on veterans as well as on civilians. Society acknowledges Fred's wartime service and is perhaps even grateful for his sacrifice. But it offers Fred no assistance in adapting to postwar life. The war has left its mark on Fred; it has also altered the Germany to which he returns. Left without a network of support, Fred sinks into greater and greater isolation and acts out his loss of agency and integrity with anger and abuse.

We later learn that Fred not only feels uncomfortable speaking but harbors a distrust of language in general. Fred's skepticism mirrors Böll's own postwar feelings concerning the potential hazards of linguistic expression. Böll's problematization of language in the novel is informed by the postwar dilemma of producing authentic literature with an adulterated native tongue. J. H. Reid writes that the "totalitarian claims of National Socialism meant that there was scarcely an area of social, intellectual or cultural life that had not been debased and discredited by association with Hitler" and includes in his examples the German language itself.[27] Böll remarks that the war left such words as "duty," "fatherland," "honor," and "obedience" completely devalued.[28] And he argues that the adjective "respectable" should be stricken from the German vocabulary altogether.[29] In his 1959 essay "Die Sprache als Hort der Freiheit" (Language as the Arsenal of Freedom), Böll insists that all who speak or write should be aware of the awesome, and sometimes dangerous, power of a single word.[30]

Fred's experiences both in and out of war have taught him that linguistic efficacy carries with it the ability to absolve oneself of suspicion and to rally others to one's cause—whether for good or evil. Language has the capacity to express emotion but also to hide it. During the war, language served as a vehicle for transmitting statistics. Translated into normal parlance, however, these same numbers spoke of an enormous loss of life. "Most of them were content to transmit death by phone. It wriggled through the telephone wires and they squeezed it into the receivers with their tinny voices—right into the ear of the person responsible for making sure that enough peopled died" (pp. 128–29). This same automated, bureaucratic speech is apparent in Fred's current employment. Fred notes that, like that of the military, the language of Catholic authority is repetitive and trite, more concerned with precautions than with meaningful conversation. The novel reveals that Fred was once faithful to Catholicism and indeed spent a large portion of his married life in church. Yet, unlike Käte, who continues to respect the language of the church and even finds some comfort in it, Fred has become cynical and suspicious. Shortly before the end of the novel, Fred confesses that such reticence provides him a sense of superiority: "There were moments when I thought I was right and everybody else was wrong, because they spoke with complete ease while I never seemed to find the words at all" (p. 164).

Concurrent with Fred's skepticism, however, is an awareness that his silence is a handicap. Fred realizes that his inability or unwillingness to communicate his trauma isolates him from others. He expresses frustration that, because he is so uncommunicative, people frequently misjudge him. Fred is also troubled that he has no real audience for his speech. And, in keeping with the tendency of trauma victims to both withdraw from and desperately seek out close relationships, Fred vacillates between extreme solitude and an overwhelming desire for intimacy. He simultaneously seeks out a room for himself and Käte and deeply regrets that he has no one to confide in, no one to whom he can convey his frustration and pain.

As mentioned earlier, it is the reader who hears these confidences. Although Fred finds it hard to speak his mind to other characters, including Käte, he is able to make public to us his private weaknesses and fears. In a sense, the reader acts as the priest Fred has ceased to find in Catholicism. Rather than going to confession, Fred makes us into his private confidante and invites us to share a privileged glimpse into his heart and mind. The danger posed by such monologues, of course, is that they lose all measure of objectivity and simply enlist the reader's sympathy. His confessions become, in effect, a kind of "countermemory" writ large.[31] Fred makes little attempt to present an objective or comprehensive view of history but rather relies upon his own private memories to construct a highly subjective, selective, and individualistic version of events. Fred's statements reveal that he is neither devoid of feelings nor blind to their significance. The problem lies, rather, in his inability to convey his suffering to those around him. Faced with the prospect of actual dialogue, Fred is most often reduced to silence.

Käte is likewise implicated in a crisis of testimony and struggles with an analogous compulsion to both expose and conceal her trauma. As mentioned earlier, Käte suffers immensely both during and after the war. She loses her home, two of her children, and, for an indeterminate period, her husband. Like Fred, Käte is at times overcome by silence. She can neither understand her feelings nor speak them aloud. While visiting with Fred at a nearby hotel, for example, Käte states that she "can't really say" why she is so sad and afraid and implores Fred to offer possible explanations for her behavior.

Just as Fred avoids conversation, Käte seeks out silence. She finds her greatest spiritual comfort not in the liturgy of the Mass but in God's soundless presence. Käte would rather hear a spiritual about Christ's silent suffering than all the sermons Catholicism can offer. And she prefers to go to church when she can be completely alone. For much of the novel, Käte suffers in silence. She hides her pain from both Fred and her children and tells the reader that she only cries when no one can hear. Käte's dilemma is amplified by her sex. While psychological trauma has been termed "an affliction of the powerless,"[32] it is evident that Käte's experiences disempower her in ways unique to her role as wife and mother. Fred states, for example, that his status as war veteran affords him a certain social benevolence and compassion. The fact that many of his rather irresponsible traits were present before the war seems to make no difference. Käte, on the other hand, receives no such treatment. She is given condescending, even disgusted, looks when she visits Fred at the hotel. She is told by her priest to take sole responsibility for her husband's absence. And she is taken to task by her neighbor for failing to prevent her recent pregnancy.

Käte is not blind to this double standard. She fulfills her obligations to her family but is also angry and bitter. She is not, as many critics claim, a paragon of the patient, self-effacing homemaker. In contrast to Schwarz, for example, who describes Käte as the actual hero of the novel, who "submits to her martyrdom without complaint,"[33] Böll makes it decidedly clear that his female protagonist has her limits. Toward the end of the novel, Käte reminds Fred of her behavior in years past, when she derived enormous pleasure from being a "brazen slut." And she ends her reminiscence by saying she "would have preferred to spit right in front of them all" (p. 130). Käte is aware that it is she who sacrifices her dignity in her current relations with Fred; her husband is not subject to the same social laws. And although Käte understands Fred's need to feel unencumbered, she denounces his self-pity and his failure to meet his responsibility as a father.

Unlike Fred, who is too overwhelmed by his own trauma to engage in the problems of others, Käte is able to step outside the confines of her own grief. Käte finds in the reader someone to whom she can finally speak. Her words address not only her own struggles but the struggles of women worldwide, whose lives and traumas are relegated to silence and whose stories thus become, in the truest sense of the word, unspeakable. Käte also learns that testimony comes with a price. When she tells Fred of her loneliness and suffering, he immediately attributes her sadness to their present economic status and claims he can provide neither comfort nor support. When Käte informs him of the children's exaggerated and disquieting humility, Fred responds that Käte's remarks are "nonsense," saying that she is merely jealous of her children's youth. As mentioned earlier, Käte also confesses her feelings to a priest. In the place of sympathy and forgiveness, however, she is criticized for harboring ill will and for failing to keep her husband at home.

Erich Santner employs the analogy of homeopathy to emphasize the centrality of an empathic environment for the working through of trauma. He states that in order to master a traumatic loss, the subject must, in the manner of homeopathy, integrate into the self the poison of loss. Santner likewise asserts that a prerequisite for this enactment of the "elegiac procedure" of mourning is a compassionate and supportive social environment.[34] Far from being placed in an empathic social setting conducive to mourning, Käte and Fred are faced with an external milieu that actively thwarts a successful working through of their personal traumas. It is evident that the postwar Germany in which Fred and Käte find themselves is a *Konsumgesellschaft* of the highest order. The voice of materialism is present at all times and in all places, telling consumers what to buy and when to buy it. Slogans such as "Trust your pharmacist" and "Take Doulorin" tout drugs as the postwar cure for Germany's ills. Germans are urged to spend not to think. This obsession with the immediate present—and concurrent avoidance of the past—can also be seen in the silent gaze of a storefront mannequin, who holds a book celebrating a "vacation from the self." It is as if the active process of bearing witness has given way to the active process of forgetting. Fred states in the final chapter of *Und sagte kein einziges Wort* that the faces of such mannequins "always call forth fear." Although his reaction may seem somewhat extreme, it can be taken as a positive sign that Fred rejects the false optimism displayed by these mannequins, thereby avoiding immersion in Germany's rampant materialism. As long as Fred remains skeptical, his detachment and denial remain incomplete. And by escaping the lure of materialism, he resists Germany's invitation to forget.

The perpetuation of business as usual is not limited to free-market capitalism. The elaborately staged religious festivals interspersed throughout Böll's novel have the same goal: to offset and disguise the tangible aftermath of war. The Catholic church, whose task it is to mediate between man's earthly existence and his immortal soul, not only has sustained physical damage but fails in the years following the war to provide the spiritual and emotional support expected from it by its followers. Well-fed, well-dressed Catholic dignitaries parade proudly by their gaunt, poorly clothed parishioners. Sermons (referred to as "watered down homilies") drone on without enthusiasm or feeling. The bishop's speech is monotonous and rehearsed and appeals to "key words" and "half truths" to control the audience's attention. Fred watches as a local priest grows irritated by and impatient with the long line of believers waiting to be forgiven. And when Käte feels compelled to confide in her local priest, the country cleric seems more concerned with the time than with her confession: "Whenever I faltered for a moment, he looked hastily at the clock; and each time I followed his glance I noticed that the hands of the clock moved slowly forward" (p. 82).

Due to the centrality of the church in *Und sagte kein einziges Wort,* it is no doubt appropriate that Käte's Catholicism precipitates her key moments of skepticism and insight. In the first of these scenes, Käte comes across the statue of an angel and is intrigued by its calm, smiling expression. When she wipes the dirt from the statue, however, she discovers that it, too, is a product (and not a very appealing one) of German commercialism. She informs the reader that her joy evaporated as "the garish colors became increasingly visible" and refers to the angel's cheap adornment as "that hideous lacquer of the piety industry" (p. 79). This scene stands in sharp contrast to Käte's earlier-mentioned efforts to clean her apartment. Her repetitive, compulsive struggle to remove all traces of dust and dirt mimics on a physical level Germany's attempts (both conscious and unconscious) to engineer a more pure and enticing present by selectively denying the past. Not surprisingly, Käte's desire for cleanliness is as futile as her country's attempts to expunge its sullied history. In this scene, which appears midway through the novel, the act of cleaning functions quite differently. Here, Käte's attempt to uncover the angel's actual appearance represents what Böll refers to elsewhere as a decisive moment of *Demaskierung* (unmasking).[35] It symbolizes Käte's attempts to expose the truth and serves as a foil for the numerous rituals, festivals, and advertisements that seek to bury German history under the lure of Catholicism and commerce. The scene is followed immediately by Käte's meeting with the priest, a man more attentive to his watch than to his parishioner's suffering. What Käte desires in both encounters is comfort: first through the aesthetic beauty of the Catholic icon, later via compassion and forgiveness. What she receives is superficiality and indifference. Significantly, however, it is only after Käte's visit to the priest that she begins a process of introspection that will eventually break through the protective walls of her denial. For the remainder of the novel, Käte continues to grow in self-understanding and self-reliance and will become increasingly intent on seeing both herself and others as they really are.

It can be argued that the selective denial embedded in Fred and Käte's environment makes the communication of their individual traumas difficult if not impossible. One can also view the isolation Fred and Käte experience within this environment as the catalyst that brings them together and forces them to speak. Despite the obstacles placed before their truth-telling, the most open and frank discussions in *Und sagte kein einziges Wort* are those between Käte and Fred. It is during Fred and Käte's time at the fairgrounds, and later at the hotel, that the couple comes closest to unraveling and bearing witness to their trauma. Käte is convinced that although the war is difficult to discuss, for herself as well as for her husband, to deny it is much more destructive. Käte seeks to explore the injuries inflicted on her family by the war and in so doing hopes to shake them from the paralysis of their traumatization. In contrast to Fred's situation, it is not life which bores Käte but the continuance of a life as victim. Rather than succumbing to past traumas, Käte confronts the reality of the present. In the words of Shoshana Felman, Käte attempts to move beyond "the shock of being stricken" and engages in the present as "an advent, a movement, and as a vital, critical necessity of moving on."[36] It is ultimately Käte who works to expose her trauma and Fred's to the light of testimony and endeavors to convert their painful, unspoken experiences into narratives conducive to recovery. Käte's persistent focus on family and religion underscores her belief that it is only through the company of others that the healing of trauma can take place.[37]

Böll concludes *Und sagte kein einziges Wort* without resolving Fred and Käte's separation. The novel neither encompasses the characters' entire personal histories nor predicts their futures. It provides, in essence, a snapshot of the trauma caused by the war and exposes the individual as well as the social reverberations felt almost a decade later. While it is possible to view the struggles of Käte and Fred to confront their trauma as a positive step toward memory, responsibility, and healing, Böll is careful to depict their progress as incomplete. *Und sagte kein einziges Wort* is no apologia for Germany's recent past. Nor does it portray the postwar years in a positive light. Böll's novel reveals how denial of history allowed Germans to vigorously embrace the present. But it also exposes how signs of Germany's traumatic secret ultimately surfaced: as manic consumerism, as debilitated spirituality, as the forced perpetuation of life as normal, as broken families, depression, and abuse. *Und sagte kein einziges Wort* is a novel about language; about coming to speech and falling into silence. The dynamics of speech and silence illuminate the characters' views of themselves and inform their relationships to both history and the present. The novel is left open-ended. And through its open-endedness, Böll underscores trauma's central paradox. Käte bears witness to her pain then silently returns to her children. Fred listens with barely a word but calls after Käte's retreating form: "Ich muß mit dir sprechen."

* * *

Scholars in recent years have emphasized the importance of trauma studies for examining the public and private narratives produced about World War II: what should be remembered and how, the ethical and aesthetic responsibilities borne by those involved (whether victims, perpetrators, collaborators, or bystanders), the importance of public memory for the creation of national identity, and the function of succeeding generations in collective remembrance and mourning.[38]

An important result of such examinations has been a reassessment of Germany's response to the central trauma of our age: the crimes committed under National Socialism. In contrast to the popularly held view that citizens of the Federal Republic engaged in a "global retreat from the past,"[39] there is now evidence that West Germans did not simply repress or forget the events of World War II and the Holocaust. Historian Robert Moeller demonstrates, for example, that 1950s Germany was a place where a "politics of commemoration" was very much alive. He details the numerous (and often governmentally sponsored) reports of German expulsion at the hands of the Red Army, advertising campaigns to free Germany's POWs, and mass-marketed movies about soldiers' experiences on the front. According to Moeller's analysis of the immediate postwar period, Germans were not so much silent as selective. It is true that the population was largely unwilling or unable to contemplate the crimes committed in the name of the German people and therefore postponed the process of individual and collective recognition and mourning. But it is also true that the events of the Third Reich did not suddenly disappear from private or public awareness. In Moeller's words, "remembering selectively was not the same as forgetting."[40]

An investigation of the German literary scene between 1945 and 1955 leads to similar conclusions. In the decade following World War II, the close proximity of a painful history appears to have precluded an adequately critical assessment of Germany's role. The stories that appeared in print were primarily tales of German suffering; either on the battlefield, in prisoner of war camps, or on the homefront. Writers did not shy away from presenting the devastation caused by the war but limited their narratives to depictions of German victimization, conspicuously avoiding the subject of Germany's victimization of others.[41] It can be argued that Germany's focus on its own suffering provided a socially acceptable, psychically tolerable means of talking about recent traumatic events without accepting responsibility for their origins. Whatever the motivation, the postwar German tendency to speak of the consequences of the Third Reich, while ignoring the population's complicity in Nazi crimes, amounted to an abbreviated story of National Socialism. It was, as Moeller writes, a carefully crafted version of history "in which Germans were ultimately victims of a war Hitler started but everyone lost."[42]

It is my belief that Böll's portrayal of German postwar life in no way precludes a critical assessment of his country's historical-political role. Although Böll relates experientially to German suffering, he insists that the trauma associated with World War II is a burden which Germany, through ignorance and malice, brought upon itself and others.[43] Böll's essays from this period draw attention to Germany's status as perpetrator and articulate the dilemma that results from being at once oppressor and victim, traumatizer and traumatized. Germany did endure the loss of life and property, but it also generated a regime responsible for widespread brutality and death. In writing of the war, Böll offers sympathy for German losses. He also underscores, quite emphatically, the suffering and loss caused to others by his country's horrific crimes. "We pray for the fallen, for those missing in action, for the victims of war. But what our numbed consciences have not yet accomplished is an open, public, and unambiguous prayer for the murdered Jews. That is what we must achieve. Whoever has eyes to see, whoever has ears to hear, must see. Must hear."[44]

Which leads one to ask: Why does Böll fail to address these same issues in his first major work of fiction?[45] Why do his political essays passionately take up the issue of the Holocaust, while *Und sagte kein einziges Wort* never mentions the Jews at all?[46] And why, after articulating a critical awareness of Germany's shameful past, would Böll focus his fictional narrative largely on the private, present-day lives of a single German couple? I would suggest that Böll's "silencing" of the Holocaust, that is, the absence in *Und sagte kein einziges Wort* of any explicit reference to Germany's persecution of the Jews, is crucial to the author's aesthetic project. In the novel Böll's task is not, in contrast to his essays, to remind Germany of its recent crimes but to dramatize through fiction the destructive tenacity of his country's growing amnesia. The novel concentrates on the domestic sphere; it is by no means limited to it. Of central importance to the novel is the convergence of the personal and political; that is, the ways in which the denial of truth and responsibility embedded in familial relations has implications for postwar society as a whole. Fred abandons his wife and children. Käte colludes in Fred's absence by claiming her husband is ill. Certain characters enjoy wealth and recognition, while others are left to live in isolation and poverty. Communication, including sexual intimacy, is mechanical and devoid of tenderness and warmth. In sum, *Und sagte kein einziges Wort* provides a disturbing portrait of Germany's failed opportunity for testimony and vividly exposes the ongoing repercussions of silence: from individual to family and beyond.[47]

NOTES

1. Cathy Caruth, *Unclaimed Experience: Trauma, Narrative and History* (Baltimore: Johns Hopkins University Press, 1996), p. 3.

2. Jean LaPlanche, *Life and Death in Psychoanalysis,* trans. Jeffrey Mehlman (Baltimore: Johns Hopkins University Press, 1976), pp. 41–42.

3. Judith Herman, *Trauma and Recovery: The Aftermath of Violence—from Domestic Abuse to Political Terror* (New York: Basic Books, 1992), p. 20.

4. Caruth, *Unclaimed Experience,* p. 7.

5. I am borrowing here from Alexander and Margarete Mitscherlich's application of Freud's distinction between denial (a defense mechanism "related to disturbing perceptions of external reality") and repression (which refers to the "unpleasure-producing perception of one's own instinctual impulses"). As trauma necessarily entails the experience of shocking or painful events within the physical environment, it is therefore correct to speak of the survivor's psychic disavowal of such events as evidence of denial rather than of repression. See Alexander Mitscherlich and Margarete Mitscherlich, *Die Unfähigkeit zu trauern: Grundlagen kollektiven Verhaltens* (Munich: R. Pier & Co. Verlag, 1967), p. 39.

6. Herman, *Trauma and Recovery,* p. 1.

7. Caruth, *Unclaimed Experience,* p. 3.

8. Caruth, *Unclaimed Experience,* p. 2.

9. Caruth, *Unclaimed Experience,* p. 3.

10. Heinrich Böll, *Und sagte kein einziges Wort* (Cologne: Kiepenheuer & Witsch, 1953). All

further references are to this edition and will be indicated parenthetically. All translations from the German are my own. Böll's novel has also been translated into English as *Acquainted with the Night.* The title provided in my essay refers to Leila Vennewitz's translation of 1978, which I prefer. Vennewitz's title not only conveys a more literal rendering of the original German, it also retains Böll's allusion to the Negro spiritual "And Never Said a Mumbalin' Word."

11. Caruth, *Unclaimed Experience,* p. 4.

12. Shoshana Felman and Dori Laub, *Testimony: Crises of Witnessing in Literature, Psychoanalysis, and History* (New York: Routledge, Chapman and Hall, 1992), p. xix.

13. "Ich habe nichts über den Krieg aufgeschrieben: Ein Gespräch mit Heinrich Böll und Hermann Lenz," *Literaturmagazin 7* (1977): 57.

14. Heinrich Böll, "Bekenntnis zur Trümmerliteratur" (1952), reprinted in *Essayistische Schriften und Reden 1952–1963,* ed. Bernd Balzer (Cologne: Kiepenheuer & Witsch, 1979), p. 35.

15. Böll, "Bekenntnis zur Trümmerliteratur," p. 35.

16. Herbert Hoven, in his commentary to Böll's letters to Ernst-Adolf Kunz, emphasizes the author's frustration with those writers and publishers who actively avoided the topic of the war. In Hoven's view, it was precisely his experience of combat that drove Böll to write and that ultimately led the future Nobel laureate to reject the "Pralinenproduktion" demanded by Germany's top publishing houses (*Die Hoffnung ist wie ein wildes Tier: Der Briefwechsel zwischen Heinrich Böll und Ernst-Adolf Kunz 1945–1953,* ed. Herbert Hoven [Cologne: Kiepenheuer & Witsch, 1994], pp. 389–427).

17. Hoven, *Die Hoffnung ist wie ein wildes Tier,* p. 18.

18. Hoven, *Die Hoffnung ist wie ein wildes Tier,* p. 143. Böll was not alone in his treatment of World War II and its aftermath. Other examples of the so-called *Trümmerliteratur* include Wolfgang Borchert's radio play *Draußen vor der Tür* (1947), the story of a soldier returning to a Germany in ruins; Hans Erich Nossack's *Der Untergang* (1949), which chronicles the firebombing of Hamburg; Elisabeth Langgässer's *Märkische Argonautenfahrt* (1950), a novel that traces the journey of Berlin refugees to the convent of Anastasiendorf; and Hans Werner Richter's *Sie fielen aus Gottes Hand* (1951), which recounts the adventures of twelve people, differing in nationality, class, and religion, from the outbreak of war to their internment in a camp for displaced persons.

19. Felman and Laub, *Testimony,* p. 67.

20. Cathy Caruth, ed., *Trauma: Explorations in Memory* (Baltimore: Johns Hopkins University Press, 1995), pp. 152–53.

21. Pierre Janet, *Psychological Healing,* trans. Eden Paul and Cedar Paul (New York: Macmillan, 1925), p. 663. Originally published as *Les médications psychologiques: études historiques, psychologiques et cliniques sur les méthodes de la psychothérapie* (Paris: F. Alcan, 1919).

22. J. H. Reid, *Heinrich Böll: A German for His Time* (New York: St. Martin's Press, 1988), p. 98.

23. Wilhelm Schwarz, *Der Erzähler Heinrich Böll* (Bern: Franke, 1967), p. 31.

24. Robert J. Lifton, *History and Human Survival* (New York: Random House, 1961), pp. 125, 162.

25. Reid argues that Fred's statement speaks to his own experience, not to Käte's, and is contradicted by what the reader himself sees. In Reid's analysis, "Käte has the energy; it is her subordinate position which prevents her from putting it to good use" (*Heinrich Böll,* p. 96). I agree with Reid that Käte's society imposes on her an inferior status but take issue with his assumption that Fred alone exhibits an apathetic or lethargic response.

26. In his correspondence with fellow veteran Ernst-Adolf Kunz, Böll repeatedly conveys similar concerns. Böll writes to Kunz of his cramped Cologne apartment, his desperate search for work, his physical fatigue, and the pressures of providing for his wife and children. The author also divulges to Kunz the key to his perseverance—coffee, nicotine, and schnapps (Hoven, *Die Hoffnung ist wie ein wildes Tier,* pp. 392–93).

27. Reid, *Heinrich Böll,* p. 38. Böll himself makes a similar statement in his essay "Befehl und Verantwortung": "The horrible thing about the National Socialist disease was that it cannot be dismissed as a mere episode in our history, as something that is over and done with. National Socialism contaminated our thoughts, the very air we breathe; it poisoned the words that we speak and write to such an extent that they cannot be made purified through legal measures alone" (*Essayistische Schriften und Reden,* p. 453).

28. Heinrich Böll, *Aufsätze, Kritiken, Reden* (Cologne: Kiepenheuer & Witsch, 1967), p. 302.

29. Böll, "Wo ist dein Bruder?" *Essayistische Schriften und Reden,* p. 172.

30. Böll, "Die Sprache als Hort der Freiheit," *Essayistische Schriften und Reden,* p. 302.

31. I am borrowing here from Reiko Tachibana's application of Foucault's notion of "counter-memory" to an examination of postwar German and Japanese literature. Tachibana shows how these narratives offer an alternative to more official versions of World War II and its aftermath. In his opinion, "postwar writers who have been repeatedly rewriting the recent past do not pretend to present an objective and unified vision of history, but rather . . . emphasize the subjectivity and the selective nature of any record of events" (Reiko Tachibana, *Narrative as Counter-Memory: A Half-Century of Postwar Writing in Germany and Japan* [Albany: State University of New York Press, 1998], p. 1).

32. Herman, *Trauma and Recovery,* p. 33.

33. Schwarz, *Der Erzähler Heinrich Böll,* p. 31.

34. Erich Santner, *Stranded Objects: Mourning, Memory and Film in Postwar Germany* (Ithaca: Cornell University Press, 1990), p. 24.

35. Böll, "Masken," *Essayistische Schriften und Reden,* p. 182.

36. Felman and Laub, *Testimony,* p. 28.

37. Käte's position offers a striking parallel to the psychological literature on trauma and recovery. Judith Herman, for example, maintains that "the solidarity of a group provides the strongest protection against terror and despair, and the strongest antidote to traumatic experience. Trauma isolates; the group recreates a sense of belonging" (Herman, *Trauma and Recovery,* p. 214).

38. See, for example, Dominick LaCapra, *Representing the Holocaust: History, Theory, Trauma* (Ithaca: Cornell University Press, 1994); and LaCapra, *History and Memory after Auschwitz* (Ithaca: Cornell University Press, 1998).

39. Perhaps the most famous proponents of this view are Mitscherlich and Mitscherlich, *Die Unfähigkeit zu trauern,* p. 19. See also Wolfgang Benz, "Postwar Society and National Socialism: Remembrance, Amnesia, Rejection," *Tel Aviver Jahrbuch für deutsche Geschichte* 19 (1990): 1–12; and Santner, *Stranded Objects.*

40. Robert Moeller, "War Stories: The Search for a Usable Past in the Federal Republic of Germany," *American Historical Review* 101 (1996), 1012–13. For further discussions of the politics of commemoration in postwar Germany see Michael Schornstheimer, *Die Leuchtenden Augen der Frontsoldaten: Nationalsozialismus und Krieg in den Illustriertenromanen der fünfziger Jahre* (Berlin: Metropol Verlag, 1995); and George L. Mosse, *Fallen Soldiers: Reshaping the Memory of the World Wars* (New York: Oxford University Press, 1990), pp. 1009–13.

41. The early activities of the famed Gruppe 47 are proof that even the most politically astute of postwar writers were profoundly shaped by the temporal vantage point from which they wrote. Despite their knowledge of the crimes committed during the Third Reich, the creative energies of these authors were directed toward depicting German suffering, not at exposing the horrors perpetrated against their country's designated enemies. The initial goal of Gruppe 47 was to remove all fascist terminology and style from the German language (displayed most blatantly in the bombast of Hitlerian oratory) and included the following suggestions: the reduction of German vocabulary to three hundred words, the production of sober and straightforward narratives, and the use of factual reportage popularized by Ernest Hemingway.

42. Moeller, "War Stories," p. 1013. Writers of the next two generations prove much more critical of Germany's causal role in the Third Reich. Fueled by the Eichmann trial of 1961 and the trial of Auschwitz guards in 1963–65, there emerged within the literary and larger cultural sphere a growing opposition to the older generation's limited political awareness. Those born during and after the war informed themselves about the crimes committed under Hitler and became increasingly aware of the cover-ups and denials rampant among their elders. In the late 1960s, the war in Vietnam and the tensions of the cold war gave rise to criticism of renewed political aggression and motivated students to question their parents and grandparents about their involvement in the authoritarian structures of Nazism. Opposition to the older generation grew and ultimately found expression not only in the student rebellions of 1968 but in a literature intent on exposing the truth. For a more detailed study of recent literary depictions of the family, see my book *Family Secrets and the Contemporary German Novel: Literary Explorations in the Aftermath of the Third Reich* (Columbia, S.C.: Camden House, 2001).

43. In his 1956 essay "Wo ist dein Bruder?" Böll argues that while National Socialism misled some Germans, others knowingly participated in its brutalities. He goes on to say that it is the political and moral task of all Germans to acknowledge what they, as a country, allowed to occur: "It remains possible for each guilty person to acknowledge what he has done; it remains possible for each person to repent. But what should never be possible, for anyone in this country, is a denial of what happened, or an attempt to justify it in any way" (*Essayistische Schriften und Reden*, p. 173).

44. Böll, "Auferstehung des Gewissens," *Essayistische Schriften und Reden*, p. 134.

45. Böll makes reference to Germany's treatment of the Jews in two of his earlier (yet commercially less successful) works: "Über die Brücke" (1950) and *Wo warst du, Adam?* (1951).

46. In addition to the essay "Auferstehung des Gewissens," in which Böll criticizes Germany's failure to openly address Nazi genocide, a considerable number of Böll's commentaries from the 1950s and early 1960s make explicit mention of the Holocaust. Such essays include his afterword to Borchert's *Draußen vor der Tür* (1955), "Wo ist dein Bruder?" (1956), "Zeichen an der Wand" (1960), "Hierzulande" (1960), and "Befehl und Verantwortung" (1961).

47. For an opposing view, see Ernestine Schlant, *The Language of Silence: West German Literature and the Holocaust* (New York: Routledge, 1999). In Schlant's estimation, Böll's fictional treatment of the Holocaust was compromised by "idealized, unrealistic stereotypes" and by ambiguous, veiled references to Nazi atrocities. Schlant concludes that despite Böll's acute social conscience and his "moral imperative to speak for the underdog," his specific narrative strategies implicate him in the silencing of Germany's crimes (p. 25).

CHAPTER 7

Memory and Existence: Implications of the *Wende*

ELIZABETH A. TEN DYKE

Think, for a moment, about grocery shopping. You grab a cart from the sidewalk in front of your local store and push through the doors. Aisle one: Produce. What do you usually buy—seedless red grapes, McIntosh apples? You ask yourself "Do we need onions?" No, the last time you checked there was a bag in the fridge. At the end of the produce aisle—one dozen large eggs, the yellow container, and a package of cheese. Aisle two: do you drink coffee or tea? What brand? Down the aisles and up, you fill your cart with the same items you buy every week. There's no need to make a list any more because shopping has become automatic. All you need to think about is "Are we out of that yet, or not?" and, occasionally, you make a special purchase—perhaps a gallon of cooking oil, or a cake mix for a birthday celebration.

What in the world does grocery shopping have to do with memory, or with memory in German history? It has to do with something often overlooked by historians, anthropologists, and others who study social aspects of memory: the crucial role of memory in facilitating the human ability to function in the world on a day-to-day basis. A considerable amount of published scholarship on social aspects of memory explores the role of memory on unique occasions or in special circumstances: commemorative ritual, public controversy over historical representation, and so forth. In this chapter I take a different approach: I explore the absolutely fundamental significance of memory to the successful performance of ordinary routines. I do so by hypothesizing a connection between a failure of memory and psychological effects of consequential social transformation.

My starting point is the host of far-reaching changes that took place in eastern Germany after 1989. During 1991 and 1992, after the *Wende* (the "turn" that led to the collapse of the German Democratic Republic and the unification of Germany), I conducted oral history interviews in Dresden, eastern Germany, as part of a larger research project.[1] Respondents who were in their thirties or older often talked about feeling *Orientierungslos*—they were experiencing radical disorientation. Given that I had an interest in the work of Martin Heidegger, I interpreted this condition as an ontological crisis. Later, I saw that their *Orientierungslosigkeit* could be linked fruitfully to memory—or the lack thereof.

I am not making a case for national amnesia in the East after 1989. Rather, I argue that the memories East Germans held, particularly those that enabled them to accomplish daily routines successfully, became irrelevant to new life circumstances in the East after 1989. In eastern Germany, a rift between memory and daily life opened up after the *Wende*. This rift can be interpreted in part through insights emerging from anthropology and cognitive neuroscience. Explored in this way, the rift generates new insight into aspects of the transition in the former German Democratic Republic (GDR) after 1989. More broadly, it contributes to understanding of the role of memory in mediating or facilitating human interactions in larger cultural and social contexts.

Ethnographic Setting

In the GDR, the year 1989 was both exhilarating and terrifying. As late as October that year it was still not clear whether or not the state would forsake violence as it responded to the increasingly insistent calls for reform voiced by its citizens. At that point no one could foresee that in a matter of months, even days, daily life in East Germany would be changed forever. On 9 November the border to the West was opened and millions of East Germans began pouring through breaches in the Berlin Wall, and at other less well known crossings, into West Germany. In March 1990 the Christian Democratic Union, the ruling party in the West, won free elections in the East. In July the economies were joined as the East German mark was replaced by the West German Deutsche mark, and on 4 October 1990 the two states were legally united under the provisions of paragraph 23 of the West German Basic Law.[2]

Despite the apparent finality of German unification, a host of profound changes were yet to come. These changes included waves of layoffs that affected millions of workers nationwide. At their peak, in some communities over a third of workers were no longer employed full-time in the positions they held prior to 1989. I offer data from the state of Saxony as an example.

In April 1991 the State Bureau of Statistics for Saxony counted 2.536 million Saxons as "*Erwerbspersonen*," or members of the work force. (The total population of Saxony was 4,730,100.) In June 1991, 214,889 Saxons (approximately 8 percent) were officially unemployed. But, in addition, a total of 39,631 Saxons had been incorporated into government work programs (*Arbeitsbeschaffungsmaßnahmen*, or ABM); an additional 586,366 Saxons were working reduced hours and 24,579 had entered programs for retraining or continuing education (see table 7.1). In other words, eight months after the unification of Germany, 865,465 Saxons, or almost 34 percent of the state's *Erwerbspersonen,* were no longer working full time in the jobs they held before the *Wende.*[3]

Those men and women fortunate enough to be employed after unification found their places of work filled with new tools, organizational strategies, processes of production, and styles of management. The workplace also became characterized by new rules of social and professional interaction. Socialist Unity Party politics and nonproductive activities including meetings of the Free German Youth and German-Soviet Friendship Society came to an end. The "all for one and one for all" mentality of the socialist collective—even if solidarity existed more in ideological pronouncements than in practice—was replaced by the mentality of the *Ellenbogengesellschaft,* or "elbow society." In other words, the paramount importance of socialist attitudes and political activities in the workplace was replaced by a competitive struggle between workers for jobs and job security.

The flood of consumer products and services that washed over the East after 1989 made it unnecessary to cultivate the networks of *Beziehungen* (relationships) so essential for subsistence in the GDR. It follows that the social interactions of *Beziehungen* and related friendships fell away too, leading to the experience of a new kind of isolation for many East Germans. It was no longer necessary to ply carpenters, electricians, or plumbers with fresh garden produce to procure their assistance with home improvement projects. Neighbors no longer stopped by to ring the bell and let friends know that the local grocer had oranges for sale. Queuing, or the time-consuming practice of waiting on line for goods or services, became a thing of the past.[4]

Practices directly pertaining to the future also vanished. Instead of applying for a car and other goods for newborn children in the hopes that the items might be available for purchase sometime after those same children came of age, families could now stroll down to a shiny new department store and purchase anything they wanted—if they had the cash. It was no longer necessary to initiate preparations for summer vacation as soon as Christmas was over—in the GDR,

Table 7.1. Employment Data, Saxony, June 1991

Category	Number	Percentage
Unemployed	214,889	8.4
Arbeitsbeschaffungsmaßnahmen	39,631	1.5
Reduced hours	586,366	23.1
Retraining/Continuing education	24,579	0.9
	865,465	33.9
Work force	2,536,000	100.0

Source: Statistisches Jahrbuch Sachsen, Statistisches Landesamt des Freistaates Sachsen (Dresden, 1992), 130, 137.

because certain foods such as jellies were available in abundance in the winter months, and scarce in spring and summer, families had started shopping for summer camping trips months in advance.[5]

In the midst of these vast changes individuals who had abandoned or sold their properties in the East any time between 1933 and 1945, and 1949 and 1989 won the right to attempt to reclaim their assets.[6] In Saxony alone over two hundred thousand properties become the focus of claims and, in just the first year after German unification, approximately twenty-six hundred were returned to their former owners.[7] In many cases former property owners or their descendants were compensated with cash instead of the real estate in question. Still, the fact that these individuals even arrived in the East, and laid claim to property, created almost unbearable levels of stress for the East German families who, in some cases, had for decades called the houses in question "home."[8]

As if these stresses were not enough, West German currency and stamps were introduced and postal codes were converted to the West German system. The cost of living increased exponentially. Prices for rent, fuel, food, clothing, books, and transportation rapidly approached or exceeded prices for comparable goods and services in the West; salaries, however, remained considerably lower. Daily papers and other media including television and radio stations were purchased by West German corporations. They were merged, shut down, or, in certain cases, continued under new management and with revised programming. Popular TV programs, including the children's bedtime show "Der Sandman," were canceled. The East German youth radio station DT-64 was silenced. Monuments to Marxism-Leninism were removed.[9] Streets and plazas were renamed but when old street signs were removed, the outlines of their letters remained, spelling out the names of famous socialists or Communists. Thus, throughout the East streets were marked with unexpected reminders of what had been.

In rural areas, once-flourishing agricultural tracts reverted to weeds after farming cooperatives were disbanded. Agricultural machinery sat unused and silent. In urban areas the sights, sounds, and aromas of the East evanesced as factories closed and the roaring of East German Trabants was replaced by the smooth hum of western cars. The din of commercial and home renovation filled the air, while scaffolding filled the sky.

Overall, the bureaucracy of the East German socialist state was replaced by the bureaucracy of the West German social welfare state. In the fall of 1991, in the midst of these vast changes, East Germans had to select new forms of health insurance for themselves. How ironic the pun: at the same time that the prevailing sentiment among virtually all East Germans with whom I came into contact was *Unsicherheit* (insecurity) almost every family I visited was pouring over a pile of papers trying to determine what kind of *Versicherung* (insurance) they should obtain. Not surprisingly, in interviews conducted during this time, respondents repeatedly focused on the *Unruhe* (agitation) they were experiencing: "It's dreadful, just dreadful. Everyone is in *Unruhe,*" commented one respondent.

In August 1991, a woman I met (who informally "adopted" me during my stay) took me on a walk around her neighborhood. We called on her friends and inquired about whether or not people knew of a room I might rent. At one house a small, gray-haired woman in her seventies answered the door. She squinted at us through very thick glasses, wrung her hands, and worried out loud. She didn't have a room for me, it was clear. She was frightened that she might lose her apartment to a West German family attempting to claim the house as their own: "Yes, it's very upsetting. There are a lot of families with these problems now. There's one woman, she lives over there, who was told that her house might be sold but they don't know for sure. She says come what may, they can't just throw me out. But people worry, worry a lot. You always have that feeling, 'What's next?'"

Later, after finding a room with a family whose son had gone off to college, I returned to speak with this elderly woman. I wrote in my notes:

> We chatted. Frau W. speaks quickly, with a full, round *sächsisch* accent. She only knows that they [the West Germans] are coming on Saturday. She doesn't know if they're coming in the morning, or the afternoon, she doesn't have any idea at all, no idea, she knows only that they want to sell the house and that they are coming on Saturday. She didn't know how the matter will be resolved, when it will be resolved and, if it is resolved in favor of the West Germans, where she will go.
>
> "Did they send a letter?" I asked. Yes, they gave notice in a letter. Otherwise she doesn't know anything. "It must be tense," I commented. There was a collective response from everyone in the room, a sharp exhalation. "Oh yes, it's tense," they said.[10]

Many respondents told me that the suicide rate increased as a result of the *Wende.* As data on suicide collected in the GDR are unreliable it is difficult, if not impossible, to ascertain whether or not the rate did actually increase. However, as the local paper started publishing reports of suicide after 1989, respondents *perceived* that the rate had increased. When asked, respondents attributed this apparent increase to the pressures of the market economy: unemployment and debt.

There are data showing that the birth rate plummeted after the *Wende.* In Saxony, there were 49,672 births reported in 1990. In 1991 only 31,278 babies were born, and in the following year that number dropped to 25,298.[11] Dr. Joachim Weller, chief of reproductive medicine at Dresden's Friedrichstadt hospital, suggested that the decline could have multiple causes. One of these was the emigration of men and women in their childbearing years. But other causes stemmed from the lack of certainty after the *Wende,* in particular with respect to the job market.[12] Beloved in the GDR, after 1989 children came to be seen as a burden, especially for women attempting to balance domestic and professional responsibilities without the inexpensive childcare that had been widely available in socialist East Germany.[13]

On top of everything else, the events of 1989 led to an altered sense of time, space, and possibility in the East, at the very least because the border to the West was opened. East Germans confronted new limits too. For the respondents I interviewed, especially men and women in their forties and older, the most significant of these was insecurity in the job market. Even elderly men and women who were, themselves, unaffected by unemployment, had children, grandchildren, friends, or neighbors in personal crisis as a result of the loss of their jobs.

In general, the overwhelming number of changes resulting from the *Wende* resulted in very high levels of distress for East Germans. Often, respondents I interviewed looked pale, fatigued, and tense. Many, like Frau W., displayed anxiety and stress by wringing their hands, shaking their heads, rubbing their foreheads, or making similarly meaningful gestures. Several had sought professional help. They told me the *Wende* had left them *"fertig"* (exhausted) and *"kaputt"* (done in or broken).

Clearly, all societies undergo change and, in many cases, change may be rapid and radical. Furthermore, the natural process of human aging, coupled with the facts of technological innovation, population movement, political conflict, and cultural development, guarantees that all of us live today in a world quite different from that in which we grew up. People often experience profound changes of other kinds too. For example immigrants, refugees, foreign students, and tourists may spend months or years in strange environments that only slowly become familiar. They may experience a variety of symptoms as a result, ranging from homesickness to physical illness, or even nervous collapse. Still, the East German case is special.

Even if tourists, foreign students, and immigrants travel away from home for a long time, or never return, they can derive some security from the knowledge that home is there. Refugees, whose homes (and families) may have been wasted behind them, are, surely, in a more precarious position psychologically than are other travelers. Citizens of other former Soviet bloc countries experienced changes after 1989, but as they did not undergo (re)unification with an economically, culturally, and politically dominant nation, the changes they experienced were less extensive and took place at a slower rate. In East Germany, in the span of just a few months, the culture of GDR society was supplanted by a culture that was at once, strangely, both foreign and familiar. As if this were not enough the mundane world, the world of daily life where people find comfort and feel secure in routine or habitual behaviors was transformed forever too. After 1989 East Germans found themselves in the utterly bizarre and unnerving situation of being "home" in eastern Germany but, because of the *Wende,* never being home again. Let us return to the example of grocery shopping.

In capitalist societies a wide variety of products are available in stores. Brand identity is created and products are differentiated through intense investment in market research, product and package design, pricing, and advertising. In the

GDR, in the absence of capitalist competition, very few varieties of a given item were available for sale in ordinary stores (the Konsum or H.O.). Those varieties offered for sale remained essentially unchanged for years; packaging was overwhelmingly simple and monotonous in materials, form, color, and symbolic representation. In general, as an element of the GDR's material culture, grocery products were fixtures of a society characterized more by constancy than innovation.[14]

The GDR was often referred to as a "shortage society" and certain goods—ranging from tropical fruits to replacement parts for automobiles—were often in short supply. Still, basic items such as such as bread, meat, soap, and clothing were commonly available. In addition, East Germans were not limited to shopping at the Konsum or H.O. Other stores, namely Exquisit and Delikat-Läden, offered a wider variety of merchandise including both luxury goods and, in some cases, products from western Germany. Intershops made western products (coffee, toys, clothes, etc.) available to foreigners and East Germans who possessed hard currency. East Germans also received western goods in gift packages.[15]

Still, with the currency union of 1 July 1990, East German Konsum and H.O. stores were emptied of eastern bloc products and filled with brands distributed by powerful West German conglomerates. No longer specialty items available only in Exquisit or Delikat stores, no longer exclusively an option for East Germans who had relatives or other contacts in the West, products including West German coffee, soap, and butter were piled up on the shelves in East German stores. As of July 1990, the socialist economy was conclusively sacked by consumer culture.

Curious East Germans poured into stores and pushed their way down the aisles. Some walked through simply to see what was there. Others shopped slowly, turning items over in their hands, carefully reading product labels, puzzling over the packaging, mulling over prices. The number and variety of items for sale in stores had exploded. If there had been one kind of yogurt previously, now there were eight! At the same time familiar brands, to which some East Germans had strong sentimental attachments, vanished. The smells of grocery shopping changed too. East German products that had given grocery stores a distinctive aroma disappeared, replaced by western products with entirely different odors. Completely new foods appeared—one respondent mentioned zucchini: "What is it? How do you eat it?" Somewhat astonished, I watched an acquaintance peel and eat a banana upside down.[16] In Dresden a cart appeared on the Prager Strasse one day, from which one could obtain informational brochures thoughtfully prepared by a West German government agency. The flyers visually depicted different kinds of fruits and vegetables, identified the seasons during which they were usually available, summarized their nutritional value, and suggested ways of preparing them for meals.

Like product packaging, in the GDR product pricing had been characterized by uniformity: a loaf of bread or a pound of butter cost the same everywhere.

After July 1990 this was no longer the case. One evening that summer I visited a pastor in Thüringen and drank lemonade while he and his wife tried to figure out whether or not it made sense to drive into town, expending gasoline, in order to save a few pennies because juice was less expensive there than in their village grocery store.

"We never had to think about things like this before," the pastor explained. "There used to be just one kind of juice and it cost the same everywhere." Similar domestic calculations went on all over the GDR that summer, as East Germans tried to make sense of the new consumer economy that had washed over their land. (In the end the pastor and his wife concluded that the cost of gasoline would offset the savings on orange juice and they decided to shop in their own village.)

Imagine if you were to shop in this situation. Instead of confidently and efficiently marching up and down the aisles, selecting your favorite and customary foods, you would find shelf after shelf filled with items you cannot recognize because you have never seen them before. You would be confused by the color and brightness of the packaging. You would perceive grocery items with minimal metaphorical or symbolic associations, such as those created through advertising to promote brand identity, because you were a novice in that particular culture. As a result, you would experience little (if any) positive or negative emotional attachment to the items you see, though you might terribly miss your old familiar laundry soap or sugar.

The thoughts and associations that used to flicker through your mind during grocery shopping—"those crackers are too salty; Jarlsburg is a good cheese"—would be absent; no stimuli would awaken the memories. You would stop and stare at the new products, puzzle at the messages conveyed by the packaging, and decide—is this what I want? Should I try that? You would not be able to fill a grocery cart by casually tossing familiar products into it—without the right memories no grocery items would be familiar. A habitual activity, once easy and smooth, would become difficult, perhaps frustrating, certainly confusing. It would take time to build a new store of relevant memories that would enable you to shop with the same level of comfort you experienced previously.

The small example of grocery shopping exemplifies the larger crisis of cataclysmic change experienced by East Germans after 1989. Familiar faces and colleagues vanished from work—victims of mass layoffs. Family and friends immigrated to the West. Daily routines were altered by unemployment, new responsibilities at work, or modified career paths. At work, in school, on the street, or on the streetcar, complex codes of verbal and nonverbal communication were altered. Old habits of greeting, of conversation, and silence became obsolete. Teachers were no longer required to begin lessons with stock phrases from the Young Pioneers or FDJ ("For freedom and socialism be prepared!" To which students answered, "Always prepared!"). It was no longer necessary to "talk through the flowers" when expressing potentially dangerous political opinions. Western clothing, hair styles, jewelry, and makeup were adopted, along with western ideas of attractiveness and beauty. Young people in particular began to experiment with hair styles, hair colors, and clothes as they "tried on" identities now part of their newly acquired culture. East Germans were compelled to make a series of massive adjustments in virtually every domain of daily life over a very short period of time. One of the consequences was the experience of profound disorientation. In a case of amnesia, or memory loss, one could experience almost total disorientation in one's own culture. But despite the rhetorical appeal of phrases such as "memory loss," it is not the case that East Germans stopped remembering after 1989. Ironically, at the same time that East Germans were called upon to "work through the past,"[17] history, in the sense of useful memories accumulated over the course of thousands of ordinary days, became extraneous. The mundane memories that enabled East Germans to function easily and unthinkingly in everyday life ceased to correspond with reality. Suddenly they were neither a wellspring of comprehension nor a reliable guide to action. How can this be understood, and what does it tell us about memory?

Social Memory—Research and Lacunae

Many of the anthropologists who work on social aspects of memory draw upon a wealth of scholarship in history and other disciplines including psychology and literary studies. Within this body of work there are several threads of interest and theoretical concern, including the extent to which constructed memory serves to create or affirm group identity and unity.[18] Others examine the ways in which social division is expressed and carried out through struggles over remembrance.[19] Attention has also been given to the media of memory in western society in different historical periods and cultural contexts.[20]

Research in anthropology benefits from this work and it makes singular and important reciprocal contributions. Among these are complex analyses of the nature of culture through which the past is received and reconstructed. By integrating symbolic analysis with attention to the material conditions of daily life and the choices of individuals in the course of social interaction, John and Jean Comaroff establish a sophisticated theoretical foundation for understanding the multiple dimensions and potential of memory.[21] Arjun Appadurai makes clear that even within a given culture recollection may be subject to contestable rules which are deployed by particular groups in service of their interests and needs.[22] Jun Jing, Andrew Lattas, Ted Swedenburg, and Rubie Watson focus on the influence of political struggle and dissent on culturally distinctive practices of remembrance (for example, in the case of Jing, Chinese genealogies and ancestral rites).[23] They also take into consideration some of the ways non-Western customs of memory influence the course of social events. Finally, Andrew Buckser, H. F. Siu, and Paul Stoller contribute analyses of memory in the context of socially and historically unique structures and processes.[24]

In many cases, anthropological research explores the minutiae of memory as it is experienced and practiced in daily life. It also brings considerable insight to bear on the larger social, cultural, and historical processes that affect practices of remembrance—and amnesia. It is crucial to study memory in natural contexts, that is, in the company of people engaged in everyday activities in their customary environments; anthropologists accomplish this task well.[25] Still, as all disciplinary specializations have strengths, they have weaknesses too. Scholarship on social aspects of memory, including much of the work published by anthropologists, often fails to take into consideration current research on psychological aspects of individual memory.

Implicit Memory

In the early to mid-1980s, cognitive neuroscientists began to work closely on a curious and significant element of human memory.[26] Implicit memory is knowledge derived from past experience that is not held consciously. People draw on implicit memories without being aware of the fact that they are doing so. Research on implicit memory makes it clear that humans possess memories, and make use of them, without conscious awareness.

Implicit memory has been tested in laboratory settings by researchers in a number of different ways, including what are referred to as stem completion tests. Subjects are exposed to a list of words. They are not instructed to memorize the words, and they are not informed that they will be tested on the words subsequently. In certain cases they are exposed to the test words while they are, at the same time, occupied with another task ("divided attention"). A few hours, days, or weeks later, without being instructed to explicitly recall the words to which they were exposed, subjects are asked to complete words where only the first few letters of the word are provided. For example, subjects may be exposed to the words "calculator, elephant, commercial." Then, when exposed to the stems "cal-, ele-, and com-" subjects are more likely to suggest the words to which they were previously exposed than other words that would successfully complete the word stems, for example "calcium, elevator, company." Tests such as these lead psychologists and neuroscientists to conclude that implicit (unconsciously held) memories derived from previous exposure to the words "prime" (facilitate) the subjects' identification of the test words.

Interestingly individuals who, due to illness or traumatic brain injury, do not have a normally functioning conscious memory still derive benefits from implicit memory. It has been shown that amnesiac patients can successfully master complex tasks at ever higher levels of proficiency—without being able to recall learning the task, or practicing it previously.[27] Clearly, there are curious and significant relationships, and differences, between memories that are consciously held and memories that are evoked and utilized without conscious awareness.

Literature in cognitive psychology and cognitive neuroscience is rife with debates surrounding research on implicit memory.[28] Are there greater priming effects when subjects are exposed to semantic rather than nonsemantic cues? Why does a change in the medium through which information is presented, then tested, adversely affect implicit recollection but not explicit recollection? (For example, when subjects are exposed to words visually then asked to recall them verbally in response to auditory stimuli, there is less priming for implicit memory than when the medium of exposure and testing is held constant.) Why is implicit memory stronger for meaningful words or objects than for nonsense words or impossible objects (such as M. C. Escher's sketches of objects that cannot exist in three dimensions)? Are there different structures in the brain for explicit and implicit recollection; or are there multiple, complex processes for creating and drawing on different kinds of memories? Can a theory of memory be formulated that will unify or transcend the perceived contradiction between neurologic structures and processes?

This is not the place to review these debates, much less to take a stance with respect to one position or another. What I wish to do, rather, is simply point to a possible connection between East Germans' subjective experience of disorientation after the *Wende* and recent research on implicit memory. In a single sentence Robert S. Lockhart made an observation crucial to the balance of this chapter: "Given that priming can be quite incidental, it would seem to follow that we are in a state of being continuously primed by our everyday environment."[29] This is true, as long as the environment in which we are functioning remains essentially constant. Unfortunately, laboratory research on activities such as stem completion tasks does not inform us about the effects of continuous environmental priming, nor does it suggest consequences that might result from the cessation of that priming.

In order to understand the significance of memory to everyday life it is essential to reflect on the possible role of implicit memory in facilitating the human ability to function with minimal difficulty while involved with mundane activities. There are several categories of memory in common use in memory studies that are relevant to ordinary life. Endel Tulving's typology—episodic, semantic, and procedural memory—is one of these.[30] Episodic memories are recollections of unique or specific occurrences, for example, an important conversation with a friend or colleague. Semantic memories are our source of general knowledge; we know there are twelve inches in a foot and tulips bloom in the spring. Finally, procedural memories enable people to do things, such as successfully order from the deli counter at a store.[31]

An additional category of memory, contributed by Paul Connerton, is habit memory.[32] Connerton argues that research on social memory tends to overemphasize its textual, cognitive, or discursive aspects at the expense of other forms. For Connerton, habit memory is "the capacity to reproduce a certain performance"; it is memory that is amassed or sedimented in the body, and it is "recalled" through actions rather than through thoughts or words.[33] The successful acquisition and deployment of habit memory is crucial to unproblematic social interaction. After all, you wouldn't greet your department chairman with the same body language with which you might greet a child.[34]

Logically, environmental stimuli such as sounds, odors, or visual images may evoke memories that are explicit (conscious) or implicit (unconscious). The memories evoked may be procedural, semantic, episodic, or habitual. Odors, in particular, powerfully evoke explicit recollections as well as generalized feelings (associated with implicit memories?) of satisfaction, happiness, comfort—or unease, anxiety, or fear.[35] Regardless of whether or not we are conscious of specific memories, recollections brought to mind (and body) by environmental stimuli play an essential role in shaping our ongoing evaluation of any given circumstance. They also influence the complex emotional and cognitive processes through which we, as humans, make choices and act in specific situations.

The fact is that most people engage successfully in the activities of their daily lives without resorting to the time-consuming and painstaking task of thinking through and planning every activity in which they participate. When we engage in ordinary activities such as grocery shopping, the continuing relevance of our memories, many of which are held and evoked outside the domain of conscious awareness, is what enables us to recognize contexts as familiar. Memories guide our behavior and choices as we respond to a wide variety of cues in a grocery store, namely the store layout, the smells of different aisles, changes in temperature (for example, as you walk past a refrigerator case), the images on product packaging, or the weight and texture of different kinds of goods. Marketing experts recognize the powerful role played by environment in the behavior of shoppers; they carefully plan product placement and the use of stimuli such as ambient music to encourage shopping. I suggest that environmental clues are effective as behavioral stimuli in part because of the implicit memories they evoke.

But grocery shopping is only one tiny domain of modern life. More generally, people sit, stand, walk, greet friends, attend business meetings, and socialize in repetitive and patterned ways with little or no conscious reflection on their gestures or motions. We can do so only because we are able to draw on a wealth of memories relevant to the situation in which we find ourselves. Hopefully, in unfamiliar circumstances, we can still access some form of relevant past experience as we interpret contextual clues and attempt to participate in a strange situation without undue difficulty or embarrassment. (Anyone who has traveled in a foreign culture knows all too well the unfortunate experience of making gross, inadvertent breaches of local custom. A corollary is the tremendous feeling of belonging when one learns how to do things right.) The fact is that without memory we could not engage in such activities easily or fluently. Every moment of our lives would require conscious analysis and decision making; every moment would be new and raw.

Discussion

After the *Wende* the physical environment in eastern Germany, including its sights, sounds, and smells, underwent a radical transformation. The material culture of the East was supplanted by the material culture of the West. East Germans actively contributed to this supplanting by favoring West German products and other goods that, previously, had circulated primarily in capitalist economies (American blue jeans, Japanese electronics, etc.). For many reasons, familiar items once produced in the GDR and other socialist countries, then sold in the GDR, ceased to be an ordinary part of daily life. Instead, over time many GDR products literally became museum pieces as they were selected for display in exhibitions on the history of GDR culture and society.[36]

A failure of memory results in confusion and bewilderment. Strangely, after 1989, it was not the memories of East Germans that failed. Rather, the world in which those memories had been relevant disappeared. As the material culture of daily life was completely transformed, the habitual practices through which East Germans had acquired and used such products fell away. At the same time, the relationships and practices of socialism came to an end, bringing an unexpected halt to hundreds, perhaps thousands of routine behaviors. Customs of speech and silence, posture and interaction characteristic of German socialism vanished. As if this were not enough, streets were renamed, addresses changed, and factories closed. Jobs vanished. Careers came to a screeching halt. Identities were routed. The future was irrevocably transformed; its relationship to the past was severed. East Germans were cast adrift in an utterly foreign present; they were strangers in their own land. As a result, it was *as if* East Germans had lost their memories.

By bringing an ethnographic and psychological perspective to the study of a rupture of memory in everyday life, we can see some of memory's existential dimensions. By focusing on the small example of grocery shopping, I have tried to bring some specificity to a discussion of the changes that took place in the GDR after 1989. Surely, the simple experience of going to the store and being confronted by hundreds of new products is not sufficient to explain the crisis of disorientation East Germans experienced during that time. But as a micro-element of this crisis it is worthy of discussion. Regardless of where or how we live, all humans anticipate the future and act in the present by drawing on past experience. Implicit memories must play a central role in enabling people to function smoothly and easily in daily life. However, multidimensional contextual changes can render a lifetime of accumulated memory irrelevant. As a result, the untroubled functioning of memory is disrupted, and disturbing psychological or physical symptoms may result.

In conclusion I wish to point out that as much as the members of a society may be shocked or traumatized by unanticipated, widespread change, people, and memories, are adaptable. One of the most extraordinary features of human memory is its mutability. New memories can be formed quickly and they promote learning in novel contexts. In addition, old memories can be reworked to apply to new situations. In all, it is the versatility of memory, in conjunction with the common but erroneous human belief in its reliability, that is one of memory's most extraordinary features. That, however, is fodder for another essay.

NOTES

Thanks to Peter Fritzsche and Alon Confino for organizing the 1998 conference that inspired the first draft of this chapter. I am grateful for their comments, and the comments of several anonymous reviewers, which enabled me to clarify my focus in this chapter.

1. Ethnographic data were collected in Dresden during fall 1989, summer 1990, the year 1991 to 1992, and winter 1998. See Elizabeth A. Ten Dyke, *Dresden: Paradoxes of Memory in History* (London: Routledge, 2001). Oral history interviews were conducted with approximately one hundred respondents who ranged in age from nine to ninety, literally. The German Academic Exchange Service and the Wenner-Gren Foundation for Anthropological Research generously supported my work.

2. For a summary of events see Dirk Philipsen, *We Were the People: Voices from East Germany's Revolutionary Autumn of 1989* (Durham, N.C.: Duke University Press, 1992).

3. Compare Helmar Drost, "The Great Depression in East Germany: The Effects of Unification on East Germany's Economy," *East European Politics and Societies* 7 (1993): 452–81.

4. See Daphne Berdahl, *Where the World Ended: Re-unification and Identity in the German Borderland* (Berkeley: University of California Press, 1999); Ina Merkel, *Utopie und Bedürfnis: die Geschichte der Konsumkultur in der DDR* (Cologne: Böhlau Verlag, 1999).

5. One family I interviewed thoroughly enjoyed the anticipation that accompanied their annual preparations and regretted that the abundance and convenience of shopping after the *Wende* deprived them of that pleasure!

6. The years 1945–49, when the East was occupied by the Soviet Army, are excluded.

7. "Wenn die Wessis kommen: wem gehören Haus und Hof?" *Sächsische Zeitung,* 18 Nov. 1991, p. 3.

8. Compare Daniela Dahn, *Wir bleiben hier, oder Wem gehört der Osten* (Hamburg: Rowohlt Taschenbuch Verlag GmbH, 1998); James Youniss, ed., *After the Wall: Family Adaptations in East and West Germany* (San Francisco: Jossey-Bass Publishers, 1995).

9. Jürgen Richter, "Dresdner Lenin soll in Garten an die Donau," *Sächsische Zeitung,* 20 Feb. 1992, p. 9.

10. Two years later, ownership of the house was transferred to the West Germans and Frau W. was forced to move to a different apartment.

11. Personal communication, Renate Recknagel, Statistisches Landesamt des Freistaates Sachsen, 1999.

12. "Christin ist eine der letzten der Baby-Boom-Generation," *Sächsische Zeitung,* 14 Oct. 1991, p. 9.

13. Simone Kruschwitz, *Frauenbericht Dresden 1991: eine Dokumentation von und über Dresdner Frauen* (Dresden: Gleichstellungsstelle/Frauenbüro in Zusammenarbeit mit dem Presseamt, 1991), p. 28.

14. Compare Georg C. Bertsch and Ernst Hedler, *SED: Schönes Einheits Design* (Cologne: Taschen Verlag, 1990).

15. Ina Merkel presents a thorough discussion of the history of consumer culture in the GDR (Merkel, *Utopie und Bedürfnis*).

16. My astonishment included the realization that I thought of bananas as having a right-side-up.

17. See for example Bernd Faulenbach, Markus Meckel, and Hermann Weber, eds., *Die Partei hatte immer recht: Aufarbeitung von Geschichte und Folgen der SED-Diktatur* (Essen: Klartext Verlag, 1994); Jeffrey Herf, *Divided Memory: The Nazi Past in the Two Germanys* (Cambridge: Harvard University Press, 1997); Christoph Klessmann, "The Burden of the Past in the Two German States," in *Studies in GDR Culture and Society 11/12,* ed. Margy Gerber and Roger Woods (New York: University Press of America, 1993), pp. 195–210; Brigitte Rauschenbach, ed., *Erinnern, Wiederholen, Durcharbeiten: Zur Psycho-Analyse deutscher Wenden* (Berlin: Aufbau Taschenbuch Verlag, 1992).

18. Richard Harvey Brown and Beth Davis-Brown, "The Making of Memory: The Politics of Archives, Libraries and Museums in the Construction of National Consciousness," *History of the Human Sciences* 11 (1998): 17–32; Andrew Buckser, "Group Identities and the Construction of the 1943 Rescue of the Danish Jews," *Ethnology* 37 (1998): 209–26; Maurice Halbwachs, *On Collective Memory,* ed. and trans. Lewis A. Coser (1952; Chicago: University of Chicago Press, 1992); Eric Hobsbawm and Terence Ranger, eds., *The Invention of Tradition* (New York: Cambridge University Press, 1983); Allan Megill, "History, Memory, Identity," *History of the Human Sciences* 11 (1998): 37–62; David Middleton and Derek Edwards, eds., *Collective Remembering* (London: Sage Publications, 1990); Leo Spitzer, *Hotel Bolivia: The Culture of Memory in a Refuge from Nazism* (New York: Hill and Wang, 1998).

19. Alon Confino, *The Nation as a Local Metaphor: Württemberg, Imperial Germany, and National Memory, 1871–1918* (Chapel Hill: University of North Carolina Press, 1997); Paul Connerton, *How Societies Remember* (New York: Cambridge University Press, 1989); John R. Gillis, "Introduction," in *Commemorations: The Politics of National Identity,* ed. Gillis (Princeton: Princeton University Press, 1994), pp. 3–23; Luisa Passerini, *Fascism in Popular Memory: The Cultural Experience of the Turin Working Class* (New York: Cambridge University Press, 1987); Popular Memory Group, "Popular Memory: Theory, Politics, Method," in *Making Histories: Studies in History-writing and Politics,* ed. Richard Johnson et al. (London: Hutchinson, 1982), pp. 205–52.

20. Mary Carruthers, *The Book of Memory: A Study of Memory in Medieval Culture* (Cambridge: Cambridge University Press, 1990); Walter Melion and Susanne Küchler, "Introduction: Memory, Cognition and Image Production," in *Images of Memory,* ed. Walter Melion and Susanne Küchler (Washington, D.C.: Smithsonian Institution Press, 1991), pp. 1–46; Jacques Le Goff, *History and Memory* (New York: Columbia University Press, 1992); Pierre Nora, ed., *Realms of Memory: Rethinking the French Past,* 3 vols., trans. Arthur Goldhammer (New York: Columbia University Press, 1996–98); Pierre Nora, "Between Memory and History: Les Lieux de Memoire," *Representations* 26 (Spring 1989): 7–25.

21. John L. Comaroff and Jean Comaroff, *Ethnography and the Historical Imagination* (Boulder, Colo.: Westview Press, 1992).

22. Arjun Appadurai, "The Past as a Scarce Resource," *Man* 16 (1982): 201–19.

23. Jun Jing, *The Temple of Memories: History, Power, and Morality in a Chinese Village* (Stanford: Stanford University Press, 1996); Andrew Lattas, "Introduction: Mnemonic Regimes and Strategies of Subversion," *Oceania* 66 (June 1996): 257–65; Ted Swedenburg, "Popular Memory and the Palestinian National Past," in *Golden Ages, Dark Ages: Imagining the Past in Anthropology and History,* ed. Jay O'Brien and William Roseberry (Berkeley: Univer-

sity of California Press, 1991), pp. 152–79; Rubie S. Watson, ed., *Memory, History and Opposition under State Socialism* (Santa Fe: School of American Research Press, 1994).

24. Buckser, "Group Identities"; H. F. Siu, "Recycling Tradition," *Comparative Studies in Society and History* 32 (1990): 765–94; Paul Stoller, *Embodying Colonial Memories: Spirit Possession, Power, and the Hauka in West Africa* (New York: Routledge, 1995).

25. See Ulric Neisser, ed., *Memory Observed: Remembering in Natural Contexts* (San Francisco: W. H. Freeman and Company, 1982).

26. P. Graf and D. L. Schacter, "Implicit and Explicit Memory for New Associations in Normal and Amnesiac Patients," *Journal of Experimental Psychology: Learning, Memory, and Cognition* 11 (1985): 501–18; K. C. Kirsner, C. Speelman, M. Maybery, A. O'Brien-Malone, M. Anderson, C. MacLeod, eds., *Implicit and Explicit Mental Processes* (Mahwah, N.J.: Lawrence Erlbaum Associates, 1998); S. Lewandowsky, J. C. Dunn, K. Kirsner, *Implicit Memory: Theoretical Issues* (Hillsdale, N.J.: Lawrence Erlbaum Associates, 1989); Daniel L. Schacter, *Searching for Memory* (New York: Basic Books, 1996); Daniel L. Schacter, "Implicit Memory: History and Current Status," *Journal of Experimental Psychology: Learning, Memory and Cognition* 13 (1987): 501–18; Michael A. Stadler and Peter A. Frensch, eds., *Handbook of Implicit Learning* (London: Sage Publications, 1998).

27. See for example N. J. Cohen, "Preserved Learning Capacity in Amnesia: Evidence for Multiple Memory Systems," in *Neuropsychology of Memory,* ed. L. R. Squire and N. Butters (New York: Guilford Press, 1984), pp. 83–103; P. Graf, L. R. Squire, and G. Mandler, "The Information That Amnesic Patients Do Not Forget," *Journal of Experimental Psychology: Learning, Memory and Cognition* 10 (1984): 164–78; Schacter, *Searching,* pp. 176–79.

28. See in particular Alan S. Brown and David B. Mitchell, "A Reevaluation of Semantic versus Nonsemantic Processing in Implicit Memory," *Memory and Cognition* 22 (1994): 533–41; Daniel L. Schacter, "Understanding Implicit Memory: A Cognitive Neuroscience Approach," *American Psychologist* 47 (1992): 559–69.

29. Robert S. Lockhart, "The Role of Theory in Understanding Implicit Memory," in *Implicit Memory,* ed. Lewandowsky, Dunn, and Kirsner, p. 9.

30. Endel Tulving, "Episodic and Semantic Memory," in *Organization of Memory,* ed. E. Tulving and W. Donaldson (New York: Academic Press, 1972), pp. 381–403.

31. One of the problems with typologies of memory is that there is considerable overlap between categories. Without relevant semantic memory, we can not evoke and use appropriate procedural memories. In other words, if we are not able to recognize a deli counter as such, the fact that we know how to order is completely irrelevant.

32. Connerton, *How Societies Remember.*

33. Connerton, *How Societies Remember,* p. 59; see also Stoller, *Embodying Colonial Memories.*

34. One hopes.

35. Frank R. Schab and Robert G. Crowder, eds., *Memory for Odors* (Mahwah, N.J.: Lawrence Erlbaum Associates, 1995), especially Rachel S. Herz and Eric Eich, "Commentary and Envoi," pp. 159–75.

36. For example, at the Stadtmuseum Dresden. After 1989 the museum revised its exhibition of postwar Germany to include artifacts from the daily life of East Germans—furnishings from a typical East German living room, children's toys, and more.

PART 3

MATERIALITY

CHAPTER 8

An Economy of Memory: Psychiatrists, Veterans, and Traumatic Narratives in Weimar Germany

PAUL LERNER

"I was a healthy man when I became a soldier, and was discharged a cripple," declared the veteran FM as he reapplied for a military pension in July 1925.[1] But unlike the *Kriegskrüppel* (war invalids) who were so central to the Weimar imaginary and were so poignantly captured in the era's iconography, FM did not display the unmistakable signs of a physical war disability: his wounds were of an elusive and less tangible nature. In July 1916 he experienced what doctors described as a "nervous shock," landing in a Bavarian war hospital where he remained for two months. Two years later, according to the fragmented case history, his nervous condition worsened considerably when he fell from a train, after which he suffered from occasional bouts of functional deafness and internal, presumably psychosomatic, pains. Between the 1916 incident and his final application for a pension almost a decade later, FM was rediagnosed numerous times—with hysteria, schizophrenia, psychopathy, and ultimately "pension neurosis"—and each time his compensation award was readjusted accordingly.

In a 1923 examination, the former ironworker complained that his poor health was seriously diminishing his earning power. "Had I never been a soldier," he added later, "and never been in the war, I would not have these nervous pains."[2] FM's statements embody a particular chronological and causal construction, in which a precipitating traumatic occurrence—the 1916 shock—permanently altered his once-healthy condition. Psychically "crippled" by the wartime event, FM implied that it was a watershed in his life which still affected his state of health many years later, making him unable to support himself long after the war.

The psychiatrists who examined FM, however, received his account with skepticism and posited an alternative story. Their version of events challenged the etiological significance of the wartime shock episode, pointing instead to the presence of a preexisting pathological constitution (*Veranlagung*) and tracing his complaints to laziness, greed, or fear. "[T]he minor accident," wrote Dr. Kraft of the psychiatric clinic at Berlin's Charité hospital, "consciously or unconsciously offered the occasion for producing psychogenic symptoms, which gave him the possibility of escaping the most unpleasant realities of war service."[3] Labeling the condition a "flight into illness," Kraft diagnosed FM with a war neurosis—the German equivalent of the English term shell shock—and concluded that like "countless neurotics," he entered the war already a sick man. The allegedly traumatic event, therefore, could not be seen as a cause, but rather an excuse: "with which the neurotic once again hopes to fulfill his wish of escaping the difficulties of daily life."[4]

At its core the dispute between Dr. Kraft and the patient FM centered around the pathological weight and economic ramifications of memory. Can horrifying events—or a subject's recollective reconstruction of them—cause enduring psychological disability? How do individuals readjust to normal life after learning to cope with and survive in extraordinary circumstances? Who must bear responsibility if this readjustment proves unsuccessful?

Psychiatrists first turned to these questions in the last third of the nineteenth century, when the advent of industrial modernity seemed to provoke a host of new mental and nervous maladies. "Railway spine"—a set of lingering, though apparently nonorganic, disabilities observed in the aftermath of train wrecks—gripped Britain in the 1860s. Neurasthenia originated in North America in the same decade and traversed the European continent soon thereafter; traumatic hysteria preoccupied the leading lights of French neurology starting in the 1880s, and ultimately conditions akin to shell shock became a regular feature of modern wars.[5] Around the same time, the concept of trauma passed from surgical medicine into neurology and psychology, and doctors in these emerging professional specialties began to study the consequences of shock on the mind and psyche.[6]

Though posed somewhat differently, these questions contain a bundle of issues which have become highly contested again, having resurfaced in the aftermath of the Vietnam War and continuing amid current controversies over cases of sexual abuse and traumatic memories.[7] We live in what many critics call a "culture of victimhood" in which great moral, cultural, and financial rewards are bestowed on survivors of traumatic ordeals.[8] Meanwhile, doctors, psychologists, lawyers, and victim advocacy groups remain locked in heated debates over the medical and financial status of victims of sexual abuse, military violence, and genocidal horror. Broadly put, memory—and in particular memories of trauma—help forge individual, communal, and national identities; thus, debates over traumatic memory carry great cultural and political significance.

Much recent scholarship on trauma and memory, particularly from the fields of psychology and anthropology, focuses on narrative. Narrative plays a key role in making memories operative and in transmitting them and thus ultimately in shaping our subjectivity. According to Michael Lambek and Paul Antze: "In forging links between past and present, between who we are and who we think we are, memory operates most frequently by means of the thread of narrative. . . . [T]here is a point at which a person's life and the stories she tells about it begin to merge."[9] Hence, narratives do not simply carry neutral memories, but by organizing them and by reflecting choices about what to include and what to exclude, they fill them with meaning.

We form these narratives, argues Ian Hacking, according to particular cultural patterns. For sufferers of Multiple Personality Disorder (MPD), Hacking writes, the connection between MPD and childhood trauma was not discovered but actually "forged." It is not a question of remembering a buried traumatic past, but of "finding" a past traumatic event and thereby making sense of a puzzling present by plugging it into a coherent historical narrative.[10] And once this connection had been forged culturally, it became operative for individual sufferers. In such a way, MPD is narratively constructed through stories of very real suffering. Drawing extensively on Hacking in his history of Posttraumatic Stress Disorder, Allan Young observes that PTSD (like MPD) is both socially constructed and real; though it is a "historical product," for Young "the reality of PTSD is confirmed by its place in people's lives, by their experiences and convictions and by the personal and collective investments that have been made in it."[11]

A similar argument can be made for German veterans of World War I. Veterans who sought financial compensation for their psychological suffering constructed (implicitly or explicitly) narratives of trauma, and these narratives brought coherence to lives shattered by the horrifying ordeal of modern warfare. By focusing on a central causal event, after which they were "no longer the same man," men like FM reframed their lives in light of their war experiences and asserted the power of traumatic events to transform identity. Locating the source of their suffering in a tangible, finite, and external occurrence supplied these men with a coherent life story, a story fraught with ontological—and indeed economic and political—meaning. Psychiatric specialists, on the other hand, systematically opposed these compensation claims and thus undermined the traumatic narratives which justified them. Significantly, this approach to veterans' narrated memories should not be seen as a way of discounting or trivializing their suffering, which was certainly quite real and often enormously debilitating. Nevertheless, by interrogating the form and content of their narrated memories, one can treat them as both real and constructed. This essay attempts just that; by reading a collection of postwar pension proceedings, it elaborates the struggle between psychiatrists and patients over the reality and significance of traumatic war memories, which it views as a contest between competing narratives of war and its traumatizing impact.

In World War I and Weimar Germany, memory carried prodigious psychological, political, and material stakes for individuals and also for the nation as a whole, and I conclude this essay by mapping the conflict over individual memories onto the broader struggle over the memory and meaning of the war in Weimar politics and culture. Psychiatrists, I will show, responded to their patients' stories by asserting a narrative of their own, a kind of counternarrative which not only opposed patient pension applications but made broader claims about war service and its significance. And just as they contested the meaning of the combat experience for individual health and identity, psychiatrists also participated in a broader Weimar-era project to recast the place of the war in Germany's collective memory and national identity.

While the study of memory in Germany continues to grow rapidly, the area remains dominated by scholarship on the memory and legacy of the Shoah,[12] and historians are only just beginning to apply critical approaches to memory and trauma to other periods of the German past.[13] To this end, I would argue, the history of mental medicine can make crucial contributions to the study of collective memory; by focusing on psychiatrists, I aim to show how a group of doctors—and the medical science responsible for the war's psychological casualties—was actively involved in contesting and forming individual and collective memories. This approach also sheds light on questions of continuity, which are unavoidable in assessing the course of recent German history. While many works have discussed the links between Germany's calamitous defeat in World War I and the rise of fascism, few authors, it seems, have taken on the obvious question of how war and military mobilization could be made to seem desirable again so soon after the devastating destruction of the Great War. Psychiatrists, I shall argue, through their counternarratives, helped lay the groundwork for this change.

Investigations into the European memory of World War I have tended to concentrate on literary sources or, more recently, on tangible sites of memory such as war memorials, cemeteries, and monuments. Scholarly debate has often revolved around the question of memory and modernity, that is, whether the catastrophe of World War I produced novel forms of commemoration, involving an ironic, modernist sensibility or rather if the devastating effects of modern mass warfare were grieved through traditional forms of religious and artistic expression.[14] While these interventions have been crucial, studying memory purely through representation risks eliding the political and ideological; the war's outcome and the different states' ways of coping with its outcome must figure into our picture of collective memory.[15] Furthermore, studies of sites of memory such as monuments and cemeteries often have little to say about the tangible consequences of particular memories for ordinary people's lives, remaining largely in the realm of elite culture.[16]

With this analysis I aim to introduce a greater degree of materiality to discussions of memory. I show how memories of World War I were bound up in the economic struggles of the Weimar period and how the category of memory itself became an object of medical and political concern. As such I draw on the ethnographic approaches to trauma discussed above, but ground them in a particular historical moment where memory figured centrally in German politics and culture. I use "trauma" in this essay not as an analytical category, but rather as an object of historical analysis.

Significantly, this essay strives to historicize the production of memory; as Alon Confino suggests in a thought-provoking methodological meditation, understanding how memory became part of the mentality of an age might be a first step in writing its history.[17] Thus, in contrast to those historians who posit the universality of trauma and bereavement in assessing the war's impact on European culture, I suggest that these very terms—"trauma," "memory," "mourning"—be problematized and historicized.[18] Memories of war trauma, I will argue, were forged, contested, and ultimately overturned in the discursive field between veterans and psychiatrists in Weimar Germany.

Memory's Material Stakes: The Pension Question

Among the sources of chaos and crisis that threatened the nascent Weimar Republic, the problem of pensioning war veterans and their widows loomed large. Since the German state had assumed full responsibility for the war wounded, pushing out independent philanthropic organizations during the war, discontent with its comparatively generous pensioning practices was aimed directly at it.[19] The hyperinflation of the postwar years further strained the state's ability to cover the colossal costs of its ambitious new pension system.

Psychiatric cases posed particular problems for both doctors and state officials. "Compensation for nervous disorders," wrote the Berlin psychiatrist Ewald Stier, "is not only the most difficult part of pensioning, but is, in short, the central problem of the whole war pension issue. It is impossible to overestimate its significance for the national economy."[20] Nearly half of all pensioned veterans, Stier observed in 1922, suffered from some form of nervous ailment (broadly defined), costing the state up to one billion marks annually. Stier's statement reflects contemporary frustration with a pension system based on the thinking of a prior age in the history of psychiatry; at the same time it points to the centrality of economics to the question of hysteria and traumatic memory.

When the Reich's Insurance Office ruled in 1889 that workers deserved compensation for the mental and nervous effects of industrial accidents—accepting neurologist Hermann Oppenheim's diagnosis of traumatic neurosis—it unleashed an enduring and acrimonious debate that divided the medical world into two camps.[21] Given the widespread preoccupation with the purported pathologies of modernity: epidemic neurasthenia, degeneration, wildly increasing incidence of mental illness, suicide, and alcoholism, the debate remained fraught with political, economic, and social consequences.[22] Oppenheim was a pioneer of trauma theory who remains virtually unknown in the English-speaking world. In his work at Berlin's Charité clinic in the 1880s on men who had survived workplace accidents, Oppenheim posited the existence of psychological and physiological connections between traumatic events and posttraumatic morbid conditions. He recognized traumatic neurosis as a distinct disease entity, in sharp contrast to his French rival, the neurologist Jean-Martin Charcot, who labeled the conditions "traumatic hysteria."[23]

Ultimately, most mainstream psychiatrists and neurologists in Germany came to accept the Charcotian position, describing posttraumatic disorders as hysterical reactions and thus locating the source of the pathology in the subject's mind and not in any external traumata. They critiqued Oppenheim on scientific grounds, but also economically, holding the idea of traumatic neurosis responsible for an epidemic of pension hysteria in a "work-shy" working class. Pension hysteria (or pension neurosis), an unofficial diagnosis, explained hysterical symptoms as a product of the desire for financial compensation, and implied that the traumatic event should be viewed less as a cause than as an excuse for any lingering illness. The next step psychiatric skeptics took was to blame the 1889 law (and Oppenheim's diagnosis) for creating these maladies. In the words of Freiburg psychiatrist Alfred Hoche: "The individuals are in fact sick, but they would be well, strangely enough, if the law did not exist."[24]

In a period marked by sharpening class antagonism and the rapid rise of working-class political and associational power, the psychiatric profession rallied to defend the status quo and supplied a vocabulary for denouncing and pathologizing new threats to the bourgeois order.[25] As such, the traumatic neurosis issue lent itself well to stigmatizing unproductive working-class Germans. Hoche, perhaps the most vituperative critic of traumatic neurosis, condemned the diagnosis as a "cancer" which caused a "nervous epidemic" that threatened to engulf the working class and thus sabotage Germany's economic health and national strength.[26] Nevertheless, Oppenheim's ideas remained officially in force and continued to have wide resonance among physicians and in the culture as a whole.

This late nineteenth-century precedent continued to influence Germany's medical leaders in the decades to come; as the conservative and deeply nationalistic profession mobilized for war, its members were determined to avoid a renewed outbreak of pension neurosis, viewing the war and its mental health consequences as an industrial accident writ large.[27] The case histories that follow show how this concern and the prewar trauma debates decisively shaped approaches to "neurotic" soldiers and how the heightened concern with the health and economic strength of the national community deeply influenced psychiatric pension policy.

The Neurological and Psychiatric Clinic of Berlin's Charité hospital was one setting where psychiatric pension claims—military as well as civilian—were sent for medical evaluation. The clinic, which was directed by psychiatry professor Karl Bonhoeffer, served in this capacity for the local Berlin Pension Office, the National Pension Office, also located in the capital city, and for many local and regional offices throughout Germany.[28] When pension appeals were evaluated there, the medical arbitrator did not actually examine the patient; instead these cases were judged based upon a perusal of the patient's complete medical history and the results of his prior examinations. These rulings (*Obergutachten*), often richly detailed discourses on patient experiences and psychiatric science, offered doctors a forum for debating the significance of war service on individual life and health; as such they present an ideal source for analyzing the formation of the war's medical memory. And although the voices of the veterans themselves have for the most part been lost, we can reconstruct their narratives by reading the psychiatric case histories against the grain.

Consider the case of EM, a tailor, who had served one year of garrison duty, when he was hit by a train door. Complaining of ensuing headaches, dizziness, and heart palpitations, he entered the Spandau garrison hospital in 1916, where a doctor noted his shaking hands and stuttering, two of the most common war neurosis symptoms. Over the following months, EM was transferred back and forth between hospitals and his unit, and was hypnotized with minor success in a neurosis station, one of the new specialized psychiatric facilities created in the middle of the war. When EM was examined at the Görden asylum near Brandenburg—the same institution where such illustrious figures as Oskar Maria Graf and George Grosz had been pronounced insane[29]—he was characterized as "a pension neurotic of the most unpleasant variety" and as "whining, weak-willed and listless."[30] Despite his difficulty in walking, he was discharged without a pension.

Psychiatrist Ewald Stier examined this patient in 1919 and concluded that there was no illness and that the symptoms were purely artificial. However, in another examination later in the same year, a different doctor, a nonspecialist sympathetic to the patient's claims, reversed Stier's ruling and estimated that EM's earning power was diminished by three-fourths and that his symptoms were in fact the result of wartime shock.

According to the pension legislation (*Reichsversorgungsgesetz*) of 1920, the result of the Weimar government's attempts to simplify and reform the unwieldy Wilhelmine system, veterans or their widows had to apply for pensions through their local offices, and doctors then determined whether the disabilities in question were causally connected to the war experience and to what extent they decreased a veteran's earning power. Loss of earning power was measured on a scale of 20 to 100 percent, and numbers were rounded to the nearest even ten. The medical determination was then passed on to pension bureaucrats who calculated the pension sum based upon the percent disability and then took into account a whole range of mitigating factors such as medical expenses, cost of living allowances, and inflationary adjustments.[31]

This complex system defined a military disability (*Dienstbeschädigung*) as a "health disorder [*Gesundheitsstörung*] which occurred in consequence of the execution of duty or through an accident that took place during the execution of duty or was caused or worsened by the conditions of military service." A war disability (*Kriegsdienstbeschädigung*) was considered a military disability that "can be traced to the particular conditions of the war and was suffered in the time between the beginning of the war and the end of the demobilization."[32] Judging cases of war disability was not an exact science. Doctors were instructed to evaluate the *probability* that an illness resulted from the conditions of war. According to pension protocols, the connection between a disability and military service "needs not be proven; it suffices when it is shown to be sufficiently probable. On the other hand, the mere possibility of a causal connection is generally not sufficient for the medical judge to assume a war disability."[33]

Hence, when EM was reexamined by Karl Bonhoeffer in the spring of 1922, the key question was whether a causal connection could be established between the 1916 accident and EM's subsequent troubles. Bonhoeffer rejected the claim and diagnosed EM with "hospital hysteria" (*Lazaretthysterie*), a condition akin to pension hysteria but believed to arise from the influence of other patients in a hospital station. He wrote:

> Experience leaves no doubt that the primary mechanism in the hospital hysteric is grounded in the desire to have the symptoms observed in others, which occasions him—whether consciously or not—to recapitulate them. During the war this wish was based on the fear of military, that is, front duty. As a consequence, with the cessation of these fears, that is, with the declaration of unfitness or after the end of the war, these symptoms observably disappear; in those isolated cases where they persist, their durability can be seen without exception as the wish for a compensatory pension.[34]

For Bonhoeffer, then, the "psychic contagion" due to the proximity of other psychopaths, rather than any catalyzing accident, was to blame for EM's hysterical symptoms; a war disability was, unsurprisingly, out of the question.

Like EM, tens of thousands of men left the war with conditions that lay between the poles of clear organic injuries and health; elusive and mysterious, war neuroses defied simple classification and did not clearly conform to the principles established for pensioning other maladies.[35] Veterans seeking pensions for somatic ailments simply had to point to a discrete event—a mine explosion, for example—that preceded the onset of their symptoms. Cases of psychic trauma, however, failed to fit this simple equation; and casuality, that is, the actual relationship between the precipitating event and the post-event symptoms, remained elusive and the subject of medical controversy, as it had been since the later nineteenth century.

Further compounding the problem, of course, was the fact that psychic trauma does not operate on the mind in the same way that a physical blow affects the body. As theorized by Freud, Charcot, and other neurologists, an event becomes "traumatic" only in the subject's imaginative reconstruction of it. Physical or emotional shocks cannot be objectified or quantified; they become psychic traumata only through internal mental processes. Thus, as Wolfgang

Schäffner has insightfully pointed out, if Freud is correct "the exact date of [a] trauma cannot be precisely located on the time axis."[36] For Freud the "reality" and objective characteristics of the traumatic event were immaterial; only the mind's memory work or the degree of its preparedness for a shock were pathologically relevant.[37] Seen in this light, cases of psychic trauma did not conform to the chronological parameters of pension criteria, since it is not the actual accident event (*Ereignis*) but rather the subjective experiencing (*Erlebnis*) of the event which leads to such conditions.[38] (The purely somatic "shell-shock" model, in which combat-related explosions were believed to cause undetectable organic change, was unanimously rejected by German psychiatrists by 1916.)

Mainstream medical thinkers who were more integral to Germany's medical landscape nonetheless shared Freud's belief in the inherent subjectivity and problematic chronological status of the traumatic event. Why, they often asked, if two men underwent exactly the same combat ordeal, did one break down and the other remain healthy? Why, furthermore, did breakdowns happen long after the traumatic event, or even in the complete absence of an identifiable trauma? Since it is the mind which transforms a shock event into a trauma, argued psychiatrists such as Karl Bonhoeffer, the source of the pathology lies within the mind. Whereas normal, healthy individuals could easily overcome such events, only minds that are so disposed provide fertile ground for the morbid wishes and fears which trigger long-standing neuroses.[39]

While a soldier with demonstrably somatic wounds would normally have no trouble proving that, say, he had two legs before a mine explosion, war neurotics were hard-pressed to establish a history of mental health, and psychiatrists were usually ready to assume a constitutional predisposition to hysteria. This was believed to be the case with OS, a construction worker who was originally discharged from service with a 30 percent pension for hysterical symptoms. Several years after the war OS was thrown in a building-site explosion, after which he lost his power of speech. Finding that his ability to earn was further reduced, and claiming that his new health problems represented a worsening of his war wounds, he applied for additional compensation, necessitating that his military pension be reevaluated. The author of this decision, Dr. Kraft, ruled out any causal connection. Kraft also took the opportunity to attack the judgments of his predecessors and to discuss the current understanding of the hysteria diagnosis: "This kind of psychopath," he wrote:

> easily break[s] down, even under normal circumstances, but especially under heightened difficulties and take[s] flight into illness, a characteristic of hysterical reactions. . . . That the granting of a pension is not only scientifically unjustified—since the so-called trauma is only a coincidental external accident to the pathological motive—but that it's also therapeutically the most dangerous conceivable step, is clear when one realizes that it sets a premium on the preservation of the hysterical symptoms; it even, according to experi-

> ence, arouses the wish for further increases, to which end the symptoms must be strengthened.[40]

The pension, in Kraft's description, emerges as not only unwarranted but also medically damaging, rewarding the subject's retention of his hysterical symptoms rather than inducing his return to work. This observed connection, combined with the perception of danger from psychic contagion and suggestibility, dictated psychiatrists' hard line in opposing nervous veterans' narratives.

According to contemporary psychiatric thinking, a psychologically healthy man might develop a fleeting "shock neurosis" after enduring a horrifying or startling event. But when such symptoms lingered and took the form of full-blown hysterical conditions, an abnormal constitution or predisposition had to be assumed.[41] As the pension protocols stated: "A more exact examination of the earlier personality reveals that even the neurotic and psychopathic disorders which seem to have been caused by the war, according to unanimous avowals, develop on the basis of a predisposed psychopathic constitution."[42] And evidence for this predisposition could normally be supplied by perusing any patient's case history; a childhood sickness or a "nervous" relative usually sufficed. As the dissenter Hermann Oppenheim protested at the 1916 "War Conference of German Psychiatrists," "we have no right to invoke a different standard for someone if it can be proven that some great uncle of the patient was a strange man or had a crooked foot. I would very much like to know how many individuals remain nonpsychopaths before the judgment of these stern men."[43] We can read Oppenheim's objection as saying that his psychiatric opponents were constructing false narratives: by "finding" and ordering the evidence to show a pathological prehistory, psychiatrists established competing, nontraumatic narratives.

Nevertheless, despite its epistemologically dubious status, a psychopathic constitution was sufficient grounds for precluding a pension during, and particularly after, the war. The mere fact that GR applied for a pension was treated with suspicion and taken as a sign of psychopathology. GR was buried in a July 1917 explosion, after which he lay unconscious for three hours. Subsequently, the sound of artillery fire triggered in him nervous symptoms such as shaking and fainting spells, which were diagnosed as hysterical. The connection GR drew between the terrifying experience of burial and his ensuing nervous symptoms was rejected by psychiatrist Kurt Pohlisch. That GR had a prior history of nervous disorder, which traced back to his childhood, together with the fact that his father had apparently died of a nervous disease, led to the assumption that he had a psychopathic constitution. According to the case history, GR applied for a pension in 1924 after he lost his job. Pohlisch wrote the final pension decision in 1926 and characterized GR's symptoms with the following description: "GR's manner of reacting to the front duty of 1917 through the hysterical symptoms which arose after artillery fire and the tremorous attacks which persisted for a long time afterwards, is a characteristic reaction to the dangers associated with the war experience in a psychopathically predisposed person." That he claimed a pension in 1924, just as his civil service position was terminated, was seen as further proof. "Such pension wishes [*Rentenwunschvorstellungen*]," wrote Pohlisch, "and the nervous symptoms associated with them are not to be understood as symptoms deserving of war-disability pensions."[44]

HE, a veteran who had served eight months in Flanders, complained after the war that his nerves no longer allowed him to work. In this case, the somatic diagnosis polyneuritis was combined with pension neurosis because the patient seemed to exhibit too great an interest in his pension proceedings and could remember relevant dates and terms for it, in contrast to his normal state of forgetfulness and disinterest.[45]

In those cases not dismissed as pension neurosis, the medical surveyor had to evaluate whether or not the symptoms existed in a probable causal relationship with the conditions and circumstances of the war. This question naturally had to be evaluated on a case-by-case basis. Even though medical consensus condemned pensions as damaging to neurotics' prognosis—since they discouraged the return to work, and regular, productive work was considered both the best means to recovery and the surest sign of recovery—pension policy did not disqualify neurotics from the beneficence of the imperial treasury.[46]

Germany's leading psychiatrists, however, were less generous than state welfare regulations. Their deep skepticism toward their patients derived from their tendency to privilege the interests of the state (or the national community) over the needs of the individual. In contrast to private clinicians like Oppenheim, who depended on the goodwill of their patients for their own livelihoods, university research psychiatrists were state officials who often had little sympathy for the largely working-class patient pool that cycled through their training clinics.

Stier, for example, complained of the generosity of general practitioners and argued that war neuroses almost never deserved financial compensation. "Not only the masses," he lamented in 1922, "but also well-educated lay people and even the overwhelming majority of doctors ascribe much too great a significance to the role of external circumstances for the development of psychoses." Indeed, he continued, "Even doctors frequently succumb to the exaggerated general opinion that sees war as having a 'damaging' effect on the nerves."[47] And in the war's final months, Stier observed, "the sad and heart-wrenching image of the stuttering, shaking, and writhing neurotics, supported by canes and crutches, which we encounter everywhere, quickly gave rise to the belief among the people that the causes of these conditions were 'burial' and 'nervous shock,' these most frightful of war disabilities, and that the greatest degree of pity and assistance was warranted for these most miserable victims of the war."[48]

Though the November Revolution seemed to bring a sudden end to the symptoms of numerous neurotics and rapidly cleared out the neurosis stations, in the difficult times that followed, many cases of neurotic symptoms were observed to reappear. The so-called neurotics of 1920, wrote neurologist Kurt Singer, were driven by the "specter of unemployment" back to the "comfortable bed of neurotic symptoms."[49] Just as in wartime, these individuals were generally judged not to be simulating but to have fallen ill as a kind of survival strategy amid adverse conditions; in this case, argued many doctors, the powerful instinct for self-preservation drew many weak individuals into neurotic illness in the face of economic hardship and the fear of starvation. Psychiatrist Karl Pönitz described this phenomenon: "'I don't shake,' explains the pension seeker, while under examination by the doctor, 'except when I get excited or have to perform strenuous labor, and then it returns.' And then the person in question shakes over the course of the examination, sometimes right at the beginning, sometimes only after several minutes."[50]

Likewise, the Heidelberg psychiatrist Viktor von Weizsäcker observed growing numbers of patients entering his clinic in the latter half of the 1920s. These patients "were not at all ill, but were broken down." He remarked that "they tried to hold on to any symptoms upon which they could base a pension claim. Illness became a legal right. Being sick became a means of survival. Many had had neuroses, but in most cases it was no longer a neurosis, but a general weariness, a breaking down, their whole existence had become a morass."[51]

Doctors and state officials condemned these postwar neurotics as a loathsome nuisance, who clogged crowded city streets with their begging, organ grinding, or picture-postcard peddling.[52] "The lay public," observed Pönitz, "see the 'pitiful shakers,' approach half out of curiosity, half out of horror, and shower the 'unfortunate' with donations."[53] Not only lay people, the neurologist Max Nonne charged, but experienced doctors also believed in the pathological impact of war trauma. Nonne, who evaluated nervous and mental disability claims after the war in Hamburg, bemoaned: "It is astonishing and sad how, in spite of the long experiences of peacetime and war, the judgments of the earning ability of . . . hysterics by doctors at the welfare offices still frequently lack the ability to see 'behind the curtain' and to judge the entire personality and all that goes with it."[54] And as he wrote to a colleague in the waning moments of the war: "The whole problem with the War Ministry is that the pension chasers [*Rentennörgler*] are—at least up to now—always satisfied."[55]

Increasingly, psychiatrists labored to prevent this from happening. In case after case the causal connections veterans claimed between wartime events and postwar disabilities—often accepted by general practitioners—were consistently overturned by leading psychiatric authorities. In fact, of the sixty-eight *Obergutachten* I have collected, only one resulted in the awarding of a pension. Once criticized for exerting an unhealthy influence on neurotic patients, pensions were, starting late in the war, condemned as actually *causing* epidemics of neurotic breakdowns in selfish, suggestible, and unpatriotic patients. As the Freiburg psychiatrist Alfred Hauptmann declared in 1925, "to give an hysteric a . . . pension does not mean compensating him, but rather debilitating him."[56]

Traumatic Narratives and Collective Memory

Over the 1920s it became more and more difficult for men to receive financial compensation for war-related psychological suffering, and psychiatric opposition to such claims grew increasingly steadfast. Denying pensions, psychiatrists argued, served both the collective good of the nation and the welfare of the individual patient. The doctor, according to Stier, "stands between two patients, which are here represented on one side by the allegedly or actually injured man and on the other side by the community of the working and tax paying population."[57]

In fact, rather than blaming the shocks and stresses of the battlefield, psychiatrists increasingly saw war as a cure, as a moral and psychological palliative to the debilitating influences of the home front. Robert Gaupp, professor of psychiatry in Tübingen, reported in 1917 that neuroses occurred less frequently in front soldiers than in those behind the lines, who were overcome by fear of going to the front.[58] Heidelberg psychiatrist Karl Wilmanns argued that neurotics "get better under the favorable conditions of the front, where the patient stands in close contact with his fighting comrades and under the influence of the front spirit."[59] Just as soldiers often rejected the pity and sympathy of their loved ones at home, medical writers asserted that war hysterics were best served by the company of other men. Safely sequestered in their all-male world and continually exposed to the "hardening" military environment, soldiers were protected from the false comforts and "damaging pity" of what war letters and diaries depicted as an increasingly alien and "feminine" world.[60]

This discourse represented the continuation of a strand of prewar thinking that viewed war as a healthy alternative to peace and prosperity. In their critiques of the perceived decadence and degeneration of Wilhelmine society, many observers—psychiatrists conspicuous among them—began to depict war as a cure, as a means not only of uniting a people fragmented by social and regional divisions but of reinvigorating bodies and minds grown soft in the luxury brought on by Germany's prosperity, and as a way of "remasculating" a nation grown weak and effeminate.[61] Indeed, critics longed for "the mighty healing power of the iron bath [*Stahlbad*] for nerves dried up and languishing in the dust from years of peace and monotonous vocational activity."[62] Writing from the comfort of their clinics and offices, many psychiatrists and neurologists glorified the wartime environment as a healthful antidote to the deteriorating conditions of Germany's expanding cities, as a corrective to the corrosive effects of technology and industrial growth on the mental and moral health of the nation. The dramatic increase in nervous and mental illness in the current generation, explained the Swiss-born psychiatrist Otto Binswanger, was due to "the nearly revolutionary changes in the conditions and standards of our lives, which the second half of the polytechnical nineteenth century has brought us."[63] War, he added, would strengthen the nervous resistance and therefore the mental health of the German people. And according to the military doctor Walter Fuchs, war was "the only means by which we, as a nation, can be saved from the physical and psychological lethargy and emasculation which are relentlessly threatening."[64]

Though it betrays a tragic ignorance of the shattering realities of modern, technological warfare, this perspective reemerged in the middle of the war and deeply influenced medical memory in the war's aftermath. Many medical authors contrasted the "authentic" and salutary experience of combat to the pathogenic world of the home front, valorizing the beneficial effects of the front environment and the community of comrades against the "numerous expressions of mawkish false pity particular to the female sex."[65] The "contagion" (*Ansteckungsstoff*) believed to cause epidemics of war neurosis was ubiquitous, according to Gustav Liebermeister, but it could be found in "high concentration" only far from the front. "The greater spread of neurosis on the front is decisively inhibited by the healthy and sturdy mental constitution of the comrades there."[66] And, as Liebermeister continued, "this concentration is the strongest in the home territory, where one finds not only our war-disabled, but also their relatives, and what's more a great part of our female population and very many other individuals who act as disease carriers."[67]

Military medical officials shared these assumptions, praising the spirit of the frontline combatants at the expense of the home front, which they constructed as a site of feminine weakness and a hotbed of pathology. Indeed, the "softening and disturbing influence of the *Heimat*," they believed, bred weakness of will, laziness, and addiction to pensions.[68] As early as 1917, new neurosis stations were designed to be free from female interference—insulated from the damaging influence of the home and characterized by hard, masculine discipline. In the words of one doctor, the mood most conducive to recovery would feature "manly guidance instead of feminine pity."[69]

Psychiatric treatment also reflected this attempt to normalize the extraordinary conditions of war, by which the "traumatic" was seen as healthy and the "normal" as pathogenic. The infamous "Kaufmann Cure," a regimen of electric current and barked military drill, sought to cure war neurosis by re-creating the conditions of the battlefield within the treatment room, demonstrating to these unfortunate patients that life in the hospital would be even less pleasant than duty in the field.[70] Verbal treatments, which generally operated through hypnosis or suggestion, aimed to convince patients that they really were not sick and strove to replace the sickly, hysterical will of the patient with the hard and manly will of the doctor.[71]

The assumptions behind these approaches to pensioning, administering, and treating psychiatric patients represent the complete negation of the war neurotics' narratives. While pension applicants asserted that a traumatic event (or series of events) had permanently altered their once-healthy state, the psychiatric response undermined this narrative in three ways. When possible, psychiatrists concluded that these men were constitutionally disposed to hysteria and were thus never truly mentally healthy. Furthermore, a once common view, which reasserted itself after the war, implied that rather than causing mental disability, war is actually physically healthful and spiritually invigorating. Finally, compensation was believed only to worsen debilitating nervous conditions—the only "cure" lay in work.

Thus, the causal connections veterans drew in their pension applications could be completely discounted. Indeed, trauma itself was seldom seen as a causal agent, and posttraumatic pathology was not accepted as a category of illness; in 1926, the 1889 decision which had made posttraumatic conditions actionable was virtually overturned, and by 1929, amid the economic crisis that helped bring down the Weimar state, the door on posttraumatic pensions was completely shut.[72] Memories that clung to shocking combat events were themselves deemed disordered and financially suspect, and less than a decade after the war's end, the shocks, fears, and horrors it had brought became a source of celebration.

On one level, this analysis is meant to point to a moment of rupture in the "history of trauma," supporting the view that traumatic memory is historically discontinuous and is constructed by particular social, cultural, and economic forces.[73] On another level, this is a specifically German story: collective memories are the result of contestation between various institutional, individual, and group memories, and the psychiatric refusal of traumatic memory played into a larger battle over the legacy of the war in Weimar political culture.[74] In its approach to the war neurosis problem, the psychiatric profession helped turn Germans' attentions away from mourning the losses of the war and toward a celebration of the physical, mental, and spiritual strengthening that war allegedly brought.

In denying the causal links between "traumatic" war events and subsequent disability, the psychiatric counternarrative had substantial material and also political consequences. Refusing to see these veterans as victims of trauma absolved the state of financial and moral responsibility for their conditions. Indeed, war neurotics failed to achieve even the limited social status of the physically war disabled and were unwelcome in the latter's organizational ranks.[75] Easily scapegoated for Germany's defeat and the collapse of the Imperial state, the war's psychiatric casualties were often equated with the revolutionary actors of 1918–19, both groups earning condemnation as shifty, psychopathic, and unpatriotic.[76] Implicitly cast into the category of "back-stabbers," along with Marxists, Jews, and other allegedly disloyal groups, war neurotics were available enemies for a war in which the German right remained mobilized.[77]

War trauma, to use historian Michael Geyer's formulation, was inverted. The "sentimental culture of death," Geyer writes, "was supplanted by that hardened and cynical notion of 'life in death.' . . . The cold, apparently affectless confrontation with death was present from the beginning [of Weimar], but it gained the upper hand, at least in intellectual circles, only in the late twenties."[78] This ascendant, inverted approach to trauma was perhaps best represented by Ernst

Jünger, who celebrated the transformative power of the front ordeal as the cornerstone of a modern, mobilized identity. Though not a specifically Nazi ideology, this celebration clearly overlaps with National Socialist myths of war and the Nazis' investment in sacralizing the war experience and in militarizing their redemptive political struggles.[79] The prevailing psychiatric view sheds light on how, so soon after the war, large movements within Germany could rewrite war's brutal consequences and embrace a radically militarist agenda.

In this analysis I have identified only several of many competing discourses on war and trauma in Weimar Germany. Clearly, individuals and groups continued to mourn the immense destruction brought by the Great War, and the wrenching sadness of wartime loss is indelibly inscribed on interwar sculpture and visual art. The "sentimental culture of death," visible in many of the Weimar period's commemorative efforts, lingered through the 1920s and 1930s.[80] Central to my argument, however, is the observation that memories of war were not simply the property of individual veterans—they were contested narratives with high material stakes which focused the political, social, and economic struggles of Germany in the interwar years. As such the medical science of memory actively participated in shaping a particular vision of the war, a collective memory in which psychological suffering was intentionally forgotten and subsumed into a celebration of war's rigors. In the process psychiatrists helped the Weimar state manage its crippling war expenses; psychiatric theory and the state's financial needs converged to dictate the denial of traumatic memory.

Denying traumatic memories on an individual level led doctors to deny the traumatizing impact of war as a whole. They even explained the experience of the war with recourse to prewar ideas which construed war service as a positive influence on the minds of individuals and the lives of nations. If war made nervous men healthy and if the desire for a pension, rather than discrete combat events, catalyzed war neuroses, then these maladies had essentially little or nothing to do with war service, meaning that in the eyes of psychiatric authorities the tens of thousands of "war neurotics" could not be considered in any real sense the war's victims. Displacing neurotic veterans from this position, psychiatrists actually sought to portray *themselves* as the victims, both of aggressive and unpatriotic hysterics—who often stubbornly resisted treatment—and of revolutionary actors, whom they considered the other side of the same coin. This association was forged when the revolutionary currents swept into psychiatric facilities, and doctors often had to run for their lives, chased by columns of hostile patients who resented psychiatric authority and brutality.[81] Ill at ease in the new republic and longing for the restoration of an imagined social status quo, psychiatrists constructed narratives which (unironically) used the language of trauma to characterize their experiences of defeat and revolution, neatly completing the wholesale inversion of the concept.

While psychiatrists had reported great success at bringing war neurotics into industrial and agricultural work during the war, in the postwar period they believed they faced more formidable obstacles.[82] "The hardships of our time," warned psychiatrist Friedrich Mörchen, "are particularly favorable circumstances for the development of neurotic reactions."[83] Peacetime, it turned out, posed a far greater health danger than the shocks and stresses of modern warfare, and psychiatrists feared the consequences of the Weimar state's toxic combination of rampant unemployment and public assistance. It seemed only fitting, then, that it would take another war to reestablish a healthy state of affairs. Long before Hitler's Germany plunged Europe into World War II, German psychiatrists declared their "war against pension hysteria," a war that began in the mid-1920s and was waged through the Weimar period and beyond.[84]

NOTES

A slightly different version of this essay has appeared in *Modernität und Trauma: Beiträge zum Zeitenbruch des Ersten Weltkrieges*, ed. Inka Mülder-Bach (Vienna: Universitäts Verlag Wien, 2000), pp. 79–103. I am grateful to Elinor Accampo, Charlotte Furth, Igal Halfin, Carla Kaplan, and the volume editors for their many helpful suggestions.

1. Archiv der Humboldt Universität zu Berlin (hereafter Archiv der HUB), Nervenklinik Bestand, Akte 19.

2. Archiv der HUB, Nervenklinik Bestand, Akte 19.

3. Archiv der HUB, Nervenklinik Bestand, Akte 19.

4. Archiv der HUB, Nervenklinik Bestand, Akte 19 (emphasis in original).

5. See, among others, George Frederick Drinka, *The Birth of Neurosis: Myth, Malady and the Victorians* (New York: Simon and Schuster, 1984); Eric Caplan, "Trains, Brains and Sprains: Railway Spine and the Origins of Psychoneuroses," *Bulletin of the History of Medicine* 69 (1995): 387–419; Mark S. Micale, *Approaching Hysteria: Disease and Its Interpretations* (Princeton: Princeton University Press, 1995); Joachim Radkau, *Das Zeitalter der Nervosität. Deutschland zwischen Bismarck und Hitler* (Munich: Hanser Verlag, 1998); and Wolfgang Schivelbusch, *The Railway Journey: The Industrialization of Time and Space in the Nineteenth Century* (Berkeley: University of California Press, 1977).

6. See Allan Young, *The Harmony of Illusions: Inventing Post-traumatic Stress Disorder* (Princeton: Princeton University Press, 1995), chap. 1.

7. An introduction to this topic with an extensive bibliography can be found in Paul Lerner and Mark S. Micale, "Trauma, Psychiatry and History: An Introduction," in *Traumatic Pasts: History, Psychiatry and Trauma in the Modern Age, 1870 1930*, ed. Mark S. Micale and Paul Lerner (New York: Cambridge University Press, 2001).

8. See for example Charles Sykes, *A Nation of Victims: The Decay of the American Character* (New York: St. Martin's Press, 1993), pp. 3–31.

9. Paul Antze and Michael Lambek, "Introduction," in *Tense Past: Cultural Essays in Trauma and Memory*, ed. Antze and Lambek, (New York: Routledge, 1996), p. xvii.

10. Ian Hacking, *Rewriting the Soul: Multiple Personality and the Sciences of Memory* (Princeton: Princeton University Press, 1995), esp. chap. 6. While Hacking discusses a case where subjects conform to a medical model of their disease, forging a kind of alliance between them and medical specialists, in my case doctors and patients are in conflict—patients cling to an older medical model that the psychiatrists of the 1920s try to displace.

11. Young, *Harmony of Illusions,* p. 5.

12. The literature on the memory of the Shoah is, of course, immense. For several outstanding examples, see Dominick LaCapra, *History and Memory after Auschwitz* (Ithaca: Cornell University Press, 1998); Saul Friedlander, *Memory, History, and the Extermination of the Jews of Europe* (Bloomington: Indiana University Press, 1993); and Saul Friedlander, ed., *Probing the Limits of Representation: Nazism and the "Final Solution"* (Cambridge: Harvard University Press, 1992).

13. See, for example, Alon Confino, *The Nation as a Local Metaphor: Württemberg, Imperial Germany and National Memory, 1871–1918* (Chapel Hill: University of North Carolina Press, 1997), and Rudy Koshar, *Germany's Transient Pasts: Preservation and National Memory in the Twentieth Century* (Chapel Hill: University of North Carolina Press, 1998). Key works on the memory of World War I in Germany include George L. Mosse, *Fallen Soldiers: Reshaping the Memory of the World Wars* (New York: Oxford University Press, 1990); Richard Bessel, "The Great War in German Memory: The Soldiers of the First World War, Demobilization and Weimar Political Culture," *German History* 6 (1988): 20–34; and Bernd Ulrich and Benjamin Ziemann, eds., *Krieg im Frieden: Die umkämpfte Erinnerung an den Ersten Weltkrieg* (Frankfurt: Fischer Verlag, 1997).

14. The classic treatment that stresses the modernist mode of memory is Paul Fussell, *The Great War and Modern Memory* (London: Oxford University Press, 1975). See also Thomas Laqueur, "Memory and Naming in the Great War," in *Commemorations: The Politics of National Identity,* ed. John R. Gillis (Princeton: Princeton University Press, 1994). Jay Winter, on the other hand, stresses the persistence of traditional forms of memory and mourning; see Jay M. Winter, *Sites of Memory, Sites of Mourning: The Great War in European Cultural History* (Cambridge: Cambridge University Press, 1995).

15. Winter, for example, tends to downplay the question of defeat, focusing instead on what German grieving had in common with French and British responses. See Winter, *Sites of Memory,* esp. p. 11, for his discussion of the "common history of mourning" among the belligerent powers. Gerd Krumeich argues that in the first five or six years after the defeat, Germans were preoccupied with the question of guilt and the material consequences of the war; the cultural and literary engagement with the war, as many have argued, came only after the mid-1920s. See G. Krumeich, "Kriegsgeschichte im Wandel," in *"Keiner fühlt sich hier mehr als Mensch . . ." Erlebnis und Wirkung des Weltkriegs,* ed. G. Hirschfeld, G. Krumeich, and I. Renz (Frankfurt: Fischer, 1996), p. 11.

16. Winter does make an attempt to collapse distinctions between elite and low culture, and his fascinating discussion of the struggles to reclaim the bodies of fallen relatives is certainly an exception to my statement. See Winter, *Sites of Memory,* esp. pp. 31–53.

17. Alon Confino, "Collective Memory and Cultural History: Problems of Method," *American Historical Review* 102 (1997): 1386–1403. See also Antze and Lambek, "Introduction," p. xv.

18. On the aftermath of World War I in Germany, Michael Geyer writes: "The experience of mass death has to be understood not as an anthropological or psychological constant, but as a cultural field of contention" ("The Place of the Second World War in German Memory and History," *New German Critique* 71 [Spring-Summer 1997]: 5–40, here at p. 12). See also Catherine Merridale, "The Collective Mind: Trauma and Shell Shock in Twentieth-Century Russia," *Journal of Contemporary History* 35 (Jan. 2000): 39–55. Russia's collectivistic approaches to trauma, Merridale argues, challenge the view that shell shock can be seen as a universal response to war.

19. Deborah Cohen, *The War Come Home: Disabled Veterans in Great Britain and Germany, 1914–1939* (Berkeley: University of California Press, 2001).

20. E. Stier, "Rentenversorgung bei nervösen und psychisch erkrankten Feldzugsteilnehmern," in *Geistes- und Nervenkrankheiten,* ed. Karl Bonhoeffer, vol. 4 of *Handbuch der ärztlichen Erfahrungen im Weltkriege, 1914–1918,* ed. Otto von Schjerning (Leipzig: Barth, 1922), p. 186.

21. For a full account of the debate over traumatic neurosis before and during World War I, see my essay "From Traumatic Neurosis to Male Hysteria: The Decline and Fall of Hermann Oppenheim," in *Traumatic Pasts,* ed. Micale and Lerner, pp. 140–71. Other works on traumatic neurosis include Esther Fischer-Homburger, *Die traumatische Neurose: Vom somatischen zum sozialem Leiden* (Bern: Huber, 1975); Greg Eghigian, "Die Bürokratie und das Entstehen von Krankheit. Die Politik und die 'Rentenneurosen,' 1890–1926," in *Stadt und Gesundheit. Zum Wandel von Volksgesundheit und kommunaler Gesundheitspolitik im 19. und frühen 20. Jahrhundert,* ed. Jürgen Reulecke and Adelheit Gräfin zu Castell-Rüdenhausen (Stuttgart: Steiner, 1991), 203–23; Gabriele Moser, "Der Arzt im Kampf gegen 'Begehrlichkeit und Rentensucht' im Deutschen Kaiserreich und in der Weimarer Republik," *Jahrbuch für kritische Medizin* 16 (1992): 161–83; Heinz-Peter Schmiedebach, "Die 'traumatische Neurose'—Soziale Versicherung und der Griff der Psychiatrie nach dem Unfallpatienten," in *Ergebnisse und Perspektiven sozialhistorischer Forschung in der Medizingeschichte. Kolloquium zum 100. Geburtstag von Henry Sigerist,* ed. Susanne Hahn and Achim Thom (Leipzig: Karl-Sudhoff-Institut, 1991), pp. 151–63.

22. For figures, see Dirk Blasius, *Umgang mit Unheilbarem. Studien zur Sozialgeschichte der Psychiatrie* (Bonn: Psychiatrie Verlag, 1986); Thomas-Peter Schindler, "Psychiatrie im Wilhelminischen Deutschland im Spiegel der Verhandlungen des 'Vereins der deutschen Irrenärzte' (ab 1903 'Deutscher Verein für Psychiatrie')" (Diss. Med., Freie Universität Berlin, 1990).

23. For Oppenheim's work with these patients, see Hermann Oppenheim, *Die traumatischen Neurosen nach den in der Nervenklinik der Charité in den 8 Jahren 1883–1888 gesammelten Beobachtungen* (Berlin: Hirschwald, 1889). Hacking singles out 1889 as the time in which "the linkage between hysteria and trauma became firmly established," but it is not entirely clear what he bases this claim on (Hacking, *Rewriting the Soul,* p. 86).

24. Alfred E. Hoche, "Geisteskrankheit und Kultur," in Hoche, *Aus der Werkstatt* (Munich: Lehmann, 1935), p. 16.

25. See, among others, Dirk Blasius, *"Einfache Seelenstörung": Geschichte der deutschen Psychiatrie, 1800–1945* (Frankfurt: Fischer, 1993); George Mosse, "Masculinity and the Decadence," in *Sexual Knowledge, Sexual Science: The History of Attitudes to Sexuality,* ed. Roy Porter and Mikulás Teich (Cambridge: Cambridge University Press, 1994), pp. 134–57; and Klaus Dörner, *Madmen and the Bourgeoisie,* trans. Joachim Neugroschel and Jean Steinberg (Oxford: Blackwell, 1981).

26. Hoche, "Geisteskrankheit und Kultur," p. 16.

27. See Lerner, "From Traumatic Neurosis to Male Hysteria" for a fuller treatment of this topic. On the politics of the medical profession in Wilhelmine Germany, see, among others, Michael Kater, "Professionalization and Socialization of Physicians in Wilhelmine and Weimar Germany," *Journal of Contemporary History* 20 (1985): 677–701; and Paul Weindling, *Health, Race and German Politics between National Unification and Nazism, 1870–1945* (Cambridge: Cambridge University Press, 1989).

28. According to the internist Wilhelm His, the Charité clinics were seen as the nation's highest authority for medical judgments on compensation claims. See Bonhoeffer, His, Hildebrandt et al., 5 Feb. 1920. Akte 1239, "Die Ausstellung von ärztlichen Attesten u. Gutachten über Kranken in der Charité (1877–1929); mit Schriftwechsel mit staatl. Dienststellen, Versicherungsämtern, und Kliniken," Blatt 342 (UI, Nr. 7421) Archiv der HUB. The Prussian State Assembly had resolved to beseech the Reich's government to make medical expert opinions accessible to patients; this suggestion was unanimously opposed at a gathering of the directors of several of the Charité clinics in February 1920.

29. Oskar Maria Graf, *Prisoners All,* trans. Margaret Green (New York: Knopf, 1928), esp. pp. 153–66; on Grosz and war neurosis, see Brigid Doherty, "Berlin Dada: Montage and the Embodiment of Modernity, 1916–1921" (Ph.D. diss., University of California at Berkeley, 1996).

30. Archiv der HUB, Nervenklinik Bestand, Akte 23.

31. Robert W. Whalen, *Bitter Wounds: German Victims of the First World War* (Ithaca: Cornell University Press, 1984), pp. 136–37.

32. "Anhaltspunkte für die militärärztliche Beurteilung der Frage der Dienstbeschädigung oder Kriegsdienstbeschädigung bei den häufigen psychischen und nervösen Erkrankungen der Heeresangehörigen. Auf Grund von Beratungen des Wissenschaftlichen Senats bei der Kaiser Wilhelms-Akademie," n.d. p. 1. Universitätsarchiv Tübingen, Nervenklinik Bestand (hereafter UA Tübingen), Akte 308/90. Although this document has no date on it, references to it in the contemporary literature make clear that it was distributed after the war. For a comparative approach to veterans, pensioning and welfare, see: Michael Geyer, "Ein Vorbote des Wohlfahrtstaates: Die Kriegsopferversorgung in Frankreich, Deutschland und Großbritannien nach dem Ersten Weltkrieg," *Geschichte und Gesellschaft* 9 (1983): 230–77; and Cohen, *War Come Home.*

33. "Anhaltspunkte für die militärärztliche Beurteilung der Frage der Dienstbeschädigung," p. 2.

34. "Anhaltspunkte für die militärärztliche Beurteilung der Frage der Dienstbeschädigung," p. 2. And in similar case, Dr. Pohlisch wrote: "E. gave the impression of psychic susceptibility during his stay in an asylum for several months. He took on that which he observed among other patients, a frequent attribute of psychopathic patients who come into these situations" (Archiv der HUB, Nervenklinik Bestand, Akte 29).

35. For a detailed treatment of the war neuroses in World War I Germany, see Paul Lerner, "Rationalizing the Therapeutic Arsenal: German Neuropsychiatry in the First World War," in *Medicine and Modernity: Public Health and Medical Care in Nineteenth- and Twentieth-Century Germany,* ed. Geoffrey Cocks and Manfred Berg (New York: Cambridge University Press, 1997), pp. 121–48; and Lerner, "Psychiatry and Casualties of War," *Journal of Contemporary History* 35 (Jan. 2000): 13–28. For other perspectives, see Doris Kaufmann, "Science as Cultural Practice: Psychiatry in the First World War and Weimar Germany," *Journal of Contemporary History* 34 (Jan. 1999): 125–44; Peter Riedesser and Axel Verderber, *"Maschinengewehre hinter der Front": Zur Geschichte der deutschen Militärpsychiatrie* (Frankfurt: Fischer, 1996); and Günther Komo, *"Für Volk und Vaterland": Militärpsychiatrie in den Weltkriegen* (Münster: Lit, 1992).

36. Wolfgang Schäffner, "Event, Series, Trauma: The Probabilistic Revolution of the Mind in the Late Nineteenth and Early Twentieth Centuries," in *Traumatic Pasts,* ed. Micale and Lerner, p. 86. See also Eva Horn, "Erlebnis und Trauma. Die narrative Konstruktion des Ereignisses in Psychiatrie und Kriegsromane," in *Modernität und Trauma,* ed. Mülder-Bach, pp. 131–62.

37. Sigmund Freud, *Beyond the Pleasure Principle,* trans. and ed. James Strachey (New York: Norton, 1961), esp. pp. 36–39.

38. On this distinction, see Walter Benjamin, "On Some Motifs in Baudelaire," in *Illuminations,* ed. Hannah Arendt, trans. Harry Zohn (New York: Schocken, 1968), esp. p. 163.

39. Bonhoeffer in "Berliner Gesellschaft für Psychiatrie und Nervenkrankheiten," *Neurologisches Zentralblatt* 34 (1915): 73.

40. Archiv der HUB, Nervenklinik Bestand, Akte 20.

41. See, for example, Robert Gaupp, "Neurasthenie und Schreckneurosen," in *Geistes- und Nervenkrankheiten,* ed. Bonhoeffer, pp. 68–101.

42. "Anhaltspunkte für die militärärztliche Beurteilung der Frage der Dienstbeschädigung," p. 17.

43. "Verhandlungen Psychiatrischer Vereine: Kriegstagung des Deutschen Vereins für Psychiatrie zu München am 21. und 22. September 1916," *Allgemeine Zeitschrift für Psychiatrie* 73 (1917): 230.

44. Archiv der HUB, Nervenklinik Bestand, Akte 19.

45. Archiv der HUB, Nervenklinik Bestand, Akte 29.

46. "Anhaltspunkte für die militärärztliche Beurteilung der Frage der Dienstbeschädigung," p. 19.

47. Stier, "Rentenversorgung bei nervösen und psychisch erkrankten Feldzugsteilnehmern," p. 171.

48. Ewald Stier, "Wie kann der Entstehung von Kriegsneurosen bei der Feldarmee vorgebeugt werden?" *Deutsche militärärztliche Zeitschrift* 47 (1918): 62.

49. Kurt Singer, "Was ist's mit dem Neurotiker von 1920," *Medizinische Klinik* 16 (1920): 951. See also Singer, "Das Kriegsende und die Neurosenfrage," *Neurologisches Zentralblatt* 38 (1919): 330–31; and E. Loewy-Hattendorf, *Krieg, Revolution und Unfallneurose* (Berlin: Schoetz, 1920), p. 21.

50. Karl Pönitz, *Die klinische Neuorientierung zum Hysterieproblem unter dem Einflusse der Kriegserfahrungen* (Berlin: Springer, 1921), p. 37. On economic and social conditions after the war, see, among others, Richard Bessel, *Germany after the First World War* (Oxford: Oxford University Press, 1993), esp. chap. 1; Gerald Feldman, *The Great Disorder: Politics, Economics, and Society in the German Inflation* (Oxford: Oxford University Press, 1993); and Whalen, *Bitter Wounds.*

51. Quoted in Karl Heinz Roth, "Psychosomatische Medizin und 'Euthanasie': Der Fall Viktor von Weizsäcker," *1999: Sozialgeschichte des 20. und 21. Jahrhunderts* 1 (Jan. 1986): 72.

52. Letter from Marquard, Kriegsmisterium, Kriegsamt, Berlin, 19 July 1917, "Kriegsbeschädigte als Hausierer und Bettler," UA Tübingen, Nervenklinik Bestand, 308/42.

53. Pönitz, *Klinische Neuorientierung,* p. 37. See also Robert Gaupp, "Krieg und Seelenleben!" *Deutsche Revue* 43 (1918): 168.

54. Max Nonne, "Therapeutische Erfahrungen an den Kriegsneurosen in den Jahren 1914–1918," in *Geistes- und Nervenkrankheiten,* ed. Bonhoeffer, p. 117.

55. Letter from Max Nonne to Ernst Kretschmer, Hamburg, 28 Oct. 1918, Kretschmer Papers, S28.4, "Briefe: Hysterie," private collection, Marburg.

56. A. Hauptmann, "Krieg der Unfalls-Hysterie!" *Deutsche Zeitschrift für Nervenheilkunde* 88 (1925): 193.

57. Stier, "Rentenversorgung bei nervösen und psychisch erkrankten Feldzugsteilnehmern," p. 169.

58. Robert Gaupp, "Die Behandlung der nervösen Schüttellähmung durch starke elektrische Ströme," UA Tübingen, 308/89, "Kriegsneurose" (emphasis in text).

59. Karl Wilmanns, "Bericht über die Sitzung des bad. Landesausschusses der Kriegsbeschädigtenfürsorge, 26 Oktober, 1917," 41, BA Berlin, Reichsarbeitsministerium, film #36069.

60. See Elisabeth Domansky, "Der Erste Weltkrieg," in *Bürgerlicher Gesellschaft in Deutschland,* ed. Lutz Niethammer et al. (Frankfurt: Fischer, 1990), pp. 317–18.

61. See Radkau, *Zeitalter der Nervosität,* and Eric J. Leed, *No Man's Land: Combat and Identity in World War I* (Cambridge: Cambridge University Press, 1979).

62. Quoted in Bernd Ulrich, "Krieg als Nervensache," *Die Zeit,* 22 Nov. 1991.

63. Otto Binswanger, *Die seelischen Wirkungen des Krieges* (Berlin: Deutsche Verlagsanstalt, 1914), p. 8.

64. Quoted in Wolfgang Mommsen, "The Topos of Inevitable War in Germany in the Decade before 1914," in *Germany in the Age of Total War,* ed. Volker Berghahn and Martin Kitchen (London: Croom Helm, 1981), 26.

65. F. Kehrer, "Zur Frage der Behandlung der Kriegshysterie," *Zeitschrift für die gesamte Neurologie und Psychiatrie* 36 (1917): 22.

66. G. Liebermeister, "Verhütung von Kriegsneurosen," *Medizinisches Correspondenzblatt des Württembergischen ärztlichen Landesvereins* 88 (1918): 308.

67. Liebermeister, "Verhütung von Kriegsneurosen," p. 308. See also Georg Berger, *Die beratenden Psychiater des deutschen Heeres 1939 bis 1945* (Frankfurt: Peter Lang, 1998), p. 59.

68. Georg Friedrich Wilhelm Schultzen, "Grundsätze für die Behandlung und Beurteilung der sogenannten Kriegsneurotiker (Neurotiker-Merkblatt)," UA Tübingen, Nervenklinik Bestand, 308/89, p. 9.

69. Ludwig Mann, "Über Granatexplosionsstörungen," *Archiv für Psychiatrie und Nervenkrankheiten* 56 (1915): 345.

70. For Kaufmann's description of the treatment, see Fritz Kaufmann, "Die planmässige Heilung komplizierter psychogener Bewegungsstörungen bei Soldaten in einer Sitzung," *Münchener medizinische Wochenschrift* 63 (1916): 802–4; and F. Kaufmann, "Zur Behandlung der motorischen Kriegsneurosen," *Münchener medizinische Wochenschrift* 64 (1917): 1520–23. For historical treatments, see Lerner, "Rationalizing the Therapeutic Arsenal," pp. 143–47; and Peter Riedesser and Axel Verderber, *Aufrüstung der Seelen: Militärpsychiatrie und Militärpsychologie in Deutschland und Amerika* (Freiburg: Dreisam Verlag, 1985).

71. On the will, psychiatric treatment, and German politics, see Paul Lerner, "Hysterical Cures: Hypnosis, Gender and Performance in World War I and Weimar Germany," *History Workshop Journal* 45 (1998): 79–101; and Lerner, "'Ein Sieg deutschen Willens': Wille und Gemeinschaft in der deutschen Kriegspsychiatrie," in *Die Medizin und der Erste Weltkrieg,* ed. Wolfgang Eckart and Christoph Gradmann (Freiburg: Centaurus-Verlag, 1996), pp. 85–107.

72. Eghigian, "Die Bürokratie und das Entstehen von Krankheit"; Moser, "Der Arzt im Kampf."

73. Young, *Harmony of Illusions,* esp. p. 5.

74. On the formation of collective memory out of competing memories, see Confino, *Nation as a Local Metaphor,* and Daniel Sherman, "Bodies and Names: The Emergence of Commemoration in Interwar France," *American Historical Review* 103 (1998): 443–66. Also see Sherman, *The Construction of Memory in Interwar France* (Chicago: University of Chicago Press, 1999).

75. On the resentment of the "really war-disabled" (*wirklich kriegsbeschädigte*) toward neurotics, see Singer, "Was ist's mit dem Neurotiker," p. 951.

76. For example, Eugen Kahn, "Psychopathen als revolutionäre Führer," *Zeitschrift für die gesamte Neurologie und Psychiatrie* 52 (1919): 90–106; Robert Gaupp, "Die Revolution und das nervöse Zusammenbruch," *Blätter für Volksgesundheitspflege* 19 (1919): 43–46; and Kurt Hildebrandt, "Forensische Begutachtung eines Spartakisten," *Allgemeine Zeitschrift für Psychiatrie* 76 (1919): 479–518.

77. The best example of this can be found in Emil Kraepelin, "Randbemerkungen zur Zeitgeschichte," *Süddeutsche Monatshefte* 16 (1919): 171–83.

78. Geyer, "Place of World War II," p. 14.

79. See, among others, Mosse, *Fallen Soldiers;* Bernd Hüppauf, "Langemarck, Verdun and the Myth of a *New Man* in Germany after the First World War," *War and Society* 6 (1988): 70–101; Albrecht Koschorke, "Der Traumatiker als Fascist: Ernst Jünger's Essay 'Über den Schmerz,'" in *Modernität und Trauma,* pp. 211–27; Klaus Theweleit, *Male Fantasies,* vol. 2: *Male Bodies: Psychoanalyzing the White Terror,* trans. Stephen Conway (Minneapolis: University of Minnesota, 1989); and Jeffrey Herf, *Reactionary Modernism: Technology, Culture and Politics in Weimar and the Third Reich* (Cambridge: Cambridge University Press, 1984).

80. See Mosse, *Fallen Soldiers;* Winter, *Sites of Memory.*

81. See, for example, Ernst Kretschmer, *Gestalten und Gedanken* (Stuttgart: Thieme Verlag, 1963), p. 94; Robert Wollenberg, *Erinnerungen eines alten Psychiaters* (Stuttgart: Enke, 1931), p. 143; and Nonne, "Therapeutische Erfahrungen an den Kriegsneurosen in den Jahren 1914–1918," esp. p. 116.

82. For a detailed treatment, see Lerner, "Rationalizing the Therapeutic Arsenal."

83. Friedrich Mörchen, "Das Problem der Hysterie," *Münchener medizinische Wochenschrift* 68 (1921): 1221.

84. Hauptmann, "Krieg der Unfalls-Hysterie!" On the "pension war" (*Rentenkrieg*) in the 1920s, see also Roth, "Psychosomatische Medizin und 'Euthanasie,'" esp. p. 73.

CHAPTER 9

Public Relations as a Site of Memory: The Case of West German Industry and National Socialism

S. JONATHAN WIESEN

In the recent flood of literature on collective memory, there is one subject that has heretofore received very little attention—the economy.[1] In their fruitful attempts to think through the relationship between the past and the present, historians have located multiple "sites" or "realms" of memory[2]—monuments, national holidays, regional festivals, and religious rituals, to name but a few.[3] But the business world has been all but overlooked as a possible site of collective memory. This oversight is perhaps not surprising. There exists to this day a view, albeit a gradually changing one, that industrial attitudes and behaviors do not lend themselves to cultural analysis. While historians have always been interested in managerial structures, marketing strategies, and the relationship between companies and society, they have resisted examining business practices with the help of newer cultural theories.[4] In this essay, I hope to counter this trend by applying the concept of memory to corporate public relations. By examining West German industry's confrontation with the legacy of National Socialism during the late 1940s and the early 1950s, I hope to demonstrate how collective memory works more broadly in a modern, capitalist system—how a group retrieves and embellishes its past and how it sells this past to a wider public and to itself.

When World War II came to an end in 1945, German industrialists bore the burden of deep complicity with the Nazi regime. They had run the factories that created the machinery of war; they had plundered businesses in occupied Europe; they had employed forced and slave laborers; and they had constructed the gas chambers where millions of Jews and other persecuted minorities were exterminated.[5] While before World War II business leaders had grown accustomed to being reproached as immoral profiteers, labor exploiters, and even warmongers, after Auschwitz the more ethically damning images of mass murder provided German industry with an unprecedented challenge. While to most postwar observers National Socialism constituted a horrifying moral collapse, for the business world it also represented a public relations disaster the likes of which had never been witnessed.[6]

In the first decade after the collapse of Nazism, politicians, Allied prosecutors, and the international media consistently reminded German business of its compromised past. Industrialists responded to this public indictment with commissioned company histories, apologetic explanations of corporate behavior under Hitler, and celebrations of free enterprise and West German productivity. By both invoking traditional stories or "myths" of capitalism and creating new ones, the business community hoped to divert public attention from the legacy of business complicity and to protect industrialists from the political uncertainties of a country under reconstruction. Imbuing companies and their representatives with moral qualities—in contrast to the heinous crimes being imputed to them—demanded the vigilant cultivation of positive images and narratives. The process of creating and marketing these images reveals memory as an *active* and collective process, aimed at both appeasing a scrutinizing public and coming to terms with a new consumer economy.

PR and Collective Memory: Working Definitions

Before discussing specific examples of how West German industry confronted the Nazi past, I will offer brief, working definitions of the terms "public relations" and the more contested "memory." Since its popularization in the United States in the 1920s, public relations has been understood as a distinctly modern tool of persuasion. Unlike older forms of "publicity," or "press agentry," through which a firm advertised its products and achievements with little attention paid to its wider reception, PR acknowledges the existence of a new and powerful entity known as "the masses." The early articulators of public relations, like Ivy Lee and Edward Bernays, saw the masses (today simply "the public") as at once impressionable and authoritarian, susceptible to persuasion through the techniques of mass psychology but also possessing the ability to make or break a company through word of mouth and purchasing behavior.[7] Through the medium of public relations, a company not only "gets the word out" about itself and its products, but it also keeps a watchful eye on the "man on the street" to determine what images he will accept or reject. In short, PR commits William Vanderbilt's legendary utterance that "the public be damned" to the dustbin of history.[8] The new age calls for "planned persuasive communications designed to influence significant publics."[9] Public relations is a deliberate and self-conscious process of creation and marketing. Its purpose is to sell a company—its products, its reputation, and its past. According to Roland Marchand, from its inception in the early part of the twentieth century, PR's ultimate goal has been to humanize capitalism—to convince a wary and powerful public that a company has a "soul."[10]

In employing the concept of "collective memory," I am drawing upon the work of French sociologist and Durkheim protégé Maurice Halbwachs. Halbwachs articulated memory as conscious, collective, and purposeful. Rather than being a passive, individual phenomenon, memory instead is located within a web of social and performative practices. For Halbwachs, private memories are, in fact, ephemeral and have no lasting life outside the group context. Memory is always embedded in a network of power relations, customs, traditions, and symbols. A group—in this case German industry—sustains itself by manipulating the images of the past for present purposes, and an individual's personal memories are mediated by broader group narratives. According to Halbwachs, therefore, memory is more appropriately seen as "commemoration"—an exercise of collective agency and rational choice, albeit always constrained by sociohistorical realities.[11]

It is at this point that public relations and collective memory converge. For by definition the "planned persuasive communication" that constitutes public relations is a process of remembering and forgetting. It is about the conscious selection of images from the past and their purposeful presentation. In their decision to put down a strike, to market a new product, or to contribute to charities, companies always draw upon lessons and images from the past. These memories can be about anything from a firm's tradition for quality, to the consequences of worker unrest on profits, to the positive results of social engagement. In short, public relations calls upon personal and institutional memories and presents them to a public or publics that, in turn, possess their own memories of and preconceptions about big business. The ultimate goal of PR is to create a symbiotic relationship based on both trust and competition between public desires and corporate profits. PR recognizes the imperative that a company sell not only its goods but its name.

Industry Constructs a Serviceable Past, 1945–49

"It is not enough to advertise a product," wrote Colonel Robert Stewart, the chairman of Standard Oil of Indiana, in 1922. "The public ought to be acquainted with the honesty and high character of the institution back of the product."[12] This remains the fundamental philosophy of public relations to this very day. But what happens when a company's "honesty and high character" have been so badly compromised that not only the firm but the very economic system in which it functions is discredited? Such was the case in West Germany after World War II. From the moment the war ended, industrialists were forced to account for their actual and putative misdeeds during the prior two decades. Communists attributed much of the blame for Hitler's success to the structural affinities between fascism and "monopoly" or "finance" capitalism and to industrialists' support of the Nazi party. In their early postwar platforms, Social Democrats (SPD) and Christian Democrats (CDU) also suggested a link, albeit less dogmatically, between capitalism and the Great Depression, class warfare, and National Socialism.[13] While the CDU and the SPD eventually abandoned their deeper suspicions of capitalism after the founding of the West German state, throughout the 1950s politicians, labor leaders, and journalists regularly used industry's misdeeds under Nazism to critique the growing power of big business. Long after the "economic miracle" took hold in the 1950s, Marxist critics, especially from East Germany, continued to publish harsh ideological attacks against free enterprise and specific companies implicated in Nazi crimes. In this heated environment, industrialists recognized the urgent need both to defend their companies' reputations and to humanize capitalism.

During the first decade after 1945 West German industry adopted essentially two public relations strategies to address its legitimation crisis.[14] The first was to deny emphatically any instance of willful wrongdoing during the Nazi years. Thus, if a company or a businessman was accused of employing slave labor, then the common response was to blame Hitler or the SS and to portray the firm as politically impotent under a totalitarian dictatorship.[15] This strategy, as I will discuss below, can be witnessed most clearly in the trials of industrialists and the accompanying apologias, commissioned by large firms and business leaders.[16] The second strategy was to adopt the more universal and time-tested practice of portraying the company, and by extension, capitalism, as possessing a long and honorable tradition of ethical and selfless behavior. This latter approach was found both in trial defenses and also in a body of literature in the 1950s and beyond devoted to creating the so-called new industrialist (*das neue Unternehmer*), who was to embody attitudes and behaviors diametrically opposed to those attributed to "fascist businessmen."[17]

A company that exemplified this dual PR strategy was Siemens, Germany's largest manufacturer of electrical products. In the summer of 1945, the directors of the badly damaged firm met amidst the rubble of its Berlin headquarters to devise ways of repairing the company's reputation. Among its activities during the war, Siemens had manufactured the majority of the electrical components used by the German military, and it had also run a network of forced and slave labor camps, including a factory at the Auschwitz subcamp Bobrek and a women's work installation at Ravensbrück. In 1945 top Siemens executives, like future managing director Wolf Dietrich von Witzleben, who had neither been arrested by the Soviets nor fled westward, prepared a document called *The Behavior of the House of Siemens during the Hitler Regime,* which attempted to justify the company's involvement in Nazi crimes. The company distributed this piece to the local press, to friends at home and abroad, and to the Allied occupation authorities.[18]

Perhaps the earliest example of postwar corporate PR, this document typifies West German industrial publicity in its depiction of industrialists alternatively as victims and opponents of the Nazis, and as the embodiment of corporate integrity. *The Behavior of the House of Siemens,* not surprisingly, denied that the firm had willingly participated in the Nazi economy. Under a totalitarian regime, the document claimed, Siemens had had no choice but to contribute to the war effort and to make use of forced and slave labor. When the Nazis demanded compliance, the company complied. Moreover, Siemens, which the Berlin press was accusing of having embraced the Nazis' political and racial aims, argued that it had in fact opposed the Nazis from start to finish, by helping Jews to emigrate or by banning the "Heil Hitler" greeting on the factory floor. In response to reports of the horrifying conditions in the forced labor camps, *The Behavior of the House of Siemens* and subsequent company reports not only denied that the workers were treated badly but, in fact, paid tribute to the firm's historically progressive track record vis-à-vis its employees.[19] It also tried to utilize the current political and economic chaos in Germany to its advantage. In 1945 the Allies were considering breaking up the company (a plan they eventually abandoned), and the PR report argued that Siemens, as the most important producer of electrical equipment, was in fact indispensable to the postwar economic recovery.[20] Finally, in response to being labeled a "war criminal firm" by the international press and the Allies, Siemens's executives emphasized the company's history of peaceful, apolitical, and humanitarian behavior.

Some of the claims contained in *The Behavior of the House of Siemens* were true, such as the company's historically liberal relationship to labor, but the majority were embellishments or outright inventions, particularly the claim of resistance to Nazism. Like every major firm, Siemens had immersed itself inextricably, and often willingly, in the Nazi economy, even if there had been isolated instances of insubordination. But historical truth was not of the highest priority in the summer of 1945. Through the example of *The Behavior of the House of Siemens,* we can witness company leaders frantically crafting a usable past[21] that would save their firm from the Allied wrecking ball and help rebuild its international reputation. By combining its progressive history with a myth of industrial resistance under National Socialism, Siemens officials hoped to prove to the public how necessary the firm was to postwar reconstruction efforts. "We hope," wrote one Siemens executive, "that none of our friends abroad are fooled by the malicious slandering of the Siemens Concern and remain convinced that the moral foundations of the House of Siemens have remained unshaken for one hundred years."[22]

The composition of this *Verteidigungsschrift* (apologia) in the rubble of Berlin clearly reveals "collective" or "institutional" memory at work. In order to counter accusations of immoral behavior, Siemens's managers, through various drafts, carefully crafted the story of a more glorious era, when the company was recognized internationally for its trade relationships with other countries, its technical ingenuity, its quality products, and its reformist social policies. Foreign trading partners who had enjoyed healthy personal and professional relationships with Siemens's executives could indeed attest to some aspects of this splendid past. But none of these cheerful evocations and strident denials could erase the reality of the firm's recent complicity during the Third Reich.

The strategies Siemens employed in the summer of 1945 were replicated by a number of firms and individual industrialists throughout the 1940s and 1950s. The most elaborate public relations efforts accompanied the series of Nuremberg trials the United States conducted against the leaders of three companies in 1947 and 1948. Prosecutors accused the executives of Krupp, Flick, and IG Farben of war crimes and crimes against humanity, including funding the Nazi party, planning a war of aggression, plundering firms in occupied Europe, and employing slave labor.[23] While some industrialists were acquitted, others, like Friedrich Flick and Alfried Krupp von Bohlen und Halbach, received multiyear sentences, which were commuted in 1951 by John J. McCloy, America's high commissioner for Germany.[24]

Again both in the defense presented during the trial and in behind-the-scenes lobbying by industrialists, we can witness the dual strategy of denial and self-promotion. On the one hand, industrialists like the Gutehoffnungshütte's Hermann Reusch, who was the most active spokesman for heavy industry, helped write and distribute apologetic pamphlets that portrayed industrialists as the collective victims of a dictatorial madman.[25] Hitler had compelled industry, through the Four Years Plan, the "forced" aryanization of Jewish businesses, to submit to the dictates of the Nazi economy.[26] On the other hand, whether in publications or in denazification courtrooms, industrialists relied on the positive strategy of elevating the accused to a heroic resister to Nazism.[27] In the employment of slave labor, the companies claimed, the firms were actually saving workers from the gas chambers of Poland;[28] in forcing Jews and non-Jews to work in German factories, they were actually providing lifelong skills to workers.

While these strategies were sometimes desperate, ad hoc defenses devised to secure the acquittal of a prominent businessman, the majority represented the carefully coordinated work of industrial publicists, corporate archivists, and company directors. What is important in all postwar PR efforts is how much these businessmen depended upon institutional memories to exculpate themselves and their firms. The lawyer for Krupp director Max Ihn, for example, used his opening defense in Nuremberg in 1947 as a chance to reflect upon Krupp's paternal concern for its workers, its "*Kruppianer.*" He went on to indicate that this same concern for workers translated into equally good treatment of its forced laborers.[29] The Bayer corporation, which as part of the IG Farben chemical conglomerate had run a synthetic rubber plant at Auschwitz, reminded the world in its publicity releases in the late 1940s and 1950s (as it still does today) that it had been the inventor of aspirin and had contributed to the public health through the manufacturing of a number of important pharmaceuticals.[30] Even Degesch, the producer of zyklon B during the war, would argue in later company reports from the 1960s that its product had once been an effective pesticide, notwithstanding its use in the gassing of millions.[31]

In each of the above examples we can see that German companies defended their reputations by infusing their histories and their products with moral substance. The companies under attack besought the public to place the Nazi years in a broader context and to measure the virtue of a firm not by any putative misdeeds in the recent past but by its longer record of a social conscience and, more importantly, by its legacy of creating superior and, indeed, humanitarian products. Postwar industry took refuge in the "made in Germany" myth as it attempted to convince the public that it was not without a soul.

Moralizing the Market Economy, 1949–55

With the founding of the West German state in 1949, and the consolidation of the market economy, industrialists' frenzied desire to explain the Nazi past began to dissipate. Businessmen had rebuilt their factories, denazification trials were winding down, and the economy was expanding. Yet during the early Adenauer years, when national leaders were debating the introduction of industrial codetermination (union representation on company boards) and the rearmament of West Germany, industrialists continued to worry that the legacy of corporate guilt might remain a permanent feature of the political landscape.

Starting in 1949, industrialists began to reflect more consciously on the power of public relations to deflect negative views from German industry and to promote businessmen as the embodiment of anti-Communism and free-market economics.[32] While industrialists continued to produce studies and company reports that purported to explain the "true story" behind business behavior under Nazism,[33] they gradually began to focus more on highlighting the benevolent aspects of their pasts and their contributions to the country's "social market economy" than on directly denying criminality. They replaced the existing practice of *Öffentlichkeitsarbeit* (publicity work), which many felt was too crassly apologetic and simplistic, with the (ostensibly) more sophisticated and more persuasive tools of American-style PR. At business meetings and PR seminars, West German industrialists formulated their desire to create a bond of trust with the public and to convince it that the market economy and its leaders would bring about unparalleled abundance while also protecting West Germany from the scourge of Soviet-style "collectivism." They turned to the United States, the spiritual home of public relations, for help in applying this new philosophy of corporate goodwill and anti-Communism. In 1950, for example, Ludwig Vaubel of the chemical firm Vereinigte Glanzstoff, enrolled in Harvard University's School of Management, where he learned the latest techniques of company leadership and promarket publicity.[34] In the 1950s industrialists representing the Federation of German Industry (BDI) regularly traveled across the Atlantic to attend seminars on public relations, human relations, and international trade and politics.[35] In newspapers, business trade journals, and commissioned biographies, industrial publicists denigrated the planned economies of the "East" and exalted capitalism as the provider of material and spiritual security. This forceful promotion of the market economy, while a reflection of cold war hostilities, also represented West German industry's attempt to move beyond the Nazi years and the memories of industrial complicity.

Affirming capitalism's moral legitimacy after the catastrophes of the 1930s and 1940s demanded more than just celebrating the market economy and its promise of material well-being. Industrialists and economic publicists had to locate role models who embodied the *Unternehmerpersönlichkeit*—the entrepreneurial personality—upon which market success depended. Here we can again witness the active work of industrial memory. From Thyssen to Krupp to Siemens, companies cast their founders and current owners as simple men, entrepreneurs, or inventors, whose dreams had never been to build large companies per se (certainly not ones implicated in the crimes of Nazism), but simply to contribute to the Fatherland and to humanity through innovations in steel production, coal mining, and textile manufacturing, and in the production of medicines. In contrast to the discredited image of the "*Herr im Hause*," the master of his domain who ruled over his workers with a quasi-beneficent/quasi-tyrannical hand, these publications portrayed their leaders as at once family fathers and avuncular owners. Love of country, family, and employees were all embodied in men like Werner von Siemens, Alfred Krupp, August Thyssen, Hugo Stinnes, and Robert Bosch.[36]

This sentimental eulogizing of the company father was already to be found in the Siemens document of 1945, which commemorated founder Werner von Siemens's contributions to humankind as inventor, entrepreneur, scholar, and technician.[37] But this strategy was particularly evident when the director of a company died. Such was the case with the late Peter Klöckner of Klöckner Steel, who had passed away in 1941. Ten years after his death, the company eulogized him in a commemorative pamphlet as the embodiment of a dying breed of *Unternehmer,* who always played an active and benevolent role in his company. "What made us great in the past," wrote industrial publicist Volkmar Muthesius in his hagiographic introduction, "and what today has allowed the revival of our economy after the collapse of 1945 is indeed that very *Unternehmergeist* that is inseparable from a market and competitive economy. . . . the great industrial personalities like Peter Klöckner can today serve as examples of an *Unternehmertum* that is at once level-headed and courageous."[38]

The personification of capitalism could be found not only in the commemoration and lionization of a "factory father" but also in a spate of business-friendly publications and workers magazines that were founded in the 1950s. In magazines like the weekly *Das Fenster* (founded in 1952) or in the publications of the *Bundesverband Junger Unternehmer* (the Federation of Young Entrepreneurs), profiles of teenage inventors and aging industrial leaders appeared next to images celebrating the success of Western consumption and production—from dishwashers, to automobiles, to smiling coal miners covered in soot.[39] These visual manifestations of West Germany's "Economic Miracle" were interspersed with articles that depicted manager and worker as partners in a crusade to defend the Federal Republic of Germany against Soviet "collectivism" and all other threats to the spirit of individualism.[40] In short, in the early 1950s industrialists' euphoria over of the FRG's economic resurgence was tempered by fears that Communists, with their rhetoric of capitalist immorality, would destroy the country's hard-earned successes. By relieving industry of its burdensome past and publicizing the FRG's economic achievement, however, the *Unternehmer* and the *Arbeiter* could together defeat their totalitarian enemy to the East.

Anxieties about the Nazi past and the image of capitalism also manifested themselves in industry's new efforts at social and cultural engagement. Individual firms like Krupp or umbrella organizations like the BDI's *Kulturkreis* (Cultural Circle) began in the early 1950s to revive a tradition of philanthropy in order to counter images of the heartless company that cared only about profits.[41] With the founding of the West German state, these organizations and companies sponsored art exhibitions, promoted their products at trade fairs, contributed to charities, produced industrial films emphasizing the tradition of "made in Germany" quality, and set up foundations to promote international education.[42]

Importantly, despite industry's newly honed PR vigilance, the tools of corporate self-promotion were by no means new. Indeed in the 1920s firms had used company newspapers, social programs, and philanthropy to project corporate goodwill.[43] But after 1945, at a time when they were being associated with the most heinous of crimes, industrialists utilized these media more self-consciously and more aggressively in order to refurbish their personal reputations and that of their firms. With the help of this proud past, they could also turn the public's attention toward the present material benefits that West German companies were providing as the economy began to soar during the *Wirtschaftswunderjahre* ("the years of the economic miracle") of the 1950s. During this period public relations, at its core, embodied a deep ambivalence. While it drew wistfully upon narratives associated with nineteenth-century capitalism—the apolitical entrepreneur who risked his own capital and took good care of his workers—it also acknowledged that there was no turning back. The means of coming to terms with National Socialism entailed confronting the past and wooing the public with the modern tools of mass communication—from books, to films, to advertisements, to industrial products themselves.

Capitalism and the Modernity of Memory

In these specific examples of West German public relations, both in the strategy of denying crimes against humanity and in investing a firm with moral purpose, one can see industrial memory at work, as selective and (at times) tendentious as it was. But in identifying post-Hitler industrial public relations as a site of memory, one can also see how corporate self-promotion in any capitalist economy is premised on the pragmatic or sentimental retrieval of the past. By recognizing PR more generally as a form of memory production, the flawed assumption that corporate publicity is merely "business as usual"—the notion that this form of self-promotion simply reflects managers' and shareholders' concern for the "bottom line"—becomes increasingly untenable. Companies, to be sure, exist to sell their products and increase their profits through a host of means and media. Marketing a brand name or donating money to a philanthropic organization is undoubtedly a reflection of a company's fundamental desire to create a business-friendly environment in which to sell its products. But PR sheds light not only on the pragmatic business mind but also on the context in which it functions. In the first decade after National Socialism, the legacy of corporate complicity in Nazism left German industrialists in a state of crisis. They desperately sought to reclaim a legitimacy that they felt had been stolen from them, first by the Nazis, and then by Communist "muckrakers." In this environment of ideological finger pointing, public relations demanded the production of a sanitized past and a morally redemptive present. PR functioned not only to increase company sales but also to draw a curtain over the Nazi past, to incite everyday Germans to strive toward material success, and to battle "collectivist" ideas that challenged the individualism undergirding a market economy.

Admittedly, distancing one's company from mass persecution and murder represents a uniquely daunting publicity challenge by any standard. But the very uniqueness of West German industry's PR crisis only illuminates how the spheres of business and economics are always imbued with memory. For even in the most extreme circumstances, West German businessmen still relied on what can be considered "standard" modes of self-promotion. Already in the late nineteenth century, as Matt Matsuda has argued in the case of France, "capitalists wrote their own visions of past and present" to challenge radical critics like Karl Marx and to credit themselves with the grand developments of their nation—from railroads, to mines, to canals.[44] Likewise in the United States, industrialists in the nineteenth century took refuge in depictions of an earlier phase of capitalism, before corporate giants replaced family-owned firms. In nineteenth-century Europe and in America, industrialists propagated Horatio Alger stories of rags-to-riches success to counter the more incriminating images of price-gouging, strike-breaking, and cigar-smoking fat cats.[45]

In a similar manner, West German industrialists, despite the horrifying singularity of their links to Nazism, wrote the history of economic recovery as a capitalist success story with universal applications. While the war required German industry to address charges of Nazi complicity, industrialists simultaneously turned their attention to the new and burgeoning world of consumer culture. Stories of past business glory would remain largely ineffective if they could not somehow resonate with the actual products of an economy increasingly driven by consumption. Already in the fall of 1950, with prosperity still more of a promise than a reality, industrialists and politicians came together to promote West German products at the first annual *Deutsche Industrieausstellung* (German Industry Exhibition) in West Berlin. Over a million visitors traveled to West Berlin to witness the first fruits of the "economic miracle," from chemicals and paints to toys and typewriters. Appealing in particular to his East German visitors, Finance Minister Ludwig Erhard lauded West German merchandise as "evidence of the meaningful and creative efforts of the German entrepreneurial spirit [*Unternehmergeist*] and the diligent hands of millions of West German workers."[46] Throughout the weeklong exhibition companies displayed their wares while industrialists and politicians delivered soaring speeches about the benefits of capitalism and the evils of the planned economy.

What did these consumer products on display have to do with memory? As Elizabeth Ten Dyke has suggested in the context of post-Communist eastern Germany, objects of consumption carry multiple meanings for individuals, both as reminders of past privations and harbingers of future economic well-being.[47] In West Germany, after years of wartime controls, postwar hunger, and food rationing, West German industry deftly recognized that the everyday items of mass consumption could evoke a range of visceral emotions in consumers. Familiar brand names could elicit positive memories of a happier time for Germans *and* deflect negative memories of corporate or individual crimes. To demonstrate how a product name penetrated the consciousness of postwar Germans, one can cite the example of Persil-brand soap and wash powder. During years of denazification in the late 1940s, a "Persilschein," (literally a "Persil certificate"—a certificate of exoneration) served as testament to one's innocence during Nazi years. This printed indication that one had both a literally and figuratively "clean" past became a coveted document during the years of postwar denazification.

In short, if public relations literature was where industrialists made a case for their moral rectitude, brand names and products themselves could constitute the tangible evidence of this. Infused with memory, products "made in Germany" evoked nostalgia for a bygone, "innocent" era, when the German economy was associated with quality, handcrafted goods, rather than tanks and crematoria.[48]

Public relations reveals that company board meetings and industrial exhibitions, no less than museums or monuments, were sites of memory. But, as a sophisticated tool of mass communication, PR also sheds light on what is, in fact, modern about memory. Perhaps most obviously, PR supports the idea that modern memory-making is a fundamentally public process. Returning to Halbwachs, one can argue that collective memory depends upon the belief that an individual and a group deserve recognition and respect in the marketplace of ideas and competing political interests. Many German industrialists, despite their compromised pasts, felt violated and abused. PR, in projecting through modern media the image of the tormented businessman and the corporate citizen, demonstrates that group memory was not a private affair; by its very nature, it was *publicly* produced and consumed—both by members of the group that did the commemorating (be it a company or an entire nation)—and by other groups or publics that accepted or rejected an act of commemoration or an assertion of entitlement.

The idea that modern memory is essentially public is supported by the work of French sociologist Pierre Bourdieu. Bourdieu's concept of the "habitus" is useful for understanding collective memory as a publicly adversarial process. Bourdieu's habitus "is a set of *dispositions* which incline agents to act and react in certain ways."[49] It is a system of attitudes, practices, and linguistic habits that inform the behavior of a particular group or an individual as it competes for various forms of "capital"—property, political and cultural authority, honor, prestige, et cetera—in the broader "field" of social conflict and political debate. As groups vie for scarce capital and political and social legitimation, they draw upon a trove of group memories and habits. In the case of Germany, industry vied with the public for control over the memory of National Socialism and the particular complicity of big business. In the early postwar years, this struggle took the form of a verbal tug of war between the accuser and the accused—between the public, the socialist and Communist press, the American prosecutors, or the buying public more generally, and the company or individual accused of criminal activity.

Once modern memory is recognized as a largely public and social affair, *language* becomes key, for it is at the level of discourse that one discovers the workings of memory. In company archives, historians can now read documents and witness how executives and publicists chose, for example, to highlight the firm's positive treatment of minorities or to delete from a PR text a provocative or controversial word or phrase. One can observe the careful selection of a euphemism that would deflect negative images away from a company. The historian can witness variations and transformations in language—from the use of the most damning term "slave labor" to "forced labor," "foreign labor," "guest labor," or even "manpower."[50] Similarly, one can chart the public's varied perceptions of industry through language. Whether one depicted industrialists as "businessmen," "managers," "entrepreneurs," "monopoly capitalists," "finance capitalists" "*Konzernherren,*" or "fascists" depended upon how one interpreted the Nazi past and capitalism more generally. In short, through the push and pull of public relations, we can see how agency and rhetoric converge, and how industrial practices, and the public's responses to them, were embedded in linguistic structures and in a series of political orientations and relationships to the past. Through public relations, one discovers the fundamentally "memorial" nature of language and image making. Postwar West German industrialists and the broader public lived and worked in a network of memories and attitudes about capitalism as an economic system—a focus on profits, a promotion of new products, the moralization of the company and its leaders, fear of strikes—that found expression in the ritualistic use of probusiness language, the recalling of founding capitalist myths, or, alternatively, in a more critical view of the free market and Western modernity.

In the wake of World War II, the legacy of industrial complicity in Nazism required West German industrialists to mobilize their defenses through images of past entrepreneurial greatness. After the founding of the FRG, this "pragmatic nostalgia" was bolstered by tangible economic growth, and Finance Minister Ludwig Erhard's promotion of a new, more humane capitalism through the "social market economy."[51] Thus despite the often calculating disingenuousness of corporate apologias, the crafted memories in postwar public relations converged with more widespread and, arguably, more deeply held beliefs and ideologies—about the liberating force of the market, individualism, *Kultur,* and family—that had accompanied the rise of capitalism and that still carried tremendous force in early postwar Germany. Regardless of the truth or falsity of industrial narratives, memory was a powerful means by which business leaders—and West Germans more generally—lent coherence to the devastating and disorienting experience of National Socialism. The legends contained in industrial PR are certainly not irrelevant. But they formed part of West Germans' broader and more genuine quest to orient themselves to a postfascist, liberal democracy.

Conclusion

In a recent article, Noa Gedi and Yigal Elam have raised the issue of whether collective memory is "but a misleading new name for the old familiar (concept of) 'myth'"?[52] In other words, does the faddishness of the word "memory" detract from older, more useful concepts like "myth" or "history"? Certainly, I have tried to demonstrate public relations as a modern form of mythmaking. Through the tropes of corporate innocence, magnified heroism, and dubious claims of industry's victimization, we can witness industrial memory as "myth" in its everyday sense—as embellishments or lies. But myth also takes the form of institutional memories, such as those of Krupp, which reveled in its dynastic history as the kaiser's arms maker,[53] or Degussa, which commemorates to this day its past as a metallurgy firm, not as part owner of a poison gas company.[54] Both forms of myth were indispensable to German industry after 1945. As Gedi and Elam argue, memory is indeed myth in its literal sense, but it is not only myth. It is also the means by which a group, such as industrialists or West Germans more generally in the early Adenauer years, (re)constituted its self-identity.

West German public relations after 1945 bears all the characteristics of modern memory. It harked back to an age of innocence, before the recent "time of troubles," when businessmen were drawn into Hitler's machinations. Industrialists longed wistfully for the return of the paternal factory father or the easy association of "made in Germany" with high quality. Memory, when viewed through the lens of public relations, becomes a series of tenuous commemorations, half-truths, lies, denials, embellishments, ritualistic celebrations, and self-inventions. Industrial memory, in the immediate postwar years, was, more than anything, an act of mourning. This lamentation was not for the victims of the Holocaust. It was a well-publicized grieving for a mythical era when big business enjoyed the freedom to produce goods, pass factories on to their sons, and to be loved and hated by the public the "good old-fashioned way"—before Auschwitz entered the picture.

NOTES

1. One recent exception is Matt K. Matsuda, *The Memory of the Modern* (Oxford: Oxford University Press, 1996), esp. chap. 2.

2. See, e.g., Jay Winter, *Sites of Memory, Sites of Mourning: The Great War in European Cultural History* (Cambridge: Cambridge University Press, 1995); and Pierre Nora, ed., *Realms of Memory: Rethinking the French Past,* vol. 1 (New York: Columbia University Press, 1996).

3. For two recent examples of the extensive literature on memory in Germany, see Rudy Koshar, *From Monuments to Traces: Artifacts of German Memory, 1870–1990* (Berkeley: University of California Press, 2000); and Alon Confino, *The Nation as a Local Metaphor: Württemberg, Imperial Germany and National Memory, 1871–1918* (Chapel Hill: University of North Carolina Press, 1997). For recent theoretical discussions of memory, see Jeffrey K. Olick, ed., *Social Science Quarterly* [special issue on Memory and the Nation] 22:4 (Winter, 1998): 377–571; Confino, "Collective Memory and Cultural History: Problems of Method" *American Historical Review* 102 (1997): 1386–1403; Susan A. Crane, "Writing the Individual Back into Collective Memory," *American Historical Review* 102 (1997): 1372–85; John R. Gillis, "Memory and Identity: The History of a Relationship," in *Commemorations: The Politics of National Identity,* ed. Gillis (Princeton: Princeton University Press, 1994), pp. 3–24; Thomas Butler, ed., *Memory: History, Culture and the Mind* (Oxford: Oxford University Press, 1989); Philip Kuberski, *The Persistence of Memory: Organism, Myth, Text* (Berkeley: University of California Press, 1992); Patrick H. Hutton, *History as an Art of Memory* (Hanover, N.H.: University Press of New England, 1993); Michael Roth, *The Ironist's Cage: Memory, Trauma, and the Construction of History* (New York: Columbia University Press, 1995); Iwona Irwin-Zarecka, *Frames of Remembrance: The Dynamics of Collective Memory* (New Brunswick, N.J.: Transaction Publishers, 1994); and Jacques Le Goff, *History and Memory* (New York: Columbia University Press, 1992).

4. This aversion to the cultural analysis of business I have heard expressed by several historians. It is also, in a way, one of the main tropes of industrial self-understanding. Businessmen portray themselves as simple people who are deeply immersed in the well-being of their company and their workers; there is nothing more to "decipher" regarding professional motivations and behaviors.

5. For a good introduction to the theme of industry and National Socialism, see Paul Erker, *Industrie-Eliten in der NS Zeit: Anpassungsbereitschaft und Eigeninteresse von Unternehemern in der rüstung-und Kriegswirtschaft, 1936–1945* (Passau: Wissenschaftsverlag Rothe, 1994); Peter Hayes, *Industry and Ideology: IG Farben in the Nazi Era* (Cambridge: Cambridge University Press, 1987); and John Gillingham, *Industry and Politics in the Third Reich* (Lon-

don: Methuen, 1985). For the reactions of German industry to defeat, dismantling, and decartelization, see Volker Berghahn, *The Americanisation of West German Industry, 1945–1973* (Cambridge: Cambridge University Press, 1983).

6. This "PR crisis" still continues today. Since 1999, the German and American governments, industrial leaders, and lawyers have met regularly to establish and administer a fund to compensate former forced and slave laborers in German factories during the Nazi period. See "Firms Offer Fund for WWII Slave Labor," *Los Angeles Times*, 11 June 1999, p. A1.

7. On mass psychology and public relations, see Edward Bernays, *Propaganda* (New York: Horace Liveright, 1928), pp. 47–61. On Bernays, see Larry Tye, *The Father of Spin: Edward L. Bernays and the Birth of Public Relations* (New York: Crown Publishers, 1998). On Ivy Lee, see Ray Eldon Hiebert, *Courtier to the Crowd: The Story of Ivy Lee and the Development of Public Relations* (Ames: Iowa State University Press, 1966).

8. On Vanderbilt's quote, see Edward Bernays, *Public Relations* (Norman: University of Oklahoma Press, 1952), pp. 51–53.

9. Quoted from John Marston, *Modern Public Relations* (New York: McGraw-Hill, 1979), p. 3.

10. Roland Marchand, *Creating the Corporate Soul: The Rise of Public Relations and Corporate Imagery in American Business* (Berkeley: University of California Press, 1998). Marchand cites a number a books relating to this idea of the "soul" even before the 1920s, including "The Heart of a 'Soulless Corporation'" (1908) and "Corporations and Souls" (1912); see p. 7.

11. See Maurice Halbwachs, *On Collective Memory*, ed. and trans. Lewis A. Coser (Chicago: University of Chicago Press, 1992); and Crane, "Writing the Individual."

12. Edward Bernays, *Biography of an Idea: Memoirs of Public Relations Counsel Edward L. Bernays* (New York: Simon and Schuster, 1965), p. 290.

13. For an introduction to the SPD and CDU's postwar positions on capitalism, see Volker Berghahn, *Modern Germany: Society, Economy and Politics in the Twentieth Century* (Cambridge: Cambridge University Press, 1987), pp. 189ff.

14. By using the term "legitimation crisis," I am not referring to a structural crisis of "advanced" or "late" capitalism, as scholars like Jürgen Habermas would later argue in the 1960s and 1970s (Habermas, *Legitimation Crisis* [Boston: Beacon Press, 1973]).

15. On the concept of totalitarianism in postwar Germany, see Abbott Gleason, *Totalitarianism: The Inner History of the Cold War* (Oxford: Oxford University Press, 1995), pp. 157–66.

16. See, e.g., August Heinrichsbauer, *Schwerindustrie und Politik* (Essen: West Verlag, 1948). On the composition of this apologia, see S. Jonathan Wiesen, *West German Industry and the Challenge of the Nazi Past, 1945–1955* (Chapel Hill: University of North Carolina Press, 2001).

17. For an example of literature on "the new industrialist," see Josef Winschuh, *Das neue Unternehmerbild: Grundzüge einer Unternehmerpolitik.* (Baden-Baden: A. Lutzeyer, 1954); and Gustav Stein and Herbert Gross, eds., *Unternehmer in der Politik* (Düsseldorf: Econ Verlag, 1954).

18. This essay's two working titles were "Die Haltung des Hauses Siemens während des Hitler-Regimes" and "Das Haus Siemens: sein Geist, seine politische Haltung und heutige Lage; Eine Denkschrift, Sommer 1945." There was also an addendum to these reports called "Einsatz ausländischer Zivilarbeiter, Kriegsgefangene, Juden und KZ-Häftlinge im Hauses Siemens." All are to be found in NL Jessen, 11/La 176, Siemens Archive, Munich (SA). For a detailed discussion of Siemens and postwar PR, see Wiesen, *West German Industry*, chap. 1.

19. On Siemens and its forced laborers, see Carola Sachse, "Zwangsarbeit jüdischer und nichtjüdischer Frauen und Männer bei der Firma Siemens 1940 bis 1945," *Internationale wissenschaftliche Korrespondenz zur Geschichte der deutschen Arbeiterbewegung* 27 (1991): 1–12; Tilla Siegel, "Die Doppelte Rationalisierung des 'Ausländereinsatzes' bei Siemens" in ibid., 12–24; Max Stein, "Report on the Employment of Slave Work by the Siemens Concern during World War II," unpublished, in Ernst Katzenstein Papers, file labeled "Siemens," Office of the Conference on Jewish Material Claims against Germany, Frankfurt. Also, see in the same file the very useful report compiled by the Claims Conference entitled "Sklavenarbeit bei Siemens."

20. On Siemens in the postwar era see the informative, if relatively uncritical, portrait of the firm written by the company archivist: Wilfried Feldenkirchen, *Siemens, 1918–1945* (Columbus: Ohio State University Press, 1998).

21. On West Germans' attempts to create a "usable past," see Robert G. Moeller, *War Stories: The Search for a Usable Past in the Federal Republic of Germany* (Berkeley: University of California Press, 2001).

22. Greuelpropaganda über den Siemens-Konzern, sent from Hanns-Henning von Pentz to Benjamin O'Seah, 8 Apr. 1947, NL Jessen, 11/La 176, SA.

23. *Trials of War Criminals before the Nürnberg Military Tribunals* (Washington, D.C.: U.S. Government Printing Office, 1950–53). See vol. 6 (*The U.S. versus Flick*), vols. 7 and 8 (*The U.S. versus Krauch*), and vol. 9 (*The U.S. versus Krupp*).

24. On the high commissioner's amnesty for industrialists and other prisoners, see Frank Buscher, *The U.S. War Crimes Trial Program in Germany, 1946–1955* (Westport, Conn.: Greenwood Press, 1989), pp. 91–113: Kai Bird, *The Chairman: John J. McCloy, the Making of the American Establishment* (New York: Simon and Schuster, 1992), pp. 359–75; and Thomas Schwartz, *America's Germany: John J. McCloy and the Federal Republic of Germany* (Cambridge: Cambridge University Press, 1991), pp. 156–84.

25. On Reusch, see Wiesen, *West German Industry*, pp. 87–91.

26. For literature from the period that promotes this interpretation, see Heinrichsbauer, *Schwerindustrie und Politik*, and Louis Lochner, *Tycoons and Tyrant: German Industry from Hitler to Adenauer* (Chicago: Henry Regnery, 1954).

27. See, e.g., the 1948 denazification trial of Fritz Thyssen, the most prominent industrialist to donate money to the Nazi party before 1933. Spruchkammerakte zu Fritz Thyssen, Hessisches Hauptstaatsarchiv, Wiesbaden.

28. See "Einsatz ausländischer Zivilarbeiter." Recently, historian Lutz Niethammer has asserted, in a much more nuanced fashion, that many people's lives were indeed saved by being employed as forced laborers. This is surely true, but we must remember that industry had no *intention* of saving lives when using this labor. See interview with Niethammer in "Entschädigung nur für Schwergeschädigte," *Die Welt Online*, 2 June 1999 <http://www.welt.de/archiv/1999/06/02/0602de84169.htm>.

29. See "Opening Statement for the Defendant Ihn," in *U.S. versus Krupp*, pp. 190–91.

30. On the debates over the self-presentation of Bayer and IG Farben after the war, see the Ulrich Haberland Papers, 27/1.1.8, Bayer Archive, Leverkusen; also S. Jonathan Wiesen, "The Richard Willstätter Affair: The Legacy of Anti-Semitism in the West German Chemical Industry," in *The German Chemical Industry in the Twentieth Century*, ed. John E. Lesch (Dordrecht, The Netherlands: Kluwer Academic Publishers, 2000), pp. 347–66.

31. "Tatsachen zum Thema Zyklon B" (Frankfurt, Apr. 1961 and Mar. 1964), and a confidential report on the subject from 15 Sept. 1945, Degussa Archive, Frankfurt.

32. On the history of public relations in West Germany, see Eva-Maria Lehming, *Carl Hundhausen: sein Leben, sein Werk, sein Lebenswerk: Public Relations in Deutschland* (Wiesbaden: Deutscher Universitäts-Verlag, 1997); Elisabeth Binder, *Die Entstehung unternehmerischer Public Relations in der Bundesrepublik Deutschland* (Münster: Lit, 1983); also Manfred Rühl, *Public Relations der Gewerkschaften und Wirtschaftsverbände* (Düsseldorf: Verlag für deutsche Wirtschaftsbiographie, 1981).

33. See Lochner, *Tycoons and Tyrant.* On West German industry's commissioning of Lochner's apologia, see the Tilo Freiherr von Wilmowsky Papers, FAH 5 37a-c, Krupp Archive, Essen, and the Louis Lochner Papers, State Historical Society of Wisconsin, Madison, esp. reels 8, 20, and 21. Also Wiesen, *West German Industry,* chap. 7.

34. See See Ludwig Vaubel, *Unternehmer gehen zur Schule: Ein Erfahrungsbericht aus USA* (Düsseldorf: Droste Verlag, 1952). See also Vaubel's unpublished writings from America: Vaubel Sammlung (ED 321/1–18), vol. 17 (Harvard-Tagebuch, 8 Sept. 1950–21 Dec. 1950), Institut für Zeitgeschichte, Munich.

35. On transatlantic business relations, see Werner Link, *The Contribution of Trade Unions and Businessmen to German-American Relations, 1945–1975* (Bloomington, Ind.: Institute of German Studies, 1978).

36. See for example, the celebration of the Krupp dynasty in a company-sponsored work, Gert von Klass's *Die drei Ringe: Lebensgeschichte eines Industrieunternehmens* (Tübingen: Wunderlich Verlag, 1953). On the Thyssen firm, see Volkmar Muthesius, *Schicksal eines Montan-Konzernes (Als Manuskript gedrückt für interne Zwecke anläßlich des 25 Jährige Jubiläums der VSAG),* unpublished copy #41 in Thyssen Archive, Duisberg. For an example of the postwar obsession with the "personality" of these famous industrialists, see Herbert Gehrig, *Die Persönlichkeit des Unternehmers* (Düsseldorf: M. Triltsch, 1955).

37. See "Die Haltung des Hauses Siemens" and "Das Haus Siemens."

38. "Vorwort zu der Schrift von Muthesius über Peter Klöckner, NL Henle, 1384/488, Bundesarchiv, Koblenz.

39. On consumption in postwar West Germany, see Erica Carter, *How German Is She? Postwar West German Reconstruction and the Consuming Woman* (Ann Arbor: University of Michigan Press, 1997); and Katherine Pence, "Labours of Consumption: Gendered Consumers in Post-War East and West German Reconstruction," in *Gender Relations in German History: Power, Agency and Experience from the Sixteenth to the Twentieth Century,* ed. Lynn Abrams and Elizabeth Harvey (London: UCL Press, 1996), pp. 211–39.

40. On the celebration of the worker as the personification of antitotalitarianism, see, e.g., Eberhard Schulz, *Das goldene Dach* (Munich: Wilhelm Steinebach Verlag, 1952).

41. On the *Kulturkreis,* see *Dokumentation über die zehnjährige Tätigkeit des Kulturkreises im Bundesverband der Deutschen Industrie* (Cologne: Bundesverband der Deutschen Industrie, 1961); and the private papers of Hermann Reusch, Gutehoffnungshütte Collection, NL Reusch, 40010146/609, Reinisch-Westfälisches Wirtschaftsarchiv, Cologne (RWWA).

42. On industrial films, see Horst A. Wessel, "Die Überlieferung von Filmquellen in Archiven von Unternehmen, Kammern und Verbänden der Wirtschaft," in *Film schätzen auf der Spur: Verzeichnis historischer Filmbestände in Nordrhein-Westfalen,* ed. Paul Hofmann (Düsseldorf: Nordrhein-Westfälisches Hauptstaatsarchiv, 1994), pp. 143–47; on international exchange programs that began in 1949, see NL Hermann Reusch, 400101460/0, RWWA.

43. See Mary Nolan, *Visions of Modernity: American Business and the Modernization of Germany* (Oxford: Oxford University Press, 1994), pp. 196–205.

44. See Matsuda, *Memory of the Modern,* pp. 44, 49.

45. On anticapitalist stereotypes throughout American history, see Mathew Josephson, *The Robber Barons* (London: Eyre & Spottiswoode, 1962); and Edward Chase Kirkland, *Dream and Thought in the Business Community, 1860–1900* (Ithaca: Cornell University Press, 1956).

46. Pressestelle der Deutschen Industrieausstellung, no. 18 (8 Sept. 1950), A1019, Landesarchiv, Berlin.

47. See Elizabeth Ten Dyke, "Memory and Existence," in this volume.

48. On the relationship between modernity and nostalgia, see Peter Fritzsche, "Chateaubriand's Ruins: Loss and Memory after the French Revolution," *History and Memory* 10 (1998): 102–17. On memory and loss, see Confino, *Nation as a Local Metaphor,* pp. 120–24.

49. Pierre Bourdieu, *Language and Symbolic Power* (Cambridge: Cambridge University Press, 1993). See John Thompson's introduction, p. 12.

50. Some of the terms in German are *Sklavenarbeit, Arbeitereinsatz, Zwangsarbeit, Fremdarbeit,* and *Gastarbeit.* See "A Short Survey of the Krupp Trial" (anonymous pamphlet, ca. 1949) for an example of the use of the term "manpower." Then and today, German industry and the government are carefully drawing these distinctions as they allocate funds to former forced and slave laborers. For an example in the 1940s, see "Opening Statement for the Defendant Ihn," *U.S. versus Krupp,* p. 188.

51. On the "social market economy" and product advertising see Dirk Schindelbeck and Volker Ilgen, *"Haste Was, Biste Was!": Werbung für die Soziale Marktwirtschaft* (Darmstadt: Primus Verlag, 1999), passim.

52. See Noa Gedi and Yigal Elam, "Collective Memory—What Is It?" *History and Memory* 8 (1996): 30–50.

53. William Manchester's *The Arms of Krupp* (New York: Little Brown, 1968) portrays this corporate ethic well.

54. See the corporate history produced by Degussa, *Im Zeichen von Sonne und Mond: Von der Frankfurter Münzscheiderei zum Weltunternehmen Degussa AG* (Frankfurt: Degussa Archive, 1993). Degussa did not manufacture poison gas but it owned part of the company Degesch, which produced zyklon B.

CHAPTER 10

Gender, Public Policy, and Memory: Waiting Wives and War Widows in the Postwar Germanys

ELIZABETH HEINEMAN

"Marriagelessness—Woman's Fate." This was the caption of a 1946 poster illustrating the demographic imbalance in the Berlin district of Schöneberg. The text continued, in smaller print, "The man-murdering Hitler war [*der Männermordende Hitlerkrieg*] has made uncounted wives into widows and condemned many young women to marriagelessness." With a graph of the pre- and postwar sexual ratios in the background, the sex ratio of Schöneberg in bold type, and a photograph of gaunt "women of the rubble" presumably representing marriageless women, the poster indicated that women were among the victims of Germany's recent past.[1] It also suggested a connection between their recent victimhood and their present and future roles: it would be their task to clean the rubble. Finally, in identifying the "Hitler war" as the culprit, the poster indicated that this was a political story.

In ensuing years, "marriageless" women would become part of a discussion reflecting the intersection of three concerns. First was memory: how should Germans remember the war that had left so many single women, the regime that had started it, and Germans' complex experiences under it? Second was national identity in the context of the cold war, as East and West Germany pointed toward their ideologies and policies regarding women, among other things, to distinguish themselves from each other as well as from the Nazi regime. Third was the lived experience of gender. The poster's photo suggested that disruptions in women's real or potential family lives required discussion of women's other roles, such as that of worker. Furthermore, reflections on men's as well as women's recent history were implicit: the "Hitler war" had "condemned" women to marriagelessness, after all, by "murdering" men, and women were clearing rubble because so few men were available for this heavy work.

In the case of war widows and married women who "stood alone" because their husbands were missing or interned in Soviet prison camps, these concerns came into particularly sharp relief. Such women did not just evoke general memories of a prewar life nicely ordered by gender and subsequently disrupted by war. They also suggested memories of individual marriages, of lived intimacy shattered by larger events. Their experiences and representations of them were strongly entwined with the cold war, as the two regimes' treatment of widows and women awaiting POWs or MIAs—like the national identities they hoped to foster—depended on their attitude toward the Soviet Union and the Nazi regime.

Finally, the question of appropriate gender roles was particularly pressing in such cases. Women who had been or still were married often had their own households and children, so the potential conflict between family and workplace roles was sharper than it was for never-married, and usually childfree, women. Furthermore, implicit in the men's absence were questions about the legitimacy of the characteristically male activity of waging war. Some women died performing military duties and left widowers, and many thousands of women were interned by the victorious Allies at the end of the war. Nevertheless, men constituted the vast majority of military casualties and POWs. The imagined gendered dichotomy of male military service and female dependency, although not fully accurate, formed the backdrop for postwar discussion of war widows and waiting wives. This essay will thus examine only widows and waiting wives, and not widowers and waiting husbands.

The following pages will argue that the construction of memory, national identity, and gender were interwoven in the postwar Germanys, and that the policy-making arena was a key site for this phenomenon. In formulating narratives of women's and men's recent history, political actors drew simultaneously on their interpretations of Nazism and the postwar settlement on the one hand, and ideologies regarding gender roles on the other. Only rarely, however, did political actors formulate these narratives in contexts where representation of the past was the primary aim, such as the building of memorials. The day-to-day business of government was policy making—and the making of policy, no less than the building of monuments, was permeated by debates about the relationship between past and present. Furthermore, policy shaped Germans' material well-being and everyday life, for example, by determining the presence and size of pension income. Thus policy may have shaped Germans' understanding of the relationship between past and present more fundamentally than did visits to memorials, which were extraordinary events.

In addition to arguing for the intersection of memory, gender, and national identity, therefore, this essay also makes a methodological argument. Historians such as James Young have revealed states' efforts to shape representations of the past by such activity as the building of memorials, and they have demonstrated that even overt representations of the past were always shaped by postwar politics.[2] Yet historians of memory must broaden their scope beyond explicit discussions of the past and attempts to represent it. They must also consider areas of state activity whose first priority might have been to address a contemporary problem, not construct a narrative of the past. In discussions of topics as diverse as Western integration, women's roles, and the formation of political parties, scholars such as Ulrich Brochhagen, Robert Moeller, and Maria Mitchell have shown that Germany's recent history was never far from the surface. Nevertheless, at the end of the day, the state needed to have a foreign policy, a social policy, and a party structure that functioned in their own right.[3] The policy-making arena did not simply influence the representation of the past, but rather, in Alon Confino's and Peter Fritzsche's formulation, transformed memory into a "set of practices."[4]

The following essay will focus on the political symbolism of and public policy regarding two groups of women in both Germanys: wives of POWs and missing men ("waiting wives") and war widows. Not surprisingly, the political division formed one boundary across which the representation and experience of such women differed. The West German regime emphasized the past losses and continuing family roles of widows and waiting wives; the East German regime discouraged a victim identity and homebound role and focused on such women's participation in the paid labor force.

Another aspect of the two groups' treatment, however, transcended political boundaries. While waiting wives and widows alike had enormous political symbolism in both states in the decade after the war, only war widows became the subject of major legislation. West Germany made aid to "victims of war" the second largest item in the state's budget; East Germany demonstratively rejected decades-long precedent and popular sentiment to eliminate special treatment for "victims of war." In the case of widows, policy thus created a forum for the discussion of the relationship between the Nazi past, public spending, and gender roles. Memory shaped the policy-making process and the popular reception of policy; in turn, the policy-making process, and the social programs they established or dismantled, shaped memory.

This dynamic was muted, if not completely absent, in the case of waiting wives. Neither state introduced policy initiatives regarding waiting wives whose impact could compare with that of the legislation regarding war widows. Narratives of waiting wives, and the memories they elicited, were not formulated and reformulated according to the evolution of social policy targeting them. Yet waiting wives had enormous symbolic potency in the intertwined realms of foreign policy, postfascist national identity, and gender roles. They were the reminders of the POWs whom the Soviets considered war criminals and who thus remained in Soviet prison camps years after war's end. They were reminders of additional hundreds of thousands of men whose fate was not known but some of whom, most Germans suspected, also lingered in Soviet camps. Narratives of waiting wives were deeply embedded in the two states' positioning in the cold war. They evolved according to the affinities or disjunctures of waiting wives' own experiences and hopes on the one hand, and their states' acceptance or rejection of Soviet claims regarding the POWs on the other. With no chance of fundamentally altering waiting wives' situation—the release of the POWs was in the Soviets' hands, not in the hands of either German government—waiting wives, the larger German public, and the two states negotiated over the more purely symbolic matter of how the story of missing men, POWs, and the women awaiting them would be told. Thus the story of war widows and waiting wives was not just one of East versus West; rather, it was also one of the varying routes via which gendered reminders of the recent past found their way into postwar life.

War Widows

In the postwar years, German women yearned for relief from their trying circumstances. For those who had not been subject to Nazi persecution, the period of intense hardship had begun with the defeat at Stalingrad in the winter of 1942–43 and the intensification of Allied air raids on German cities around the same time. With the end of the war, the bombs ceased to fall, but hunger, deprivation, and uncertainty characterized the ensuing years. Nonpersecuted German women experienced and remembered the "crisis years" of 1943–48—from Stalingrad to currency reform—as a chaotic period of extreme hardship.[5]

German women's sense of the world around them, in which the wartime traumas of air raids, evacuation, flight from the East, and rape segued into the postwar traumas of homelessness and hunger, reflected the immediacy of their own corporeal experience.[6] The corporeal experience of others, such as victims of the Germans' aggressive war or of the genocide, did not loom as large in the consciousness of nonpersecuted Germans who now faced their own struggle for survival. The specifics differed for men and for women: men worried about their survival at the front or in Soviet prison camp, while women worried about their survival through bombing raids, while fleeing the Soviet armies, or in the decimated cities after the war.[7] Nevertheless, the larger phenomenon of Germans' focus on their own trials, rather than on the sufferings Germans had inflicted on others, transcended sexual difference.

However unsurprising this focus on one's own traumas may be, it raised significant questions of how to interpret the larger contours of Germany's recent history. In a postwar world marked both by cold war divisions and by a striking demographic imbalance between the sexes, this question provoked discussion not only of Nazi-era Germans and the Nazis' many victims but also of East and West, and of male and female.

One such discussion centered around military pensions. As part of their program of demilitarization, the occupation governments suspended special military pensions.[8] This was social policy—members of the military should no longer have a privileged place in German society—but it was also an attempt to shape memory. Germans should recall recent *Wehrmacht* activities as the sort of thing that did *not* earn one special privilege. Germans, however, recalled no such thing. Rather, they interpreted wounded veterans, widows, and orphans as doubly victimized: first by the war, then by the allies' revocation of their pensions. Those "who had borne the main burden of the war on the front and made a sacrifice in blood," protested a former officer, were now forced "to bear the entire burden of the defeat."[9]

As James Diehl has demonstrated, the young West German state was sympathetic to popular bitterness against this provision and sought to distinguish an "honorable" German tradition of loyal military service from Nazi crimes. As its first major piece of social legislation, the Federal Republic introduced a comprehensive program for veterans and survivors of military personnel. Passed years before a law that made payments to selected victims of Nazism, and with far less controversy, the 1950 "Law to Aid Victims of War" both responded to material needs and made clear that "victims of war"—rather than other victims of the recent past—would receive the first attentions of the new state.[10] The law excluded no one on the basis of organizational affiliation (e.g., the Nazi Party or the SS), nor did the application form inquire into applicants' activities during the previous regime. The law left the evaluation of complicity to the denazification courts, whose sentence could include a revocation of pensions.

The inclusion of war widows in part reflected the reflexive adoption of models from other pension plans, including pensions related to service in World War I.[11] Widows should be compensated for the loss of their means of support, just as wounded men were compensated for their reduced earning power. In addition, men going to war should be assured that, if their service cost them their lives, their dependents would be cared for. The inclusion of widows, however, also reflected assumptions of women's political voicelessness in the Nazi period. The Bundestag debated the possibility that some men's service was too tarnished by Nazism to qualify them for benefits. An early draft, for example, had excluded members of the Waffen-SS.[12] This measure would also have excluded survivors of members of the Waffen-SS from the plan—but it would have done so because of suspicions of the men's complicity in Nazi crimes, not because the potential beneficiaries, widows and orphans, were suspect. No one suggested that widows, by virtue of their own complicity in Nazi crimes, might have disqualified themselves from pensions.[13] As we shall see, the East German Socialist Unity Party (SED) made precisely this insinuation.

War widows' pensions, however, did not only refer to widows' past losses. They also sought to shape widows' present and future lives by enabling them to maintain a domestic role. What better way for the state to honor fallen soldiers than to "reconstruct" their families, with the state, via its provision of a pension, standing in for the missing man? As a later report of one of the provincial pension offices explained, pensions were to "enable . . . [widows] . . . to carry on their households and support them in the raising and educating of their children."[14] The Law to Aid Victims of War complemented West German family law by purportedly enabling widows as well as wives to fulfill the ideal female role of a housewife—a role that contrasted markedly with that offered by East Germany.[15]

The Bundestag and federal ministries deliberated the draft Law to Aid Victims of War in 1950. During the debates, it emerged that characterizing widows as victims when the victorious allies denied them pensions was one thing; doing the same when a German government was responsible for pensions was another. As the Finance Ministry sought ways to limit expenditures, its eye fell on two groups: widows who were young, physically fit, and unburdened by childrearing responsibilities and veterans whose injuries were minimal and thus did not significantly limit their earning power. The financial argument regarding members of the two groups was similar: both could earn their own livings if need be. Nevertheless, arguments favoring pensions for young, employable widows without orphaned children proved less persuasive than did those for the lightly wounded. For one thing, these widows constituted a much smaller voting bloc than did lightly wounded veterans, and while there were veterans aplenty in the ministries and in the Bundestag, war widows had little if any presence.[16] In addition, though, would-be cost-cutters had difficulty countering narratives of veterans' loyal service and sacrifice. By contrast, they were able to draw on critical memories of young widows, resurrecting in parliamentary committee popular wartime accusations that women wed soldiers simply to become eligible for state aid.[17]

The deliberations thus produced mixed narratives of war widows. The dominant narrative, indeed the very premise (and name) of the pension program, was one of victimization. There was also space, however, for reminders of some widows' alleged misdeeds, in the form of opportunistic wartime marriages. In the end, the law awarded able-bodied widows under forty with no children who were legally recognized war orphans only a token sum (20 DM/month). Just as significantly, it suspended such widows' benefits indefinitely. This limitation provoked criticism from veterans' associations, women's groups, and some parliamentarians, and benefits were finally activated in August 1953.[18] In the meantime, the majority of war widows—those who had legally recognized war orphans as children, who were over forty, or who were physically disabled—earned full recognition as "victims of war." By 1954, nearly 1.2 million West German women were entitled to benefits as war widows.[19]

The federal government had endowed "victims of war" with official significance and committed taxpayer money to them. Thus both memories of widows' past sufferings and impressions of their present-day behavior were a matter of public concern. Yet this combination of past and present was tricky, and compensating widows for the loss of their husbands was, in some ways, more complicated than compensating veterans for wounds inflicted on their own bodies. Penalizing widows most suspect of having entered opportunistic marriages did not settle the matter. Even with "deserving" widows—those who were older, who were raising so-called half-orphans, or who were physically disabled—pensions commemorating *men's* service encountered difficulties when memories of *women's* actions intervened.

Among those collecting orphans' pensions were "apparently legitimate" children (*scheineheliche Kinder*). "Apparently legitimate" children were born within marriage but were not the offspring of their mothers' husbands. In other words, they had resulted from adultery. Since the marriage of a woman and a man at war, imprisoned, or missing remained legally intact until the man was officially declared dead, children born years after the last meeting of the child's mother and her husband could be legitimate. If their mothers' husbands were later declared to have died at war, the children had the status of, and received the benefits of, war orphans. The Federal Bureau of Statistics estimated in 1955 that twenty thousand "apparently legitimate" children passed as war orphans.[20]

Already in 1952–53, however, the Ministry of Labor, responsible for administering pensions for victims of war, mounted a campaign to prevent such children's widowed mothers from drawing orphans' pensions for their children—and sometimes from drawing widows' pensions on their own. The ministry's hope: that the judiciary would declare husbands dead or children illegitimate in cases where failure to do so allowed "apparently legitimate" children and their mothers to draw pensions. The ammunition: reminders of women's unfaithfulness to their husbands when the latter were at war or in a POW camp.

The debate about "apparently legitimate" children involved several federal ministries, the Bundestag and Bundesrat, and provincial judiciaries and pension offices. Most participants in the debate agreed that such widows were pension cheats, though the possibility that some "apparently legitimate" children had resulted from Soviet rapes rather than willed adultery gave pause for thought. But nearly all objected to the Ministry of Labor's plan for action. The other ministries and the judiciary contended that the state's interest in preventing pension fraud did not justify state interference in family matters like declarations of death for men and revocations of legitimate status for children. In 1953, the Bundestag approved a compromise solution. Pension offices could revoke "apparently legitimate" children's allowances without having the children declared illegitimate or the husbands dead.[21]

If the debate regarding "apparently legitimate" children led portions of the state bureaucracy to focus on widows' infidelity rather than their losses, cohabiting widows brought the matter to the wider public.[22] War widows became front-page news in the mid-1950s, as the press reported that perhaps one hundred thousand of them were cohabiting because they would lose their pensions upon remarriage. The resulting public uproar alternately highlighted widows' sexual misbehavior and the state's disincentive to remarriage.

The Family Ministry and a portion of the larger public objected to the suggestion that cohabitants be offered incentives to marry, such as a continuation of the pension or a larger one-time "marriage settlement" upon remarriage. Arguing that such women were hardly the "deserving widows" who had a claim to state funds, a women's organization wrote to the Family Ministry in 1955 that "the war widows are the worst practitioners of concubinage; they take women's husbands, above all the husbands' money, move them into their apartments . . . and live as if married. These women don't think about marriage at all, because they certainly don't ever want to lose their 'well-earned pension,' which they acquired through the death of their fallen husbands."[23] By contrast, cohabiting widows' defenders portrayed them as upright people trapped by bad pension law. "The State Makes the Merry Widows," proclaimed a 1953 headline that proved representative of editorial opinion.[24] Eventually, the Bundestag revised the law to encourage remarriage, but not before the term "Uncle Marriage"—thus named because the widow's children presumably called the new man "uncle"—had entered the popular vocabulary.

By the mid-1950s, mention of war widows in West Germany elicited images of illicit sexual behavior and crude materialism at least as often as it summoned memories of sacrifice and suffering. The bumpy road of war widows' pensions reflected contradictions between roles remembered and roles presently played, between idealized collective identity and real individual behavior. With considerable state resources devoted to victims of war, memories of victims of war did not remain static. The people collecting the pensions lived *now,* in 1952 or 1957: their pensions supported their present-day households and supplemented their present-day wages. Contradictions between memory and present-day perception arose especially easily in the case of women, because their remembered role was a mediated one—it was really their husbands' service that was commemorated—but their present role was their own. Widows, not their late husbands, either were or weren't devoting themselves full-time to their children, did or did not exhibit sexual propriety. Men had died violent deaths in an era of terror and suffering; their widows were now consumers in the land of the economic miracle.[25] Present-day misbehaviors were easily interpreted as offenses against widows' late husbands. Unfaithful widows did not just cost the taxpayer; they also mocked the identity of "victim of war," which the Law to Aid Victims of War had invested with official significance.

The fact that widows were the beneficiaries of a major social program made it necessary, and worthwhile, to revisit their histories. Furthermore, it helped to determine the questions that would be asked of those histories, and thus the narratives that emerged. In the late 1940s, memories of war widows, bereft of pensions by Allied policy and visibly struggling to feed their children, focused on their experiences of victimization. The Law to Aid Victims of War gave formal state sanction to the narrative of victimization, but in their deliberations around the law, ministries and parliamentarians also took note of the woman who had allegedly married a man at war in order to reap state aid. By the mid-1950s, public discussion of widows, whose pensions supported children of adultery and nonmarital households in an era of growing consumption, focused on their misdeeds. Pensions ensured that memories of widows would be dynamic rather than fixed.

In East Germany, war widows were also the subject of major social legislation. In the East German case, however, the crucial moment was the abolition of the category "victim of war" as a legal and public entity. This act had no less profound ramifications for memories of war widows and for widows' own experience than did the West German reification of that category. Once accomplished, however, it eliminated an important avenue for the further evolution of memories of war widows: the implementation and revision of the pension plan.

The East German state had no interest in enabling widows to remain housewives. Rather than encouraging domesticity for women, it tried to coax ever more women into the labor force. It had even less desire to award special prestige to those whose husbands and fathers had died in the Nazis' war.

In April 1947, the Soviet occupation released a decree regulating war victims' assistance.[26] The decree folded assistance for victims of war into the work of the social insurance offices. This was part of a larger plan to create a unified insurance system out of the existing crazy quilt of separate schemes, each with its own regulations and bureaucracy, which discriminated against members of the lower social classes. Consolidation thus had more than bureaucratic charms: the decree pointedly eliminated the privileged status of veterans and civil servants, granting them the same pensions as victims of industrial accidents and requiring that all categories of pensioners appear at the same offices.

The provisions of the 1947 decree, further elaborated in 1948, were meager, and few war widows received a pension at all. Not only were survivors of members of the Nazi party and its affiliated organizations excluded but pensions were available only to survivors who were incapable of paid work. For a widow under sixty to gain this status, she had to have one child under the age of three, two under the age of eight, or be an invalid. Invalidism was defined as a long-term physical condition that prevented her from earning one-third of the earnings an able-bodied worker.[27] In 1954, when West Germany's population was three times that of East Germany, nearly 1.2 million West Germans, but only 59,369 East Germans, were entitled to benefits as war widows.[28]

The SED's arguments against war widows' pensions referred to memories of the Nazi past, to the current opposition of East German socialism to West German capitalism, and to women's roles past and future. In keeping with the Marxist analysis linking fascism with capitalism, the party challenged earlier pension plans—and current plans in West Germany—that awarded veterans, civil servants, and their survivors superior treatment. Why should an invalid veteran or civil servant receive DM 90, as many petitioners demanded, when the victim of an industrial accident had to make do with DM 40 or 50?[29] In addition, opponents of military pensions suggested that such plans implicated women in militarism: "We must explain to women why we do this," cautioned a party functionary: "[I]n order that women don't say, 'If war comes and my husband doesn't return, then I'll be taken care of by the state.' Then one is a little less willing to have a new war."[30] Women, evidently, were *not* innocent of the crimes of an aggressive regime: they had not done all they could to resist, because pensions had promised material security even upon their husbands' death.

But socialism would not only transform women by making them pacifist. It would also make them full members of the productive economy, an essential step to women's emancipation. Furthermore, widows were needed in the labor force, and the number of people paying into social insurance schemes was inadequate to support so many pensioners. Indeed, the East German social insurance scheme eliminated pensions to all able-bodied widows without young children, not just war widows.

East Germans, however, interpreted restrictions on war widows' pensions as something quite different from female emancipation or the destruction of fascism. More often, they regarded it as akin to forced labor: widows denied pensions would have to go to work. But East Germans' dissatisfaction did not just refer to widows' material deprivation. It also reflected bitterness about the lack of recognition for people most East Germans saw as innocent victims of war.

During the Weimar and Nazi periods, "victims of war" had attracted official praise, and the pension had been the marker of their special status. By stripping from "victims of war" the status they had previously enjoyed, the 1947 decree was instrumental in shaping memories of war widows in East Germany. To be sure, the 1947 decree did not prescribe popular memory. Intended by its authors to "correct" the notion that wounded veterans and survivors were victims, it instead reinforced exactly this perception, adding yet another name to the list of victimizers: not only the war and the occupation, but now also the new East German authorities, who implemented the provisions established under Soviet occupation. East Germans' awareness of West Germany's provision of pensions only intensified their bitterness; pensions for "victims of war" became one item in a long catalogue of what was denied them but available in the "Golden West." And although the elimination of special military pensions affected wounded veterans as well as widows, wounded veterans at least received the same recognition as workers injured in industrial accidents. Most widows received nothing at all. Denied symbolic recognition by their government, East German war widows instead symbolized the chasm between official and popular narratives of recent history.

But the 1947 decree did not just fail to elicit the desired response. It also stunted the evolution of memories of war widows. In the months surrounding the release of the decree, party functionaries reported vociferous objections at party assemblies.[31] Soon, however, it became clear that the matter was closed, and widows and their defenders gave up their protests. There was no point in lobbying for women whose husbands had died trying to exterminate Communism and had caused unprecedented suffering to the Soviet Union.

Furthermore, the denial of special benefits to war widows meant that there was no need to elaborate or adjust the nature of the assistance, a process which, in the West German case, prompted revision of the narratives of war widows. East German war widows, like their West German counterparts, cohabited with men to whom they were not married and raised children of adultery. But they received no public assistance, and their late husbands, in the state's eyes at least, were perpetrators of war, not victims. Neither the fiscal interests of the state nor the honor of the widows' deceased husbands demanded that perceptions of widows be revisited in light of widows' behavior.

Memories of war widows thus remained more static in East Germany than in the West. East Germans knew individual war widows in a variety of roles: some were full-time housewives while some took up paid labor, some remained faithful to their husbands' memories while others entered new liaisons, some lived in dire poverty while others found a secure economic footing. But these appeared as individual life histories, not the history of women sharing a collective identity of "war widow." While the emphasis of West German narratives of "war widows" as a group shifted from victimhood to misbehavior, East German narratives of "war widows" as a group remained more consistent: they were those beings who had first lost their husbands and then were denied pensions by an unpopular government.

Waiting Wives

Unlike widows, waiting wives were not the subject of major legislative innovation in either postwar state. In West Germany, they received benefits late, in small amounts, and with little fanfare. In East Germany, the denial of benefits did not fly in the face of precedent. Politics, nevertheless, shaped narratives of waiting wives.

In the case of West Germany, the shared popular and official abhorrence of the USSR's refusal to release the last POWs created an environment for an uncontested narrative of waiting wives as victims. In East Germany, the official denial that the USSR held prisoners other than condemned war criminals and the popular fury at this position paralleled the chasm separating official from popular narratives of war widows. In the case of waiting wives, however, more was at stake. What was a pension compared to a husband's return? Waiting wives challenged the official narratives more persistently than did war widows, and as a result East German narratives of the former were more dynamic than were those of the latter.

In the third quarter of 1945, the victorious Allies officially held 8,699,732 German prisoners of war. About 40 percent were married.[32] By the end of 1946, the Western allies had released most of their prisoners. At the end of 1948, however, when the Western allies had freed the last of their prisoners, the Soviet Union officially acknowledged nearly half a million still in its camps. By the end of 1949, the USSR declared that it had released all prisoners except convicted war criminals, whose families knew of the sentence. These men's defenders, including their wives, expressed skepticism at the fairness of the trials and sentencing, and petitioned for the convicted men's release. Furthermore, the Western allies, the West German government, and East and West Germans were convinced that, aside from convicted war criminals, many more—possibly millions—languished in Soviet camps well into the 1950s.[33] Since there was no accurate count of war dead, even wildly inflated estimates seemed plausible, and rumors of "secret camps" from which prisoners could not send mail caused women to cling to the hope that their husbands might still live.[34] When the Soviets released twelve thousand prisoners in the fall of 1953, Germans' skepticism regarding Soviet honesty in matters regarding the POWs only increased.[35] Wives of "missing" men could not know whether their husbands had been killed in action but listed as missing in the Wehrmacht's attempts to hide the extent of its casualties, whether their husbands had been captured but had subsequently died in prison, or whether their husbands were still alive somewhere in the Soviet Union.

In terms of lived experience, the boundaries between being a waiting wife and being a war widow were often fleeting. Many waiting wives *were* in fact widows: they simply did not yet know that their husbands were dead. Given the difficulties in obtaining information about one's husband, the difference between being a waiting wife and being a war widow was often a state of mind. If the woman still believed in her husband's survival and hoped for his return, she was a waiting wife; if she doubted that her husband had survived or felt it necessary to proceed under the assumption that he had not, she was a widow. Even if her husband returned, she might become a war widow if he subsequently died of war wounds. Aside from the complicated matter of formulating an identity with inadequate information about one's husband, material conditions helped to blur the distinction between waiting wives and war widows. Whatever their knowledge of or hopes for their husbands, women's most pressing tasks in the postwar years were feeding, clothing, and housing themselves and their dependents. This daily grind did not differentiate according to whether a woman had never married, was widowed, knew her husband was in prison camp, or had no information whatsoever.

In terms of the relationship between political symbolism and legal status, however, there was a great difference between waiting wives and war widows. Waiting wives had enormous symbolic importance and irritated open political wounds in the cold war, but there was relatively little effort to regulate their legal status. The social status of waiting wives—especially those who had no information about their husbands—was, by definition, unclear. As the East German government frequently reiterated, wives of missing men could clarify their status in one simple way: by having their husbands declared dead. When waiting wives became widows, they and everyone else would know where they stood.[36] The West German government, perhaps more tactful but also aware that waiting wives' unique propagandistic value in the cold war would be lost if they were reclassified as widows, refrained from actively pushing wives of missing men to have their husbands declared dead.[37] The fact remained, however, that in West Germany, as in East Germany, a declaration of death clarified the status of the wife of a missing man considerably. As discussions in both states made clear, this was not a purely legalistic matter. A declaration of death also freed a woman emotionally to seek meaning in work, to accustom her children to the idea of their fathers' death, and perhaps to remarry.

In practical terms, it mattered little where such a wife resided: she had no power to gain her husband's release if he was classified as a war criminal, or even to find out whether a missing husband was alive or dead. In political terms, however, it made a great difference. In the West, reminders of men who were or might still be imprisoned became symbols of Soviet perfidy, and thus reminders of the superiority of the western alliance in the cold war. Furthermore, the constant reiteration of Soviet guilt in not repatriating prisoners of war also helped to displace thoughts of German guilt: it became less necessary to ask what the Germans had been doing in the USSR in the first place.[38]

In comparison to war widows, however, waiting wives were the object of relatively little social policy in West Germany. To be sure, there was little precedent for such policy. During the war, wives of POWs and MIAs had continued to participate in the system of family allowances for military men. Family allowances were higher than widows' and orphans' pensions, so this measure was expensive—but the Nazi state found it useful to maintain families' hopes that their military relatives might still be alive.[39] With the end of hostilities, family allowances—designed to serve dependents of men in active service—ceased to exist. Yet although there were no more dependents of men in active service, there were millions of destitute dependents of POWs and MIAs. During the military occupation, as provinces developed interim programs for victims of war, some included dependents of MIAs and POWs in their provisions for widows and orphans.[40] Yet the status of "waiting wives" as beneficiaries of the welfare state remained unclear in the early years of the Federal Republic. Finally, in 1952, almost as a delayed afterthought to the 1950 legislation introducing benefits for victims of war at the federal level, the Bundestag made West German wives of POWs and MIAs eligible for most of the same benefits as war widows. Waiting wives still, however, remained ineligible for important need-based programs.[41] The campaign to remove children of suspicious fatherhood from the pension rolls technically affected wives of missing men and POWs as well as widows, as did the uproar about cohabitation. The language of both controversies, however, identified *widows* as the culprits, thus reflecting and further reinforcing waiting wives' legal invisibility.

Yet outside the arena of social policy, waiting wives attracted considerable attention in West Germany. Waiting wives were often featured in POW commemorations.[42] While waiting wives were a ready symbol of Soviet meanness in not repatriating POWs, however, media outlets did not simply exploit waiting wives for their symbolic value in the cold war. Veterans', women's, and social workers' magazines instead developed several tropes regarding the family and loyalty. One such trope consisted of tales of heroism and sacrifice, as waiting wives conquered the emotional strain of uncertainty about their husbands' fate to pull their families through. In the maudlin words of West Germany's largest women's magazine, "Where these women hold with unalterable loyalty onto the lost one, we wish to silently bow down before them and their pure feeling."[43] A second theme was unfaithfulness, as women developed relationships with new men. If widows who formed new liaisons betrayed their husbands' memories, then wives of POWs who did so betrayed real live men. As an article in a journal for the protection of youth put it, the culmination of the POW's years of suffering was to find a new man in his bed. "One can only portray with difficulty what passes through the heart of a man who, upon his return, not only stands before the ruins of his house, but also must see that, in the great collapse [at the end of the war], the family happiness of which he'd dreamed has slipped away."[44] Finally, there were sympathetic articles about women who had remarried in the sincere belief that their missing husbands were dead—only to have those husbands reappear years later.[45]

Narratives of waiting wives, like narratives of war widows, thus might describe victimhood or infidelity. Yet while narratives of waiting wives were hardly uniform, the range and balance remained relatively static. By contrast, the establishment of pensions for "victims of war" in 1950, followed by the uproar about pensions for "apparently legitimate" children and cohabiting widows in the mid-1950s, brought first a preponderance of narratives of suffering, then a preponderance of narratives emphasizing infidelity and materialism. Furthermore, with few public moneys at stake, discussions of waiting wives were quieter. Most significantly, there was no parallel to the scandal about cohabiting war widows who collected pensions, a scandal that put war widows on the front pages and editorial pages of mainstream newspapers. Through most of the first postwar decade, waiting wives appeared in more specialized outlets, such as women's magazines, veterans' magazines, social work magazines, and advice books.

Waiting wives hit the front pages only with the release of twelve thousand prisoners in 1953, and especially with the release of the last 9,626 POWs in 1955. Even then, however, POWs were the protagonists; waiting wives were supporting characters. While widows' behavior had provoked a reexamination of narratives regarding them, the release of POWs required that wives be part of the story, but not necessarily that narratives regarding them be revised. The media described wives who greeted their husbands with small children bearing witness to the women's infidelity, triumphantly reported long-awaited reunions by couples who had stayed their course—and noted the many single men anxious to begin a "normal" family life.[46]

In short, with the return of POWs a highly politicized issue, waiting wives played a key role in West German memories of the Nazi era and the state's use of these memories in the establishment of cold war national identity. But waiting wives' pensions came late and quietly, and there was no other major social program for them. As a result, these women's missteps—like cohabiting with new men before they had definitive news about their husbands—attracted less attention than milder sins on the part of war widows, such as cohabiting with new men once they knew their husbands were dead. Popular and official narratives of German victimhood and Soviet guilt, women's struggles to survive, men's release from prison camp, and family reunion: all coexisted harmoniously.

In the Soviet zone and later East Germany, waiting wives received no public financial support. Officially speaking, there was no such thing as a wife of a missing man in the GDR. The USSR, according to its version of events, released the last of the POWs in 1949 and continued to hold only convicted war criminals. According to the East German state, most "waiting wives" were simply women who would not or could not accept their husbands' death. A few were the wives of war criminals who, to be sure, awaited their husbands' return—but then, so did the wife of any man serving a prison sentence.

In this context, it is hardly surprising that there was no social program designed for waiting wives in East Germany. There was no social program for war widows, either, but this did not make the situation of the two groups parallel. By losing their pensions, war widows lost a benefit they had formerly enjoyed, not just under the Nazis but following the wars of unification and World War I as well.[47] Waiting wives had lost their access to family allowances, but this did not represent the end of a longer tradition of pensions for this group. Furthermore, widows' official status, and not just their material well-being, was intimately connected to the pension: an "officially recognized war widow" was one who had a claim to a pension. Waiting wives had no such marker. Ironically, once widows' vehicle for articulating grievances was removed from the table, waiting wives, who had never had such a vehicle, were better able to continue to articulate their complaint.

The disjuncture between the popular belief that the USSR held more prisoners than it admitted and the official denial of the same—a disjuncture missing in the West German case—forced the state to elaborate a narrative about waiting wives and their husbands, even absent any explicit material interest. The narrative evolved over time, in relation to the official stance on POWs, the forum and nature of waiting wives' demands, and the evolution of other aspects of policy regarding women.

As early as 1946, when the USSR (like the Western allies) still acknowledged that it held prisoners of war, women frequently raised the matter at SED party forums. The SED employed several strategies in response. First, it claimed credit for negotiating the release of some of the men. Beyond this, the party expressed its understanding for the "spiritual burdens" of relatives of men still imprisoned while reminding listeners that the current suffering was the fault of Hitler and the Nazis, not the Soviet Union.[48] In August 1948, a delegation of the party women's organization (*Demokratischer Frauenbund Deutschlands* or DFD, the Democratic Women's League of Germany) visited Soviet prison camps and produced a rosy report intended to put to rest the notion that prisoners suffered wretched conditions.[49] At this point, it was still possible to acknowledge that prisoners were being held, but it was necessary to counter East Germans' belief that conditions in Soviet camps were far worse than conditions in Western camps. By the 1950s, however, party organizations no longer defended conditions in the camps or reminded the civilian population that the POWs had been captured during an aggressive war against the USSR—because according to the official story, POWs were no longer being held anyway; only war criminals were. Now, the SED simply denied that POWs were still in the USSR, and it blamed West German "anti-Soviet agitation [*antisowjetische Hetze*]" for East German women's beliefs that their husbands might still be imprisoned.[50]

Waiting wives' behavior differed significantly from that of war widows in East Germany. While war widows resented the denial of a pension, they rather quickly accommodated themselves to it and ceased to petition their government for a change in policy. The matter was clearly not open for discussion and, in the end, it was only money: a pension would not bring a dead husband back to life. War widows turned to other matters that promised greater material reward, like finding a job—exactly the behavior anticipated by party officials when they developed such a limited pension plan. Party institutions did not need to defend or elaborate their pension policy after the late 1940s, and they did not need to revise the narrative of war widows' experience that accompanied the pension policy.

Waiting wives, by contrast, were a constant thorn in the party's side. Throughout the late 1940s and well into the 1950s, waiting wives (and mothers) raised the issue of the POWs at party assemblies, in DFD meetings, and in letters to party officials.[51] This was *not* just about money: it was about their husbands' (and sons') lives. Furthermore, waiting wives were not convinced that the matter was closed, even if the SED insisted that it was. West German agitation was not responsible for East Germans' belief that the USSR still held POWs, SED claims not withstanding. Nevertheless, the knowledge that West Germany was exerting pressure for POWs' release surely emboldened East German women to maintain hope that persistent pressure might eventually bring results.

The SED found it necessary to respond to protests at party assemblies and in letters to party organizations. In doing so, it refined not only the narrative of POWs and their Soviet captors but also the narrative of the waiting wives articulating the protests. In reports of party assemblies of 1946, waiting wives were portrayed as rather quick to forget who had started the war, but indeed shouldering heavy burdens. Later in the decade, party functionaries had less to say about waiting wives' burdens. Waiting wives were understandably concerned about their husbands' circumstances, but they were a little too willing to accept at face value anti-Soviet rumors regarding conditions in the camps. By the 1950s, women who claimed to be waiting wives were victims of Western lies at best, disseminators of anti-Soviet propaganda at worst.[52]

Furthermore, party officials linked the narrative of waiting wives' concern for their husbands with other evolving narratives, like those concerning the transformation of the individual under socialism. Frank Biess has perceptively observed the ways the regime's programs to reintegrate returning veterans—which focused on their working and political lives, and studiously ignored their family lives—minimized the interdependence of family groups. Instead, such programs posited the priority of the relationship of the individual to the political or productive collective.[53] In the case of waiting wives, another factor contributed to the downplaying of spousal interdependence: claims of the emancipation of women under socialism. Unlike women under Nazism or in the capitalist West, a woman in socialism could make her own way: she need not pathetically wait for her husband to make things better. In the late 1940s, women's magazines explained how to divorce a husband known to be alive in a POW camp.[54] In 1950, a publication aimed at waiting wives emphasized that, rather than remain in limbo for years after war's end, women should use new, streamlined regulations for having their husbands declared dead.[55] By employing such measures, a later history explained, women could "close the chapter—however painfully—on the effects of the Second World War" and get on with their lives.[56] They could take advantage of new legislation encouraging a greater female presence in the labor force; they could even obtain vocational training that had been denied to them in prior German regimes, and that was still denied their sisters in the West.

Indeed, they could do more than carve out a better life for themselves: they could help to build socialism and ensure future peace. As the DFD shifted its energies from working on women's behalf to organizing women to work on socialism's behalf, it claimed pacifist agitation as a type of "women's work."[57] Waiting wives should have a special interest in this task. Responding to a 1955 correspondent who expressed despair at her husband's continued absence, Ilse Thiele, since 1953 the head of the DFD, pointed out the suffering inflicted on millions of others by members of the Wehrmacht, such as the correspondent's husband. She also noted, typically, that West German lies were responsible for the belief that Germans other than convicted war criminals remained in the USSR. Finally, Thiele suggested that the correspondent was positioned to play a special, and very important, role in light of West Germany's impending military integration into NATO: "Certainly your individual fate is to be lamented, like that of many people. But complaining and looking back doesn't help us! All of us, and especially women such as yourself, must help to fight against the new [Western] preparations for war, to spare women and mothers the suffering that you yourself experience."[58]

To be sure, the transformations of the official narratives of waiting wives did not enter the popular consciousness in East Germany, as new narratives of war widows did in West Germany. In large part, this was because such transformations were fine-tunings of a narrative which most East Germans fundamentally disbelieved. The popular (if not publicly spoken) memory of waiting wives, like that of war widows in East Germany, remained one of multiple victimization: first by the war, now by the state, which denied the legitimacy of waiting wives' claims and instead accused them of petitioning on behalf of war criminals. Women's protests referred not only to their husbands' imprisonment but also to the gap between official claims of international socialist friendship on the one hand and popular perceptions of enmity on the other. "Now put yourself for once in the position of a mother whose son is stuck somewhere deep in Russia and is working hard and can't send out any sign of life," wrote an anonymous correspondent to Elli Schmidt, then head of the DFD, in 1952. "Ask your conscience—is that a true 'people's friendship?'"[59]

But there was another reason transformations of the narrative of waiting wives did not enter the popular consciousness, and this reason draws our attention to the significance of social programs. The actions of East German waiting wives, like those of West German war widows, demanded revision of the official narrative. Despite their common dynamism, however, official narratives of the East German waiting wife and the West German war widow evolved in very different discursive spaces. With public funds and the officially sanctioned identity of "victims of war" at stake, West German war widows' reputation was transformed on the front pages of newspapers. Narratives of East German waiting wives were transformed in letters to individual constituents or, at most, in comments at party assemblies. This relatively hushed dialogue was *necessary* because waiting wives' protests contradicted the officially sanctioned version of history, but it was *possible* because changing narratives had no policy implications. New or amended policies *were* published and explained in the GDR, even if without the unusual level of publicity that accompanied changes in war widows' pensions in the West. Absent any need to adapt policy, evolving narratives of waiting wives in East Germany did not need to be aired to a larger public.[60]

Conclusion

Alon Confino has called for historians of memory to integrate the political, the social, and the cultural, and to acknowledge the simultaneously fragmenting and unifying nature of memory.[61] An examination of waiting wives and war widows, where gender, politics, and social policy intersect, illustrates the importance of his plea.

Gender denies the possibility of studying the political, the social, or the cultural in isolation. The social is political, as access to economic resources depends in part on gender privilege in political life: West German war widows were less well-placed than veterans to contest limitations to their pensions. The political is cultural: gendered notions of fallen soldiers' "honor" made it intolerable for the West German state to financially support widows' cohabitation with new men.[62]

Furthermore, while gender is experienced on the most individual level in intimate relationships, it is simultaneously one of the most important axes of social organization. Existing at the intersection of the individual and the collective, it demands a discussion of the relationship between individual and collective memory.[63] Thus East and West German widows alike remembered their marriages, their bereavements, and the course their lives had taken since the war; but collective memories of war widows differed in East and West Germany because of the two states' distinct policies regarding war widows.

Finally, since gender coexists with other axes of social organization, including national identity, it illustrates the simultaneously fragmentary and unifying nature of collective memory. Men and women necessarily have different memories of experiences that differed according to sex. Yet the political fissures that often bring competing narratives of the past may transcend gender lines, unifying women and men around partisan narratives which themselves fragment the nation.[64] Thus East German party functionaries, regardless of sex, could agree that the USSR had proven a fine friend in liberating Germany from the Nazis. Meanwhile, the larger mass of East Germans might share memories of defeat by the Soviets as a painful, humiliating moment—even as women recalled rape by the victor and men recalled imprisonment. In turn, gendered experiences that transcend partisan identity, such as military service for men or tending the home front for women, can be crucial to constructing national identity based on shared memory. In the West German case, men's experience in POW camp, and women's experience awaiting their men's return, both confirmed German victimhood at the hands of the Soviets and thus helped to establish a West German national identity in the cold war.

Public policies such as the establishment or dismantling of widows' pensions are not primarily attempts to shape memory, as war memorials are. Precisely for this reason, it is impossible to divorce the ways in which public policies reflect and shape memory from the ways they address material issues, such as single women's poverty. At the same time, discussion of public policy measures occupies some of the same space as discussion of cultural artifacts such as films or texts. In their morning newspapers, Germans could read coverage of Bundestag debates and then turn to reviews of new films.

Consideration of public policy offers at least a partial solution to the problems of reception that plague cultural historians. We might not know what viewers thought of a particular film (even if we are lucky enough to know how many tickets were sold), but we often know what citizens thought of public policies: they petitioned their governments; they wrote letters to editors; they responded to pollsters. In doing so, they did not respond in a "pure" manner to the merits or demerits of particular programs. Rather, they also responded to the representation of those programs in the media. A widely reported policy debate with hints of scandal, such as the debate on West German widows' pensions, elicited a different response than a dry debate that received little news coverage. To be sure, such evidence does not solve the problem of representativity. Furthermore, it requires sensitivity to the environment in which citizens made their voices heard: whether the media was censored and by whom; whether the political situation appeared fluid enough for citizens to believe their voices might make a difference; and so on. Thus one must interpret East German widows' relative quiet on the denial of pensions with caution: it reflects recognition of the hopelessness of the situation, not approval. Nevertheless, such evidence as constituent letters and letters to the editor provide important windows to cultural, and not just social and political, history.

"Memory stands at the beginning of this book, memory of that which was or was to have been: A life for two, with each other and for each other in joy and in sorrow!"[65] So opened a book entitled *The Courageous Life: Life Questions of Women and Mothers Standing Alone,* published in West Germany in 1957. Yet although memory stood at the beginning of the book, most of the text was devoted to questions of the present. What public assistance might women standing alone expect? Did the large number of single women mean it was time to revise illegitimacy law? What should one say to say to nosy neighbors who disapproved of a widow's dating? This was no memorial to past suffering; it was a guide to practical living. The millions of "women standing alone" who constituted the book's target audience would not come to terms with the past by building or visiting a memorial, by making or viewing a film. They would come to terms with the past as they conquered daily life. And in that task, the state, which distributed or withheld pensions, and which set the stage for public discussion of widows' sexual lives and waiting wives' heroism, played a powerful role.

NOTES

I am grateful to Andrew Bergerson, Frank Biess, James Diehl, Robert Moeller, Vanessa Schwartz, and the editors of this volume for their responses to inquiries and for their comments on earlier versions of this essay. All translations are by the author.

1. The poster is reproduced in Elizabeth Heineman, *What Difference Does a Husband Make? Women and Marital Status in Nazi and Postwar Germany* (Berkeley: University of California Press, 1999), p. 11. The first postwar census, performed in October 1946, showed roughly seven million more women than men in the occupation zones, occupation soldiers excluded. See *Volks- und Berufszählung vom 29. Oktober 1946 in den vier Besatzungszonen und Groß-Berlin* (Berlin: Duncker and Humblot, 1946).

2. E.g., James Young, *The Texture of Memory: Holocaust Memorials and Meaning* (New Ha-

ven: Yale University Press, 1993). On postwar German states' activities in collecting individuals' memories—which expressed official priorities about whose memories must be preserved and what stories they should tell—see Robert Moeller, "War Stories: The Search for a Usable Past in the Federal Republic of Germany," *American Historical Review* 101 (1996): 1008–48, esp. pp. 1021–30; Catherine Epstein, "The Production of 'Official Memory' in East Germany: Old Communists and the Dilemmas of Memoir-Writing," *Central European History* 32 (1999): 181–202.

3. On these topics, see in order: Ulrich Brochhagen, *Nach Nürnberg: Vergangenheitsbewältigung und Westintegration in der Ära Adenauer* (Hamburg: Junius, 1994); Robert G. Moeller, *Protecting Motherhood: Women and the Family in the Politics of Postwar West Germany* (Berkeley: University of California Press, 1993); and Maria Mitchell, "Materialism and Secularism: CDU Politicians and National Socialism, 1945–1949," *Journal of Modern History* 67 (1995): 278–308. More generally on public policy and memory, see Norbert Frei, *Vergangenheitspolitik: die Anfänge der Bundesrepublik und die NS-Vergangenheit* (Munich: Beck, 1996); Jeffrey Herf, *Divided Memory: The Nazi Past in the Two Germanys* (Cambridge: Harvard University Press, 1997); and Christian Pross, *Paying for the Past: The Struggle over Reparations for Surviving Victims of the Nazi Terror* (Baltimore: Johns Hopkins University Press, 1998).

4. See the introduction to this volume.

5. *Von Stalingrad zur Währungsreform: Zur Sozialgeschichte des Umbruchs in Deutschland,* ed. Martin Broszat, Klaus-Dietmar Henke, and Hans Woller (Munich: Oldenbourg, 1988).

6. On the importance of trauma in determining which portions of experience will dominate individual or collective memories, see Iwona Irwin-Zarecka, *Frames of Remembrance: The Dynamics of Collective Memory* (New Brunswick, N.J.: Transaction Publishers, 1994), pp. 16, 49. On women's prominence during this period, see Sibylle Meyer and Eva Schulze, *Wie wir das alles geschafft haben: Alleinstehende Frauen berichten über ihr Leben nach 1945* (Munich: Beck, 1984); *"Das Schicksal Deutschlands liegt in der Hand seiner Frauen": Frauen in der deutschen Nachkriegsgeschichte,* ed. Anna-Elisabeth Freier and Annette Kuhn (Dusseldorf: Schwann, 1984); Heineman, *What Difference,* pp. 75–136.

7. Moeller, "War Stories"; Elizabeth Heineman, "The Hour of the Woman: Memories of Germany's 'Crisis Years' and West German National Identity," *American Historical Review* 101 (1996): 354–95.

8. The Joint Chiefs of Staff Document 1067 of April 1945 prohibited military pensions except in case of disability, and in such cases in amounts not to exceed benefits awarded those whose disabilities stemmed from non-military causes. Control Council Law 34 (20 Aug. 1946) formally closed the Wehrmacht's pension offices and transferred disability pensions to other offices. See *Documents on Germany under Occupation, 1945–1954,* ed. Beate Ruhm von Oppen (London: Oxford University Press, 1955), pp. 13–28, 151–52.

9. As quoted in James M. Diehl, *The Thanks of the Fatherland: German Veterans after the Second World War* (Chapel Hill: University of North Carolina Press, 1993), p. 61.

10. For a detailed examination of the Law to Aid Victims of War, see Diehl, *Thanks of the Fatherland,* pp. 109–40. On payments to victims of Nazism, see Constantin Goschler, *Wiedergutmachung: Westdeutschland und die Verfolgten des Nationalsozialismus (1945–1954)* (Munich: Oldenbourg, 1992). Already during the military occupation, western authorities had backpedaled on their strict prohibition against military pensions and permitted provincial-level programs in their zones (Rainer Hudemann, *Sozialpolitik im deutschen Südwesten* [Mainz: von Hase und Koehler Verlag, 1988]; Diehl, *Thanks of the Fatherland,* pp. 76–78, 87–108).

11. More extended discussion of war widows' pensions can be found in Heineman, *What*

Difference, pp. 162–73; Elizabeth Heineman, "Complete Families, Half Families, No Families at All," *Central European History* 29 (1996): 19–60.

12. E.g., Erich Mende's remarks, *Verhandlungen des deutschen Bundestages, 84. Sitzung, 13. September 1950* (Bonn, 1949–90), p. 3178. On the rehabilitation of the Waffen-SS, see David Large, "Reckoning without the Past: The HIAG of the Waffen-SS and the Politics of Rehabilitation in the Bonn Republic, 1950–1961," *Journal of Modern History* 59 (1987): 79–113.

13. For the best-known scholarly challenge to claims of nonpolitical women's innocence in the functioning of the Nazi regime, see Claudia Koonz, *Mothers in the Fatherland* (New York: St. Martin's, 1987); for a discussion among West German feminists on the subject see *TöchterFragen NS-Frauengeschichte,* ed. Lerke Gravenhorst and Carmen Tatschmurat (Freiburg am Breisgau: Kore, 1990).

14. *Drei Jahre Landeswohlfahrtsverband Hessen, 1953–56* (Kassel: Landeswohlfahrtsverband Hessen, 1956), p. 51. See also Maria Probst, "Die Stellung der Christlich-Sozialen-Union zur Kriegsopferversorgung," draft article for *Festschrift Bayern-Kurier* [n.d.; late Oct. 1955], NL219/16, Bundesarchiv (hereafter B Arch). The term "reconstruction of the family" is Robert Moeller's; see "Reconstructing the Family in Reconstruction Germany: Women and Social Policy in the Federal Republic, 1949–1955," *Feminist Studies* 15, no. 1 (1989): 137–69.

15. In fact, pensions were inadequate to constitute widows' sole means of support (Heineman, *What Difference,* p. 165).

16. There were 80,000 fit, childfree war widows under forty and 661,000 lightly wounded veterans. For the statistics regarding widows, see *Verhandlungen des (26.) Ausschusses für Kriegsopfer- und Kriegsgefangenenfragen des Deutschen Bundestages über das Bundesversorgungsgesetz,* 107D, I/87A, Lfd. 10, Parlamentsarchiv-Bonn (hereafter PA). For the statistics on veterans, see Diehl, *Thanks of the Fatherland,* p. 228.

17. Stenographisches Protokoll (Abschrift), p. 32. Sitzung des Ausschusses für Kriegsopfer- und Kriegsgefangenenfragen, 28 Sept. 1950, I/87A, Bd. 2, p. 61, PA; Stenographisches Protokoll (Abschrift), 37. Sitzung des Ausschusses für Kriegsopfer- und Kriegsgefangenenfragen, 11 Oct. 1950 I/87A, Bd. 2, pp. 19, 21, PA. In fact, wartime provisions awarded only token amounts to women who had not lived with or been supported by their husbands and who had no marital children (Heineman, *What Difference,* p. 62).

18. By this time, the number of eligible widows had declined to about thirty-eight thousand. See Waldemar Schönleiter, "Zweites Gesetz zur Änderung und Ergänzung des Bundesversorgungsgesetzes," *Bulletin des Presse- und Informationsamtes der Bundesregierung* (hereafter *BPIB*) 164 (29 Aug. 1953): 1377–78.

19. For statistical overviews of beneficiaries of the law, see W[aldemar] Schönleiter, *Die Kriegsopferversorgung* (Stuttgart: Kohlhammer, 1961); *Die Leistungen der Bundesrepublik Deutschland auf dem Gebiet der Kriegsopferversorgung 1.4.1950–31.12.1956* (Bonn: H. Köllen, n.d., [prob. 1957]); "Kriegsopferversorgung 1950–1977," (pamphlet, RKZSH, n.d., [prob. 1977]), ZSg 1-156/8(1), B Arch.

20. Dr. Fürst, Statistisches Bundesamt—der Präsident (VII K 04/03), 21 Mar. 1955, B141/15635, B Arch.

21. Bundesministerium für Arbeit (IV b 2—1793/53) RR. Dr. Wilke an den Herrn Bundesminister für Justiz Thomas Dehler, 14 April 1953, B149/1876 fols. 112–13, B Arch. For greater detail, see Heineman, *What Difference,* pp. 171–72.

22. For greater detail, see Heineman, *What Difference,* pp. 168–73. Press reports typically gave an estimate of one hundred thousand such cohabiting widows, but the source of this number is unclear.

23. Die Niedersächsische Frauenvereinigung an Franz-Joseph Würmeling, 10 November 1955, B153/1113 fols. 134–35, B Arch.

24. "Der Staat macht die lustigen Witwen," *Der Mittag* (3–4 Jan. 1953), 15, B149/1881, B Arch. This file contains numerous clippings illustrating editorial support for improved provisions.

25. On the simultaneous allure and fear of a consumption gendered female in reconstruction West Germany, see Erica Carter, *How German Is She? Postwar West German Reconstruction and the Consuming Woman* (Ann Arbor: University of Michigan Press, 1997).

26. 22 Apr. 1947 Befehl Nr. 92 des Obersten Chefs der SMAD betr.: Maßnahmen zur Verbesserung der Sozialfürsorge für die deutsche Bevölkerung in der sowjetischen Besatzungszone Deutschlands, reprinted in *Jahrbuch Arbeit und Sozialfürsorge* 2–3 (1947–48): 350–51. See n. 8 above for similar measures applicable in all occupation zones, which were, however, quickly superseded by more generous programs in the western zones. For a useful, if hostile, overview of the trend toward unified insurance in East Germany, see Alfred Leutwein (pseud. Siegfried Mampel), *Die sozialen Leistungen in der sowjetischen Besatzungszone* (Bonn: Bundesministerium für Gesamtdeutsche Fragen, 1955); for a sympathetic East German introduction, see S. Wiederhold, "Verbesserung der Sozialfürsorge nach Befehl 92," *Jahrbuch Arbeit und Sozialfürsorge* 2–3 (1947–48): 285–91. The Federal Republic's pension reform of 1957 equalized pensions for salaried employees and wage workers (but not "victims of war") in the West German state.

27. "Verordnung über die Zahlung von Renten an Kriegsinvaliden und Kriegshinterbliebenen," *Arbeit und Sozialfürsorge* 3 (1948): 345–46. A draft had included only mothers whose children could not be placed in an orphanage or in child care (18 Nov. 1947, 2. Entwurf: Verordnung über die Leistungsgewährung an Kriegsbeschädigte, Wehrmachtsbeschädigte und deren Hinterbliebene, DQ2 138 fols. 38–41, B Arch). For further detail on war widows' assistance in the GDR, see Heineman, *What Difference*, pp. 195–201.

28. *Die Leistungen der Bundesrepublik Deutschland auf dem Gebiet der Kriegsopferversorgung 1.4.1950–31.12.1956* (Bonn: H. Köllen, n.d., [prob. 1957]); Leutwein, *Die sozialen Leistungen*, pp. 128, 133.

29. Jenny Matern, remarks in "Stenographische Niederschrift über die Sitzung des Frauensekretariats der Ostzone am 4./5. November 1947," IV 2/1.01/61 fols. 3ff., here fol. 65, Stiftung Archiv der Partei und Massenorganisationen der Deutschen Demokratischen Republik im Bundesarchiv (hereafter SAPMO).

30. "Protokoll der Arbeitskonferenz des FDGB-Bundesvorstandes über Fraueneinsatz, 13. Juni 1951," Halle/Saale, FDGB A 1505, SAPMO.

31. Käthe Kern, remarks in "Sitzung des Bundesausschusses des DFD am 24. September 1948," DFD, BV no. 95, fols. 251–306, here fol. 269, SAPMO; 25 Nov. 1948, "Bericht über die erste sächsische Landesschwerbeschädigten-Konferenz in Dresden am 29. Oktober 1948," DQ2 3774, B Arch; 29 Nov. 1949 FDGB Görlitz an Wilhelm Pieck, DQ2 3774, B Arch; F. Bohlmann, "Die Versicherten haben das Wort," *Arbeit und Sozialfürsorge* 4 (1949): 474–75.

32. "Die standesamtlich beurkundeten Kriegssterbefälle und gerichtlichen Todeserklärungen in den Jahren 1939 bis 1954," *Wirtschaft und Statistik* 7 (1956): 302–4. 47.6 percent of those registered as missing were married, but since married men were more likely to be registered than were single men (who had no wives to register them), a disproportionate number of single missing men probably escaped detection ("Im Bundesgebiet vermißte Wehrmachtsangehörige," *Wirtschaft und Statistik* 2 [1950]: 153–55).

33. Kurt W. Böhne, *Die deutschen Kriegsgefangenen in sowjetischer Hand* (Bielefeld: E. und

W. Gieseking, 1966); Arthur Smith, *Heimkehr aus dem zweiten Weltkrieg* (Stuttgart: Deutsche Verlags-Anstalt, 1985).

34. Frank Biess, "The Protracted War: Returning POWs and the Making of East and West German Citizens, 1945–1955" (Ph.D diss., Brown University, 2000), p. 355. On missing men's wives' experience, see also Margarete Dörr, *"Wer die Zeit nicht miterlebt hat . . .": Frauenerfahrungen im Zweiten Weltkrieg und in den Jahren danach,* vol. 2: *Kriegsalltag* (Frankfurt: Campus, 1998), pp. 235–40.

35. Biess, "Protracted War," pp. 448–49. Most of these prisoners had in fact been convicted of war crimes (p. 426).

36. "Todeserklärung für Kriegsteilnehmer," *Suchzeitung 14/4 (November 1950), V278/2/73, SAPMO; "Todeserklärung?" Suchzeitung* 10/4 (July 1950), V278/2/73, SAPMO; see also Frank Biess's discussion of Politburo decrees of 1951 in "'Pioneers of a New Germany': Returning POWs from the Soviet Union and the Making of East German Citizens, 1945–1950," *Central European History* 32 (1999): 143–80, here p. 163.

37. Matter-of-fact explanations of the law regarding declarations of death appear in: "Wann wird der Vermisste als tot erklärt?" *Constanze* 1 (Nov. 1948): 3; "Wenn eine Todeserklärung notwendig ist" *Frauenstimme* 4, no. 9 (Sept. 1952): 8–9; Dr. Besecke, "Sie und das Recht," *Sie,* 10 Feb. 1946, p. 5. On the GDR's and FRG's policies on declarations of death, see also Biess, "Protracted War," pp. 357–59.

38. Moeller, "War Stories."

39. "Neue Gebürnisregelung für vermißte Wehrmachtsangehörige," *Mitteilungen des deutschen Vereins für öffentliche und private Fürsorge* 24, no. 9 (Sept. 1943): 131; "Hinterbliebenen- und Unfallrenten bei Vermißten," ibid. 25, no. 2 (Feb. 1944): 24.

40. "Unterhaltsbeihilfe für Angehörige von Kriegsgefangenen," *BPIB* 11 (26 Jan. 1952): 108.

41. "Unterhaltsbeihilfe für Angehörige von Kriegsgefangenen," *BPIB* 27 (6 Mar. 1952): 271; "Unterhaltsbeihilfe für Angehörige von Kriegsgefangenen," *BPIB* 51 (6 May 1952): 545.

42. Biess, "Protracted War," p. 362.

43. Petra Lund, "Die hat ja Herz im Liebe!" *Constanze* 1 (Nov. 1948): 3; see also Ruth Andreas-Friedrich, "Warum sie ledig bleiben," *Constanze* 6 (May 1953): 7; *Das tapfere Leben: Lebensfragen alleinstehender Frauen und Mütter,* ed. Lothar Franke and Helmut Bazille (Cologne-Hoffnungsthal: Werner Scheuermann, 1957), p. 14.

44. Carl Speitkamp, "Scheidung von Kriegsgefangenen-Ehen," *Jugendwohl* 29 (Sept.–Oct. 1948): 21–22.

45. E.g., "Wenn der totgeglaubte Mann zurückkehrt," *Reichsbund,* Apr. 1948: 9.

46. Robert G. Moeller, "'The Last Soldiers of the Great War' and Tales of Family Reunions in the Federal Republic of Germany," *Signs* 24, no. 1 (1998): 129–46. For the lower-key coverage of the release of prisoners in 1953, see Biess, "Protracted War," pp. 406–14.

47. On World War I pensions, see Birthe Kundrus, *Kriegefrauen: Familienpolitik und Geschlechtsverhältnisse im Ersten und Zweiten Weltkrieg* (Hamburg: Christians, 1995).

48. Käthe Kern, "Frauen überwinden die Not," Vortrag im Rundfunk gesendet am 6 Aug. 1946, VI 217/26 fols. 13–16, SAPMO; Elli Schmidt, "Frauen denkt daran!" *Neues Deutschland,* 1 Sept. 1946, NY 4106/4 fol. 141, SAPMO; Elli Schmidt, "Unsere Aufgaben zur Gewinning der Frauen bei den Gemeindewahlen," 20 Oct. 1946, NY 4106/4, SAPMO; Elli Schmidt, Flugblattentwurf für Berlin, Oct. 1946, NY 106/4 fols. 271–87, here fols. 284–85, SAPMO; "Entschliessung angenommen auf dem Gründungskongress des DFD, 9. März 1947," reprinted in *Dokumente der revolutionären Arbeiterbewegung zur Frauenfrage 1848–1974* (Leipzig:

Verlag für die Frau, 1975), pp. 160–61; "Resolution des II. Parteitages der SED zur Frauenfrage, 24. September 1947," reprinted in *Dokumente*, pp. 162–63.

49. Ilse Wittwika, *Was ich mit eigenen Augen sah* (Berlin: Deutscher Frauen-Verlag, 1950).

50. E.g., "Kriegsgefangenenfrage—Vermißtenproblem," *Suchzeitung* 9, no. 4 (June 1950), DY 55/V278/2/73, SAPMO; "Das Kriegsgefangenen-Problem," *Frau von heute* 6 (Nov. 1951): 17; "Entlarvt die Lügen der Kriegstreiber!" *Frau von heute* 7, no. 8 (Feb. 1952): 4; *Geschichte des DFD* (Leipzig: Verlag für die Frau, 1989), p. 86.

51. On waiting wives' letters to party officials, see also Biess, "Protracted War," pp. 391–400.

52. On other facets of the evolution of East German narratives of POWs, see also Beate Ihme-Tuchel, "Die SED und die deutschen Kriegsgefangenen in der Sowjetunion zwischen 1949 und 1955," *Deutschland-Archiv* 27 (1994): 490–503.

53. Biess, "Protracted War," pp. 195–271.

54. "Die Aussprache," *Frau von heute* 3 (Mar. 1948): 24.

55. "Todeserklärung für Kriegsteilnehmer," *Suchzeitung* 14 (Nov. 1950), V278/2/73, SAPMO; "Todeserklärung?" *Suchzeitung* 10 (July 1950), V278/2/73, SAPMO.

56. *Zur Geschichte der Rechtspflege der DDR 1945–1949* (Berlin: Staatsverlag, 1976), p. 305.

57. Donna Harsch, "Approach/Avoidance: German Communists between Women's Anti-Communism and Proletarian Anti-Feminism in the Soviet Zone of Occupation," *Social History* 25, no. 2 (2000): 156–82.

58. 3 Feb. 1955, Ilse Thiele to A.H., DFD, BV #557, fols. 126–27. See also DFD-Ortsgruppe Steinfurth, 17 Dec. 1952, to Elli Schmidt and Elfriede Gerber's response, 9 Jan. 1953, DFD, BV #540 fols. 36–37, SAPMO.

59. Anonymous letter, received 2 Feb. 1952 by Elli Schmidt, DFD/BV 540 fol. 72, SAPMO.

60. On similarly muted—but not completely suppressed—discourses of abortion in the GDR, see Donna Harsch, "Society, the State, and Abortion in East Germany, 1950–1972," *American Historical Review* 102 (1997): 53–84.

61. Alon Confino, "Collective Memory and Cultural History: Problems of Method," *American Historical Review* 102 (1997): 1386–1403.

62. On male honor, see Edward Berenson, *The Trial of Madame Caillaux* (Berkeley: University of California Press, 1992); Ute Frevert, *Men of Honor: A Social and Political History of the Duel*, trans. Anthony Williams (Cambridge, Mass.: Polity Press, 1995).

63. Susan Crane, "Writing the Individual Back into Collective Memory," *American Historical Review* 102 (1997): 1372–85.

64. On partisan narratives of the past, see for example Robert Gildea, *The Past in French History* (New Haven: Yale University Press, 1994); Herf, *Divided Memory*.

65. *Das tapfere Leben*, p. 12.

Epilogue: Dangerous Memories

STEVEN T. OSTOVICH

The role of memory increasingly is at issue in contemporary reflection on what it means to do history. The interest in memory has become so intense that Dominick LaCapra writes of the temptation to react to the "problem of memory" with "a suspicious view and refer to fixation," and he expresses the concern that "the immersion in memory and its sites may at times have the quality of junk-Proustian *Schwärmerei*."[1] Charles Maier views this obsession with memory in pathological terms as indicating that "we have in a sense become addicted to memory."[2] These concerns are themselves testimonies to the necessity of working through the relationship of memory and history. This is especially the case in the German context. Crafting an identity for a (re-) unified Germany involves turning to the past, and *Vergangenheitsbewältigung* returns as an intellectual and political issue. And there is the particular aspect of this past that resists mastering, that is, the trauma of Auschwitz.

Working through the relationship of history and memory is made difficult by the ambiguity of these terms. "History" is the determination of the facts of the past using a critical method (at least in modernity), but it also is concerned with situating events in a meaningful and explanatory nexus of causes and effects. The latter task connects history and narrative structure. At a metahistorical level this complexity results in the indeterminacy (or perhaps overdeterminacy) of "history" as a concept. Hegel, for example, attempts to sublate the antithesis between the "objective" and "subjective" poles of history in a philosophy of history, but more recently there is a hermeneutical willingness to explore this tension. Ranke attempted to prescind from these difficulties into a historicist concern with the way things actually were, but there also is an embracing of the literary quality of historical narrative in, for example, Hayden White's discussion of tropics of discourse in history.

The meaning of "memory" is even less clear despite the rapid growth of contemporary memory work. Memory often is located in the individual as a private psychic or physiological phenomenon extending at most to the family. On the other hand, there has been much recent interest in "collective memory," especially as this seems to be a field for relating memory and history. As with history, there is a connection between memory and identity, gender, and power. And issues of the relationship of history and literary form return both in terms of the critical use of memories that have their own distinct forms (e.g., testimony) and in terms of how best to write historical narratives incorporating memories.

This essay contributes to the discussion of memory and its relation to history by proposing that memory can be dangerous, that is, there are dangerous memories that resist the mastering of historical narrative. "Dangerous memories" are not a particular kind or function of memory that can be isolated and defined (and thereby critically controlled); they are rather a disruptive practice of and from memory. Any memory can become dangerous. These memories are neither simply individual nor collective but political in the Aristotelian sense of crossing the boundary between individual and collective through an understanding of the human person as a political animal (Aristotle's *politikon zoon*). There is therefore an intrinsic connection between dangerous memories and the political virtue of justice. Dangerous memories also challenge the notion that historical time is either empty or teleological with an understanding of time and history as eschatological. And dangerous memories are not simply sources of information to be employed instrumentally in critical historiography; rather, they offer a criterion of critical understanding in the practice of "remembrancing" in which the past (and the dead) has present implications and future content.

The disruptive potential of dangerous memories is evident in many of the recent struggles of German historiography in trying to come to terms with the Nazi era. The *Historikerstreit,* the conflict between professional historians and the general public in the reception of Daniel Goldhagen's *Hitler's Willing Executioners,* and the general unrest surrounding the *Wehrmachtausstellung* all can be read as testifying to the tensions between writing history and what people remember (or want to forget). And these tensions are exacerbated by the relative absence of the practices of remembering the Nazi era in the former DDR and by the coming to power of a German generation too young to have personal memories of the Third Reich.

The first section of the essay resurrects images of dangerous memories from the writing of Walter Benjamin. Benjamin has been overworked in cultural studies, perhaps, and many of the images below are familiar already. Still, placing these images together in the context of a concern with dangerous memories is revealing. The first section also will show the traces of Benjamin's dangerous memories in the work of the contemporary political theologian Johann Baptist Metz. The second section will move to a concern with the intimate connection between dangerous memories and historical trauma with a focus on the Holocaust (which is itself the context for much recent work on memory). The last section finds the key to employing "dangerous memory" as a critical category for historical reason in the context of this volume's general concern with the modern connections between memory and death.

Memory as Dangerous

Walter Benjamin's understanding of memory is bound up with his philosophy of language and history and his theology, but it is based on an experience he characterizes as the "chaos of memories."[3] There is a resistance to narrative ordering and control associated with memory for Benjamin. He specifies this resistance further: "I find in my memory rigidly fixed words, expressions, verses that, like a malleable mass which has later cooled and hardened, preserve in me the imprint of the collision between a larger collective and myself" in which "isolated words have remained in place as marks of catastrophic encounters."[4] Catastrophe engenders memories whose rough and hardened edges preclude placement in smooth-flowing narratives as a form of coming to terms with the past. These memories are disturbing in a manner similar to dreams. Like dreams, these memories involve crossing a threshold and stepping outside the closed world of normalcy. They "arrest" thought: "Thinking involves not only the flow of thoughts, but their arrest as well. Where thinking suddenly stops in a configuration pregnant with tensions, it gives that configuration a shock, by which it crystallizes into a monad."[5] The political theologian Johann Baptist Metz, under the influence of Benjamin, describes these memories as follows:

> There are memories in which earlier experiences break through the centre-point of our lives and reveal new and dangerous insights for our present. They illuminate for a few moments and with a harsh steady light the questionable nature of things we have apparently come to terms with, and show up the banality of our supposed "realism." They break through the canon of all that is taken as self-evident, and unmask as deception the certainty of those "whose hour is always there" (John 7.6). They seem to subvert our structures of plausibility. Such memories are like dangerous and incalculable visitants from the past.[6]

These memories are dangerous in their threat to attempts to master the past through constructing historical narratives.

History in the context of dangerous memories is catastrophe. "The concept of progress should be grounded in the idea of catastrophe. That things 'just keep on going' is the catastrophe."[7] The now classic image for this catastrophic understanding of history in Benjamin is the ninth of his *Theses on the Philosophy of History:* "A Klee painting named 'Angelus Novus' shows an angel looking as though he is about to move away from something he is fixedly contemplating.

His eyes are staring, his mouth is open, his wings are spread. This is how one pictures the angel of history. His face is turned toward the past. Where we perceive a chain of events, he sees one single catastrophe which keeps piling wreckage upon wreckage at his feet."[8] The dream-image of history appears to be a nightmare. In this context, the role of memory is to provide the awakening shock.

Dangerous memories also entail an understanding of historical time informed by Jewish messianic and mystical traditions, that is, time as eschatological. Dangerous memories arrest the flow of time. They interrupt historical narratives. In more religious terms, they represent a "Messianic cessation of happening" and illumine the present as "shot through with chips of Messianic time" in which each second is "the strait gate through which the Messiah might enter."[9] History is eschatological, not teleological, that is, the "end" of history is not a goal (*telos*) but a disruption (*eschaton*).

Eschatology informs Benjamin's dismissal of philosophy of history as progress and of historicism. Attempts to employ memory in the construction of narratives of progress oriented toward some future end that grounds meaning run afoul of dangerous memories embodying catastrophes. The past will not be controlled through a myth of progress because dangerous memories interrupt any controlling narrative. In light of this disruptive power of memory, "Progress does not reside in the continuity of temporal succession, but rather in its moments of interference."[10] The same holds true regarding historicism, with its concept of time as an "empty" vessel to be filled with the "objective facts" determined positively by the historical-critical method. Benjamin rejects this historicism whose "method is additive" as it "musters a mass of data to fill homogenous, empty time." For Benjamin, "To articulate the past historically does not mean to recognize it 'the way it really was' (Ranke). It means to seize hold of a memory as it flashes up at a moment of danger."[11]

Benjamin's historian is not interested in exercising control over the past through the use of an ostensibly critical and objective method. The task of the historian rather is to strike a spark by bringing past and present together in an image of truth, an image in which "the Then (*das Gewesene*) and the Now (*das Jetzt*) come into a constellation like a flash of lightning."[12] The "lightning flash" in effect "rescues" the past not by fitting the past into the flow of events but by interrupting that flow. And the constellations are constantly being reformed. Benjamin's historian is not the social scientist following a positive method to construct the truth of the past out of the raw material of, for example, memories. Neither is the historian the hermeneutical deployer of narrative strategies to give memories meaning in an interpretive framework. The historian is rather the *chiffonnier*, the ragpicker, rummaging through the detritus of history looking for the cast-off, the discarded, and that which is in danger of being lost. Put another way, the task of the historian is to "brush history against the grain."[13]

Metz helps clarify how this brushing "against the grain" has political as well as historiographical ramifications. Metz characterizes the modern way of being human in the world as an "anthropology of domination"—"Man is by subjugating. All non-dominating human virtues . . . recede into the background."[14] The application of this logic to writing history results in *Siegergeschichte,* the triumphant history written by the "victors" in the struggle for domination in which memories of suffering are suppressed. It is this suppressing that makes such memories of suffering dangerous, however, as these memories come from the victims of subjugation. Dangerous memories keep alive the *Leidensgeschichte* or history of suffering that resists being buried in a history of progress. For Metz, "the memory of the 'history of suffering of the world' becomes a medium for the realization of reason and freedom that critically opposes an unreflective as well as banal idea of the undialectical 'progress of reason.'"[15] Dangerous memories call for a "solidarity backward" or "anamnestic solidarity" with the dead, with the victims of injustice, as the struggle for justice continues. Benjamin anticipated this in some of his discussions with members of the Frankfurt School. Max Horkheimer, for example, claimed that "Past injustice is dead and finished. Those who have been beaten to death are truly dead." Benjamin rejected this forgetting: "The corrective of this [Horkheimer's] line of thought lies in the reflection that history is not only a science, but equally a form of remembrance. Remembrance can make the incomplete (happiness) complete, and render the complete (suffering) incomplete."[16] And this is clearest with regard to dangerous memories, because, as Metz indicates, "They are memories we have to take into account; memories, as it were, with future content."[17]

History and time are understood eschatologically by Metz as by Benjamin, although Metz is more explicit about the religious roots of his understanding. Metz finds in the Jewish and Christian scriptures an encounter with God as a "God of history." Biblical history is not the empty time of historicism or the progressive time of dialectical philosophy (spiritual or material). The biblical image of history is history as promise: "the words of Revelation in the Old Testament are not primarily words of statement or information, nor are they mainly words of appeal or of personal self-communication by God, but they are *words of promise.*"[18] These words are the "eschatological promises of the biblical tradition—freedom, peace, justice, reconciliation" which "cannot be reduced to a private matter" but "constantly force themselves into the sense of social responsibility" so that "*every eschatological theology must become a political theology in the sense of a theology of social criticism* [emphasis in original]."[19] The principle of this social criticism is the "eschatological proviso," that is, the principle that social and political conditions, although real, remain provisional and subject to criticism in light of the promise of justice in history. This is a critically negative promise, because justice cannot be defined positively but only in terms of the experience of its absence. And critical negativity helps Metz avoid the dualism of traditional salvation history: "there is not a world history and 'next to' this or 'over' this a salvation history. The salvation history of which Christian theology speaks is rather itself world history as marked by a threatened and restricted but also indestructible promised hope for universal justice (as God's justice that includes the dead and past suffering), and that calls the living to an undivided commitment to justice."[20] God's promise is not the disclosure of suprahistorical reality or the deposit of salvation history into otherwise empty time, but is rather the transformation of history. And as the promised justice extends to the dead, it has an anamnestic character that makes it dangerous.

Dangerous memories also can be embodied in rituals in which words may play a role but in which actions carry the power of remembrancing. Metz describes how the Christian celebration of the Lord's Supper or Eucharist is this type of ritual, that is, a ritual that is based on and communicates a particular dangerous memory. This shared meal enacts the *memoria passionis,* the memory of the suffering and death of Jesus as a promise of the resurrection. The ritualistic sharing of bread and wine is an act of solidarity in suffering, a solidarity that extends backwards in time as the ritual carries the participant back to the Last Supper and makes the suffering Christ present (in some albeit disputed manner) to those sharing the meal. Metz contrasts the bread of suffering in the Lord's Supper to the bread of domination consumed by Nietzsche's Zarathustra.[21] The logic of domination that informs modern reason needs to be transformed into a reason based on a logic of anamnestic solidarity. This is the transformative effect of the praxis of dangerous memories.

Another aspect of memory as dangerous is its relationship to nostalgia. Connecting memory with ruins, dreams, and the past casts memory in the seemingly romantic light of nostalgia. The result of this casting could be to rob memory of its danger, to smooth the rough edges of memories not so much to fit them into continuous narratives but to offer the possibility of resignation given the distance and irrelevance of the remembered past to present concerns. Metz, for example, worries about "memories which bathe everything from the past in a soft, conciliatory light" from which "everything dangerous, oppressive and demanding has vanished" because they are "deprived of all future."[22]

That this need not be the case is established by Peter Fritzsche's essay above. According to Fritzsche, nostalgia can lead to critical engagement with history—the present and future as well as the past. This is because nostalgia arises from an awareness of distance between the past and the present, an awareness that something has been "shattered" and is in danger of being lost. And it is this shattering that creates the distance necessary for criticism. The dominant narrative of historical experience is rejected as naive but not in the service of some counternarrative. Fritzsche uses words like "exile" to describe the being in the world of nostalgics like Chateaubriand. Living among the debris of the past, the nostalgic's challenge is to construct a world and an identity out of this debris. Put in terms from Benjamin, it is possible to speak of the "shock" of nostalgia.

Milan Kundera provides an example of the shock of nostalgia at the beginning of *The Unbearable Lightness of Being.* In the course of discussing Nietzsche's notion of eternal return, Kundera writes, "Not long ago, I caught myself experiencing a most incredible sensation. Leafing through a book on Hitler, I was touched by some of the portraits: they reminded me of my childhood. I grew up during the war; several members of my family perished in Hitler's concentration camps; but what were their deaths compared with the memories of a lost period in my life, a period that would never return?" The "lesson" Kundera derives from this experience: "This reconciliation with Hitler reveals the profound moral perversity of a world that rests essentially on the nonexistence of return, for in this world everything is pardoned in advance and therefore everything cynically permitted."[23] "Nostalgia" is the refusal to let the past be simply past while resisting its incorporation into the present. There is a future content to nostalgia that can be dangerous.

This is why Hannah Arendt is mistaken when she describes Benjamin's historian as a pearl diver. In seeking to give an image for Benjamin's thought in this regard, Arendt describes the historian as one "who descends to the bottom of the sea, not to excavate the bottom and bring it to light but to pry loose the rich and the strange, the pearls and corals in the depths."[24] But pearls fit a preexistent framework of value, that is, they are worth something in the market—they are commodities. Dangerous memories even as nostalgia disrupt such systems of exchange. The determination of what is a "pearl" for Benjamin occurs only when the found object or memory is brought to the surface and the historian becomes aware of the potential for the "pearl" to create new categories of "value" as it flashes in the light of history. Pearls are not traditionally determined cultural treasures; to the oyster, pearls are an irritation.

A difficulty here is determining in advance when nostalgia will be dangerous and when it will be enervating. There is no neutral algorithm for this purpose, or, put another way, even though nostalgia creates the space of criticism it is not subject to instrumental control. Fritzsche acknowledges how modern culture turns nostalgic images into fashions to be consumed. This does not seem to be a case of two kinds of nostalgia, a "good" and a "bad" consumable past. Rather, any particular memory can be turned into kitsch—and, conversely, can become dangerous. The images Fritzsche uses to describe nostalgia work are often passive—the castaway floating amidst the wreckage left by a storm, the attic as a place of nostalgic retreat. But the point remains the necessity and value of actively swimming among the flotsam and rummaging in the attic for those memories in danger of being lost or turned into commodities. This non-instrumentally controlled work unleashes the future content of nostalgia described by Fritzsche.

Memory work is an *activity* in Arendt's sense of this term, that is, it is constructive of political life and is concerned with political issues like freedom and justice (as distinct from labor and work and their concerns for what is necessary or useful). Memories are not simply the usable raw materials or resources for writing history. Rather, the activity of remembering is itself part of political life. This results in a certain formal ambiguity regarding dangerous memories:

stories, rituals, the objects of nostalgia from photographs to letters and travel journals, and as the next section will discuss, oral testimony, in short, all the flotsam and jetsam associated with the streams of memory, can become dangerous through the activity of being remembered. As is generally true of politics, the activity of (dangerous) memory requires judgment, and this in turn requires a model of the responsible historical subject and a critical theory of the praxis of memory. These, then, are the concerns discussed below, first in relating memory and trauma and then memory and death.

Memory and Trauma

Memory as dangerous, as disruptive, as connected to dreams and to death indicates the connection between dangerous memories and trauma. Given a concern with the relationship of memory and history and given the context of German history as the site for exercising this concern, the connection between memory and trauma becomes specified in the question of Auschwitz or the Holocaust. The Holocaust has been an originating context for the development of memory studies for a variety of reasons. There is the difficulty in coming to terms with the Holocaust as a historical event as it resists incorporation into any kind of smooth narrative. This difficulty is exacerbated by the tensions regarding the past and the formation of German identity in the present (after 1989). And there is the issue of testimony to the Holocaust as the generation of victims, perpetrators, and witnesses passes. The Holocaust is an essential site, therefore, for drawing out the character and implications of dangerous memories.

Lawrence Langer, in his book *Holocaust Testimonies: The Ruins of Memory,* addresses directly what "memory" means in the context of Holocaust testimony. The focus of the book is on oral testimony by those who experienced the Holocaust directly and the difference of this oral testimony from written testimony and historical accounts of these events. Langer identifies in these oral accounts what he labels "deep memory" or occasions when memory becomes dangerous to a stable sense of historical subjectivity. Listening to and viewing videotapes of interviews with witnesses to the Holocaust, Langer writes of being struck with the difficulty many of the testifiers had in accomplishing something they obviously wanted very much to do, that is, tell a coherent story of their experience that made sense of it and that communicated it to the audience. Instead the testifiers would talk of their frustration and of their sense of living in two worlds, the world of the concentration camps, the ghettoes, and other sites of terror, and the world of temporal continuity, the world of the present that sometimes connected with the world before the camps but never directly with the camps themselves. The two worlds were not temporally related in a linear manner but existed separately—one was not before or after the other but alongside it.

Langer identifies common memory as the basis for the quest for continuity and the restoration of habits after a trauma. Common memory establishes communal as well as temporal connections. These testimonies, however, also contain examples of deep memory. Deep memories speak to experiences that isolate individuals because they are incommunicable and that alienate individuals from community because they transgress moral interpretive frameworks. They testify to occasions when there was no "good" choice because there was no real choice at all. Deep memories disrupt narratives and threaten identity. They cannot be written about effectively because the act of writing exercises a kind of control and these memories lie beyond the pale of such control. At most they can be talked about, given the immediacy of oral interaction, but sometimes even this fails and all that is left is silence. Langer develops the testifiers' sense of living in "two adjacent worlds" and of carrying on a "parallel existence" by characterizing it as a "moral and emotional chiaroscuro" in an "atmosphere of eschatology."[25] At any moment the world of deep memory can disrupt the world of habit, of control, of common memory. Deep memories are disruptive for the audience as well as the testifier, and Langer reports the discomfort of the interviewers faced with the surfacing of deep memories in many of the tapes.

Langer's deep memories fall under the rubric of dangerous memories, but this category of memory does not exhaust the potential for memories to become dangerous. For example, deep memories are intensely personal to the point where it is hard for victims of a trauma like the Holocaust to share their experiences even with each other, but there are also dangerous memories that are communal, whose power to disrupt lies in their offering an alternative polity (at least potentially) to that which is dominant. Also, deep memories are fixed and can never become part of common memory. But there are shifting memories that can be both common and innocuous at one moment and dangerous at another, even for the same person of group. The Lord's Supper as a ritual of dangerous memory serves as an example of a communal dangerous memory—the rite itself is meant to establish community through a shared meal even though it often is privatized as an act of personal devotion and solitary communion with God especially in Protestant denominations; and of a memory that can shift in its orientation—as controlled by a priesthood in Roman Catholicism and Eastern Orthodox churches, the Eucharist often is used as an instrument of control and subjugation. The disruptive power of this rite and the dangerous memory it enacts remains, however.

This example should not be taken to mean the Christian ritual of the Lord's Supper provides a response to the trauma of the Holocaust. Metz is again helpful in this context for he has continually engaged the question that Auschwitz poses for Christian theology in his own political theology. For Metz, the situation to which Christianity must speak is the situation "after Auschwitz" in which questions of suffering and injustice are central. And these questions resist answers. They become instead cries to or indictments of God, and they raise again the question of theodicy. Metz writes, "As I became conscious of the situation after

Auschwitz, the God-question forced itself on me in its strangest, most ancient and most controversial form, as the theodicy question; not in its existential but, to a certain degree, in its political garb: discourse about God as the cry for the salvation of others, of those who suffer unjustly, of the victims and vanquished in our history. . . . For discourse about God is either about a vision and promise of universal justice, touching even the sufferings of the past, or it is empty and void of promise, even for those alive today."[26]

The issue between deep and dangerous memories might be one of images. Langer describes deep memories as pieces in a mosaic and, more specifically, a "damaged" mosaic. The emphasis in this image is on pieces that no longer fit together to give a meaningful picture which seems appropriate given his description of deep memories. Still, the image is static. The pieces do not change, and, like deep memories, no longer relate to other pieces meaningfully. Mosaic pieces have the rough edges and hardness of dangerous memories. Missing from this image, however, is a dynamism that some dangerous memories also exhibit, a dynamism that takes the form of entering into new relationships with other "pieces" or being incorporated into different "pictures." Benjamin similarly writes of "monads" when describing the effects of dangerous memories, but his emphasis seems as much temporal as spatial, that is, dangerous memories deliver shocks to inertial systems that otherwise would keep on moving as they were (one of Benjamin's definitions of catastrophe). More useful for purposes of comparison are Benjamin's images like the montage and the constellation that he uses to describe relations among ideas and concepts as well as dangerous memories. Montages involve perceptual movement, and this better captures the potential dynamism of some dangerous memories. Constellations are even more interesting as they construct meaningful "order" among bodies that are in motion, that change, and do this from a particular perspective that also is subject to change. Deep memories are dangerous memories, but there are other practices of remembrancing that can be dangerous as well.

Langer's response to the awareness of deep memories is important for discussing dangerous memories and their role in historiography. For Langer, deep memories preclude coming to any closure regarding historical trauma. Langer cites Albert Camus as a model of "lucidity" regarding the indifference of the universe to human concerns for meaning and a defense of the human in the face of inhumanity—what Camus labels the ability to live "without appeal."[27] Memory usually serves to establish a sense of normalcy and to help us develop the trustworthy habits we need to get by in the world. This is what the testifiers to the Holocaust were looking for from their memories. Deep memory intervenes. Drew Bergerson and Elizabeth Ten Dyke illustrate the quest for normalcy through memory in their essays for this volume. Bergerson in particular describes the failure of those who try to use memory to reconstruct Alt-Hildesheim as a site of normalcy and how they run afoul of their own dangerous memories (and, like Langer, Bergerson uses Camus to respond to this failure). Normalcy is disrupted by memory.

Langer uses theological language to describe the resistance of deep memory (and dangerous memory) to quests for meaning. "Redemption" and "salvation" no longer work in the context of deep memory. These words promise closure and offer the hope of meaning, the very possibility of which deep and dangerous memories call into question. Langer and Metz end up in similar places after Auschwitz. Neither can accept explanations, interpretations, or justifications of events or God as anything other than ghastly abstractions. Metz turns to theodicy as a questioning of God and a "suffering unto God," while Langer calls for us to share the darkness without being "crippled" by it.

Dominick LaCapra offers a similar response to Auschwitz but one that is couched in psychoanalytical rather than theological language. In *History and Memory after Auschwitz* LaCapra treats Auschwitz under the category of trauma in which "an extreme threshold or outer limit of transgression was crossed."[28] The crossing of this threshold moots questions of uniqueness and comparability (the issues of the *Historikerstreit*). The extreme character of transgression here means that living "after" this trauma also affects what came before. For example, reading Nietzsche and Heidegger changes in light of Auschwitz. The therapeutic response to trauma is a working through that LaCapra also characterizes as mourning and associates with both rites and places of mourning. This mourning brings with it "the possibility of engaging trauma and achieving a reinvestment in, or 'recathexis' of, life."[29]

The notion of a "recathexis" of life is important to LaCapra as the ground for reconstructing a sense of responsible historical subjectivity. It also shapes his criticism of Langer. For LaCapra, "historiography involves work on memory that inquires into its operations, attempts to retrieve what it has repressed or ignored, and supplements it in ways that may provide a measure of critical distance on experience and a basis of responsible action."[30] Trauma does not destroy the capacity for responsible action and historical judgment. Responsibility demands, however, a (Freudian) theoretical working through of trauma in a process of mourning "that would attempt, however self-questioningly and haltingly, to specify its haunting objects and (even if only symbolically) to give them a 'proper' burial."[31] According to LaCapra, it is just this theoretical concern that is lacking in Langer. Without the theoretical possibility of mourning, Langer remains trapped, "symptomatically staying within trauma by acting out a repetition compulsion with its fragmentation or fracturing of all possibilities of bonding and renewal."[32] This is a politically naive and dangerous position to be in, as it provides no grounds for resisting the misappropriation of trauma by, for example, fascism. Responsible subjectivity requires (at least potentially) closure through mourning.

LaCapra is making a critical error here, however. He is concerned with overcoming the dualistic thinking that limits the theoretical possibilities for doing history in light of trauma to either the totalizing discourse that seeks to make sense of everything (and therefore ends up denying trauma) or the complete despair that anything makes historical sense in light of trauma. His Freudian theory of "working through" and "mourning" is an attempt to offer a third, responsible option. LaCapra remains stuck in a dualism of his own, however: either successful mourning or melancholy resignation. Martin Jay, in an article on Benjamin's refusal to mourn (the suicides of friends protesting World War I), points out that another critical distinction is possible, "between a refusal to mourn that knows all too well what its object is . . . and is afraid that mourning will close the case prematurely . . . and a refusal to mourn based on a denial that there was anything lost in the first place."[33] The refusal to mourn, which in Benjamin's case takes the form of melancholy, is not resignation and it need not be enervating. It is instead the willingness to face the demands of responsible judgment even while recognizing the open-ended quality of history and subjectivity.

LaCapra seemingly recognizes this open-ended quality in describing the work of the historian. The working through of trauma happens belatedly after a period of latency in which the traumatic event is repressed or denied. Testimony or witnessing to trauma also is delayed, therefore, which presents particular challenges for the historian. First there is the issue of how to be critical about sources for writing history that arise only long after the events to which they testify. LaCapra's focus is on another aspect of this problem for criticism, and that is what he describes as the issue of transference. Testimony to trauma raises in a heightened way the issue of the historian's subject-relation with respect to the witness. As with the behavior Langer observed among the interviewers, there is a tendency for the historian or interviewer to become personally and even emotionally involved in listening to the testimony. The historian typically is cast as a neutral bystander or onlooker to events and to the testimony of those caught up in the events, but such "objectivity" is difficult to attain with respect to historical traumas. LaCapra uses the language of psychoanalysis here to charge the historian with "negotiating transference" by "coming to term with his or her implication in the tragic grid of participant positions" as preparation for "overcoming the entire complex of relations defined by the grid: perpetrator—collaborator—victim—bystander—resister." This demands an open-ended and ongoing response to traumatic events: "Working through the past in any desirable fashion would thus be a process (not an accomplished state) and involve not definitive closure or full self-possession but a recurrent yet variable attempt to relate accurate, critical memory-work to the requirements of desirable action in the present."[34] As with Langer and Metz, memories of trauma preclude closure of the historical narrative while demanding critical responsibility on the part of the historian. The historian must continually work through the testimony of those who remember.

Memory and Death

Theodor Adorno worried Benjamin about the lack of theoretical superstructure in the latter's *Arcades Project.* Adorno's concern was that this lack of framework would make Benjamin's memory work available for appropriation by fascism because Benjamin provided no way to make critical judgments regarding the use of dangerous memories. Jürgen Habermas raises a similar issue regarding Benjamin and dangerous memories in the contemporary context of Germany's reconstruction of its past. There are attempts to move Germany away from the democratic traditions of Western Europe and the United States favored by Habermas and toward the earlier notion of a *Sonderweg* in German history. This is based on a feeling that Germany has suffered enough at the hands of the victors in the twentieth century's wars.[35] The desire to leave the recent past behind and recover a slightly more distant and certainly more pleasant past threatens liberal democracy with a return of blind nationalism. Memory work has political consequences. If the past cannot be mastered to provide a stable ground for historical criticism, and if memories can resist instrumental integration into contemporary schemes of meaning, how is critical judgment possible regarding dangerous memories, history, and politics? The problem of responsible historical subjectivity returns here in a new context.

The challenge is to spell out the theory enacted in the praxis of dangerous memories, as Adorno suggested. This theory might be described in general terms as rational responsibility to the past. The past is here understood not in a quasi-metaphysical sense as an objective ground for historical judgment. Neither is it the object for positivistic research in which method guarantees truth. Rather the past should be understood in a specifically historical sense as change, that is, as neither over and done with nor repeatable but still with future content that cannot be exhausted in the present. "Responsibility to the past" remains abstract, however, especially given the demands for political action contained in dangerous memories. Those to whom the historian responds are more concretely described as the dead.

Several of the essays in this volume allude to the relationship of memory, death, and modernity. The most explicit of these is Craig Koslofsky's essay on memory in the German Reformation. Koslofsky draws out the theoretical change that defines modernity as enacted in the change in funeral and burial practices among the Reform communities in German Christianity. The shift from a medieval sense of *memoria* in which the dead remain part of the community to Reformed death practices based on the temporal finality and individuality of death resulted in the changed stance toward the past that marks modernity. The past must be kept past and can no longer be changed by the present (for example, Purgatory and the possibility of interceding for the souls there is dismissed by the Protestants as a Roman church tool for economic and political oppression). The modern past "can be remembered and interpreted, but never set right." Koslofsky's argument is applicable to other practices at issue in the Reformation like the Eucharist or Lord's Supper, as he indicates. Debates over the nature or "reality" of Christ's presence in the elements of this ritual illustrate the Protestant move toward the past as finished. If the bread and wine undergo the miracle of transubstantiation at the hands of the priest (or even the more moderate Lutheran notion of consubstantiation), the "real" presence eliminates the temporal distance between the Last Supper and the present of celebration. This destruction of time occurs in any effective ritual. Changing the rite to an act of commemoration in which the Christological presence in the elements is spiritual rather than actual, as did Zwingli and others, heightens the sense of separation from the past act of institution at the Last Supper. The same can be said about Luther's principle of *sola scriptura,* the Bible (made accessible to the individual through translation into the vernacular) as the sole standard of faith sufficient unto itself and not needing a tradition of ecclesiastical control of interpretation. The effect here, too, can be to heighten the sense of temporal distance between the era of (biblical) revelation and the present and to limit present rational activity to the interpretation of the now-closed past.

Koslofsky also raises the question of what a parallel failure of modern practices of social memory might mean. This is the question Metz addresses in referring to the Lord's Supper as a *memoria passionis.* Metz is a Roman Catholic priest who is very conscious of how the Roman church has lagged behind modernity. Put more positively, it is working from this place outside modernity that makes it possible to work through the questions Koslofsky and others raise. The "return" of *memoria* (if return is the correct word for something that never disappeared entirely from religious practice) does not mean a return to the Middle Ages. This would be impossible. Metz, too, realizes the past must remain past as one of the central insights of modernity. And yet the past has a future content that places demands on the present. *Memoria* is a praxis of memory demanding responsibility to the dead and their claim on the future, that is, it is a form of dangerous memory. Metz describes this as a praxis of anamnestic solidarity characterized by anamnestic rationality. The rational principle of historical criticism is justice for the dead.

There is a foundational ambiguity regarding subjectivity in the history of suffering, as has been seen above. Solidarity with victims as a principle depends on being able to identify who are the victims in history. Insofar as anamnestic rationality questions modernity, however, it raises questions about modern definitions of the historical subject. Koslofsky writes of how narrative and biography take the place of *memoria* in modernity and of how this is a matter of redefining subjectivity. The same connection between modernity and a particular version of subjectivity is made in Fritzsche's essay and others. Calling into question modern history on the basis of dangerous memories entails, therefore, questioning the modern concept of the subject, a concept that in politics takes the form of liberal individualism.

The logic of dangerous memories demands leaving the subject position open, as has already been made clear in other contexts above. Legal definitions of victims in terms of entitlement end in the performative contradiction of everyone being able to claim status as a victim in some context, even the perpetrators of crimes against humanity. Liberal individualism as defined by law fails to allow for rational judgments regarding justice. Class identification also fails the test of anamnestic solidarity. The notion that a particular class represents the best hope for the future is simply another myth defining history in terms of enmity and excluding the claims of others who have suffered in the past. At the same time, there can be no justice and no history without subjects. Metz, for example, in reflecting on Auschwitz, worries about the potential loss of historical subjects capable of guilt in contemporary posthistoricism with its myth of empty time (although his concern for the "defense of the human subject" leads Metz to close the subject position too soon).

Responding to this problem means reexamining the role of narrative in history. Dangerous memories disrupt mastering historical narratives, but this does not mean dispensing with narrative in writing history. Narrative is too closely bound up with subjectivity to be dismissed as necessarily controlling and inadequate to all aspects of memory. Memories do not speak alone but through stories that construct historical subjects and worlds. Put in other terms, the issue here is one of "voice." Dangerous memories require that in writing history there be heightened awareness of whose voice is being heard. With specific regard to Auschwitz, Saul Friedlander points to the very different quality of the voices of perpetrators and victims and the threat of being seduced by the "aesthetic enticement" of the former while the latter "carry only the horror and the pity."[36] In the same context, Metz challenges the notion that *Leidensgeschichte* can be reduced to a single story. "The catastrophe of Auschwitz directs theology [and history] away from the singular of 'history' to the plural of 'histories of sufferings' which cannot be idealistically explained but rather only remembered with a practical intention."[37] Historiography is not charged with writing the single story of "the way it really was" and what it means, but with the writing of multiple, changing, and sometimes conflicting histories in response to dangerous memories.

Naming memories as "dangerous" is another way of claiming that the past cannot be mastered but at best worked through and lived with. The response of historians remains rational, however, because rationality itself changes historically in response to the demand of the dead for justice. David D. Roberts describes what the practice of "responding to the world as historical" entails concerning the rational criteria by which historical judgments are made: "Those criteria are continually being hammered out within history as part of the interaction. Deciding on the rules is part of the game. . . . The same is true for deciding on the rules for determining the rules—take it as many steps as you like." This is not a scandal for reason, however, because "There is no way to transcend the process of interaction and specify what counts as rational or competent once and for all. But though the ongoing interaction never yields suprahistorical rules or criteria, its weak, provisional resultants afford the measure of coherence necessary for dialogue and learning—and for a continuing history."[38] This "weak" historical reason constitutes part of what Benjamin called our "*weak* Messianic power, a power to which the past has a claim."[39] And it is a critical power.

The disruptive potential of dangerous memories can be liberating for historical practice. Writing modern pasts is made difficult by the political implications of historiography, as is evident in the case of Germany today. These tensions are exacerbated by the internal conflicts among historians who seem to be caught in a dichotomy: either reason is defined in terms of a critical method capable of objectively uncovering the truth and meaning of the past as fact, or reason is abandoned in recognition of the constructed character of all histories. Dangerous memories offer a model of historical practice in which the past is real but open, an openness that makes reason a practice of critical negotiation rather than methodological objectivism or literary constructivism. At the same time the eschatological character of time revealed by dangerous memories makes doing history on the basis of either idealist or materialist teleologies uncritical. And dangerous memories are by definition incapable of being buried in the historicist past as it was. Faith in method and faith in facts is replaced by respect for the dead on the part of responsible historical subjects (including historians) able to make critical judgments.

NOTES

1. Dominick LaCapra, *History and Memory after Auschwitz* (Ithaca: Cornell University Press, 1998), p. 8.

2. Charles Maier, "A Surfeit of Memory?: Reflections on History, Melancholy and Denial," *History and Memory* 5 (1993): 140.

3. Walter Benjamin, "Unpacking My Library," in *Selected Writings,* vol. 2: *1927–1934,* trans. Rodney Livingstone et al., ed. Michael W. Jennings, Howard Eiland, and Gary Smith (Cambridge: Belknap Press of Harvard University Press, 1999), p. 486.

4. Walter Benjamin, "A Berlin Chronicle," in *Selected Writings,* vol. 2: *1927–1934,* p. 602.

5. Walter Benjamin, "Theses on the Philosophy of History," in *Illuminations,* trans. Harry Zohn, ed. Hannah Arendt (New York: Schocken Books, 1968), p. 262.

6. Johann Baptist Metz, "The Future in the Memory of Suffering," *Concilium* 76 (1972): 15.

7. Walter Benjamin, "N [Re the Theory of Knowledge, Theory of Progress]," trans. Leigh Hafrey and Richard Sieburth, in *Benjamin: Philosophy, Aesthetics, History,* ed. Gary Smith (Chicago: University of Chicago Press, 1989), p. 64.

8. Benjamin, "Theses on the Philosophy of History," pp. 257–58.

9. Benjamin, "Theses on the Philosophy of History," p. 263.

10. Benjamin, "N," p. 65.

11. Benjamin, "Theses on the Philosophy of History," pp. 262, 255.

12. Benjamin, "N," p. 49.

13. Benjamin, "Theses on the Philosophy of History," p. 257.

14. Johann Baptist Metz, *The Emergent Church: The Future of Christianity in a Postbourgeois World,* trans. Peter Mann (New York: Crossroad, 1981), p. 35.

15. Johann Baptist Metz, *Glaube in Geschichte und Gesellschaft* (Mainz: Matthias-Grünewald, 1977), p. 171.

16. Quoted in Rolf Tiedemann, "Historical Materialism or Political Messianism? An Interpretation of the Theses 'On the Concept of History,'" in *Benjamin: Philosophy, Aesthetics, History,* pp. 181–82.

17. Metz, "Future in the Memory of Suffering," p. 15.

18. Johann Baptist Metz, "The Church and the World," in *Love's Strategy: The Political Theology of Johann Baptist Metz,* ed. John K. Downey (Harrisburg: Trinity Press International, 1999), p. 17.

19. Johann Baptist Metz, "The Church's Social Function in the Light of a 'Political Theology,'" in *Love's Strategy,* ed. Downey, p. 31.

20. Johann Baptist Metz, "Kampf um jüdische Traditionen in der christlichen Gottesrede," *Kirche und Israel* 2 (1987): 16.

21. Metz, "Bread of Survival," *Emergent Church,* pp. 34–47. Liberation theologians frequently discuss the revolutionary power of the Eucharist or Lord's Supper. Graham Greene describes this revolutionary power in his novel, *The Honorary Consul:* rebel peasants force their ex-priest leader to continue saying Mass; he finds the ritual distracting and superstitious, but they find it empowering. Craig Koslofsky's claims regarding modernity, identity, and rites of the dead apply equally well here—see his essay above and further comments below. All this also might be said about another ritual "bread," the *matzoth* of Passover/Unleavened Bread.

22. Metz, "Future in the Memory of Suffering," p. 14.

23. Milan Kundera, *The Unbearable Lightness of Being,* trans. Michael Henry Heim (New York: Harper, 1984), p. 4.

24. Hannah Arendt, "Introduction: Walter Benjamin, 1892–1940," *Illuminations,* pp. 50–51.

25. Lawrence Langer, *Holocaust Testimonies: The Ruins of Memory* (New Haven: Yale University Press, 1991), pp. 34–38. The rupture in the world of the audience caused by testimony to these deep memories can be compared to Art Spiegelman's wrestling with his father's testimony in *Maus* (2 vols. [New York: Pantheon, 1986 and 1991]). Langer writes of a "drama of avoidance" among the interviewers who do not want to let their own belief in an order of meaning and morality be disrupted by these testimonies. Spiegelman writes of his frustration because his father's Holocaust experiences get bound up with more contemporary concerns in the telling. Both reactions testify to a desire for control and isolation that these testimonies disrupt.

26. Johann Baptist Metz, "Theology as Theodicy?" in *A Passion for God: The Mystical-Political Dimension of Christianity,* trans. J. Matthew Ashley (New York: Paulist Press, 1998), p. 55. See also the essay "The Church after Auschwitz" in *A Passion for God:* "We Christians have certainly preserved this remembrance-structure of our faith in our cult ('Do this in remembrance of me.'). But have we cultivated it enough in the public sphere?" (p. 131).

27. See Albert Camus, "The Myth of Sisyphus," in *The Myth of Sisyphus and Other Essays,* trans. Justin O'Brien (New York: Vintage Books, 1983), pp. 1–138. Also Shoshana Felman, "Camus' *The Plague,* or A Monument to Witnessing," in Shoshana Felman and Dori Laub,

Testimony: Crises of Witnessing in Literature, Psychoanalysis, and History (New York: Routledge, 1992), pp. 93–119.

28. LaCapra, *History and Memory after Auschwitz,* p. 6.

29. LaCapra, *History and Memory after Auschwitz,* p. 45.

30. Dominick LaCapra, "The Return of the Historically Repressed," *Representing the Holocaust: History, Theory, Trauma* (Ithaca: Cornell University Press, 1994), p. 175.

31. LaCapra, "Return of the Historically Repressed," p. 193.

32. LaCapra, "Return of the Historically Repressed," p. 195. LaCapra later acknowledges, "The nuances in Langer's argument may suggest . . . we are still in search of a language with which to render, however inadequately, both what happened to people in the camps and what implications we may draw from these events" (p. 202).

33. Martin Jay, "Against Consolation: Walter Benjamin and the Refusal to Mourn," in *War and Remembrance in the Twentieth Century,* ed. Jay Winter and Emmanuel Sivan (Cambridge: Cambridge University Press, 1999), p. 237.

34. LaCapra, *History and Memory after Auschwitz,* pp. 41–42.

35. Jürgen Habermas, *A Berlin Republic: Writings on Germany,* trans. Steven Rendall (Lincoln: University of Nebraska Press, 1997).

36. Saul Friedlander, "Introduction" to *Probing the Limits of Representation,* ed. Saul Friedlander (Cambridge: Harvard University Press, 1992), p. 16.

37. Metz, "Communicating a Dangerous Memory," in *Love's Strategy,* ed. Downey, p. 139.

38. David D. Roberts, *Nothing but History: Reconstruction and Extremity after Metaphysics* (Berkeley: University of California Press, 1995), p. 309.

39. Benjamin, "Theses on the Philosophy of History," p. 254.

CONTRIBUTORS

Andrew Stuart Bergerson is an assistant professor of modern European history at the University of Missouri–Kansas City, specializing in *Alltagsgeschichte* and ethnographic history in twentieth-century Germany. He has published articles on his Hildesheim research in *New German Critique, German Studies Review,* and *Issues in Integrative Studies.* He is currently completing the manuscript for his forthcoming book, *Ordinary Germans in Extraordinary Times,* which will tell the history of conviviality and normalcy in Hildesheim from 1900 to 1950. His next research project will be a history of German bread in modern Württemberg.

Alon Confino teaches modern German and European history at the University of Virginia. He has written on modern German history, nationalism, film and history, historical memory, and problems of method in social and cultural history. His book *The Nation as a Local Metaphor: Württemberg, Imperial Germany and National Memory, 1871–1918* won the Smith Book Prize of the Southern Historical Association. He is a co-editor of "The Local Life of Nationhood: the Cultural, the Historical, and Problems of Method," a special issue of *National Identities,* and "Consumer Culture in Twentieth Century Germany," a special issue of *German History.* He is now at work on how traveling culture, closely associated with the notions of modernity and experience, illuminates the twentieth century's major systems of life and thought—Nazism, Communism, and liberal democracy.

Peter Fritzsche is professor of history at the University of Illinois, Urbana-Champaign. He is the author of numerous books in German history, including *Reading Berlin 1900* and *Germans into Nazis.* He was awarded a Guggenheim fellowship in 1999 to complete his latest book on nostalgia, exile, and the experience of modern time.

Marcus Funck is a historian affiliated with the Technical University in Berlin. His publications include "Schock und Chance. Der preussische Militaeradel in der Weimarer Republik zwischen Stand und Profession," in Heinz Reif, ed., *Adel und Buergertum in Deutschland: Entwicklungslinien und Wendepunkte,* and "The Meaning of Dying: East-Elbian Noble Families as 'War Tribes,'" in Matt Berg, Greg Eghigian, and Steve Reinhardt, eds., *Sacrifice and National Belonging in Twentieth-Century Germany.* His research interests include the history of the nobility, military history and theory, and the history of cities in the nineteenth and twentieth centuries.

Elizabeth Heineman is associate professor of history at the University of Iowa. She is author of *What Difference Does a Husband Make? Women and Marital Status in Nazi and Postwar Germany,* "The Hour of the Woman: Memories of Germany's 'Crisis Years' and West German National Identity," *American Historical Review,* and numerous other articles. She is now working on a book tentatively entitled *Sex Objects: Beate Uhse, Business, and the Material Culture of Sexuality in Germany.*

Jonathan M. Hess is associate professor of German at the University of North Carolina at Chapel Hill. He is the author of *Reconstituting the Body Politic: Enlightenment, Public Culture and the Invention of Aesthetic Autonomy* and numerous articles on eighteenth- and nineteenth-century literature, aesthetics, and intellectual history. He is currently completing a monograph entitled *Germans, Jews and the Claims of Modernity.*

Elizabeth Snyder Hook is assistant professor of German at the University of North Carolina Asheville. She has published a book on literary reactions to the Holocaust, *Family Secrets and the Contemporary German Novel: Literary Explorations in the Aftermath of the Third Reich,* as well as articles on German-Jewish writers Nelly Sachs and Else Lasker-Schueler. Professor Snyder Hook also writes and teaches on filmic representations of the Holocaust and is currently writing a book on the anti-Nazi Resistance.

Craig Koslofsky, assistant professor of history at the University of Illinois, Urbana-Champaign, specializes in late medieval and early modern German history. His work *The Reformation of the Dead: Death and Ritual in Early Modern Germany, 1450–1700* was published in 2000. He is also co-editor (with Bernhard Jussen) of a study of the medieval cultural origins of the German Reformation: *Kulturelle Reformation: Sinnformationen im Umbruch 1400–1600.*

Paul Lerner is assistant professor of history at the University of Southern California and specializes in modern German history, the history of psychiatry, and German-Jewish history. He co-edited, with Mark S. Micale, *Traumatic Pasts: History, Psychiatry and Trauma in the Modern Age, 1870–1930,* and is currently completing a manuscript entitled *Hysterical Men: War, Psychiatry and the Politics of Trauma in Germany, 1890–1932.*

Stephan Malinowksi completed his dissertation, "Vom Koenig zum Fuehrer? Soazialer Zerfall und politische Radikalisierung im deutschen Adel 1900–1934," at the Technical University in Berlin in 2001. He is the author of "'Fuehrertum' and 'Neuer Adel': Die Deutsche Adelsgenossenschaft und der Deutsche Herrenklub in der Weimarer Republik," in Heinz Reif, ed., *Adel und Buergertum in Deutschland: Entwicklungslinien und Wendepunkte,* and, with Marcus Funck, "Geschichte von oben. Autobiographien als Quelle einer Sozial- und Kulturgeschichte des deutschen Adels in Kaiserreich und Weimarer Republik," in *Historische Anthropologie.*

Steven T. Ostovich is a professor of philosophy and religious studies at the College of St. Scholastica in Duluth, Minnesota. His areas of interest are critical theory, political philosophy, and political theology. He has published articles on Walter Benjamin, Johann Baptist Metz, Jüergen Habermas, and Carl Schmitt and on philosophy of religion and higher education reform. He is the author of *Reason in History: Theology and Science as Community Activities.*

Elizabeth A. Ten Dyke is the author of *Dresden: Paradoxes of Memory in History,* in addition to several articles on the transition in eastern Germany after 1989. Most recently, she has worked on social studies curriculum development for the Kingston City Schools and she is developing a study of spatial or geographic aspects of memory in urban settings.

S. Jonathan Wiesen is assistant professor of history at Southern Illinois University. He is the author of one book, *West German Industry and the Challenge of the Nazi Past, 1945–1955,* and a number of articles, including "Overcoming Nazism: Big Business, Public Relations, and the Politics of Memory, 1945–1955," *Central European History;* and "Study Tours, Trade Fairs, Publicity Campaigns: Business Encounters and Cold War Anxieties, 1945–1968," forthcoming in Detlev Junker, ed., *The United States and Germany in the Era of the Cold War.* His current research project examines discourses about mass society and cultural decline in twentieth century Germany.

INDEX

The University of Illinois Press
is a founding member of the
Association of American University Presses.

Composed in 10.5/12.5 Minion
with Gill Sans display
by Jim Proefrock
at the University of Illinois Press
Manufactured by Maple-Vail
Book Manufacturing Group

University of Illinois Press
1325 South Oak Street
Champaign, IL 61820-6903
www.press.uillinois.edu